Classroom
Uses of
Behavior
Modification

Mary B. Harris
University of New Mexico

Charles E. Merrill Publishing Company
A Bell & Howell Company
Columbus, Ohio

International Standard Book Number: 0–675–09156–X

Library of Congress Catalog Card Number: 77–182944

2 3 4 5 6 7 8 9 10/76 75 74

Printed in the United States of America

Preface

This book is written for students of psychology and education as well as for practicing teachers. The first two sections give an introduction to the methods and principles embodied in the articles which follow in order to provide a foundation for those who do not possess a background in educational psychology and experience in reading journal articles. Comments are also given for each article to assist the reader in seeing some of the implications of the paper for the practicing teacher. The focus of the book throughout is on applicability to the classroom situation; this does not imply that theory is ignored but that the implications of the theory to actual situations are made specific. By seeing the actual research on which conclusions are based, the reader should have a clearer idea of the way in which behavior modification studies are carried out and the validity of the interpretations.

An attempt has been made to secure as wide as possible a range of ages, problems, and methods with the provisos that they be pertinent to the classroom situation. Research on behavior therapy in private practice or mental hospitals and laboratory research projects only tangentially relevant to the classroom situation have been omitted. Particular preference has been given to articles which describe in detail their techniques and problems of implementation. The articles reprinted in this book should represent the variety of programs involving classroom uses of behavior modification today.

My thanks are due to the authors and editors who gave me permission to reprint the articles and to Richard, Jennifer, and Christopher Harris for constantly demonstrating the importance of positive reinforcement.

Mary B. Harris

iii

Contents

v

Classroom
Uses of
Behavior
Modification

PART 1

Basic Principles of Learning

In recent years a new approach to solving human problems has become important in both psychology and education. This approach, originally called behavior therapy, was at first emphasized within the area of psychotherapy, as an alternative to more traditional analytic, client-centered and group therapy approaches. Behavior therapy essentially focused on the actual behaviors which were disturbing to the patient or client and rejected the idea of attempting to diagnose or treat hypothetical internal states or illnesses; instead an attempt was made to describe the behaviors of the patient, the situations in which they occurred, and their consequences. A body of specific techniques which were largely based on principles of learning established through laboratory research was gradually developed. Although behavior therapy has been criticized for its ignoring the "inner needs" and feelings of the patient, for its "superficiality," and for the fact that not all the techniques used followed directly from learning theory, there is little doubt that in many cases the techniques of behavior therapy have been very successful.

Teachers and educators soon realized that many of the techniques used by behavior therapists were appropriate in dealing with problem behavior not only in the therapy situation but also in the classroom. Indeed many of the techniques had been advocated by B. F. Skinner for classroom teaching before the advent of behavior therapy and many, in fact, were the kinds of suggestions which parents and teachers had been using without a conscious rationale for many years. When the techniques used were modified to fit situations other than the therapist's office or mental hospital, it was realized that the term behavior therapy was no longer appropriate. "Behavior change techniques," "operant conditioning," "precision teaching" and other terms have also been used to refer to this general group of techniques; however, the phrase which has found widest application and seems to encompass the broadest range of possibilities is the one that will be used in this book: behavior modification.

Behavior modification implies both a philosophical and procedural focus and also a group of techniques. Essentially behavior modification assumes as its task the production of changes in a person's behavior, rather than curing his illness, giving him some motivation, increasing his interest in the material, drumming something into his thick skull, etc. Practitioners of behavior modification, whether working in the classroom, the laboratory, or the therapist's office, all take as their first step the specification of the person's actual behaviors and the behaviors to be substituted for them. It may be the case, of course, that certain internal states, which are reflected in the behavior, are responsible for his actions in a sense; at present psychologists often disagree strongly on the existence and meaningfulness of such hypothetical states as interest, happiness, motivation, understanding, etc. Nevertheless, regardless of their personal opinions of the value of considering such states of the person, all behavior modifiers follow the cardinal rule of focusing on actions rather than feelings. This means that instead of calling a student inattentive they would say that he faces the back of the classroom, doodles on a piece of paper, does not speak when spoken to, etc. A behavior modifier, in short, defines the behaviors he wishes changed in very explicit terms and takes as his measure of success the amount of measurable change in these behaviors. Problems of specifying, observing, and evaluating behavior change will be considered in Chapter 2.

BASIC PRINCIPLES OF LEARNING

The methods used to produce changes in behavior are for the most part derived from learning theory. A brief review of the most important facets of learning theory will serve to indicate the basis for much of the theory and many of the techniques of behavior modification.

Although there is less than complete agreement among psychologists and educators on how learning should be defined, it is generally considered to be a relatively permanent change in performance (behavior) occurring as a result of practice or experience rather than of maturation or temporary states of the person such as those caused by fatigue, hunger, drugs, etc. Learning, as such, cannot be measured directly but must be inferred from performance; since this is the case, and since the physiological changes occurring as a result of learning have not yet been isolated, behavior modifiers use performance changes as their criteria of success, rather than attempting to assess changes within the person.

Conditioning

The simplest or most basic kind of learning is called conditioning. There are two different kinds of conditioning; classical, or Pavlovian, and instrumental or operant. In classical conditioning a stimulus (the conditioned stimulus) acquires the ability to elicit a new response (the conditioned response) through pairing with a stimulus (the unconditioned stimulus) which elicits a similar response (the unconditioned response). The classical example of classical conditioning is the experiment by Pavlov in which he would ring a bell (the CS) shortly before putting meat powder (the UCS) in a dog's mouth, which always caused him to salivate (the UCR). After several pairings, the bell alone began to elicit salivation (the CR), which it had never done before. Although deliberate use of classical conditioning in the classroom is rare, many emotional responses to stimuli appear to be learned through such a process. An actual example is that of a high school Latin teacher who always wore a red tie on test days; after several pairings of the sight of the tie with the horrors of a "surprise" test, the sight of the tie alone began to elicit fear and trembling on the part of his students.

The closest thing to a "classical" operant conditioning experiment is based on the work of B. F. Skinner; it consists of putting a rat in a box with a lever rigged so that a push on the lever will release a pellet of food. After his first accidental push on the lever, the rat begins to push on it more and more frequently, as long as some percentage of the lever presses are rewarded or reinforced with food. In operant conditioning, the essential factor is that the animal is presented with an object or event called a reinforcer *contingent* (dependent) upon his performance (or for some purposes, nonperformance) of a response. Unlike the classical conditioning situation, there is not necessarily a conditioned stimulus which comes to elicit the response; however the reinforcer can be thought of as analogous to the UCS, which elicits its own response, and in both cases, the frequency of performing a response (the CR) is changed. The basic difference between classical and instrumental conditioning, however, is that in the latter the reinforcement is *contingent* upon the performance of the response. Whereas in classical conditioning the UCS is presented regardless of whether or not the CR is performed, in operant conditioning the reinforcement comes only if the subject performs the response. In other words, the subject actually operates on the environment; his behavior is instrumental (essential) to obtaining the reward. The great majority of studies utilizing behavior modification in the classroom have involved the application of operant conditioning.

Reinforcement

As was stated before, the essential element of operant conditioning is the principle of reinforcement, sometimes called the law of effect. Essentially, this principle states that a response which is followed by the presentation of any one of a group of objects or events called positive reinforcers or rewards, or by the withdrawal of one of a group of objects or events called negative reinforcers or aversive stimuli, will be more likely to be repeated in the future. The law of effect also works in reverse; the term "punishment" refers to the presentation of an aversive stimulus or the withdrawal of a positive reinforcer, either of which is followed by a decrease in the probability of the preceding response.

Extinction

Punishment, however, has been shown only to suppress a response rather than to eliminate it entirely. When the threat of punishment is gone, the response reappears. The only way to permanently get rid of a response appears to be by a process called *extinction*, which refers to the presentation of the CS without the UCS (in classical conditioning) or the nonpresentation of the reinforcer after the response is made (in operant conditioning). The term "extinction" is also used to refer to the disappearance of the response in such a situation, as well as to the conditions causing such a disappearance. Because extinction is the only way known to cause the permanent disappearance of a response, it is used when feasible by behavior modifiers, often in conjunction with positive reinforcement of alternative or incompatible responses.

Partial Reinforcement

Reinforcement, of course, does not have to be administered every time the response is made. In fact, it would be almost impossible for a teacher to reinforce every single correct answer of all her students every day. If reinforcement is delivered on only some of the trials, a procedure called "partial reinforcement" or "intermittent reinforcement," then two effects typically are noticed. First, and not surprisingly, learning is slower under partial reinforcement than under continuous reinforcement. The second phenomenon, one which has been called the "partial reinforcement effect," is more startling; resistance to extinction is greatly augmented if reinforcement has been only intermittent. Although there is some disagreement on the reasons for this effect, it seems reasonable to conclude that it is harder to tell when extinction begins if there is no obvious switch from continuous reinforcement; also, under partial reinforcement one learns to persist in responding even after several non-reinforced trials. Since we would like many of the behaviors we teach in school to persist even if reinforcement is sometimes infrequent, reinforcing only intermittently may be a convenient way to increase resistance to extinction.

Schedules of Reinforcement

If reinforcement is not given on every trial, it may be presented randomly or according to some schedule. There are basically two different ways of classifying schedules. In the first classification reinforcement is dispensed either according to time elapsed since the last reinforcement (an interval schedule) or according to the number of responses performed (a ratio schedule). By the second method of classification the reinforcement is given regularly (a fixed schedule) or irregularly (a variable schedule). On a fixed interval schedule, the reinforcer is given for the first response after every N minutes; on a variable interval schedule the reinforcer is given for the first response after a varying number of minutes which averages out to N minutes. Similarly, a fixed ratio schedule involves reinforcing the person for every Nth response; a variable ratio schedule involves reinforcing him after a varying number of responses, averaging one reinforcement per N responses. Although there are subtle differences in the patterns of behavior evoked by different reinforcement schedules and by the size of the ratio or interval involved, the schedule which is clearly least appropriate where one wants people to keep working at a steady pace is the fixed interval schedule. If a fixed interval schedule is used in the classroom, e.g., calling on someone only once a day, then one would expect that the person would quickly learn to take a very long rest, e.g., not raise his hand, after every reinforcement, rather than to continue responding.

Delay of Reinforcement

Not only the schedule of reinforcement but also its delay determines effectiveness. Unlike animals, humans can often be affected by reinforcers which are delayed by hours, days, weeks or even years; however, immediate reinforcement is invariably much more effective and may even be essential for changing the behavior of children. Many behavior modification procedures are specifically designed to reduce the usual delay that occurs before a behavior can be reinforced in the classroom. Once a response has been learned, however, delaying reinforcement for it may increase resistance to extinction; thus many procedures which at first involve immediate reinforcement of responses later deliver reinforcement only after delays of increasing length.

Generalization and Discrimination

Once a behavior has been learned, it is rarely performed under all conditions. The phenomena of stimulus generalization and discrimination help one to determine when a response is likely to be performed. Stimulus generalization refers to a tendency to perform a response in situations similar to that in which it has been reinforced. Since the environment is constantly changing from instant to instant and no one is ever in exactly the same stimulus situation twice, it seems obvious that some degree of generalization is essential for permanent behavior changes to occur. A related phenomenon is that of response generalization; a person is likely to perform other responses similar to those for which he has been reinforced. Discrimination is just the opposite of generalization; it refers to the tendency to respond differently to two situations in which different reinforcement contingencies are in effect. One of the most important tasks of education is to foster appropriate discriminations; that is, to enable students to know how to behave in different circumstances. Many of the behavior problems often noticed in the classroom can be considered as the result of inadequate discriminations and can be improved by making clearer or altering the contingencies governing responses in different situations.

A term widely used by behavior modifiers to describe the effects that stimuli have on behavior is "stimulus control." Sometimes stimuli control behavior very directly by eliciting certain unconditioned responses, such as salivation at the sight and smell of a hamburger; more often they serve as discriminative stimuli, indicating the kinds of reinforcement contingencies now in effect, as do the familiar red, yellow and green traffic lights. In the classroom, the presence or absence of certain teachers, the time of day, the teacher's expression, etc., may all exercise stimulus control over behavior by indicating the probable consequences of certain behaviors. It is important to realize that stimuli often control behavior without the conscious awareness of the person; we can see this when the relationship between certain stimuli and behavior is suddenly made clear to us, as exemplified by the many responses that are often made to emotionally upsetting stimuli by people who are unaware of them—smoking, talking louder, nail biting, etc.

The principles and facets of learning which are briefly summarized here by no means constitute an adequate list of the important characteristics of learning; however, an understanding of these terms is essential to enable one to comprehend and utilize the techniques of behavior modification in the classroom, techniques which for the most part follow directly from these principles.

BEHAVIOR MODIFICATION TECHNIQUES

Although no one method of classifying techniques for changing behavior has been universally used, a logical division of such techniques would seem to be a separation of those which are used to increase the frequencies of certain behaviors from those which are used to decrease the frequencies of specific behaviors. Some techniques, such as modeling and stimulus control procedures, appear to be adaptable for both purposes. Although particular studies often utilize several methods and may have several goals, the separation of techniques into these categories should assist in helping one to assess the components of these studies.

Techniques Designed to Increase the Frequency of Certain Behaviors

In essence, all the techniques which fall under this heading utilize the principle of positive reinforcement. The most direct method of utilizing positive reinforcement is to simply present a reinforcer contingent upon the performance of the desired response. For many children feedback or knowledge of their performance ("right," "correct," etc.) is an adequate reinforcer. Material reinforcers, such as food, candy, trinkets, money, etc. are very frequently used in therapy with retarded or disturbed children but due to their disruptive effects are less common in the normal classroom, although several studies at the nursery school level have used them. Social rewards, such as praise, hugs, and positive comments, are among the easiest to administer in the classroom; in addition, they have the advantages of being natural and not interfering with normal classroom activity. However praise from the teacher may not be rewarding for all children, particularly if the peer group considers such praise as "sissy stuff." A fourth type of positive reinforcer which can be directly administered by the teacher consists of the opportunity to engage in preferred behaviors. The Premack Principle, named after David

Premack, states that activities which are highly probable when a person has a choice of many behaviors can serve as reinforcers for less probable behaviors. Thus running and screaming, talking, recess, playing games, or whatever students choose to do can serve as reinforcers for less preferred activities like studying or reciting in class.

Token Reinforcements

A more complex use of reinforcement than simply presenting a reward for a desired response involves the use of a token reinforcement system. Essentially, a token can be any object which is not intrinsically valuable but which is made valuable by the fact that the researcher, therapist, or teacher agrees to let it be exchanged for any of a number of rewards called "back up" reinforcers. Tokens used in the classroom have included points, checkmarks, plastic chips, paper tickets, and a great variety of other objects; back up reinforcers have consisted of a large variety of material rewards and high probability behaviors. Token reinforcement systems have become extremely popular in schools because they have the virtues of ease and convenience, enabling one to reward immediately and continuously at first, gradually increasing the amount of work that must be done to earn a token and/or the number of tokens necessary to earn a reward (children understand inflation), in order to increase resistance to extinction. In addition, because the token reward systems permit the use of very powerful reinforcers as well as such a variety of reinforcers, there is sure to be at least one appropriate for every child. Additional advantages may involve learning about saving, planning, deferring rewards, etc. In some instances, however, the use of a token reinforcement system may be both more expensive and more complex than that of more direct rewards, so that it is not necessarily appropriate for all classrooms.

Contracting

Other programs to increase the frequency of desired classroom behaviors have been less concerned with the type of reinforcement used and more with the setting of contingencies. One method for doing this which differs from the usual procedure of having the teacher make all the decisions is the use of a contract system. With such a system the student and teachers decide jointly what type of rewards will be forthcoming for what specific behaviors. A written contract, spelling out both sides of the agreement may even be signed. Although such an approach has been most often used at the college level with grades as a reinforcer, there is no necessary reason why this need be so; it may be particularly appropriate at the high school and junior high school level where students are very concerned about setting goals for themselves.

Group Contingencies

Another type of approach concerns the use of group contingencies. Instead of having the child's behavior affect only his own reinforcement, such a program usually involves having rewards for the whole class made dependent upon the behavior of one or more (sometimes all) of the children in the class. Such a procedure is particularly useful where disruptive behavior has been maintained by social reinforcement from peers thus rendering the teacher's praise or criticism relatively impotent. A related idea is the use of parents to mediate behavioral changes, either as observers of the behavior or as dispensers of reward. Either way, the parent is now engaged actively in helping to change the behavior and is much less likely to counteract the effects of the program by inadvertently extinguishing or even punishing the desired behaviors.

Programmed Instruction

A large number of different approaches to presenting subject material can all be classified under the heading of programmed instruction. Many studies have utilized teaching devices called "teaching machines;" others have utilized computers, and still others have used programmed textbooks. Essentially all these methods have in common the fact that they manage to provide individualized instruction to each student without the necessity of having an individual tutor for each person. In all these methods the material is presented in small steps and the student has to make a correct response before he is permitted to progress to the next step. *Linear* programs follow the same series of steps for everyone; *branching* programs vary the sequence depending upon the answers given. The advantages of programmed learning are many: 1) the material must be presented in a graduated, organized fashion, unlike the case in many classrooms; 2) the student gets immediate and frequent feedback or reinforcement; 3) the student must actively participate—the lesson won't go on while he daydreams; 4) since a good program is designed to permit very few errors, the student is unlikely to experience feelings of failure; 5) the subject matter, speed, and method of presentation, etc., can be varied to suit the individual. Disadvantages of programmed instruction include the fact that a poorly written lesson can be even more boring than a dull book or lecture, particularly to the bright student, and that the advantages of personal contact with a teacher may be lost.

Shaping

To a large extent the previous discussion has centered upon how to increase the frequency of behaviors the person already has in his repertoire. Sometimes, however, one wants to teach a student to do something completely new. The phenomena of reinforcement and response generalization suggest one way of accomplishing this; by rewarding closer and closer approximations to the desired behavior one can gradually shape or mold a response to approximate the desired criteria. A very common example occurs in language training; at first anything resembling "wawa" is reinforced; gradually only responses similar to "water" are rewarded, and eventually only complete sentences embodying such terms as "please" produce reinforcement. By using the principle of successive approximations or shaping, pigeons have been taught to play ping-pong, rats have been taught to perform extremely complex maneuvers, and adult humans have been taught to dance. As will be mentioned later, the technique of modeling provides the other commonly used way of teaching people totally new responses.

Techniques to Decrease the Frequency of Responses

In an ideal classroom, a lucky teacher can focus his attention on teaching new responses rather than on trying to get the children to stop behaving in ways detrimental to the teaching-learning process. Unfortunately, however, most teachers are faced with the program of eliminating disruptive or undesirable behaviors as well as instilling new ones. Responses which interfere with learning may include daydreaming, talking, standing up, fighting, teasing, wisecracking, giving incorrect answers, cheating, etc. Behavior modifiers have suggested a variety of methods to be used in eliminating these and other undesirable behaviors. Although many of the methods used are more extreme than would be appropriate for a classroom situation, since they were based on therapy carried out with severely disturbed patients, others of them are relevant and appropriate for use by both teachers and parents.

Extinction

As was mentioned earlier, the only way to completely eliminate a response from a person or animal's repertoire is to ensure that the response will no longer be reinforced. It is generally assumed that if a response persists, it is indeed being reinforced in some way. A first step, then, in extinguishing a response is to identify the reinforcer for it. Very often, in the classroom, undesirable responses are being reinforced by attention from either the teacher or other students or both. Even criticism or reprimands from the teacher may be serving as a positive reinforcer for the child; in other words the teacher's comments and attention, even if negative from her point of view, are often rewarding for children. At other times, peer attention may be serving as the reinforcer; in this case rewarding the other students for ignoring the one whose behavior is disruptive may be necessary to extinguish his behavior. Another procedure, called "time-out" or "isolation" may be used: This involves removing the child from the classroom upon misbehaving so that he can no longer be rewarded by peer attention.

A teacher should be alert to cues that point out how she is unconsciously rewarding undesirable behavior; commenting on such behavior, dismissing the class when it is noisy, ending a lesson when the children seem restless, etc., are practices which, if stopped, will lead to the extinction of some undesirable behaviors. A large number of studies have shown that extinction procedures, although sometimes leading to a temporary increase in the intensity of the behaviors, provide a safe, effective means of eliminating an unwanted behavior without any undesirable side effects. The effect of extinction, moreover, is greatly enhanced when it is combined with positive reinforcement for appropriate behavior.

Punishment

Unfortunately, not all behaviors can easily be eliminated by extinction, since some of them seem to bring about their own reward. Examples of such behaviors include cheating and stealing, as well as many behaviors which are reinforced by the reduction of anxiety. Such avoidance and escape behaviors may include playing truant or just ignoring the teacher, talking with others during class, giving the first answer which comes into one's head, etc. Moreover, extinction may take a long time to accomplish, and some teachers may find that the temporary increase in the intensity of responding which may be the immediate reaction to nonreinforcement is too disturbing. In any of these instances, punishment techniques coupled with reinforcement for appropriate behaviors may be more effective than the use of extinction.

Although punishment alone merely suppresses behavior, if alternative responses which will be rewarded are available, then presentation of an aversive stimulus, such as criticism, or requiring the child to perform some aversive activity such as helping to clean the classroom, may be effective in reducing the frequency of some unwanted act. Aside from the ethical implications of using such techniques, however, there are some practical difficulties: presentation of a negative reinforcer may cause the classroom, teacher, and school to be aversive to the child; he may learn withdrawal responses to the situation or he may become very fearful of performing any behaviors at all. However, the term "punishment" does not refer only to the procedure of presenting an aversive or noxious stimulus after the undesirable response. A better type of punishment consists of withdrawing or withholding positive reinforcers contingent on performance of the unwanted response; this technique has also been called "deprivation of privileges" or "response cost." If a child is kept from recess, forced to forfeit some privilege, or not permitted a treat because of some undesirable behavior he is less likely to try to avoid the entire situation and more likely to want to do whatever will regain his reinforcers for him. It is easy to see how explicit specification of just what alternative behaviors are effective to earn rewards would be very effective in combination with punishment. In addition, a contract system utilizing punishment, in which the child himself endorses the terms and is fully aware of them, is likely to produce much less resentment than punishment imposed by the teacher.

Reinforcement of Incompatible Behavior

Another technique which is sometimes useful in the classroom is to reward the child for performing some behavior which is incompatible with the one you wish to eliminate. In psychotherapy, behavior therapists use a technique called "cognitive desensitization," in which they train a person to relax in the presence of cues which formerly caused anxiety responses. In the classroom one might try rewarding a quiet child for speaking up, praising a bully for ordinary politeness, or reinforcing a show-off for listening to someone else.

Other Techniques

Several other methods for preventing certain responses are not particularly appropriate for most classroom situations. At times it may be necessary to physically prevent a response, such as breaking up a fight. A technique called "satiation" or "flooding" has been used with hoarders in mental hospitals; by giving them unlimited quantities of what they desire, their hoarding was finally eliminated. Related to this is a technique called "implosive therapy" in which anxious patients are required to imagine the source of their fear in great and terrifying detail, until their anxiety finally diminishes. Aversive counterconditioning involves pairing an undesired response or a stimulus which one wishes to become aversive (drugs, cigarettes, alcohol, etc.) with an aversive stimulus like electric shock through a classical conditioning paradigm. All of these latter methods, as well as the more extreme forms of punishment, are more appropriate to the therapy situation than to the classroom.

Modeling

Two final methods for modifying behavior are particularly useful, since they both can be used to either increase or decrease the frequencies of behaviors. The technique of modeling involves performing the behavior to be imitated so that the person you are trying to teach can see and observe it. The effects of modeling have been demonstrated for an extremely wide range of situations and behaviors, including altruism, aggression, language, self reward, delaying gratification, reducing or increasing fears, and many other instances. Moreover, the modeling/ imitation phenomenon does not appear to depend on reinforcement; people learn from observing a model regardless of whether or not they are reinforced for doing so. However, they are much more likely to perform a behavior for which they see a model reinforced (called "vicarious reinforcement"), and are themselves promised a reward for imitation. Similarly, they are less likely to perform a behavior if they see a model refrain from making the response, particularly if he is rewarded for his resistance; the tendency to perform a behavior they see a model punished for may also be inhibited.

Modeling is consciously used as a teaching technique in most classrooms; the teacher may demonstrate the desired response and ask students to deliberately imitate it; he may "make an example" of one student by rewarding or punishing him; he may tacitly assume that hearing one student recite correctly will improve the performance of others in the class. Since the effects of modeling do not depend upon the awareness or desire of the person observed that he serve as a model, the teacher should realize that he and everyone else in the class are constantly serving as models for other students. Thus, the type of language used, disciplinary techniques, degree of enthusiasm for the subject matter, prejudices, and almost every aspect of his behavior will be observed and possibly imitated by the students. Similarly, the consequences to another student of his behaviors will also be observed and will affect whether or not these behaviors are imitated. Just as parents discover that their children are picking up all their good and bad habits, a teacher should be aware of his influence as a model and possibly attempt to use it deliberately to modify the behavior of his students.

Stimulus Control

The study of stimulus discrimination has made it clear that certain behaviors are much more likely to occur in the presence of certain stimuli than in their absence. This control of behavior by stimuli may often develop without the conscious involvement of the person concerned; if he has formed a habit of behaving in a certain way whenever he is in the presence of a particular stimulus, the stimulus soon will serve to elicit the behavior whenever it is present. Similarly, if a person is used to acting in a certain way only when in the presence of a certain stimulus, he will cease responding in that fashion when the controlling stimulus is no longer present. Stimulus control procedures have been used to increase studying by having a person designate a certain place, time of day, etc., where and when he will be sure to study. They have also been used to reduce the frequency of undesirable behaviors like smoking or overeating by reducing the number of situations in which these behaviors occur. The use of certain areas of the classroom for certain activities, scheduling definite times for some activities, refusing to permit unwanted behaviors such as talking except at certain times and places, are examples of stimulus control procedures in the classroom. Alternatively, changing the stimulus situation very drastically might prove an effective way of getting students out of their rut and instigating new ways of behaving.

SUMMARY

This chapter has focused on providing an overview of the major principles of learning theory and the behavior change techniques derived from them which have been found useful for modifying behavior in the classroom situation. Most of these techniques have been used deliberately outside the classroom situation by employers, therapists, mental hospital personnel and others. Many of them have been used unconsciously by parents and teachers, who may not have been fully aware of the consequences of their own behaviors. The parent who cuddles his child for getting into his pajamas and the parent who cuddles his child who has been screaming in bed for an hour are both using positive reinforcement techniques and probably both warm loving parents; however the end results of their use of these techniques will be very different. As the above example illustrates, the fact that these methods are so widely used does not ensure that they will always be used efficiently.

It is hoped that for a person with a general understanding of the fundamental methods of behavior modification, the articles reprinted here should be useful in illustrating practical and innovative ways to apply these techniques. The subjects in these studies have ranged from nursery school children to college students, from middle class children to juvenile delinquents to members of minority groups. The users of these techniques have been psychologists, teachers, aides and parents; the behaviors involved have ranged from reading to getting out of one's seat to social interaction. In the next chapter, some of the practical and ethical difficulties in using these methods as well as in designing studies to assess their effectiveness will be discussed along with suggestions as to how to read and interpret research articles on behavior modification.

PART 2

Conducting and Evaluating Behavior Modification Projects

ETHICAL ISSUES

In order to successfully apply the techniques of behavior modification, the teacher or therapist has to consider a variety of problems and issues. First among these are the ethical and moral questions which arise whenever someone is trying to change another person in some way.

CONTROL

Probably the most controversial moral issue raised by the use of behavior modification techniques is the question of whether it is justifiable to control or manipulate someone's behavior. By treating people as if they are objects or animals to be manipulated, isn't the teacher or therapist denying their very humanity, their free will? Or, more mildly put, can children truly benefit from being forced to learn or forced to change? Wouldn't they then lose the joy of discovering things for themselves, the sense of creativity which comes when someone is following his own direction and inclinations without having someone else deliberately modifying his behavior? Isn't this "manipulation" the antithesis of the "free school," where self-actualization and self-exploration are encouraged?

The answer to the problems of whether or not it is "right" to control another person is one which every teacher, therapist, and parent has to face for himself. Those who practice behavior modification point out that such questions arise only when effective techniques of behavior control are available; if a person cannot deliberately affect another's behavior, then he need be less concerned about taking responsibility for the effects of his own actions on another. Before people were aware of the possibility of deliberately using the techniques of behavior modification to change behavior, the problem of the morality of such control was rarely raised. They emphasize that this issue of control is really a question that no one can escape, since we are all always affecting the behavior of everyone with whom we interact. Regardless of our knowledge of or intention to use the principles of learning, we still have effects on others every time we smile or pay attention to someone, every time we look bored or walk away, every time our own actions and the consequences to us are observed. This is particularly true in the classroom, where a teacher is constantly attending to some children and not to others, making decisions about whom to call on, and presenting himself or herself as a model every time he or she speaks. In short, we are already manipulating and controlling other people all the time; we may as well do it deliberately to encourage behaviors we want, as to let the process continue haphazardly.

A second answer to the above questions is that it is the teacher's job to change students. If students are no different when the school year is over, they are considered traditionally to have "failed" and may be requested to repeat the year until they do show some change. Even beyond the cognitive changes a teacher is supposed to effect in her students are the changes in the affective domain; the importance attached to changing student's feelings and values is reflected in the presentation of courses such as citizenship, art appreciation, social studies, etc. If the teacher is trying to change behaviors, then, why shouldn't the most effective means for doing so be used? Isn't this really the purpose of courses in learning theory and methods of teaching?

A third response to the question of control is to suggest that the person involved set his own goals and that the teacher or therapist or behavioral engineer act, in a sense, as a consultant to help him establish the means. People hire doctors, lawyers, plumbers and other experts to help them deal with problems or achieve goals, when assistance is needed. In fact, some philosophical views of the teacher see him as just that: a person who assists the learner to change his behaviors, to acquire new knowledge to further his own ends. In actual practice, many practitioners of behavior modification can go a step beyond merely specifying a particular means for change, by giving the "client" or student a choice of alternative ways to achieve his objective. Surely, if it is the person himself who desires to change, there is little moral dilemma about providing him with a list of possible methods for producing this change.

One more answer to the question of freedom versus control is to point out that changing someone's behavior, particularly the kind of change we call education, may actually expand his freedom. A child who is unable to make his thoughts understood, to interact with other children, to read or do arithmetic, is likely to have a difficult time as he gets older. In most modern societies, many options are closed to the person with few skills, little education, and little ability to get along with others. If a person's behavior is modified so that he now possesses these abilities, then his freedom to choose whether or not to exercise them and the type of life he would like to lead will be much greater. By "controlling" someone's behavior, it may be that the teacher or therapist is in fact releasing him from the control of circumstances.

TECHNIQUES

A second ethical issue which arises in addition to the question of manipulation is the morality of the various techniques used for changing behavior. Some of these objections are to techniques not applicable to the usual classroom situation, such as aversive classical conditioning and implosive therapy. The same criticism that is made of these techniques, namely, that the experiences involved are unpleasant for the client, has also been made of one technique which has frequently been used in the classroom—the application of punishment. Some of the practical difficulties with the use of punishment have already been discussed and might suggest that there are times when punishment should not be used, simply because its side effects may make it inefficient. However, the moral question of whether or when punishment is justifiable can not be easily resolved. The fact that physical punishment and ridicule, as exemplified by hickory sticks and dunce caps, have been a traditional part of American education, is hardly a reasonable argument for their continuance.

There may really be two problems involved in considering the use of punishment: the situations in which it is applicable and the types of punishment which are appropriate. The point of view which the author shares is that punishment should be used only in those situations where other techniques will not be or cannot be effective or where it is urgent that the behavior be stopped immediately. Examples might include behaviors which bring about their own reward, such as stealing or cheating, behaviors for which other techniques have been tried and found unsuccessful (for example, when there is no acceptable social behavior to be positively reinforced), and behaviors which might have serious and harmful consequences for others, such as beating another child or destroying someone's property.

Concerning the matter of what kind of punishment to use, it is generally felt that withdrawal of privileges is ethically more justifiable than presentation of an aversive event, such as physical punishment or ridicule. Moreover, you have the "fringe benefit" that you can use reinstatement of privileges to positively reinforce some other behavior. Similarly, there is general agreement that the use of "No, that answer is wrong" or other information (feedback) about the correctness of an academic behavior is unlikely to be upsetting to a child; in fact a number of studies have shown that in problem-solving tasks, informing someone when he is wrong usually produces better learning than telling him when he is right. A third type of punishment which most people feel is justifiable is reparative or constructive punishment, in which the child is asked to do something to "make up for" the unacceptable behavior. This might include something like earning money or doing work to pay back damage done to someone else's property or doing extra lessons or work to remedy an academic deficit. Apologies, if sincere, would fall into this category. Types of punishment which many people feel are never acceptable are ridicule (criticizing someone on the basis of his intelligence, race, sex, etc.) and physical punishment. The latter is particularly inappropriate because it teaches students that this is an acceptable way of dealing with people who cannot retaliate.

Two more points can be made about the use of punishment. First, punishment seems a much more ethical technique if the student concerned agrees on its use and is involved in the decision as to what behavior to punish and what punishment to use. If the class as a whole decides on rules and penalties, then imposition of these penalties seems ethical. A second point which can be made is that punishment should always be used in conjunction with reward for appropriate behaviors, for reasons of both efficiency and morality.

The other technique to which ethical objections have been raised is, paradoxically enough, the use of reward. Ordinarily, social rewards such as praise are not criticized seriously, as their use is so common. However, many parents and teachers have objected strenuously to the use of material and token rewards. Of course, to act reasonably and responsibly is to make sure that the particular rewards are acceptable to the parents of the children who receive them; many parents would not want their children receiving candy, cokes, toy guns, etc. The objection more frequently met, though, is that it is immoral to "bribe children for doing what they ought to do anyway." In response, it might be said that adults do not object to being "bribed" with money, vacations, etc., for doing their jobs. If the behavior you want to teach or instill is a valuable one, then it seems only fair to show the person that some value is attached to it. Too often children, at home as well as in school, are ignored when they are being good and given attention only for misbehaving. Surely it is just as ethical to let someone know when you like what he is doing, by a smile, a comment, or a material reward, then to inform him only when you disapprove. Closely related to this objection is the idea, often expressed only implicitly, that the value or meaning and perhaps even the fun of an activity will be reduced if external rewards are offered for doing it. Certainly there are times when people feel insulted or unhappy at receiving a reward for an activity which was done without expectation of reward, particularly in the case of a helpful or altruistic act. One suggestion for dealing with such situations is to use social rewards such as praise or thanks, since objections to these are extremely rare. Another suggestion is that when presenting extrinsic rewards to a person for an action done without expectation of reward, you make it explicit that you know that he was not working *for* a reward but nevertheless his behavior was good enough to *deserve* one. Few people would object to being rewarded for their accomplishments when their good intentions are also recognized.

SECRECY

A third ethical issue, which is particularly but not solely applicable to research projects, is the question of the awareness and possible consent of the participants to the use of the techniques. Certainly, there is no reason why students in the classroom cannot be told exactly what the consequences of their good and bad behavior will be, exactly what the teacher is attempting to model or teach, and so forth. In fact, they can often be involved in setting goals and deciding on rules and techniques for achieving them. On the other hand, when a research study is going on, it may be much better for reaching accurate conclusions, if the students are not informed about the hypotheses, purposes, means, and even the existence of the research. Most universities and most public school systems now have committees to screen research and be sure that no objectionable techniques or unnecessary secrecy are involved. Generally, unless the project involves only behaviors and events typical to the normal classroom (e.g. teachers comments, smiles, etc.), the parents are informed of and requested to consent to their child's participation.

Sometimes, of course, telling children or parents the details of the research will spoil it (e.g. "I'm going to model lots of pronouns and see if the students then use more pronouns.") Very often in such cases, the project can be explained afterwards and the implications discussed with the people concerned. If this cannot be done, then the potential benefits of the project should be weighed very carefully against the possible disadvantages of secrecy before a decision is made.

ETHICS OF DOING RESEARCH

In addition to the issue of openness or secrecy, which arises in both research and non-research situations, there are several other ethical problems which are primarily relevant when doing research in behavior modification. These are concerned with the questions of getting some means of comparison to find out whether or not your program was successful without the possibility of penalizing or harming children by not exposing them to the most effective techniques all the time. Two general methods are used for making these comparisons in research: one is to compare a student's performance when the program is in effect with that before (the base rate period) and after (the reversal period) and the second is to have one or more "control" groups not exposed to the same program or technique. The dilemma is clear: How can one find out whether or not a technique really has an effect if there is no basis of comparison?

One solution to the problem is to institute a reversal phase, when the technique will no longer be used, and to watch very carefully during this period to see that the child's behavior, if he reverts back to the older and less desirable ways of behaving, is not such as to have any unwanted permanent effects. If your target behavior has been to have children stay in their seats, it is unlikely that a return to the older standing up behavior during the reversal phase will cause any harm. On the other hand, if the behavior involved was to have a child interact socially with others, a long reversal phase might seriously destroy this capacity. Sometimes, when one does not want to use a reversal phase for ethical reasons, the research purpose can be served by working on several different behaviors one at a time and seeing whether or not each one changes only when it is the specific target of the techniques.

One answer to the control group problem of having some children forgo exposure to some possibly helpful technique is to do a comparative study and try out different techniques (not necessarily all based on behavior modification), so that everyone is receiving some possibly beneficial experience. Another response to the problem is to recognize that some studies find that the technique the researchers expected to be beneficial in fact was less effective than the traditional ways of dealing with the problem. In a sense you are always comparing two different techniques, when you are dealing with classroom behavior, and until there is some evidence that the "new" technique is better or worse than the "traditional" one, there seems to be no moral reason for choosing one over the other.

Other ethical issues besides these four are found when one is using behavior modification techniques or any other techniques in the classroom. The decision about what goals to implement and what values to teach, if any, are ones faced by every teacher, therapist, and parent. Seeking advice from experts or from the individuals concerned may help with solving these problems. Being aware of the ways in which your own values are expressed in your behavior and are affecting other people may also be useful in deciding on moral issues. In the final analysis, however, every individual is faced with making these ethical decisions himself, even though a teacher's decisions may have great effects on his students.

PRACTICAL PROBLEMS

Once the ethical questions have been considered, if a teacher has decided to use behavior modification in the classroom, certain practical problems commonly arise. The articles in the latter part of the book will discuss some of these problems and give some specific examples of what difficulties arose and how they were dealt with. More generally, the following problems have been found to be typical in deciding how to implement such a program.

CHOOSING TARGET BEHAVIORS AND TECHNIQUES

On one level, most teachers are aware of the changes they would like their students to exhibit. They want them to learn mathematics or stop talking in class, to work more independently or to pay closer attention to the teacher. On another level, however, many teachers and others have some trouble at first in specifying particular behaviors that they would like to see altered. A term commonly used to refer to the goals which teaching or other behavior change techniques should implement is "behavioral objectives." As the term implies, the objectives of the teacher should be described in terms of actual behaviors which can be observed, so that such observations can be used to gather evidence as to whether or not your technique is having any effect. This does not mean that a teacher need be concerned only with trivia or that all the important objectives of education are easily measurable. However, if a teacher cannot specify the nature of the specific behavior changes he expects his teaching to produce, then it is unlikely that he will have any way of knowing whether his goals have been achieved. Many examples of objective target behaviors will be given in the following articles; among these are things like correct answers either on written tests or orally in class, raising one's hand, decreasing the amount of talking, sitting in one's seat, being able to read aloud, and answering questions on material read.

Once the teacher has decided what behaviors he wants to change, the practical question of what techniques to use arises. The first chapter specified some of the applications, advantages, and disadvantages of the various possible techniques. As a practical matter, many teachers prefer to begin with methods which can be carried out naturally in the classroom without making obvious changes in the normal procedures. Positive reinforcement and shaping using praise and "free time" as reinforcers, along with modeling and stimulus control, can be used to increase certain behaviors without being obvious; the latter two techniques plus punishment in the form of feedback or deprivation of privileges ("no recess until you've answered this problem correctly") can also be used unobtrusively to decrease the frequency of some activities. These particular techniques and reinforcers also have the great advantage of costing nothing.

For more dramatic results, particularly with younger children, material rewards are often more effective than natural ones. Similarly, tokens are particularly effective if you have a diverse class of students who are not all responsive to the same rewards. They may also be used for their educational value in teaching about monetary exchange, delay of gratification, etc. Although they usually require some degree of financial outlay, inventive teachers have printed classroom money on the school ditto machine and used it in auctions of assorted jobs and privileges within the class.

Other decisions about the choice of techniques include whether to use extinction or punishment to eliminate a particular undesirable behavior; whether to use shaping, modeling or some combination to remedy a behavior deficit, i.e. to teach an appropriate response when none exists; what type of reward or punishment is most appropriate for a particular child; whether to use group or individual contingencies or some combination (e.g., reward the whole group for one individual's performance); whether to use stimulus control and if so what stimuli to alter or present; whether to use a contract system or decide on the goals and methods yourself; and a large number of issues that have to be faced in individual cases. Looking over the studies here may help you decide what target behaviors and techniques would be most appropriate in your situation.

KEEPING RECORDS

Once the choice of behavioral objective and techniques has been made, the keeping of some kind of records becomes important. An immediate question which comes to mind is whether or not such record keeping is necessary or even helpful. Most people who have used behavior modification will answer yes to both questions. There are many examples of teachers, parents and therapists thinking that their activities were or were not having any effect on their students, children or patients and then finding out from accurate records that their impressions were wrong. Psychologists and educational researchers are well aware of the fact that people's expectations may color their actual perceptions. Thus, until the benefit of a particular program has been well established, some form of record is necessary to determine how well it is being implemented and the effects it is having.

In order to keep records, some kind of recording device is necessary. For most classroom purposes, a piece of paper called a rating schedule or observational schedule will be most helpful. It is essential that such a schedule be easy and quick to use, as well as provide the necessary information. Usually either a rating scale is used, in which the teacher rates each of several behaviors with respect to various dimensions, or a check list, in which a mark is made every time a certain behavior occurs. It is very important that the behaviors be specified in sufficient detail that few problems arise in deciding how to count or score them, both to simplify recording and to insure that the records be accurate.

An important aspect of any record sheet is that it be objective or reliable; in other words, that the score recorded be independent of who is doing the observing or recording. One way of finding out whether or not this is so is to have two observers watch the same behavior and see whether or not their records agree. Usually the percentage of agreement is given. Another way to assess objectivity, if a product rather than a process is being observed, is to have the same person attempt to re-score or re-measure the same product at a later time. Unless a recording device is reliable, in the sense that the same behavior will always be recorded or scored in the same way, then it is worthless for all practical purposes. Generally, the only way to find out whether or not a recording schedule will work is to try it out ahead of time and revise it until it is quick, easy, and reliable.

FEASIBILITY

Another group of practical problems which arise, in addition to specifying objectives and techniques and developing some kind of recording chart or device, concern the ease and feasibility of carrying out such a project. Almost any kind of change in the classroom is going to create some problems of administration, requiring at least initially some time and inconvenience. Even a very simplified record chart cannot be filled out instantaneously. One question which arises is whether the use of behavior modification techniques might not create more inconvenience than they resolve. Most of the studies which are published indicate that this is not the case and that, in fact, the reduction in the amount of the teacher's time devoted to discipline and to drill is much greater than the time needed to administer the program. Many programs, in fact, are designed so that the students themselves can take over and run them; this is particularly true of token reinforcement and contract systems. In the articles that follow more specific descriptions will be given of practical problems which arose, how they were dealt with, and the resulting administrative conveniences and inconveniences.

READING AND EVALUATING RESEARCH STUDIES

For people who have had little experience with reading research reports, learning how to get the most important information from such a study without being lost in a morass of jargon, statistics, and details may take some practice. For those of you who feel a bit overwhelmed when you look at all those Es, Ss, ts, and ps, here are a few comments which may make such reading easier.

One thing to remember when reading a journal article is that the author has probably been forced to shorten his manuscript drastically; therein lies the reason for many of the abbreviations and condensations. Nevertheless, although not all articles have all parts formally subdivided, there are typically five basic parts to a research report. Usually, the article begins with an abstract, although some older papers use a summary at the end in place of an abstract at the beginning. The abstract contains, in one paragraph, the author's own summary of the most important aspects of his article—usually, what he was looking for and what he found. If intelligible, it serves as a good framework by which to evaluate the rest of the paper.

Sections of a Typical Article

The first section of the main body of the article will be the introduction, often not formally identified as such. In the introduction, the author discusses the reasons for his investigation, gives a very sketchy review of the literature, tells very generally what he actually did, and sets forth in some detail his hypotheses or predictions about what the results should be. Ordinarily the value and adequacy of his theorizing and his methodology are judged by whether or not the results confirm his hypotheses; however, sometimes critical readers can think of other explanations for his results, even though they did turn out as predicted.

After the introduction comes the methods section, in which the details of the study are actually spelled out. Even the most zealous editor will usually spare this section, since it is essential to know exactly what was done in order to interpret the study. Usually, details about the subjects or participants (S), the experimenter (E), and the setting will be given, along with a description of the actual procedures. In the methods section, be sure to look for a description of the dependent measure, the actual behavior or test score which was measured or observed. Sometimes you may find that an author's discussion of the changes he found imply much more drastic changes than those actually observed. It is important to read the methods section carefully, since this is the part of the paper which describes what the author really did.

The next section of a typical article is the one which usually causes the most trouble to the inexperienced reader—the results. There is often a great temptation, in looking at all the Greek letters, the numbers, graphs and charts, to abandon the article at this point. Instead, if you're someone who knows little or nothing about statistics, try skimming the writing to see if there are several summary sentences which present the results. A handy hint is to remember that almost all statistical tests are performed to discover whether or not the results would have occurred by chance alone or are really due to something else, such as the experimenter's manipulations. Therefore, look for the ps, the probabilities that the results were due to chance alone. The smaller the p value, the less likely it is that the results were due to chance and the more likely that they would be found again if the study were repeated. Ordinarily, if less than five times in a hundred such results would occur by chance alone ($p < .05$), they would be considered statistically significant. Thus, if you go through the results section and find those results which had p values of less than .05 ($p < .05$), you will know which ones are significant, even if you don't understand the details of the particular significance test involved.

A second way to glean something from the results section is to look at the tables and graphs, paying close attention to the title. Often average scores (means or medians) for the different groups will be put in a graph or table. Sometimes before and after scores (called "pretest and posttest scores") will be presented. By looking at the actual numbers, you can often get an idea of the size of the difference, as well as its statistical significance. Sometimes a change or difference or relationship may be so small as to be of little practical importance, even though it is statistically significant.

The discussion section, which comes at the end, is usually the broadest and most far-reaching part of the article. Often, it begins with a brief restatement of the major results, which is a sop or boon, depending on your interpretation, to the less statistically-minded who haven't perused the results section too carefully. Usually, in the discussion the author relates the results to the hypotheses and attempts to account for any discrepancies. He also relates his findings to his and other's theoretical interpretations and often suggests new research which should be done to clear up matters left unexplained by the present study. With fingers crossed, it is probably safe to say that an article never concludes with the statements that the problem has been solved, no further research is necessary, and psychologists and educators can best occupy themselves by investigating some other topic.

INTERPRETATION

Due to the fact that psychologists and educators do most of their research with people, there are many sources of bias which can lead the researcher to faulty conclusions. Often he will point out some of these possible flaws in the discussion, but it is helpful for the reader to be aware of some of the problems which might confound the interpretation of the findings. Some common sources of bias in psychological and educational research are:

1. Non-random assignment. If the subjects have not been *randomly* assigned to groups, then there is a likelihood that the groups differ in some other way than just exposure to different treatments by the experimenter.
2. Inappropriate generalization of the results. If the research was a case study, involving just one subject or one small group, such generalization is particularly likely; you can only generalize legitimately to a population from which the particular subjects were randomly selected. If, as is usually the case, the subjects were not randomly chosen but were selected on the basis of availability and convenience, then you should be cautious about generalizing, especially to people who seem different in some way from the ones in the research study.
3. Hawthorne, placebo, and novelty effects. Often a program designed to bring about some kind of improvement (such as psychotherapy or education) will cause such an improvement not because of anything specific to the program but because it is new (novelty effect), because the subjects are given lots of

attention and know it (Hawthorne effect) and/or because they *believe* it will help (placebo effect). If the results are due to these effects rather than to the specific program, you can often save time and money by keeping the attention and enthusiasm but dropping the rest of the program.

4. Inaccurate scoring or observing. If the people who score the test or observe the behavior know what differences or changes are expected, they may tend to misperceive them in the direction expected. One specific example of this is called the halo effect, in which a person who does well on one thing is perceived as doing well on everything. These effects are minimized by having several independent scorers or observers use objective tests or observation schedules, and having the observers ignorant of the purpose (and, ideally, the existence) of the research.

5. Regression toward the mean. People who get extreme scores on a test can be expected to get scores somewhat closer to the average if they are given the same or a similar test again. Thus if the lowest five percent of a class is selected for remedial work, you would expect their scores on a second test to be higher even if nothing whatsoever was done in the meantime.

6. Experimenter or interviewer effects. It has been shown that the beliefs and expectations of an experimenter or interviewer affect the behavior of the subjects or interviewees. Results from a "naive" experimenter or at least one with no axe to grind are likely to be more valid.

7. Response biases. People have tendencies to answer tests or questionnaires in certain ways, almost independent of the content of the item; some say "yes" or "no" most of the time; others use extreme responses or always choose the middle category; some guess when they're uncertain and others don't; some misunderstand questions; some try to answer in the socially acceptable or desirable direction, rather than representing themselves as less desirable or correct. This is particularly a problem with interviews or questionnaires which are not anonymous.

8. Faulty reasoning. A common example is the mistaken idea that because A and B are correlated, A must cause B; actually B could cause A or C could cause both A and B. However, each researcher may have his own special tendencies to misinterpret his data; be alert.

Lest this sound too severe, let me add that most published research studies are carefully thought out and well designed, and that the researchers themselves are usually well aware of these possible flaws and have done their best to avoid them. Other problems, such as inappropriate use of statistical tests, may be both more common and more difficult to recognize. Yet the reader of an article should always keep in mind other possible interpretations of the results of a study and consider the author's conclusions as justified only when alternative explanations of the results seem less reasonable and more far-fetched than the author's interpretation. In short, the questions the reader should ask himself and be able to answer when reading an article are: 1) What was he trying to find out? 2) How did he go about it? 3) What did he find? 4) What does he think it meant? 5) Are there any obvious problems which might make his conclusions invalid? If you can answer these questions, you've understood the article.

PART 3

Studies Attempting to Increase Certain Behaviors

As a teacher looks over his class and observes what they do in the course of an hour or day or semester, he often can think of changes he would like to see in their behavior. The first group of articles reprinted here have a common purpose: to increase the amount of some behavior or improve performance on some measure. The first study, by Harris and Miksovic, attempted to increase social interaction in mentally retarded nursery school children. The next two studies, by Hall, Lund, and Jackson and Bushell, Wrobel, and Michaelis, attempted to increase the amount of time spent studying by elementary school and preschool children. The next group of three studies focused more directly on academic behaviors and learning, although none concentrated solely on a particular academic response. One step beyond these is Biehler's study, in which grades were both the dependent measure and also the reinforcer. Finally, we come to the articles by Staats and Butterfield and Bandura and Harris, which focus on specific behaviors related to academic and classroom performance but manipulated or taught by the authors outside of the classroom.

The techniques used in this group of articles vary almost as widely as the age ranges of the subjects and the types of responses to be changed. Praise and attention from the teacher, tokens or other material rewards for the individual or for the whole class, grades and even modeling have all been utilized. One feeling common to most of the articles, in spite of their diversity in techniques, has been the pleasure of teachers, students, and parents in focusing on desirable behaviors rather than on what the child is doing wrong. For this reason, as well as the demonstrated success of the methods used by these authors, the techniques designed to make desirable behaviors more frequent can be expected to continue to increase in popularity.

Mentally retarded children of preschool age are often lacking in the social skills as well as the intellectual ones which normal children of that age possess. This study used reinforcement of social activities involving other children to increase the amount of group interaction among the participants. For all of these children, hugs and attention from adults, which appeared to be rewarding, were used along with food as reinforcers. Some amount of shaping was necessary, as the children at first needed to be rewarded for physical proximity and looking at other children; later on reward was given only for true interaction.

The authors point out the great convenience of the technique. Although mentally retarded children of nursery school age usually require individual instruction, no additional staff above the usual two teachers for four children was required for this program. In fact the techniques proved so successful that the size of the class has since been expanded from four to six without any additional personnel. Since social skills evidently can be taught even to children with such low mental ages, there seems to be a definite value to using behavior modification techniques to develop these abilities in mentally retarded children before they can be stigmatized on the basis of social as well as mental disabilities.

Operant Conditioning of Social Interaction in Preschool Retarded Children

Mary B. Harris
and
*Ruth S. Miksovic**

ABSTRACT

A program utilizing contingent teacher attention for social interaction among retarded preschool children produced an increase in social behaviors for both the two children who received the treatment and the other two children in their nursery school class. During a reversal phase social behaviors did not increase and during a second treatment phase they again increased. Social interaction with adults and non-social behaviors, which were treated by extinction or isolation, showed a decrease in both treatment phases and an increase during reversal. The results suggest that social interaction among preschool retardates can indeed be instituted and maintained by this simple, inexpensive procedure.

*This project was conducted while both authors were at the University of New Mexico.

In recent years a great deal of interest has arisen in the use of operant techniques to modify children's behavior, both in and out of the classroom (Gelfand, 1968; Leff, 1968). A significant number of these have concentrated on preschool children, although relatively few have dealt specifically with the attempt to condition social behaviors (Allen et al., 1964). Techniques used have usually consisted of reinforcing the child for appropriate behaviors and ignoring or isolating him for undesirable behaviors; the most typical reinforcers have been teacher praise and attention. Although the reported programs are almost universally successful, they tend to deal with rather isolated specific behavior problems of particular individuals even when they occur in a group setting. The current study, on the other hand, dealt with the broad category of social interaction among children and utilized specific reinforcement techniques with two of four retarded children in a nursery school class.

Although many attempts have been made to change the behavior of young autistic children (Leff, 1968), relatively few studies have attempted to deal with preschool retarded children by any means or specifically to focus on social behavior. One project (Kirk, 1958) did find that attendance at a nursery school increased rates of intellectual and social growth of a group of retardates but that children from an inadequate control group appeared to show equivalent gains after beginning public school classes. Operant techniques, particulary food rewards, have been used with preschool retarded children to teach perceptual-motor and conceptual behaviors (O'Hare, 1966), including language behaviors (Witt, 1965; Hubschman, 1967), but have not been employed to train social behaviors. The present study was designed to utilize the operant approach, specifically the use of contingent teacher attention, to increase the amount of social, rather than intellectual, behaviors displayed by these children.

An additional advantage of the current program was that no additional staff nor extensive training was necessary for its instigation or maintenance. Many behavior modification programs require an expenditure of funds, a large number of paid or volunteer workers to augment the staff or serve as observers, and a period of training and outside consultation which often continues indefinitely. The present study attempted to assess the feasibility of using behavior modification techniques with no additional expenditures of time or money, and no extra personnel.

METHOD

SUBJECTS

The subjects for this study were three boys and one girl with a mean C.A. of 4.1 years (range 3-10 to 4-9 years) and a mean I.Q. of 68.2 (range 64-71). They had been in a special nursery school for an average of six months on two consecutive days a week for two hours a day. No other children attended the class at these times. The nursery school class was administered by one of the authors (R.M.); in addition at every class an assistant was present, although the particular assistant varied from day to day.

Facilitating the social development of these children was one of the primary goals of the nursery school. Nevertheless, in spite of an average of six months attendance at this school, the children typically either played by themselves or interacted with the teachers who approached them. Although the children often played near the other children at the urging of the teacher, there was little spontaneous parallel or mutual play. All the children were, however, responsive to adult attention. It was felt that a program in which adult attention and praise were made contingent on interaction with other children might prove instrumental in instituting and maintaining such interaction. This program was carried out from 9:30 until 10:00 on the days when the class met, as this was the time which was supposed to be devoted to "free play."

OBSERVATIONS

The specific behaviors observed fell into three general areas: interactions with children, interactions with adults, and non-social behaviors. The behaviors observed with respect to both adults and other children were 1) standing within three feet, 2) looking and/or smiling, 3) touching, 4) "talking to," 5) touching other's toy, 6) sharing, defined as handing an object to another child, 7) parallel play, defined as playing with similar objects but with no vocal or physical interaction, and 8) mutual play, defined as play which necessarily involved two or more children. Grabbing (9) was also checked as related to an adult or another child but was considered a non-social behavior, along with 10) playing alone, 11) tantrum or other undesirable behavior, and 12) doing nothing. The social behaviors listed are not mutually exclusive, with the exception of mutual and parallel play; nor are the categories of "looking" and "within three feet" incompatible with the category of "playing alone." Because of this fact, total interaction scores were tabulated both including and excluding these two measures. During each twenty second time sample, those behaviors which were observed to occur were checked; only one check was given per category, even if, for example, a child were to share twice.

A base rate observation was carried out for two weeks. During this period and throughout the study, a time sampling procedure was used in which each of the children was observed for two twenty second periods each day at two intervals chosen randomly every day to begin at a time between 9:30 and 9:58. Because of a lack of personnel and because only a half-hour of the two-hour nursery school program was devoted to "free play," no more extensive observation procedure could be carried out; however, even these brief samples proved to be sufficient to show trends in children's behavior.

One of the authors (R.M.) served as the observer for almost all of the observations, but an assistant made about five percent of the observations when the author was unable to do so. To increase reliability, behavior definitions were written for the assistants and practice sessions using the forms were carried out and discussed during and after the observations. A brief reliability check of about ten time samples revealed 100 percent agreement between the two observers. Unfortunately, lack of personnel precluded more extensive reliability testing.

After the base rate observation, two of the children (Ernie and Ellen) were randomly chosen to serve as experimental subjects and two as controls (Craig and Carl). It was realized that with preschool retarded children, individual differences might well be so great as to overshadow any effects of a treatment program, and, as it happened, the two children assigned to receive the experimental treatment were the least social of the four, in the opinion of the teacher. Ellen, in particular, rarely showed any interaction with the other four children. Moreover, one would expect changes in the behavior of the control subjects both due to vicarious reinforcement (Bandura, 1969) and due to the fact that the other children were being reinforced for interacting with them. Nevertheless, it was felt that this practice of using the program for only two of the children at least provided minimal controls and the opportunity to assess any dramatic difference due to the program alone.

Procedures

The procedures to be used for the experimental pair were listed and given to the assistants. The rules to be followed were divided into two categories: those dealing with positive reinforcement of social interactions with other children and those dealing with ignoring the child for all other behaviors. It was stated that specific comments (so that the child would be aware of what was being reinforced) should be made for standing within three feet of another child, looking or smiling (these two only for the first few sessions), "talking to" another child, sharing, parallel play, and mutual play. Detailed examples of such comments were also given.

The rules concerning procedures for dealing with other than child-child interactions were also spelled out in terms of the specific behaviors involved. The teachers were to ignore the child when he was playing alone or doing nothing and to avoid one child-one teacher situations. If approached by a child, the teacher was to suggest joining the other children or take the child to the nearest child and get them started playing together. They were to take a passive role in play and to withdraw if mutual or parallel play was going strongly.

Two rules dealing with less desirable behavior were observed for the control children as well. If grabbing and pushing slightly did not appear to upset the parallel or mutual play, it was to be ignored. Behavior which hurt another child physically or psychologically (e.g. made him cry) or which was considered very undesirable (e.g. tantrums, throwing toys) was to be treated by a time out procedure. This procedure consisted of saying, "No, don't ——" and then seating him in a chair for a brief period of about twenty seconds. Until the teacher came to get him or told him to get up he was not to leave his seat or to receive any attention.

The procedures to follow for the control pair were also written out, although, except for isolation, they were the same procedures that the nursery school had been using previously. The rules stated that the teachers should make no special effort to get the child to play with others and that she should go to the child, play with him, hug or pat him when alone or when he approached her.

No trouble was encountered in carrying out the procedures except for a slight feeling of awkwardness at first and the reluctance on the part of one assistant, who felt that the children would be hurt by the lack of teacher attention when alone. After six weeks of the program, during which time there were a few absences and a holiday, a reversal phase was instituted for one week (two days of class). In the reversal period the procedures formerly applied to the control pair were used with all four children. Due to the decrease in social behavior, particularly on the part of Ellen, who appeared to be unhappy about playing alone and was not consoled by teacher attention, the treatment procedures were reinstated the next week, rather than continuing the reversal. During the second treatment phase, the treatment procedures were applied to all four children. The program had to be terminated after two weeks of treatment II, due to the end of the school year.

RESULTS

The data were tabulated by adding up the number of categories which were checked within each twenty second period for each of the three general areas: social interactions with children, social interactions with adults, and non-social behaviors. The mean number of behavior categories checked per twenty second observation period during each phase of the project was then calculated for each general area.

Except for a few absences, there were eight base rate observations, twenty-four observations during treatment I, four during reversal and eight during treatment II. Table 1 shows the mean levels of interaction with adults per observation for each of the children during the four phases of the study.

Table 1

Mean Levels of Interaction With Adults

	Subject	Baseline	Treatment I	Reversal	Treatment II
Total	Ernie	1.500	.458	1.750	.250
Subtotal *		.250	.042	.750	.000
Total	Ellen	1.625	.600	2.250	.500
Subtotal		.375	.250	.500	.125
Total	Craig	2.375	1.249	2.000	.875
Subtotal		1.000	2.49	.750	.250
Total	Carl	.750	.708	1.250	.375
Subtotal		.125	.125	.000	.125

* Total excluding the categories of "within three feet" and "looking and/or smiling."

All four children decreased their total interaction with adults during the first treatment phase, increased it during the reversal phase and decreased it again during treatment II. Table 2 presents the mean levels of interaction with other children for each of the subjects during each of the phases of the study.

All subjects increased their interaction with other children in treatment I over the base rate and in treatment II over the reversal period and also the base rate. However, only Ellen showed a sharp drop in all indices of social behavior during the reversal period and Carl dropped on only one of the indices. Figure I shows the changes in social indicators (talking, parallel play, and mutual play) throughout the study; all children increased their frequency of these behaviors during both treatment phases. Table 3 shows the mean amounts of non-social behaviors per observation for all four children during the four phases of

Table 2

Mean Levels of Social Interaction With Children

	Subject	Baseline	Treatment I	Reversal	Treatment II
Total	Ernie	1.750	1.999	1.750	3.000
Subtotal *		.375	.958	1.250	1.375
Social					
Indicators **		.250	.708	.500	1.000
Total	Ellen	.750	2.050	1.500	1.750
Subtotal		.000	.900	.250	.750
Social					
Indicators		.000	.550	.250	.625
Total	Craig	1.375	2.458	2.250	3.250
Subtotal		.250	1.125	1.000	1.500
Social					
Indicators		.250	.709	.750	1.125
Total	Carl	1.625	2.501	3.750	3.875
Subtotal		.875	1.334	1.750	2.000
Social					
Indicators		.500	1.042	1.000	1.375

* Total excluding "within three feet" and "looking and/or smiling."
** "Talks to" plus "parallel play" plus "mutual play."

the experiment. For all the children except Ernie, who showed a steady decline in non-social behaviors, the amount of such behaviors decreased during treatment I, increased during reversal and decreased during treatment II.

Subjective impressions corroborate the time sampling data. One day all four children by themselves went into the bathroom, closed the door and played together by throwing toilet paper into the bowl. A music group was initiated by Ernie, joined by the other three children and continued at least five minutes with Ernie's urging the others to keep going. No

Table 3

Mean Levels of Non-Social Behaviors

Subject	Baseline	Treatment I	Reversal	Treatment II
Ernie	.750	.334	.250	.250
Ellen	.750	.300	1.000	.500
Craig	.375	.375	.500	.000
Carl	.500	.250	.750	.125

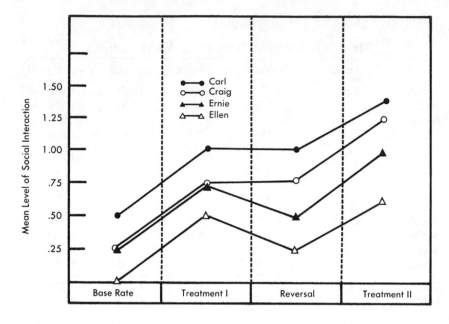

Figure I

Changes in social indicators (talking, parallel play, and mutual play).

such spontaneous total group play had ever been observed prior to the start of the program. One child, Ernie, after apparently grabbing a toy from Carl and making him cry, spontaneously isolated himself when asked what had happened and after the isolation went back to Carl, apologized and hugged him. Since there had been no previous mention of apology during the program or reinforcement for it, it appears that a real concern for and interest in the other children was developing. The mother of the least social child, Ellen, reported her beginning to talk about the other children at home for the first time. Moreover, the assistants, whose opinions had ranged from somewhat dubious to downright distrustful of the program, had been very impressed with the results.

DISCUSSION

The present program of social reinforcement did appear to initiate and maintain social interaction among a group of preschool retarded children who previously showed little or no interaction. The procedures appeared to operate equally well for the experimental children, to whom they were specifically applied, and for the control children, who were not themselves deliberately reinforced for social interaction. The effectiveness of the program for the control children might have been due in part to a modeling and vicarious reinforcement effect as well as to the fact that Ellen and Ernie received reinforcement for playing with the control children as well as with each other. One advantage of the program is that it required no additional personnel, even to serve as observers. Indeed, as the program progressed, the teachers had more and more free time, as the children were playing with each other. Previously, it had appeared that each teacher was having to divide her time between two children; now, the children were entertaining each other while the teachers had the opportunity either to observe the group play or to provide a greater variety of experience for the children, such as music.

The fact that mentally retarded persons are often as handicapped by social inadequacies as by intellectual ones (Johnson, 1950) would suggest that such a program to increase social behaviors in young retarded children might go a long way toward reducing the problems they might encounter as adults (Young, 1958). The ease and economy of conducting this program and of training teachers to implement it, as well as the decided improvement shown by the children, would suggest that these procedures might successfully be used with other retarded preschoolers.

POSTSCRIPT

In the year and a half since the research study was completed, the techniques developed during the program have continued in use at the nursery school. Occasional informal monitoring of teacher and student behaviors suggest that both the convenience and the successful results of the program have continued, even though different assistant teachers and different children are now at the school. In fact, the greater ease and success of such a program has made it possible to expand the size of the class from four to six. Although the possibility of biased observations or of teacher expectancies affecting the results cannot be ruled out, the long-term success of the program does strongly suggest the effectiveness of the procedures.

References

Allen, K., Hart, B., Buell, J., Harris F., & Wolf, M. "Effects of social reinforcement on isolate behavior in a nursery school child." *Child Development*, 1964, 35, 511–518.

Bandura, A. *Principles of behavior modification.* New York: Holt, Rinehart & Winston, 1969.

Gelfand, D. M., & Hartman, D. P. "Behavior therapy with children." *Psychological Bulletin*, 1968, 69, 3, 204–215.

Hubschman, E. "Experimental language development program at the nursery." Paper presented at the annual meeting of the American Association for Mental Deficiency, Denver, Colorado, 1967.

Johnson, G. O. "A study of the social position of mentally handicapped children in the regular grades." *American Journal of Mental Deficiency*, 1950, 55, 60–89.

Kirk, S. A. *"Early education of the mentally retarded."* University of Illinois Press, Urbana, Illinois, 1958.

Leff, R. "Behavior modification and psychoses of childhood." *Psychological Bulletin*, 1968, 69, 396–409.

O'Hare, M. G. "Concept formation in children with Down's syndrome." *Dissertation Abstracts*, 1966, 27, 2143B.

Witt, B. S., & Witt, B. "Home program for development of speech and language in the mentally retarded preschool child." Paper presented at American Association of Mental Deficiency meeting in Chicago, 1966.

Young, M. A., "Academic requirements of jobs held by the educable retarded in the state of Connecticut." *American Journal of Mental Deficiency*, 1958, 62, 792–802.

What kinds of behaviors in a classroom attract the attention of the teacher? Typically, teachers tend to ignore students in their classes who appear to be studying and pay attention to them when they are dawdling or disruptive. Hall, Lund, and Jackson report the effects of changing this usual procedure and having the teacher pay attention to the students for studying. For most of the teachers involved, an observer in the classroom provided a signal to indicate when the child should be reinforced. Later on the use of such cueing was discontinued with no apparent ill effects. The authors point out that even with the signal one teacher was unable to apply the procedures, because her use of praise and approval was so rare. They suggest that for some teachers training in the use of praise may be necessary before they will be able to apply it appropriately.

Several case studies are reported here which illustrate a variety of specific problem behaviors of the children involved. Regardless of the specific child, teacher, or problem behavior, in all cases a reversal procedure in which the teacher commented to the child only on his non-study behavior produced an increase in the amount of inappropriate activity. In most of the cases there was an improvement noted in academic performance as well as in simple time devoted to studying, as reflected in higher grades.

The teachers participating in the program were themselves reinforced by getting daily feedback on the performance of their students and by direct praise from the project staff for their own appropriate use of reinforcement. The visible change in the students' behavior during a reversal phase may have also been motivating to the teachers. Although this procedure required the presence of at least one other person throughout (the observer), a time-sampling procedure might permit the teacher to serve as her own recorder and thereby lessen the dependence on an outside staff.

Effects of Teacher Attention on Study Behavior[1]

R. Vance Hall,
Diane Lund,
and
Deloris Jackson*†

ABSTRACT

The effects of contingent teacher attention on study behavior were investigated. Individual rates of study were recorded for one first-grade and five third-grade pupils who had high rates of disruptive or dawdling behavior. A reinforcement period (in which teacher attention followed study behavior and non-study behaviors were ignored) resulted in sharply increased study rates. A brief reversal of the

* R. Vance Hall, Diane Lund, and Deloris Jackson, "Effects of Teacher Attention on Study Behavior," *Journal of Applied Behavior Analysis* 1 (1968): 1–12. Reprinted with permission. Copyright 1968 by the Society for the Experimental Analysis of Behavior, Inc.

† University of Kansas.

[1] The authors wish to express appreciation to Dr. O. L. Plucker, Ted Gray, Alonzo Plough, Clarence Glasse, Carl Bruce, Natalie Barge, Lawrence Franklin, and Audrey Jackson of the Kansas City, Kansas Public Schools and Wallace Henning, University of Kansas, without whose cooperation and active participation these studies would not have been possible. Special tribute is due to Dr. Montrose M. Wolf and Dr. Todd R. Risley for their many contributions in developing research strategy and for their continuing encouragement. We are also indebted to Dr. R. L. Schiefelbusch, Director of the Bureau of Child Research, and administrative director of the project, who provided essential administrative support and counsel. Reprints may be obtained from R. Vance Hall, 2021 North Third St., Kansas City, Kansas 66101.

contingency (attention occurred
only after periods of non-study
behavior) again produced low rates
of study. Reinstatement of teacher
attention as reinforcement for study
once again markedly increased study
behavior. Follow-up observations
indicated that the higher study rates
were maintained after the formal
program terminated.

A series of studies carried out in preschools by Harris, Wolf, and Baer
(1964) and their colleagues demonstrated the effectiveness of contingent
teacher attention in modifying behavior problems of preschool children.
In these studies inappropriate and/or undesirable rates of isolate play
(Allen, Hart, Buell, Harris, and Wolf, 1964), crying (Hart, Allen, Buell,
Harris, and Wolf, 1964), crawling (Harris, Johnston, Kelley, and Wolf,
1964), and a number of other problem behaviors were modified by
systematically manipulating teacher-attention consequences of the
behaviors. Similarly, teacher and peer attention were manipulated by
Zimmerman and Zimmerman (1962), Patterson (1965), and Hall and
Broden (1967) to reduce problem behaviors and increase appropriate
responses of children enrolled in special classrooms.

To date, however, there has been little systematic research in the
application of social reinforcement by teachers in the regular school
classroom beyond the successful case studies reported by Becker, Madsen
Arnold, and Thomas (1967) in which no attempt was made to evaluate
the reliability of these procedures through experimental reversals.

The present studies analyzed experimentally the reliability with which
teachers could modify the study behavior of children of poverty-area
classrooms by systematic manipulation of contingent attention.

GENERAL PROCEDURES

SUBJECTS AND SETTING

The studies were carried out in classrooms of two elementary schools
located in the most economically deprived area of Kansas City, Kansas.[2]

[2] The research was carried out as part of the Juniper Gardens Children's Project, a
program of research on the development of culturally deprived children and was par-

Teachers who participated were recommended by their principals. The teachers nominated pupils who were disruptive or dawdled. They were told that one or two observers would come regularly to their classrooms to record behavior rates of these pupils.

OBSERVATION

The observers used recording sheets lined with triple rows of squares, as shown in Fig. 1. Each square represented an interval of 10 sec. The first row was used to record the behavior of the student. (The definition of study behavior was somewhat different for each student and depended on the subject matter taught. Generally, study behavior was defined as orientation toward the appropriate object or person: assigned course materials, lecturing teacher, or reciting classmates, as well as class participation by the student when requested by the teacher. Since each pupil was observed during the same class period, however, the response definition was consistent for each student throughout the course of an experiment.) Teacher verbalizations to the student were recorded in the second row. The third row was used to record occasions when the teacher was within a 3-ft proximity to the student.

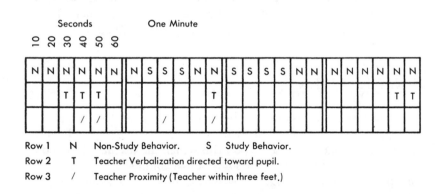

Row 1	N	Non-Study Behavior.	S	Study Behavior.
Row 2	T	Teacher Verbalization directed toward pupil.
Row 3	/	Teacher Proximity (Teacher within three feet.)

Figure 1

Observer recording sheet and symbol key.

tially supported by the Office of Economic Opportunity: (OEO KAN CAP 694/1, Bureau of Child Research, Kansas University Medical Center) and the National Institute of Child Health and Human Development: (HD-00870-(04) and HD 03144-01, Bureau of Child Research, University of Kansas).

These observations were made during each 10-sec interval of each session. The observers sat at the rear or the side of the classroom, and avoided eye contact or any other interaction with pupils during observation sessions.

Inter-observer agreement was analyzed by having a second observer periodically make a simultaneous observation record. Agreement of the two records was checked interval by interval. The percentage of agreement of the records [# agreements × 100 ÷ (# agreements + # disagreements)] yielded the percentage of inter-observer agreement.

EXPERIMENTAL CONDITIONS

BASELINE

Rates of study were obtained for the selected pupils. Thirty-minute observations were scheduled at a time each day when the pupils were to be working in their seats. In most cases observations were made two to four times per week. After obtaining a minimum of two weeks of baseline, the students' study rates were presented graphically to the teachers. Then, selected studies (Hart *et al.*, 1964; Allen *et al.*, 1964; Hall and Broden, 1967) were presented to the teachers, the fundamentals of social reinforcement were discussed, and a pupil was selected for systematic study.

REINFORCEMENT$_1$

During reinforcement sessions the observer held up a small square of colored paper in a manner not likely to be noticed by the pupil whenever the pupil was engaged in study. Upon this signal, the teacher attended to the child, moved to his desk, made some verbal comment, gave him a pat on the shoulder, or the like. During weekly after-school sessions, experimenters and teachers discussed the rate of study achieved by the pupil and the effectiveness of attention provided by the teacher, and made occasional adjustments in instructions as required.

REVERSAL

When a satisfactory rate of study had been achieved, the observer discontinued signaling and (as much as possible) the teacher returned to her former pattern, which typically consisted of attending to non-study behavior.

REINFORCEMENT$_2$

When the effect of the reversal condition had been observed, social reinforcement of study was reinstituted. When high study rates were achieved again, the teacher continued reinforcement of study behavior without the observer's signals.

POST CHECKS

Whenever possible, periodic post-checks were made through the remainder of the year to determine whether the new levels of study were being maintained.

CORRELATED BEHAVIORAL CHANGES

Where possible, other behavioral changes, including teacher reports, grades, and other records of academic achievement were recorded. Because such data are difficult to evaluate, their importance should not be unduly stressed.

INDIVIDUAL EXPERIMENTS

ROBBIE

Robbie was chosen because he was considered a particularly disruptive pupil who studied very little. Figure 2 presents a record of Robbie's study behavior, defined as having pencil on paper during 5 sec or more of the 10-sec interval. During baseline, study behavior occurred in 25% of the intervals observed during the class spelling period. The behaviors which occupied the other 75% of his time included snapping rubber bands, playing with toys from his pocket, talking and laughing with peers, slowly drinking the half-pint of milk served earlier in the morning, and subsequently playing with the empty carton.

During the baseline period the teacher would often urge Robbie to work, put his milk carton away, etc. In fact, 55% of the teacher attention he received followed non-study behavior. Robbie engaged in continuous study for 60 sec or more only two or three times during a 30-min observation.

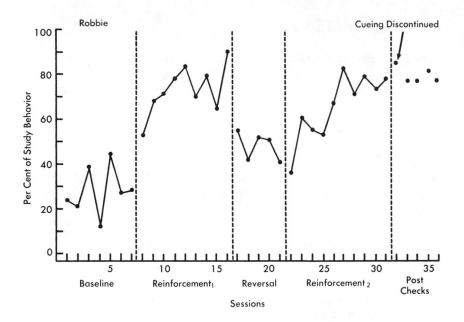

Figure 2

A record of study behavior for Robbie. Post-check observations were made during the fourth, sixth, seventh, twelfth, and fourteenth weeks after the completion of Reinforcement₂ condition.

Following baseline determination, whenever Robbie had engaged in 1 min of continuous study the observer signaled his teacher. On this cue, the teacher approached Robbie, saying, "Very good work Robbie", "I see you are studying", or some similar remark. She discontinued giving attention for non-study behaviors including those which were disruptive to the class.

Figure 2 shows an increased study rate during the first day of the first reinforcement period. The study rate continued to rise thereafter and was recorded in 71% of the intervals during this period.

During the brief reversal period, when reinforcement of study was discontinued, the study rate dropped to a mean of 50%. However, when reinforcement for study was reinstituted, Robbie's study rate again increased, stabilizing at a rate ranging between 70% and 80% of the observation sessions. Subsequent follow-up checks made during the 14 weeks that followed (after signaling of the teacher was discontinued) indicated that study was being maintained at a mean rate of 79%. Periodic checks made during each condition of the experiment revealed that agreement of observation ranged from 89% to 93%.

Robbie's teacher reported behavior changes correlated with his increased rate of study. During Baseline, she reported that Robbie did not complete written assignments. He missed 2 of 10, 5 of 10, and 6 of 10 words on three spelling tests given during Baseline. By the final week of Reinforcement$_2$, she reported that he typically finished his initial assignment and then continued on to other assigned work without prompting. Disruptive behavior had diminished and it was noted that he continued to study while he drank his milk and did not play with the carton when finished. He missed 1 of 10 words on his weekly spelling test.

ROSE

Rose was a classmate of Robbie. Baseline observations were made during the math and/or spelling study periods. The mean rate of study during Baseline was 30%, fluctuating from 0% to 71%. Her non-study behaviors included laying her head on the desk, taking off her shoes, talking, and being out of her seat.

On the day her teacher was first to reinforce Rose's study behavior, Rose did not study at all, and the teacher was thus unable to provide reinforcement. Therefore, beginning with the second reinforcement session, the teacher attended to behavior that approximated study (e.g., getting out pencil or paper, or opening her book to the correct page). Once these behaviors were reinforced, study behavior quickly followed, was in turn reinforced, and had risen to 57% by the third reinforcement session.

During the fourth session, however, study dropped to 25%. An analysis of the data indicated Rose had increased in out-of-seat behavior, to have her papers checked and to ask questions. Consequently her teacher thereafter ignored Rose when she approached but attended to her immediately if she raised her hand while seated. There was an immediate drop in out-of-seat behavior and a concurrent increase in study behavior. As can be seen in Fig. 3, during the last 10 sessions of Reinforcement$_1$, study behavior ranged between 74% and 92%, the mean rate for the entire period being approximately 71%. A high rate of study was maintained after the observer discontinued signaling after the thirteenth reinforcement session.

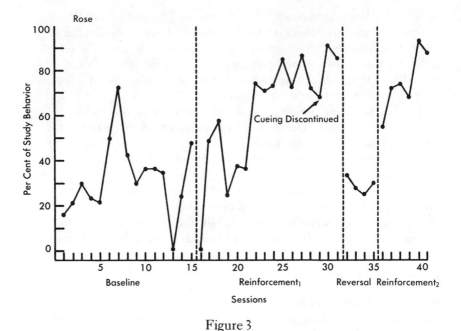

Figure 3

A record of study behavior for Rose.

During the four reversal sessions, study was recorded in only 29% of the intervals. However, a return to attention for study immediately increased study behavior and during the second reinforcement period study was recorded in 72% of the observed intervals. Observer agreement measured under each condition ranged from 90% to 95%.

An analysis of the attention provided Rose by her teacher demonstrated that it was not the amount of attention, but its delivery contingent on study which produced the changes in this behavior. Figure 4 shows these amounts, and the general lack of relationship between amount of attention and experimental procedures.

In fact these data show that when teacher attention occurred primarily during non-study intervals there was a low rate of study. When teacher attention occurred primarily during study intervals there was a higher rate of study. Figure 4 also shows that the mean rate of total teacher attention remained relatively stable throughout the various experimental phases, rising somewhat in the Reinforcement$_1$ and Reversal phases and declining to baseline levels in the Reinforcement$_2$ phase.

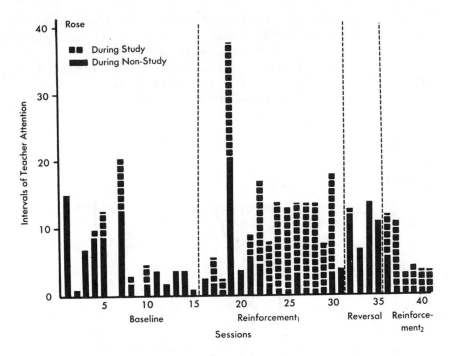

Figure 4
A record of teacher attention for Rose.

Rose's grades at the end of the baseline phase were D in arithmetic and D in spelling. Her grades for the reinforcement phase of the experiment were C— in arithmetic and B in spelling.

KEN

Ken was one of the other 41 pupils in Rose's class. He had a wide range of disruptive behaviors including playing with toys from his pockets, rolling pencils on the floor and desk, and jiggling and wiggling in his seat. His teacher had tried isolating him from his peers, reprimanding by the principal, and spanking to control his behavior. These efforts apparently had been ineffective. Study behavior ranged from 10% to 60%, with a mean rate of 37%, as seen in Fig. 5.

Reinforcement of study behavior was begun at the same time for both Ken and Rose. The observer used different colored cards to signal when the behavior of each pupil was to be reinforced. Ken's study increased to a mean rate of 71% under reinforcement conditions. However, during his brief reversal, Ken's rate of study was again about 37%. The re-introduction of the reinforcement for study recovered study behavior in 70% of the observed intervals. Agreement between observers measured during each of the conditions ranged from 90% to 92%.

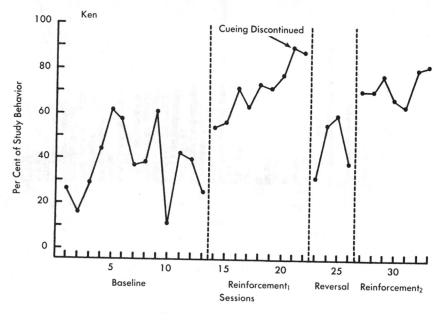

Figure 5

A record of study behavior for Ken.

Ken's teacher reported several correlated behavior changes. Before the experiment she had stated that he rarely, if ever, finished an assignment. His grades for the baseline period included D in math, D in spelling and U (unsatisfactory) in conduct. After reinforcement was instituted his teacher reported a marked decrease in disruptive behavior and stated, "He's getting his work done on time now." Ken's report card grades subsequently were C in spelling, C in arithmetic and S (satisfactory) in conduct.

GARY

Gary, a third-grade boy in another classroom of 39 pupils was chosen as a subject because he failed to complete assignments. The course of Gary's program is shown in Fig. 6. Observations made during the 30-min morning math period indicated that Gary engaged in study during 43% of the 10-sec intervals observed. Non-study behaviors included beating his desk with a pencil, chewing and licking pages of books, moving his chair back and forth in unison with a classmate, banging his chair on the floor, blowing bubbles and making noises while drinking his milk, and

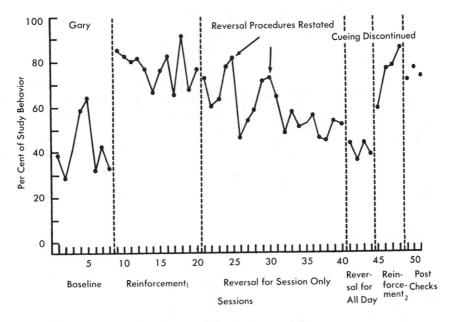

Figure 6

A record of study behavior for Gary. Post-check observations were made during the first, fourth, and tenth weeks after completion of Reinforcement$_2$ condition.

punching holes in the carton so that milk flowed onto the desk. He would also gaze out the window or around the room and would say "This is too hard", "Shoot, I can't do this", and "How did you say to work it?"

Gary had been observed to engage in appropriate study for 60 sec or more at least one to three times during most study periods. The observer thus signaled the teacher whenever Gary had engaged in study for six consecutive 10-sec intervals, and he was attended to by the teacher only on those occasions.

As shown in Fig. 6, reinforcement produced a marked increase in studying. With the rise, almost all disruptive behavior disappeared. He still talked out of turn in class but typically to say "I know how to do it",

"He's wrong", "Can I do it, teacher?", "Oh, this is easy." Gary engaged in study during approximately 77% of the 10-sec intervals observed during Reinforcement$_1$.

After the twentieth session a reversal was programmed, and the teacher was signaled whenever Gary engaged in non-study behavior for 30 sec. When this occurred, the teacher gave Gary a reminder to get back to work. No attention was given for study behavior.

As can be seen, this resulted in a fluctuating but declining rate of study during the 30-min math period. At this point it was noted that Gary's rate of study was again rising, and that the teacher was in fact providing intermittent reinforcement for study. Therefore, on two occasions the procedures for reversal were gone over once again in conference with the teacher and a subsequent slow but steady decline in study rate was achieved. There also appeared to be an increase in disruptive behavior. The mean rate of study at this point of Reversal was about 60%.

It was then noted that a more rapid reversal effect had been brought about in the previous studies, probably because that teacher had carried out reversal procedures for the entire day whereas Gary's teacher practiced reversal only during the 30-min observation period. Reversal of reinforcement conditions was, therefore, extended to the entire day. The mean rate for these sessions was approximately 42%. However, resumption of reinforcement immediately recovered a study rate of 60% which increased as reinforcement continued. After the first day of this reinforcement phase the teacher expressed confidence in being able to work without cues from the observer. Signaling was therefore discontinued without loss of effect. Periodic checks made during subsequent weeks indicated study behavior was being maintained at a level higher than 70%. The reliability of observation measured during each condition ranged from 92% to 96%.

JOAN

Joan, one of Gary's classmates, did not disrupt the class or bother other pupils but was selected because she dawdled. Typically, during arithmetic study period, she would lay her head on her desk and stare toward the windows or her classmates. At other times she would pull at or straighten her clothing, dig in her desk, pick or pull at her hair, nose or fingernails, draw on the desk top or play with her purse. During baseline her study rate was approximately 35%.

During the Reinforcement$_1$ phase, after the observer signaled that 60 sec of continuous study had occurred, the teacher made comments such as, "That's a good girl", and often tugged lightly at Joan's hair or patted her shoulder. As can be seen in Fig. 7 this resulted in an immediate increase in study behavior. The observer discontinued signaling after Session 20 when the teacher stated it was no longer necessary. Though the study rate fluctuated in subsequent sessions it generally remained higher than in Baseline. The lowest rate of study came in Session 26 when Joan was without a pencil through the first part of the session. Study was observed in 73% of the intervals of the Reinforcement$_1$ phase.

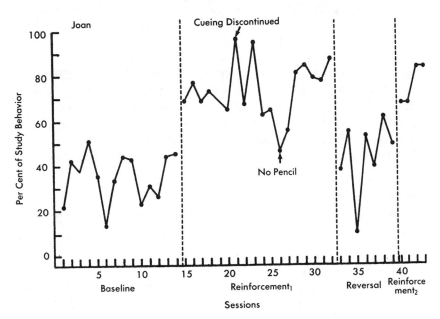

Figure 7

A record of study behavior for Joan

During Reversal, Joan's study rate declined markedly and play with clothes, pencils, and head on desk behaviors appeared to increase. The mean study rate for the reversal sessions was approximately 43%. Reinstatement of reinforcement for study, however, resulted in a rapid return to a study rate of approximately 73%. No post-checks were obtained because of the close of school. Observer agreement ranged from 93% to 97%.

Joan's arithmetic-paper grades provided interesting correlated data. During Baseline a sampling of her arithmetic papers showed an average grade of F. During Reinforcement$_1$ they averaged C. All her arithmetic papers graded during Reversal were graded F. In Reinforcement$_2$ the average grade on arithmetic papers was C—.

LEVI

Levi was a first-grade boy who was selected because of his disruptive behaviors. Although he achieved at a fairly high level, he often disturbed the class by making loud noises, by getting out of his seat, and by talking to other students. The school counselor suggested using reinforcement techniques after counselling with the pupil and teacher brought about no apparent improvement in Levi's behavior.

The counselor was trained in the observation procedures and he obtained baseline rates of Levi's study and disruptive behaviors during seatwork time. A second observer was used to supplement data gathering. During Baseline, Levi's rate of study was approximately 68%, ranging from 34% to 79%. An analysis of teacher attention during baseline showed that although Levi had a relatively high rate of study, he received almost no teacher attention except when he was disruptive (*i.e.*, made

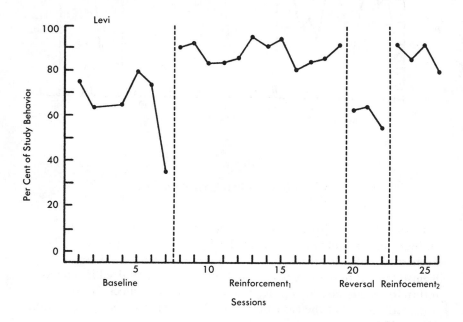

Figure 8

A record of study behavior for Levi

noise or other behaviors which overtly disturbed his neighbors and/or the teacher).

During Reinforcement$_1$ the teacher provided social reinforcement for study and, as much as possible, ignored all disruptive behavior. No signals were used since Levi had a relatively high study rate and the teacher was confident she could carry out reinforcement without cues. Figure 8 shows that study occurred in approximately 88% of the intervals of Reinforcement$_1$ and at no time went below that of the highest baseline rate. A brief reversal produced a marked decrease in study to a mean rate of 60%. However, when reinforcement for study was reinstated study again rose to above the baseline rate (approximately 85%).

Figure 9 presents the disruptive behavior data for the four periods of the experiment. Disruptive behavior was defined to occur when Levi made noises, got out of his seat or talked to other students and the response appeared to be noticed by the teacher or another student. During Baseline the mean rate of disruptive behavior was 7%. During Reinforcement$_1$ the mean rate declined to 2.2%. During the brief Reversal phase the mean rate rose to 3.2%. In Reinforcement$_2$ the rate

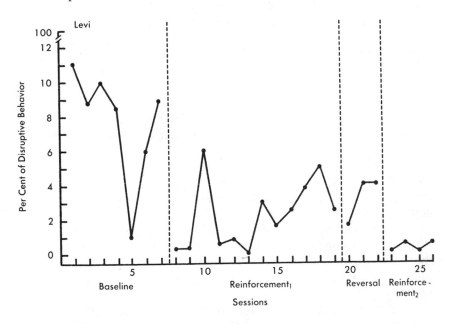

Figure 9

A record of disruptive behavior for Levi.

declined to an almost negligible 0.25%. No follow-up data were obtained because of the close of the school year. Observer agreement measured under each condition was consistently over 80%.

The teacher and the school counselor reported at the conclusion of the experiment that in their opinion Levi was no longer a disruptive pupil.

DISCUSSION

These studies indicated clearly that the contingent use of teacher attention can be a quick and effective means of developing desirable classroom behavior. Effective teachers have long known that casually praising desired behaviors and generally ignoring disruptive ones can be useful procedures for helping maintain good classroom discipline. What may appear surprising to school personnel, however, is the degree to which student behavior responds to thoroughly systematic teacher attention.

One purpose of these studies was to determine whether the procedures could be carried out by teachers in public school classrooms. Although these teachers were initially unfamiliar with reinforcement principles and had had no prior experience with the procedures, they were clearly able to carry them out with important effect. The fact that they were carried out in crowded classrooms of schools of an urban poverty area underscores this point. In such areas one would expect a high incidence of disruptive behaviors and low interest in academic achievement, conditions generally conceded to make teaching and motivation for study difficult. Yet, with relatively slight adjustment of the social environment, it was possible to increase rates of study with comparative ease.

The teachers in these studies did not have poor general control of their classrooms. Most of their pupils seemed to apply themselves fairly well, although a few did not. When their baseline data were analyzed, it became clear that these pupils were in effect being motivated not to study. It became apparent that for these pupils, most teacher attention was received during non-study intervals rather than when they were studying. This was not surprising since many of the non-study behaviors were disruptive and thus seemed to the teacher to require some reprimand.

Several aspects of the teacher training program appear worthy of mention. During baseline, as far as the teacher was concerned, the primary purpose was to determine study rates. After baseline, a simple procedure designed to increase those study rates was emphasized (rather than the fact that the teacher had in all probability been reinforcing the very behaviors which were causing concern).

The teacher was constantly informed of the results of each day's sessions and its graphed outcome. These daily contacts, plus weekly conferences in which the procedures were discussed and the teacher was praised for bringing about the desired behavioral changes, may have been central to the process of a successful study.

The teachers readily accepted the advisability of carrying out a brief reversal when it was presented as a means of testing for a causal relationship between teacher attention and pupil behavior. All, however, felt reversal sessions were aversive and were glad when they were terminated.

These procedures did not seem to interfere greatly with ongoing teaching duties. For one thing they did not necessarily result in more total teacher attention for a pupil. In fact, the teachers had more time for constructive teaching of all pupils because of the decrease in disruptive behaviors in the classroom.

Two teachers reported they were able to utilize systematic attention to increase appropriate study of other pupils in their classrooms who were not included in these studies. No corroborative data were collected to verify their reports. Investigation of the degree to which this kind of generalization occurs should be a goal of further research, however, since such a result would be highly desirable.

In the first five subjects, cueing of the teacher was initially used to make certain that the teacher could discriminate when study behavior was occurring. Later, cueing was discontinued without loss of effectiveness. In the case of Levi, cueing was never used. Further research will be needed to determine how often cueing contributes to the efficiency of the procedures.

In one classroom, a teacher was unable to carry out the procedures in spite of the fact that the same orientation and training processes were used which had previously proved successful. Although the teacher seemed sincere in her efforts to reinforce study, she observably continued to give a high rate of attention for non-study behaviors. Observations indicated that the teacher gave almost no praise or positive attention to any member of the class. Virtually her entire verbal repertoire consisted of commands, reprimands, and admonitions. Consequently the teacher was instructed to provide positive verbal reinforcement for appropriate behavior of all class members. This did result in a measurable increase in the number of positive statements made to individuals and to the class. According to both the teacher and the observers, this greatly improved general classroom behavior. Only slight increases in study were recorded for the two pupils for whom data were available, however, and the close of the school year prevented further manipulations.

This failure prompted the authors to begin developing a system for recording appropriate behavior rates for an entire class. It also indicates that there may be certain teachers who need different or more intensive training to carry out these procedures effectively.

Finally, it should be noted that the pupils of this study did have at least a minimal level of proficiency in performing the academic tasks and thus seemed to profit from the increased time they spent in study. The teachers apparently assigned study tasks within the range of the pupils' skills, and correlated gains in academic achievement were noted. If teachers were to use the procedures but failed to provide materials within the range of the pupil's level of skill, it is unlikely that much gain in achievement would result.

References

Allen, K. E., Hart, B. M., Buell, J.S., Harris, F. R., and Wolf, M.M. Effects of social reinforcement on isolate behavior of a nursery school child. *Child Development*, 1964, 35, 511–518.

Becker, W. C., Madsen, C. H., Jr., Arnold, R., and Thomas, D. R. The contingent use of teacher attention and praise in reducing classroom behavior problems. *Journal of Special Education*, 1967, 1, 287–307.

Hall, R. V. and Broden, M. Behavior changes in brain-injured children through social reinforcement. *Journal of Experimental Child Psychology*, 1967, 5, 463–479.

Harris, F. R., Johnston, M. K., Kelley, C. S., and Wolf, M. M. Effects of positive social reinforcement on regressed crawling of a nursery school child. *Journal of Educational Psychology*, 1964, 55, 35–41.

Harris, F. R., Wolf, M. M., and Baer, D. M. Effects of adult social reinforcement on child behavior. *Young Children*, 1964, 20, 8–17.

Hart, Betty M., Allen, K. Eileen, Buell, Joan S., Harris, Florence R., and Wolf, M. M. Effects of social reinforcement on operant crying. *Journal of Experimental Child Psychology*, 1964, 1, 145–153.

Patterson, G. R. An application of conditioning techniques to the control of a hyperactive child, Ullman, L. P., and Krasner, L. (Eds.), *Case studies in behavior modification*, New York: Holt, Rinehart and Winston, Inc., 1966. Pp. 370–375.

Zimmerman, Elaine H. and Zimmerman, J. The alteration of behavior in a special classroom situation. *Journal of the Experimental Analysis of Behavior*, 1962, 5, 59–60.

Token reinforcement programs have been successfully used to increase the amount of academic behaviors of older children, but their use to reward preschool children for studying is still quite rare. The twelve subjects in the present study were given tokens contingent on studying on a variable interval schedule; however any mention of the token by the student deprived him temporarily of his opportunity to receive one. Tokens were redeemable for a late-afternoon snack as well as admission to the special event of the day. During a second part of the study, as a control, the children were given the snacks and special events noncontingently, and the tokens were no longer legal tender. After seven days, the contingencies were reinstated, for another measure of the experimental condition. As expected, a greater amount of studying was found during those phases in which the tokens given for studying were necessary to obtain rewards.

Several procedures were used by the authors to ensure that the data derived from their time-sampling methods were valid and reliable. More detailed records were made on three of the children, which appeared to parallel the time-sample data very closely. The class scores obtained by the four observers for each day were also compared. Nine months after the study four new coders and two of the original observers re-coded the original descriptions. To assure that the results were not due to averaging across the group, the individual records were also examined. All of these checks on the reliability of the scores led to the same conclusion; the decrease in percentage of time spent studying when the special event and snack were no longer contingent upon the child's behavior is seen regardless of the observing and coding method used. It is possible that different teachers will prefer different definitions of study behavior and that another teacher might choose to consistently reward writing, for instance. It does seem clear, though, that the behaviors for which the children received tokens were those which did increase in frequency under contingent reinforcement conditions and that the author's description of study behaviors would be considered appropriate by many for children older than those in the present study. If preschool children can be induced to spend eighty percent of their time studying by such a procedure, surely older children could benefit even more.

Applying "Group" Contingencies to the Classroom Study Behavior of Preschool Children[1]

Don Bushell, Jr.,
Patricia Ann Wrobel,
and
Mary Louise Michaelis*†

ABSTRACT

A group of 12 children were enrolled in a preschool class. During the first experimental stage they participated in special events contingent on token earning. Tokens were acquired by engaging in a variety of study behaviors. After a level of study behavior was established under this contingency, the special events were provided noncontingently. Study behavior declined throughout the noncontingent stage. Reestablishing

* Don Bushell, Jr., Patricia Ann Wrobel, and Mary Louise Michaelis, "Applying 'Group' Contingencies to the Classroom Study Behavior of Preschool Children," *Journal of Applied Behavior Analysis* 1(1968): 55-61. Reprinted with permission. Copyright 1968 by the Society for the Experimental Analysis of Behavior, Inc.

† University of Kansas and Webster College.

[1] This study was carried out as a part of the program of the Webster College Student Behavior Laboratory, and preparation of the report was supported in part by the Institute for Sociological Research, The University of Washington. The authors gratefully acknowledge the able assistance of the observers who made this study possible: Alice Adcock, Sandra Albright, Sister Eleanor Marie Craig, S. L., Jim Felling, and Cleta Pouppart. We are particularly indebted to Donald M. Baer who encouraged us to commit this study to paper and subsequently gave thoughtful criticism to the manuscript. Reprints may be obtained from Don Bushell, Jr., Dept. of Human Development, University of Kansas, Lawrence, Kansas 66044.

*the original contingencies produced
an immediate return to the initial
level of study behavior.
Noncontingent special events
reduced the amount of independent
study, group participation, and
cooperative study. The study
behavior of each child was altered in
the same direction, though
differences in the magnitude of
effects from child to child were
observed.*

The experimental analysis of behavior has concentrated on the
examination of responses emitted by a single subject. Recently,
extensions of this research have begun to deal with groups of individuals.
Behavioral research with adult psychiatric patients (Ayllon and Azrin,
1965), and retarded children (Birnbrauer, Wolf, Kidder, and Tague,
1965) has indicated that certain operant techniques can be applied
effectively well beyond the "artificial" conditions of the experimentally
isolated subject.

In most group situations it is not practical to program individually
special contingencies for the responses of each group member. Uniform
criteria must be designed according to which a number of individuals are
to be rewarded or punished. Schools, prisons, hospitals, business, and
military organizations all maintain systems of response contingencies
which are quite similar for all the individuals of a certain category within
the organization. The objective of this research was to determine whether
operant techniques may be applied to a group of individuals with effects
similar to those expected when a single subject is under study. The
specific behavior under analysis was the study behavior of a group of
preschool children.

The dependent variables were behaviors such as attending quietly to
instructions, working independently or in cooperation with others as
appropriate, remaining with and attending to assigned tasks, and reciting
after assignments had been completed. Counter examples are behaviors
such as disrupting others who are at work, changing an activity before its
completion, and engaging in "escape" behavior such as trips to the
bathroom or drinking fountain, or gazing out the window. To the extent
that the first constellation of behaviors is present and the second is
absent, a student might be classified as industrious, highly motivated, or
conscientious; in short, he has good study habits.

METHOD

CHILDREN AND SETTING

The subjects were 12 children enrolled in a summer session. Three other children were not considered in this report because they did not attend at least half of the sessions due to illness and family vacations. Four of the 12 children were 3-yr old, two were 4-yr old, five were 5-yr old, and one was 6-yr old. These 10 girls and two boys would be described as middle class; all had been enrolled in the preschool the preceding spring semester, all scored above average on standardized intelligence tests, and all had experienced some form of token system during the previous semester.

Classes were conducted from 12:45 to 3:30 p.m., five days a week for seven weeks. A large room adjoining the classroom afforded oneway sight and sound monitoring of the class. The program was directed by two head teachers who were assisted for 25 min each day by a specialist who conducted the Spanish lesson. All of the teachers were undergraduates.

DAILY PROGRAM

Data were collected in three phases during the first 75 min of each of the last 20 class days of the summer session. During the first 20 min, individual activities were made available to the children for independent study, and the amount of social interaction, student-student or student-teacher, was very slight. The next 25 min were devoted to Spanish instruction. The interaction pattern during this period was much like that of a typical classroom, with the teacher at the front of the assembled children sometimes addressing a specific individual but more often talking to the entire group. The remaining 30 min were given over to "study teams", with the children paired so the one more skilled at a particular task would teach the less skilled. Composition of the groups and their tasks varied from day to day according to the developing skills of the children.

Following this 75 min, a special event was made available to the children. Special events included: a short movie, a trip to a nearby park, a local theater group rehearsal, an art project, a story, or a gym class. The special event was always 30 min long and was always conducted outside the regular classroom. The children were not told what the activity would be for the day until immediately before it occurred.

TOKEN REINFORCEMENT

The tokens, colored plastic washers about 1.5-in. in diameter, served as a monetary exchange unit within the classroom. As the children engaged in individual activities, Spanish, and study teams, the teachers moved about the room giving tokens to those who appeared to be actively working at their various tasks, but not to those who were not judged to be attending to the assignment at the moment.

To minimize unproductive talking about the tokens, the teachers avoided mentioning them. Tokens were never given when requested. If a child presented a piece of work and then asked for a token, the request was ignored and additional work was provided if needed. Similarly, the presentation of tasks was never accompanied by any mention of tokens, such as, "If you do thus and so, I will give you a token." The tokens were simply given out as the children worked and, where possible, the presentation was accompanied by such verbal statements as "good", "you're doing fine, keep it up", "that's right", *etc.* The teachers avoided a set pattern in dispensing the tokens so that their approach would not become discriminative for studying. They would watch for appropriate behavior, move to that child, present a token and encouragement, then look for another instance not too nearby. During Spanish, the two teachers were able to present tokens for appropriate responding to the children who were assembled in front of the Spanish teacher. During study teams the teachers presented tokens as they circulated from group to group, and also at a checking session at the end of the period. Here, the student-learner recited what had been learned and both children were given tokens according to the performance of the learner. Each teacher distributed from 110 to 120 tokens during the 75 min.

The tokens could be used to purchase the special-event ticket. The price varied from 12 to 20 tokens around an average of 15 each day so the children would not leave their study activities as soon as they acquired the necessary amount. Children who did not earn enough to purchase the special-event ticket remained in the classroom when the others left with the teachers. There were no recriminations or admonishments by either the teachers or the students, and the one or two children left behind typically found some toy or book to occupy themselves until the rest of the class returned. After the special event, additional activities enabled the children to earn tokens for a 3:00 p.m. snack of cookies, ice cream, milk, or lemonade, and a chair to sit on while eating. Tokens could be accumulated from day to day.

As tokens became more valuable, theft, borrowing, lending (sometimes at interest), hiring of services and a variety of other economic activities were observed. No attempt was made to control any of these except theft, which was eliminated simply by providing the children with aprons which had pockets for the tokens.

OBSERVATION AND RECORDING PROCEDURES

The four principal observers were seated in an observation room. Each wore earphones which enabled audio monitoring of the class and also prevented inter-observer communication. On a signal at the beginning of each 5-min period, each observer looked for the first child listed on the roster and noted that child's behavior on the data sheet, then looked for the second child on the list and noted its behavior; and so on for each child. All observers were able to complete the total observational cycle in less than 3 min. During the 75 min of observation, the children's behavior was described by noting what the child was looking at, to whom he was talking, and what he was doing with his hands. Fourteen daily observations of each child by each observer produced 672 items of data each day.

Criteria were established by which each behavioral description on the data sheets could be coded as either "S", indicating study behavior, or "NS", indicating nonstudy behavior. Behaviors such as writing, putting a piece in a puzzle, reciting to a teacher, singing a Spanish song with the class, and tracing around a pattern with a pencil were classified as "S", if they were observed in the appropriate setting. Descriptions of behaviors such as counting tokens, putting away materials, walking around the room, drinking at the fountain, looking out the window, rolling on the floor and attending to another child, were classified as "NS". Singing a Spanish song was scored "S" if it occurred during the Spanish period when called for, but "NS" if it occurred during an earlier or later period. Similarly, if one child was interacting with another over instructional materials during the study teams period, the behavior was labeled "S", but the same behavior during another period was classified "NS".

If a given child's behavior was described 14 times and eight of these descriptions were coded "S", then the amount of study time for that child was $8/14$ for that day. The amount of study behavior for the entire class on a given day was the sum of the 12 individual scores.

TIME-SAMPLING VALIDITY CHECK

Time-sampling assumes that, in a given situation, the behavior observed at fixed spacings in time adequately represents the behavior occurring during the total interval. To check the validity of this assumption, a fifth observer described the behavior of only three children much more frequently. At the beginning of each 15-sec interval an automatic timing device beside the fifth observer emitted a click and flashed a small light. The observer then described the ongoing behavior of the first of the three target children of the day, noting essentially the child's looking, talking, and hand behaviors. The procedure was repeated for the second child, then the third. At the onset of the next 15-sec interval, the sequence was repeated. The tape ran continuously. Consequently, during the same interval when the principal observers made 14 observations, the fifth made slightly more than 300 observations of each of the three children. This procedure was used during nine of the 20 experimental sessions, and the three children chosen for this type of observation varied.

The data sheets completed by the four regular observers and the tapes recorded by the fifth observer were coded each day by the four principal observers who assigned either an "S" or "NS" to each description. Coding was accomplished independently by each observer without consultation. The fifth observer did not participate in classifying any of the tape descriptions.

DESIGN

The study, a within-group design, consisted of three stages. During the first stage, participation in the special event was contingent upon the purchase of the necessary ticket with tokens. After nine days under these conditions, participation in the special event was made noncontingent. During the seven days of the noncontingent stage, the children were presented with special-event tickets and snack tickets as they arrived for school. Tokens and verbal statements of praise and encouragement were still given for the same behaviors as during the first phase, but the tokens no longer had any purchasing power. All the privileges of the classroom were available to every child regardless of how much or how little study behavior he or she displayed.

The decision to continue dispensing tokens but devalue them by providing everything free was made in order to retain all of the original procedures except the contingent special event. Had the tokens been given on a noncontingent basis at the beginning of each session, or eliminated entirely, this might have altered the behavior of the teachers toward the children throughout the remainder of the session.

After the sixteenth day of the study, the aprons containing the accumulated tokens were "sent to the cleaners" and all of the tokens were removed. As the children arrived the next day and asked where their tickets were, they were told they would have to buy them. When the children noted that they couldn't because they had no tokens, the teachers responded by saying: "Perhaps you can earn some. Your (activity—name) is over there." Thus, for the final four days, the last days of the summer session, the initial conditions were restored with special-event and snack tickets again being made contingent upon tokens acquired by the students for study behavior.

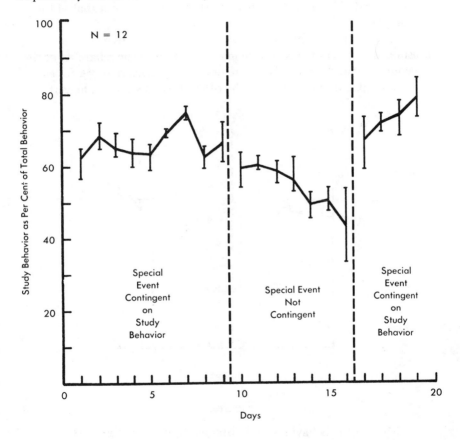

Figure 1

Mean per cent of 12 children's study behavior over 20 school days. Vertical lines indicate the range of scores obtained by the four observers each day.

RESULTS

Figure 1 shows that study behavior was influenced by whether or not the special event was contingent upon it. During the first nine-day stage, offering the special event contingent on study behavior resulted in an average score for the class as a whole of 67%. During the noncontingent stage, the observed study behavior declined 25 percentage points over seven days to a low of 42%. Restoring the original contingencies on Day 17 was associated with a 22% increase in study behavior over that of the previous day.

Because the study behavior data were derived from observational measures, a number of checks were made to establish the reliability of the procedures. First, the total class score obtained by each observer for each day was compared to the scores of the other three observers. The vertical

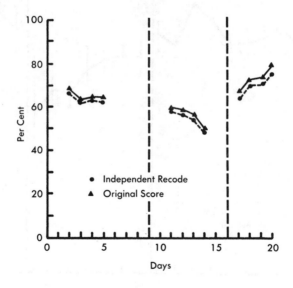

Figure 2

Mean study behavior scores obtained by original observers compared with scores obtained by a panel of coders nine months after the completion of the study. ▲ indicates scores obtained by two of the original observers who recoded the original data sheets nine months after the completion of the study.

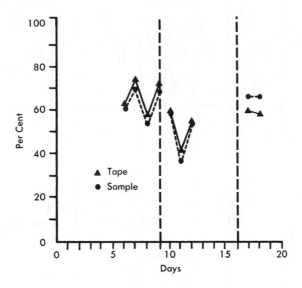

Figure 3

Mean study behavior of various trios of children based on taped observations each day compared with written time-samples during the same period.

lines at each point in Fig. 1 describe the range of group scores obtained by the four observers each day. Inspection of these lines indicated that the same pattern was described even if the summary class score for any given day was drawn at random from the four available scores. Indeed, the data of any one, or any combination, of the four observers presented the same pattern with respect to the effects of contingent reinforcement upon study behavior.

The fact that the behavior descriptions of each day were coded within a few hours after they were obtained might have been an additional source of error. A description might have been coded "NS" on Day 15 and "S" on Day 19 simply because the observer expected study behavior to increase during the final contingent stage. To check for such effects, four new coders were empaneled nine months after the study was completed. These new coders had no knowledge of the details of the original investigation. They were trained to read behavioral descriptions like those appearing on the original data sheets and assign an "S" or "NS" to each according to the criteria outlined in the previous section. Once

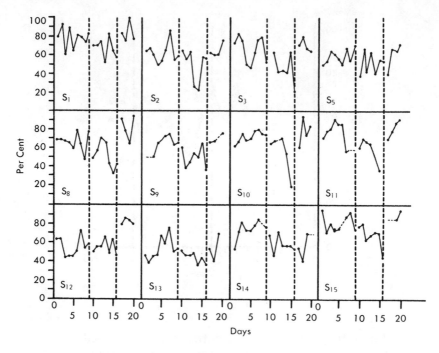

Figure 4

Percent of each individual child's behavior classified as study behavior under all conditions. Dotted lines without points indicate absence.

they agreed within 5% on the independent scoring of a given data sheet, they were each given nine of the original sheets.

The data sheets given to the new coders were in scrambled order with all dates and other identifying marks obscured so they had no way of determining which stage a sheet came from even if they understood the significance of the experimental conditions. Sheets from Days 3, 4, 5, 12, 13, 14, 18, 19, and 20 (three from each stage) were recoded in this fashion. The procedure guaranteed that the expectations of the coder would not influence the scores obtained. The comparison of the original scores and those obtained by the new coders are shown in Fig. 2.

As a further check on coding bias, two of the original observers were recalled after a nine-month interval to recode one set of four data sheets from each of the three stages of the study, 12 sheets in all, also presented in random order. These two observers each recoded the descriptions of one of the other observers and their own data sheets completed at the time of the original study. The results are also shown in Fig. 2 for Days 2, 11, and 17. These points, marked ▲, indicate that the results obtained by having the original observers recode their own and someone else's data do not differ from those obtained when newly trained coders score the original data. In all cases the scores obtained described the effects of contingent and noncontingent reinforcement in the same way.

The comparison of the total score for the three target children obtained by the regular method and the tapes is shown in Fig. 3 and supports the validity of the 5-min time-sampling technique.

The data describing the effects of the different contingencies upon each of the three instructional styles (individual activities, group instruction, teams), failed to demonstrate that this was an important dimension in the present study. Day-to-day variability was greater for these smaller periods than for the entire session, but in all cases the proportion of study behavior dropped similarly in the absence of the contingent special event and rose during the final four days.

Just as the day-to-day variability increased as the analysis moved from the whole class to periods within each day's class, individual study behavior was more variable than the aggregate data for all 12 children. It is to be expected that students of different age, sex, and educational background will perform differently in comparable settings, but all 12 records shown in Fig. 4 indicate that noncontingent reinforcement was less effective in sustaining study behavior than contingent reinforcement. There was no case in which an individual student displayed more study behavior during the second stage of the study than was displayed during the first and third stages.

DISCUSSION

The results indicate that the contingent special event controlled much of the study behavior. In the time available it was not possible to continue the noncontingent stage until study behavior stabilized. With such an extension, study behavior might have gone lower.

A token system has much to recommend it from a practical standpoint, for there are many school activities (recess, early dismissal, extra-curricular events) which might be employed to develop and maintain higher levels of study behavior. Further, the classroom teacher responsible for the behavior of many students can manage a token system, but faces some difficulty in relying solely on verbal praise and attention as reinforcers.

Behavior modification with social reinforcement requires constant monitoring of the subjects's responding (Baer and Wolf, 1967). This can be done only on a very limited scale in a classroom by a single teacher.

The day-to-day variability in individual records requires further study. At first glance it would appear that the individual fluctuations could indict the smoother curve of the group as resulting from the canceling effect of numerous measurement errors at the individual level. However, the several measurement checks suggest that other factors may have been more important in explaining the variability. For example, the practice of allowing the children to accumulate tokens from day to day may have produced some variability. It allowed the children to work hard and lend one day, and loaf and borrow the next; work hard and save one day, loaf and spend their savings the next. This would tend to produce a smooth curve for the group, since not everyone could lend at the same time nor could all borrow at once. The present practice in the preschool is to remove all tokens from the children's pockets after each day's session.

The next approximation toward a useful classroom observational technique will require additional measures to determine the effects of the students' changing behavior on the attending and helping behavior of the teachers. This work is now in progress.

It may be concluded that: (1) practical reinforcement contingencies can be established in a classroom; (2) the effects of various contingencies can be ascertained by direct observational techniques where the use of automated recording equipment is not practicable.

References

Ayllon, T. and Azrin, N. H. The measurement and reinforcement of behavior of psychotics. *Journal of the Experimental Analysis of Behavior*, 1965, 8, 357–383.

Baer, D. M. and Wolf, M. M. The reinforcement contingency in preschool and remedial education. In Robert D. Hess and Roberta Meyer Baer (Eds.), *Early education: current theory, research, and practice*. Chicago: Aldine. In press.

Birnbrauer, J. S., Wolf, M. M., Kidder, J. D., and Tague, C. E. Classroom behavior of retarded pupils with token reinforcement. *Journal of Experimental Child Psychology*, 1965, 2, 219–235.

This study is one of the few which have made group rewards contingent on the performance of a single child. Both early dismissal from class and a story reading period appeared to increase academic behaviors of fourth and sixth grade children. Because the authors did not attempt to reward only the individual student, we cannot discover whether or not the fact that the whole group was rewarded had any additional effect. The authors' comment that the fourth-grade students did encourage the experimental student in their class to do well suggests that the social rewards from their peers may have indeed had an additional effect. Certainly the fact that the subjects who were receiving rewards which were not contingent on their performance (that is, the rest of the class) did not show any improvement suggests that the contingency rather than the "positive" atmosphere engendered by the rewards was responsible for the behavior change.

The lack of generalization once the contingencies were changed caused the authors to suggest two possibilities for making the improvement more permanent: continuing to ask questions and gradually "thinning" the reinforcement schedule. Other possibilities might involve the substitution of social reinforcement from the teacher and the other students and the expansion of the system to include the performance of the whole class. After all, if everyone has learned the material it is reasonable to let the whole class out early.

One problem may arise with the use of escape from academic work as a reinforcer. Although such escape is obviously rewarding, it is a sad comment on the classroom situation that this is so. If other activities within the classroom can serve as positive reinforcers, such as the story telling of Experiment 2 in the Evans and Oswalt study or the opportunity to do a special science project, publish a class newspaper, etc., then the teacher is conveying the idea that classroom activites need not be negative reinforcers. Of course, the only way to discover the effect that a certain event or object has is to actually try it out and see. The procedure used by Evans and Oswalt was clearly convenient, effective, and inexpensive; teachers at all grade levels may want to try it.

Acceleration of Academic Progress through the Manipulation of Peer Influence[1]

Gary W. Evans
and
Gaylon L. Oswalt [2]*†

ABSTRACT

Discontinuance of regular classroom duties for the entire class (early dismissal or story reading) was made contingent upon the performance of under-achieving children in two sections of a fourth-grade class and two sections of a sixth-grade class. Experimental Ss' weekly test scores increased to a statistically significant extent in relation to the test scores of control Ss.

Behavior modification techniques have been successfully applied to a variety of behavior problems associated with the classroom, e.g. hyperactivity (Homme, et al., 1963; Patterson, et al., 1965), peer isolation (Allen, et al., 1965; Patterson and Brodsky, 1966), and school phobia

* Gary W. Evans and Gaylon L. Oswalt, "Acceleration of Academic Progress through the Manipulation of Peer Influence," Behavior Research and Therapy 6(1968): 189–195. Reprinted with permission.

†Bureau of Child Research, University of Kansas and Parsons State Hospital and Training Center.

[1] This study was conducted and supported under NICHHD Grant No. 00870 04.

[2] The authors wish to thank Miss Joella Ragan, Mrs. Linda Ney, Mrs. Nancy Thompson and Mr. Gordon Huggins of the Parsons, Kansas Public School System for their cooperation during the course of this study.

83

(Patterson, 1965). In spite of the successes in these areas, few attempts to manipulate academic achievement have been reported. Zimmerman and Zimmerman (1964) reported a case study of academic progress obtained by selective teacher-approval of correctly spelled words. The study by Patterson, *et al.* (1965), indicates that peer influence is helpful in reducing hyperactivity in the classroom, but its effect on academic achievement was not investigated.

This paper reports an attempt to accelerate academic progress of selected individuals by arranging contingencies in such a manner that peer influence is brought to bear on the subjects' academic performance. The specific procedures used in the following experiments resulted from the assumptions that: (a) most grade-school children will approve of behavior which leads to a story period or early dismissal from class; (b) peer approval has reinforcing properties for the underachieving child.

EXPERIMENT 1

SUBJECTS

The Ss were 22 students from a fourth-grade spelling class. Two experimental Ss (S_1 and S_2) were selected by the classroom teacher and the other 20 students served as control Ss. Experimental Ss were students who were, according to the teacher, "capable of doing considerably better work than they are presently doing."

PROCEDURE

This experiment was conducted over a 13-week period. On the final day of each school week during this period, the teacher constructed and administered a 10-word spelling test covering words that had been presented during that school week.

The first four weeks (Phase 1) was a baseline period in which weekly test scores were recorded but no treatment was introduced. During weeks five through nine (Phase 2), the teacher announced daily, 5 min prior to the morning recess, that the class would be dismissed for recess immediately if S_1 could correctly spell a specified word (or words). The teacher then presented a word for S_1 to attempt to spell (the word was selected from those covered during the preceding period). If S_1 spelled the word correctly, the class was dismissed immediately. If his spelling of the word was incorrect, classwork was continued until the customary dismissal time. During weeks ten through thirteen (Phase 3), the procedure was identical to that of Phase 2, with the exception that early dismissal was made contingent on S_2's responses rather than S_1's. No questions were asked of S_1 in Phase 3.

RESULTS

The results are illustrated in Fig. 1. The results clearly show that the test performance of both S_1 and S_2 showed considerable improvement when the experimental treatment was in effect. Once the experimental condition was discontinued however, S_1's performance declined to its previous level relative to the control Ss. The control Ss showed a slight decline in test performance throughout the experiment. Whatever the reason was for this decline (e.g. more difficult tests, spring weather), it does serve to illustrate that the improvement manifested by S_1 and S_2 during the experimental phases was not due to the presence of elements common to the class as a whole.

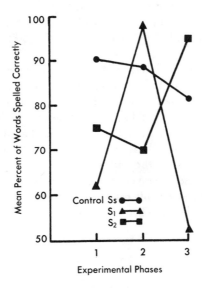

Figure 1

Mean percent of correctly spelled words on weekly tests under phase 1 (baseline), phase 2 (experimental treatment applied to S_2), and phase 3 (experimental treatment applied to S_3).

EXPERIMENT 2

SUBJECTS

The Ss were 20 students from a fourth-grade arithmetic class. Two experimental Ss (S_3 and S_4) were selected by the classroom teacher (the teacher of this class also taught the spelling class described in Experiment 1). Again, the two experimental Ss were students who the teacher believed were performing below their capabilities. The remaining 18 students in the class served as control Ss.

PROCEDURE

This experiment was conducted over a 14-week period. On the final day of each school week during this period, the teacher constructed and administered a ten-problem arithmetic examination covering material that had been presented during the school week.

Again, the first 4 weeks (Phase 1) was a baseline period in which weekly test scores were recorded but no treatment was introduced. During weeks five through nine (Phase 2), the teacher announced daily, 5 min before the class was scheduled to be terminated, that she (the teacher) would read a story to the class for the remainder of the period if S_3 could solve a specified arithmetic problem. The teacher then presented a problem, selected from material presented during the period, for S_3 to attempt to solve. If S_3's solution were correct, the teacher read aloud to the class for the remainder of the period. If S_3's solution were incorrect, normal classwork was contined until the end of the period. During weeks ten through fourteen (Phase 3), story reading was made contingent on S_4's responses, rather than S_3's. Daily questions were asked of S_3 in Phase 3, but no experimental consequences were associated with her answers.

RESULTS

The results are illustrated in Fig. 2. Again, the results clearly show that the experimental Ss showed considerable improvement when placed under the experimental condition. Notice, however, that S_3's performance did not deteriorate in Phase 3 when the treatment discontinued. This finding differs from that of Experiment 1 where S_1 failed to maintain his improved performance when the treatment was discontinued. The control Ss' test performance remained quite stable over the three phases of the experiment illustrating that improvement manifested by S_3 and S_4 was not due to the presence [of] elements in the situation common to the class as a whole.

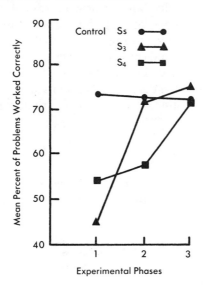

Figure 2

Mean percent of correctly solved arithmetic problems on weekly tests under phase 1 (baseline), phase 2 (experimental treatment applied to S_3), and phase 3 (experimental treatment applied to S_4).

EXPERIMENT 3

SUBJECTS

The Ss were 24 students from a sixth-grade, social-science class. One experimental S (S_5) was selected by the teacher on the basis that he had not been doing as well as he should have been doing in his classwork. The remaining 23 students served as control Ss.

PROCEDURE

This experiment was conducted over a 10-week period. On the final day of each week, the teacher administered a ten-item test covering material presented during the week.

Again the first four weeks (Phase 1) was a baseline period in which weekly test scores were recorded but a treatment was not introduced. During weeks five through ten (Phase 2), the teacher announced daily, 5 min prior to the customary noon dismissal time, that the class would be dismissed 5 min early if S_5 could correctly answer a question over material covered during the class period. The teacher then asked S_5 a question and, if he responded correctly, the class was dismissed. If he responded inappropriately to the question, classwork was continued until the customary dismissal time.

RESULTS

The results are illustrated in Fig 3. The results show that S_5 showed some improvement relative to the control Ss, but the extent of the

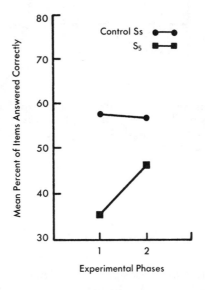

Figure 3

Mean percent of correctly answered items on weekly social science tests under phase 1 (baseline) and phase 2 (experimental treatment applied to S_5).

improvement was considerably less than that manifested by experimental Ss in the first two experiments.

EXPERIMENT 4

SUBJECTS

The Ss were 24 students from a sixth-grade, general-science class. An experimental S (S_6) was selected by the teacher (the teacher of this class also taught the social-science class described in Experiment 3). Again, the experimental S was a student who the teacher believed should be doing better work than he was currently doing. The remaining 23 students served as control Ss.

PROCEDURE

The procedure and time periods were identical to those employed in Experiment 3 with the exception that dismissal time was contingent on a

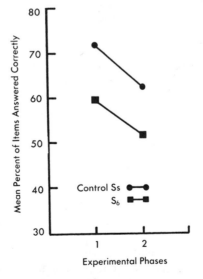

Figure 4

Mean percent of correctly answered items on weekly science tests under phase 1 (baseline) and phase 2 (experimental treatment applied to S_6).

correct response from S_6 5 min prior to afternoon recess, rather than noon hour.

RESULTS

Figure 4 illustrates that the test performance of both S_6 and the control group declined during Phase 2. Since there was little change in S_6's standing relative to the control group, the decline was probably due to an environmental element (such as more difficult examinations) other than the experimental treatment.

ANALYSIS OF RESULTS

A mean change score was obtained for each experimental S by subtracting his mean test score during the preceding baseline phase(s) from his mean test score during the treatment phase. Thus, the mean change score for S_1 was his mean test score in Phase 2, minus his mean test score in Phase 1. The mean change score for S_2 was his mean test score in Phase 3, minus his mean test score in Phases 1 and 2 combined. Mean change scores were also obtained for the control groups so that mean change scores for each experimental S could be compared with an appropriate group change score.

The difference between each experimental S's change score and the change score of the appropriate control group was obtained. These six difference scores were analyzed statistically by means of the paired t-test. The mean difference was found to be statistically significant beyond the 0.02 level of confidence ($t = 3.678$; df = 5). Whereas the experimental Ss showed a mean gain of 1.73 items per test (17.3%) under the treatment conditions, the control Ss showed a mean loss of 0.37 items per test (3.7%) under these conditions.

DISCUSSION

The results of these experiments demonstrate that the procedures described can accelerate the academic performance of underachieving grade-school children. The lack of uniformity of results may have been due to:
1. Age or educational differences between fourth-grade and sixth-grade children.

2. Teacher differences in attitude toward or execution of the program.
3. Subject matter differences.
4. Individual differences among subjects.

The question of the relative effects of these different variables cannot be answered by the data obtained in these experiments. A confounding of effects is present due to the fact that one teacher taught both fourth-grade classes and the other teacher taught both sixth-grade classes. The difference in responsiveness to the treatment may have been due to certain attitudinal differences between the teachers, or the fact that the program was more effective with fourth-grade Ss than with sixth-grade Ss may have led to attitudinal differences between the teachers.

Anecdotal reports by the teachers indicate there was a difference in the manner in which the fourth-grade and sixth-grade children reacted to the program. The fourth-grade teacher reported several attempts by peers to influence the experimental Ss' success (e.g. urging S to study his material and offering assistance). No such attempts by peers was noticed by the sixth-grade teacher. Both teachers reported, however, that their classes were pleased when early dismissal occurred. Differences in teacher attitudes toward the program were indicated by their verbal reports. The fourth-grade teacher spoke very favorably of the program, while the sixth-grade teacher was unimpressed. Further experimentation to isolate teacher, grade, and subject matter differences is planned.

Experimentation is also planned to identify procedures which will prevent relapses after the treatment is discontinued, such as the one exhibited by S_1. At least two possibilities suggest themselves. One possibility is to continue to ask the child questions but eliminate the consequences of his answer. This treatment was applied to S_3 in Phase 3 (Experiment 2) and her performance did not deteriorate. A second possible preventative of severe deterioration after the treatment conditon is removed is gradually to decrease the treatment frequency until the desired behavior comes under the control of positive natural consequences.

A comment on the generalization of learned behavior seems appropriate at this point. Note that the dependent variable employed in this study, weekly test performance, was not the behavior that was actually reinforced. The finding that reinforcing daily performance will affect behavior on weekly tests which is not reinforced, though not particularly surprising, demonstrates that behavioral generalization does occur under the conditions of these experiments.

Acquisition of control over an individual's behavior by making a class-reinforcer contingent on the behavior of the individual is a treatment technique that lends itself to a variety of behavior and learning problems in the classroom. In addition to its versatility, the technique has the advantage of requiring very little of the teacher's time or energy. Tests and records are necessary only to evaluate the effectiveness of the procedure. Once the conditions under which the procedure is effective are established, tests and records are not a necessary part of the program. Hopefully, these features will serve to make the technique both effective and practical for general use in the classroom situation.

References

Allen K. E., Hart B. M., Buell J. A., Harris F. R. and Wolf M. M. (1965) Effects of social reinforcement on isolate behavior of a nursery school child. In *Case studies in behavior modification* (Eds. Ullmann and Krasner), pp. 307–312.

Homme L. E., C.de Baca P., Devine T. V., Steinhorst R. and Rickert E. J. (1963) Use of the Premack principle in controlling the behavior of nursery school children. *J. exp. Analysis Behav.* 6, 544.

Patterson G. R. and Brodsky G. A behavior modification program for a child with multiple problem behaviors. *J. Child Psychol. Psychiat.* (In press).

Patterson G. R., Jones J. W., Whittier J. and Wright M. A. (1965) A behavior modification technique for the hyperactive child. *Behav. Res. & Therapy* 2, 217–226.

Zimmerman E. H. and Zimmerman T. (1962) The alteration of behavior in a special classroom situation. *J. exp. Analysis Behav.* 5, 59–60.

What can a teacher do with a class composed of students whose behavior problems are too severe for them to be permitted to attend regular classes? What can a teacher do who wishes to utilize the technique of token reinforcement but for philosophical or financial reasons does not wish to utilize material rewards? The study by Vernon suggests an answer to both these questions. The first part of the answer, which involves dividing the year's work into a sequence of written exercises, may not be appropriate for all teachers, some of whom may wish to reward other behaviors than written answers. The second part, on the other hand, involves the kind of creativity in the selection of rewards that most teachers could make use of; however, it is unlikely that most school boards would be willing to buy the teacher a new convertible even if being chauffeured home turned out to be as popular a reward as in Vernon's study. The device of "charging" for tantrums is another suggestion which may well be appropriate in many other classrooms.

The academic results reported by Vernon seem almost too good to be true. If all of a group of fourth grade problem children can complete fifth grade work, why do normal children in a normal classroom take so much longer to do so? Is it that the small class and individualized instruction greatly reduce the distractions and tedium of a typical class situation, as he suggests? Is it that the contingencies, immediate feedback and desirable rewards vastly increase the student's motivation to learn? Or is it that perhaps the exercises developed do not in fact cover all the work traditionally taught at that grade level? Regardless of the answer, the reported improvement in both behavior and academic work for no material rewards suggests seriously that such a procedure might be appropriate in a classroom of normal as well as problem children.

Non-Material Token Reward Systems with Severe Classroom Problems

Walter M. Vernon*

A relatively new approach in classroom motivation has come into use during this decade. The approach employs the use of operant principles in place of the more traditional appeals to "natural inquisitiveness," insight into educational relevance," and the like. Thus far the formal use of operant principles has been mainly with the disadvantaged, the retarded, and in classrooms for special education of the maladjusted. The subjects in these cases have been in the most imperative need of help, and the operant approach has met with striking success. Skinner (1968) has pointed out a need for similar changes in the average classroom as well. A few such applications of formal programs have recently been attempted, also with striking success.

Common to most of these efforts have been token economies with *material* back up reinforcers; that is, tokens are exchangable for such prizes as candy bars, model airplane kits, story books, and even money. Sometimes the token intermediation is dispensed with and very small rewards are directly administered. These are the famous M and M's, Hershey's "Kisses," pennies, etc.—again, all *material* end-rewards. Most of us know the difficulty involved in gaining an appreciable level of cooperation from school administrators when material rewards are to be involved. The resolution of this dilemma is obviously to build up a powerful program using non-material back up reinforcers. One or two teachers of my personal acquaintance have attempted to use tokens exchangable for additional points toward the grade in the course. These effects have been inconsistent and generally disappointing. It has become

*Illinois State University

obvious that in the public school classroom letter grades are not reinforcing to the extent we might have imagined. The present research represents an effort to extend the principles of a token economy operation into a system using an array of non-material back up reinforcers that work.

The class was made up of ten children starting in the first week of October, 1968. During the next five weeks two more children were added to the group. All were 9 or 10 year olds who had begun the year in 4th grade classrooms in the large University laboratory school on the campus. All of these children were termed extremely disruptive and given to tantrums or other means of resistance to authority. Moreover, all but one were classed as "slow learners," although it was not clear to what extent their discipline problems might have contributed to their achievement deficit. The children were being removed from the regular classrooms because of their behavior problems. The token economy class was the only alternative for the parents who wanted to keep their children in the laboratory school.

On the first day of the special class a few minutes were taken to explain the economy. All the standard subjects of elementary education were broken down into rigidly sequenced exercise sheets with instructions for working the exercises and examples where necessary written out at the top. These exercise sheets were developed by a team of certified, experienced elementary teachers. There were no lecture demonstrations. Class began each day with each child being given an exercise sheet. The child works until finished with the problems. The child then goes directly to the teacher with his sheet. Answer boxes on the sheet are checked against a key. A criterion of 90% is usually set, or 100% if the exercise is a continuation of previously established principles. If the sheet meets the criterion of accuracy, the child is given "paper coins" in the amount indicated on the corner of the exercise sheet. Most sheets are rated for 10 points. If a child's work does not meet the criterion a fresh duplicate exercise sheet is given with the ones missed underlined, and the child returns to his seat to start the exercise over. On rare occasions where a child persists in an error pattern the teacher spends a few minutes presenting an extra example or two. We usually take this to mean that the explanation at the top of that particular exercise sheet needs revision. As soon as the child completes an exercise and is awarded the tokens, he is given a new exercise sheet of the teacher's choice.

Thus far little has been described that is not completely familiar. It might be pointed out that the technique just described (1) allows a child to progress as rapidly as he develops his skills, (2) allows individualized instruction with the teacher "prescribing" exactly those exercises that represent relative deficits in knowledge, and (3) develops reading skills; for most of the children it was the first time that retention after reading was visibly vital to future rewards. Almost as a side effect of standard subject matter, it was found that reading comprehension showed a marked increase.

It was in the matter of back up reinforcers that we hoped to develop some useful methods. We refused to have the children act as role-appropriate prisoners. Thus, drinks of water, visits to the pencil sharpener and the rest rooms, which have occasionally been described as token redemption items, were allowed gratis. Some of the back up reinforcers we did employ were:

1. Recess, 10 points.
2. Double length recess, 20 points.
3. Feed the three caged animals in the classroom, 20 points.
4. Hot lunch at noon in the cafeteria, 15 points.
5. Dessert after lunch, 15 points.
6. Playground privilege after lunch, 10 points.

We enlisted the suggestions of the children and arrived at three others:

7. Serve as teacher's assistant, scoring the simpler exercise sheets and dispensing tokens for one-half hour, 20 points.
8. Join another class's field trip after getting permission from both the other teacher and the parent, 30 points.
9. Be chauffeured home after school in the teacher's new convertible, 25 points.

During the early weeks of the token economy program prices were readjusted to represent relative popularities of the activites. Of course we maintained lunches and recesses at an economy cost, and there were no cases of children skipping lunch in favor of some other redemption.

What of our results? Remind yourself of the initial conditions of the children just before acceptance into the program. By the second day of the token economy the class was quiet except for occasional enthusiastic exclamations following token successes. Work was rendered rapidly and eagerly. The change just in the facial expressions when the children approached the teacher for interaction was in sharp contrast to the attitudes that had been described for us by previous teachers of these children. School, exercise problems, reading, and the teacher became associated with fun, rewards, success, and an absence of coercive control. One of the class's new arrivals three weeks after the project began was a tantrum-thrower whose screaming, kicking and crying several times every day had terrorized his teachers from the first grade on. The official school records used the word "uncontrollable" in describing his status. Following his first tantrum in the token economy class he was told that he could have it free, but subsequent tantrums would have to be paid for at a price of 10 points each. It was emphasized that he would be allowed to purchase as many as he cared to pay for. Two tantrums were observed during that week. Since that time none have occurred, nor has there been any "symptom substitution." The pattern of change observed with this child is the pattern for all—aggression has ceased, stop-work resistance has ceased, and daydreaming has ceased. Disruptive behavior, in general, has virtually disappeared.

Traditionally the classroom teacher has looked upon discipline and academic motivation as separate processes. The research described in this paper proceeded under a different assumption—one that is familiar to all operant behaviorists. That is, a high level of classroom achievement, just by virtue of its existence, will effectively displace incompatible patterns such as disruptive behavior.

As far as academic achievement is concerned, the results have been completely satisfactory. Instead of spending time listening to largely unnecessary explanations and multiple examples being rendered by a teacher, and rather than be attracted by the numerous distractions offered by peers in a classroom plagued by tedium, the children are almost constantly engaged in individualized learning. They resent distracting interferences. *All* ten children have gone completely through the 4th and 5th grade boxes of exercise sheets. Five of the ten have completed the 6th grade boxes and it is almost certain that the number will be eight of the ten by the end of the school term. Two children may complete the 7th grade materials. I would point out that these materials make up the complete subject matter concepts expected in the appropriate grades, with the exception of art, music and physical education activities. The material has also been mastered to a much higher criterion (90% to 100%) than is represented by the test averages in the regular classrooms.

The program has now lasted for 7½ months with about ½ month to go. In the last two months we have begun to phase the students into partial reinforcement schedules that mimic traditional settings. For example, students began to get "credits" which were computed during the entire day; on the day following, the student would be given one big pay-off at 8:30 a.m. of his previous day's earnings. Two day, then four day intervals before pay-day have been developed. In this manner we hope to ease the transition into traditionally taught classrooms in September. All of our students have been deemed appropriate for placement in high track accelerated classes next year.

Sometimes we are asked what will happen to these children when they must switch from a token economy and are put back into the old-style classrooms. We are optimistic about their future, but are beginning to ask a question of our own. What will happen when they go back to the traditional classroom? Why should any of them have to?

Reference

Skinner, B. F. *The Technology of Teaching*. New York: Appleton-Century-Crofts, 1968.

Hawkins, Sluyter, and Smith in this article describe a way in which parents and teachers can cooperate to improve student's academic performance. As they point out, many parents who are sincerely concerned about their children's school performance would be willing to help them improve their performance if effective and convenient ways to do so were available to them. The technique selected by the authors was to have the teacher send a note home to the parent if the child's behavior met certain standards and to have the parents reinforce the child for bringing home the notes. The particular behaviors reinforced included paying attention and being quiet, as well as academic performance in several areas. The parents, of course, selected rewards appropriate to the particular child, which varied from permission to play outdoors to stuffed animals to praise.

The study clearly demonstrated that delays of a few hours need not mean that the reinforcement would no longer affect behavior. Since this appears to be true, it may be much more convenient and just as effective for teachers using this technique to hand the notes to the child only at the end of class. Certainly the administrative labor on the part of the teacher is much less with such a program than with a more traditional token system in which the teacher dispenses the back-up reinforcers as well as the tokens.

An additional advantage of such a program is the involvement of the parents. For one thing, it forces parents to pay attention to the scholastic progress of their child. Another advantage is that it focuses attention on the good aspects of the child's behavior and on the use of reward rather than punishment. The use of reward for appropriate behavior often brings about changes in the parent-child relationship, particularly if it has been previously based on criticism and punishment. Often the parent's attitudes toward their children become more positive and their disciplinary techniques shift in the direction of positive reinforcement. In turn the child may improve both his behavior and his respect and liking for the parent. Although the case studies reported by Hawkins et al. did not appear to involve parents who were uninterested, unconcerned or particularly inept at discipline, this approach might be quite effective with such parents, if they are willing to attempt it.

Modification of Achievement by a Simple Technique Involving Parents and Teacher[1]

Robert P. Hawkins
David J Sluyter[2]
and
Carroll D. Smith*

ABSTRACT

Seven experiments were conducted to help answer the question, "What can parents and teachers of an underachieving child do to help that child?" Though many school programs exist for such children, many remain underachievers despite absence of serious "emotional" or socio-economic problems.

A simple, inexpensive reinforcement technique was designed to raise achievement in those children whose primary problem was low motivation. Its

* Adapted by authors from Robert P. Hawkins, David J. Sluyter and Carroll D. Smith, "Modification of Achievement by a Simple Technique Involving Parents and Teacher," *Journal of Learning Disabilities*, in press. Reprinted with permission.

[1] Based upon a paper presented at the American Educational Research Association convention, Minneapolis, March, 1970. This research was made possible by the financial and moral support of Marland E. Bluhm, Director of Special Education, and Albert L. Bradfield, Superintendent, Kalamazoo Valley Intermediate School District and was conducted as part of the School Adjustment Research Project. It was also facilitated by the cooperation of the following personnel in Comstock Public Schools: Larry Lindeman, Ron Reese, and Mainord Weaver, principals; Pat McQueen, Elsie Lewis, Marsha DeHaven, Ruth Hibart, Mary Cole, and Muril Robinson, teachers.

[2] Presently Acting Director, Behavior Treatment Project, Coldwater State Home and Training School, Coldwater, Michigan.

adoption could be initiated by either parents or teachers, since no specialized knowledge and very little effort was required of either party. The technique involved daily dispensing of dittoed notes to the child at school regarding his performance in the area of interest. These notes were taken home and parents arranged reinforcing consequences there.

A single-subject research design was used. Dependent variables, chosen on the basis of individual subject's achievement problems, included mathematics performance, spelling performance, reading performance, social studies performance, talking out of turn, and inattentiveness. Six of the seven cases showed significant improvement resulting from application of technique. Four of the cases are presented here to illustrate the technique and various effects it produced.

Variations of this simple technique should be tried in many schools to determine its general effectiveness. It can be initiated by counselors, psychologists, social workers and principals as well as teachers and parents. It should be applicable to most grade levels, but this remains to be determined.

What can the parents of an underachieving child do to help that child improve in his academic work at school? While the parents of some underachievers are not interested in the fact that their child is an underachiever or in what they might do about it, many parents of underachievers are genuinely interested in helping their child and very open to suggestions as to how they might provide this help. The interested parents will often indicate to their child's teacher, principal, school social worker, remedial reading teacher, counselor, or school psychologist that they would be very happy to help their child if only they knew what to do.

Sometimes school personnel will suggest to the parents that they help the child with his school work at home, in the evening; but many educators have found this method to be unsatisfactory. Parents of an underachieving child are very likely to do more harm than good when they attempt to instruct the child at home, because they expect too much of the child, do not understand the work well themselves, are inconsistent, do the work for the child, or become very punitive. The result often is very unfavorable for the child, the parents and the teacher.

An alternative method by which the parents might help their underachiever would be to simply motivate him. They could completely avoid the area of instruction, and restrict themselves to activities that would serve to motivate better academic performance on the child's part. Of course, this idea is not new to parents; most interested parents of underachievers have probably encouraged, cajoled, warned, threatened, and offered sizable rewards to their child in order to get him to perform. It is probably also accurate to say that most underachievers would really like to do better academically. The basic difficulty that both the parents and the child have is that they do not understand enough about the way human behavior works. Their knowledge of how to arrange the environment so that the child's behavior changes, is inadequate.

Over the past few years a number of researchers have been using available knowledge of "how behavior works" to rearrange school and home environments in such a way as to motivate improved learning and performance in children. Employing principles and techniques of behavioral science, these researchers have modified a wide variety of child behaviors in school settings. For example, Wolf, Giles and Hall (1968) showed that performance in different academic subjects depended upon the amount of reinforcement provided in each subject; Hall and Broden (1967) guided teachers and parents in modifying the "brain-damaged behavior" of three children through manipulation of social reinforcers; Surratt, Ulrich and Hawkins (1969) found that the attentive working behavior of first grade children could be modified by making certain privileges contingent upon attentiveness or inattentiveness; and Madsen, Becker and Thomas (1968) demonstrated that stating of rules has very little effect on classroom behavior, while showing approval of appropriate behavior exerts a great deal of control over classroom behavior.

The motivational manipulations used in these studies differ in several important respects from the kinds of things that parents of the underachieving child are likely to have tried. The person making systematic use of behavioral principles and techniques is not likely to do any cajoling, threatening or persuading. Nor is he likely to use much punishment. He *is* likely to offer rewards for accomplishment, but the rewards will usually be small ones offered for very small improvements in performance, and the rewards will typically be given much more immediately and consistently than those given by most parents or teachers.

The parents of the underachieving child are at a disadvantage in carrying out the kind of behavioral engineering used in the studies cited, however. They are in a position that has two serious drawbacks. Though they can avoid cajoling, threatening, persuading, and punishing, and they can offer small rewards for small improvements in performance; they cannot give the rewards immediately, and they will have difficulty knowing when performance has been adequate to earn a reward. That is, the parents typically cannot be present in the classroom and give immediate rewards; and they need some way to monitor the behavior if they are to give any rewards at all. The present studies were done to determine whether a practical, inexpensive technique could be devised that would overcome these difficulties.

Three local school children were located who met the following criteria: their daily performance in one or more academic areas was far below average (though their achievement test scores might not be); their I.Q. scores were average or above; and their teachers and parents were willing to try an experiment. Two of these experiments will be presented to illustrate the method and general findings, but results with the third subject were comparable to those obtained with the first subject.[3]

EXPERIMENT I: SHERRY

METHOD

Subject

Sherry was a nine-year-old fourth grader whose work in both social studies and arithmetic was well below her capabilities. Performance in these two areas was chosen as the target behavior.

---

[3] These studies were conducted by Carroll Dean Smith in partial fulfillment of the requirements for the degree of Master of Arts from Western Michigan University.

Procedure

Baseline. Sherry's performance in both social studies and arithmetic was measured in terms of the percentage of her work she did correctly. In social studies the teacher gave short quizzes several times each week, so the percent of questions Sherry answered correctly on each quiz constituted one dependent variable. Written arithmetic assignments were given daily and Sherry's accuracy on those assignments constituted the second dependent measure. For 16 days no manipulations were made; the teacher simply scored Sherry's social studies and arithmetic papers after school and recorded these scores. When an adequate estimate of Sherry's performance in these two subject areas had been obtained, the first manipulation was introduced.

Child-Parent Feedback. On the 17th day the teacher told Sherry that if she did better work in social studies or arithmetic she would receive a note to take home to her parents. The teacher began correcting Sherry's social studies and arithmetic papers as soon as they were turned in. If Sherry's performance met a specified criterion in either subject, the teacher would fill out a note and give it to Sherry with the instruction to take the note home and show it to her parents.

The notes were dittoed in advance and simply said "Sherry did very well in arithmetic today" or "Sherry did very well in social studies today." The teacher dated and signed the arithmetic note, if Sherry's arithmetic performance met criterion, and handed the note to Sherry. The same was done for social studies. The criteria in this phase of the experiment were that she have at least 37 percent correct in social studies and 46 percent correct in arithmetic; however Sherry was not informed what these criteria were.

This technique was not what the experimenters were most interested in testing; it lacked one element of the technique of interest. Thus it was an attempted component analysis of the whole technique (Baer, Wolf, and Risley, 1968). The whole technique was to include the dispensing of reinforcers, by the child's parents, contingent upon the child's bringing home a note.[4] The Child-Parent Feedback phase would reveal whether the reinforcement provided at home was an essential ingredient. It could be sufficient for a teacher to merely grade the underachieving child's work immediately and give the child a note saying he had done well. This

---

[4] The use of weekly token reinforcers (grades) at school that were exchangeable for "backup reinforcers" (money) at home has also been investigated by McKenzie, Clark, Wolf, Kothera and Benson (1968). They measured the effect of this contingency upon attentiveness to reading and arithmetic assignments.

phase also served as a test for the Hawthorn effect, since any new procedure in the classroom—and especially one that focused attention on the target behaviors—might have an effect on the child's performance.

In order to develop a technique that required as little as possible of a teacher, the experimenters instructed Sherry's teacher not to even use any praise. The teacher was to merely score the child's paper and give her a note, if she had earned it, without commenting to the child, patting her on the back, or giving any kind of social reinforcement.

After nine days of applying the Child-Parent Feedback condition sufficient information on its effectiveness had been accumulated. The technique of interest was then employed.

Reinforcement. Those familiar with the concept of token reinforcement will recognize that the note given Sherry for good performance was a type of token reinforcer. It had no reinforcement value in itself, as demonstrated in the Child-Parent Feedback condition; but it could be made valuable if it gained the child access to other stimuli that were reinforcers. During the Reinforcement phase the experimenters arranged for the note to acquire value. The parents were asked to give Sherry certain rewards if she brought home a note. They agreed to give her praise and allow her to play outside before dinner if she brought home one note. If she brought home both notes she was allowed to play outside after dinner as well. She was allowed to play outside on weekends only if she brought home a certain number of notes during the preceding week.

As Sherry's performance improved, the criteria for receiving notes were shifted upward. In arithmetic the criterion began at 46% and shifted finally to 85%. In social studies the criterion began at 38% and shifted gradually to 72%.

RESULTS AND DISCUSSION

During Baseline Sherry's performance in social studies averaged 37 percent correct. In arithmetic her performance averaged 47 percent (Figure 1). She was in the lowest 10 percent of her class in social studies and the lowest 15 percent of her class in arithmetic. The conditions of the Child-Parent Feedback phase had no apparent effect on Sherry's performance. Thus, the immediate scoring of her work, the focusing of attention on arithmetic and social studies performance, and the dispensing of notes to take home were not adequate to change her behavior.[5]

---

[5] The fact that no praise was given with the notes may be very significant. Obviously a better technique for modifying the behavior would be to praise the child while giv-

When Sherry's parents informed her of the new contingencies, in the Reinforcement phase, her performance in both subjects improved immediately. Subsequently there were two consecutive days in which her social studies scores were zero. Sherry was a child accustomed to having "her own way," and it is suspected that she was merely "testing" whether her parents actually meant to follow through on the contingencies they stated. They did follow through; Sherry not only lost half of her outdoor privileges on those two nights, but also lost outdoor privileges through the weekend, because those two days were Thursday and Friday.

After that her performance in both social studies and arithmetic improved drastically. By the end of the study Sherry was among the top 10 percent of the class in arithmetic and in the top half of the class in social studies.

EXPERIMENT II: JIM

METHOD

Subject

Jim was a six-year-old first grader described by his teacher as "lazy" and "uninterested." His two most difficult subjects were arithmetic and reading.

Procedure

Baseline. For twelve days Jim's scores in both arithmetic and reading (workbook and work sheets) were recorded by the teacher. This was sufficient to provide an evaluation of Jim's pre-experimental performance.

Child-Parent Feedback. The teacher gave Jim notes for performance above criterion, and he was instructed to take these home to show his parents. Criteria in arithmetic and reading were 47% and 15% respectively. Again, the teacher was to give no social reinforcement with the notes. The parents were given no guidance about what to do when Jim brought home notes.

Reinforcement. When the Reinforcement phase was begun the experimenters talked with Jim's parents to see what they had been doing

---

ing her the note. This was not included in the research design because the experimenters wished to develop a technique that could be implemented in even a classroom where the teacher's approval had little reinforcing effect.

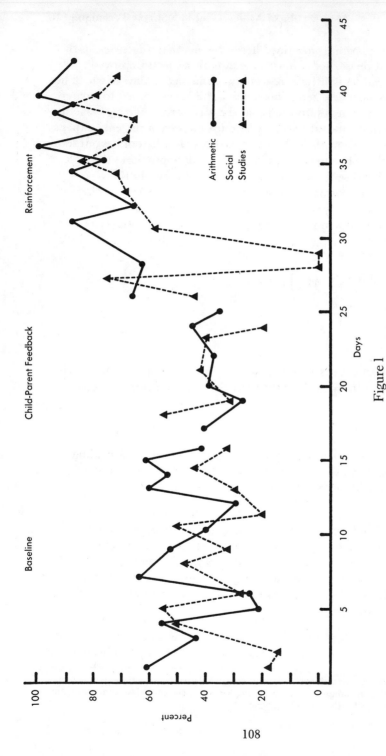

Figure 1

Sherry's performance in two academic areas under three experimental conditions; no specially programed feedback (Baseline), feedback to the child in the form of notes about good achievement in either activity (Child-Feedback), and home consequences contingent upon bringing home notes. Data indicate what percentage of her written assignment was completed correctly. No data point is shown for an activity on days when that activity did not occur.

when Jim brought home notes. It was found that they were already doing exactly the kinds of things that the experimenters had planned to recommend they do during the Reinforcement phase. They praised Jim when he brought home a note, and they placed it on a family bulletin board. They allowed him to stay up half an hour later on nights when he brought home a note, and on Saturday's he was allowed to watch television until late in the evening if he had received several notes during the preceding week. Other privileges, such as going to the store or going with his father on errands in the car, were occasionally added as reinforcers. When Jim failed to bring home a note, his parents expressed disappointment and questioned him about the reasons for his not receiving a note. It was suggested that they stop this last procedure, because under some conditions (such as when a child is angry at the parent) lengthy expressions of disappointment and discussions of problems appear to act as reinforcers rather than as punishers or aversive consequences. Other than making this one recommendation, the experimenters did nothing but encourage the parents to continue what they were doing and be very consistent and enthusiastic in applying the reinforcers.

Jim continued receiving the notes at school for performance above criterion and continued receiving the privileges and social recognition at home as "backup reinforcers."

RESULTS AND DISCUSSION

During Baseline Jim got an average of only 13 percent of his reading answers correct and 52 percent of his arithmetic (Figure 2), though he typically completed the assignments. He was in the lowest 10 percent of his class in both subjects. During the Child-Parent Feedback condition, his performance in both areas improved rapidly. When the Reinforcement phase was begun, the parents were interviewed and it was discovered that they had actually been rewarding Jim in very appropriate ways for his good work. The experimenters had expected that none of the parents of these underachievers would spontaneously use consequences that were sufficiently positive and consistent to have much effect on their child's performance, but this prediction proved inaccurate in Jim's case.

Counseling the parents to use only praise for good performance and be very consistent, during the Reinforcement phase, appears to have resulted in even further improvement in Jim's academic performance. His arithmetic performance during this phase averaged 84 percent correct and his reading, 63 percent. He averaged in the top 20 percent of his class in arithmetic and the top 20 percent of his group in reading.

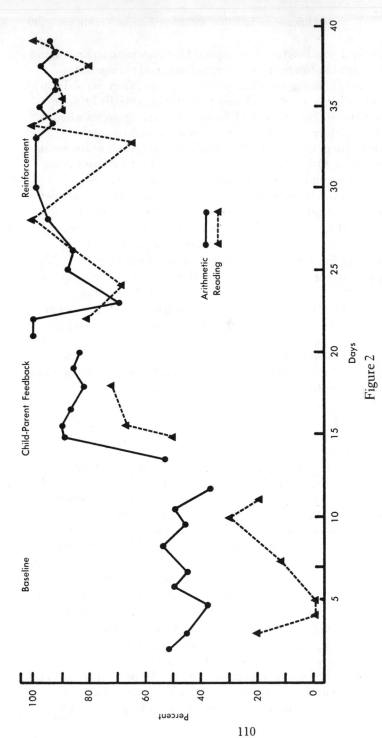

Figure 2

Jim's performance in two academic areas under three experimental conditions; no specially programed feedback (Baseline), feedback to the child in the form of notes about good achievement in either activity (Child-Feedback), and home consequences contingent upon bringing home notes. Data indicate what percentage of his written assignment was completed correctly. No data point is shown for an activity on days when that activity did not occur.

After still a third successful case, the experimenters wondered just how simple and convenient this technique could be made without losing its effect. In the first three experiments the reinforcement had been applied to performance in two subject areas at the same time. What if it were applied to only one subject area? And what if the experimenters made it even less demanding on the teacher by asking her to give the child his note at the *end* of the day rather than immediately after the child completed his assignment? Of course one of the basic principles of behavior is that either reinforcement or punishment is more effective the more immediate it is, but there is some evidence that with verbal human subjects a delayed reinforcement contingency can still be effective (Schwarz and Hawkins, 1970). The experimenters decided to find a few more underachievers.

Four additional underachievers were located. This time the technique would involve a delayed reinforcement, in which the child did not find out whether he had earned a note or not until the end of the school day. The contingency was applied to performance in only one subject area, but measurement of performance in a second area was taken in order to assess generalization of behavior changes and as a further test for a Hawthorn effect.[6] Also, a further component analysis of the independent variable was conducted in two of the experiments to determine whether the child's simply receiving a note would affect his behavior even if he were not allowed to take it home; because in Experiment II it could be argued that Jim's simply receiving the note produced the behavior change found in the Child-Parent Feedback phase, and that the parental consequation (reported, in retrospect, but not programmed by the experimenters) was irrelevant.

EXPERIMENT III: DIANNE

METHOD

Subject

Dianne was an 11 year old sixth grader performing poorly in arithmetic and spelling, but not in other subjects.

Procedure

Baseline. Dianne's performance in arithmetic and spelling was recorded. In this and all subsequent studies of academic performance it was also

---

[6] These four experiments were conducted by David J. Sluyter in partial fulfillment of the requirements for the degree of Master of Arts from Western Michigan University.

determined how the rest of the class was performing, so that the child's relative standing in the class could be assessed continuously. That way it would be more certain that changes in our subject's performance were not simply a reflection of increased or decreased difficulty of the teacher's assignments; for if the assignments became, say, more difficult, everyone's performance should show a decline, and the subject's relative standing in the class would hopefully be unaffected.

Contrary to instructions, during the Baseline Dianne's parents told her that her poor school work had attracted the attention of a psychologist and that she should work harder. This occurred on day 8, and when the experimenters found out about it, it was decided to extend the Baseline period longer than planned so that it could be determined whether this inadvertent manipulation would have any effect.

Child-Feedback. After a 20 day Baseline the first intentional manipulation, the Child-Feedback condition, was begun. Every day that no more than 80 percent of the class scored higher than Dianne in arithmetic, Dianne received a note *after* school saying "You did well today in arithmetic." Thus she could earn a note only in arithmetic, and this note was not dispensed until the end of the school day, a few hours after the actual behavior upon which it was contingent. The teacher gave her no indication, prior to that time, whether or not she had reached criterion for a note (in fact, the teacher did not check the papers immediately and could not give such feedback). After Dianne read the note, she was required to return it to the teacher.

Reinforcement. During the Reinforcement phase Dianne was to receive a small toy, stuffed animal (which she had a collection of) after bringing home two notes, a larger one after the fourth note, and a still larger one after the sixth note. Her parents did not specify to her what she would receive thereafter. The teacher continued dispensing notes at the end of the day if arithmetic performance was above criterion.

RESULTS AND DISCUSSION

During Baseline, 67 percent of the class scored higher than Dianne in arithmetic, on the average, and 32 percent scored higher during spelling (Figure 3). Since her performance after day 8, when her parents urged her to improve, was not clearly better or worse than her performance before day 8, it may be concluded that these urgings were ineffective.[7]

---

[7] This result is compatible with the finding of Ayllon and Azrin (1964) that instructions often are ineffectual in modifying behavior unless accompanied by appropriate

Also ineffective was the Child-Feedback condition, in which Dianne was given a note at the end of the day but was not allowed to take it home. An average of 69% scored higher than she in arithmetic, and 30% in spelling, during Child-Feedback. These percentages are very close to those from the Baseline.

When backup reinforcers were provided at home, in the Reinforcement phase, Dianne's class standing in arithmetic improved. Only 25% scored higher than she in arithmetic. Because of the variability of the data, it is somewhat difficult to interpret them by visual inspection, so a Mann Whitney U Test was applied and revealed that during Reinforcement Dianne's standing in arithmetic was significantly improved over her standing during the Child-Feedback phase ($p < .002$, $U = 2.0$, $N_1 = 6$, $N_2 = 11$, two tailed). Apparently the delay in the note reinforcement and application of the technique to only one behavior did not prevent its affecting the behavior.

No notes or backup reinforcers were given Dianne for her spelling performance, and her relative performance in that subject was unaffected by the dispensing of notes and reinforcers for arithmetic performance. Her performance in spelling was still exceeded by 29% of her classmates. Thus the effect that was obtained in arithmetic did not generalize to spelling.

EXPERIMENT IV: TIM

METHOD

Subject

This study was done with a ten-year-old fourth grade boy whose work in all academic areas was poor. He was inattentive and disruptive in class. It was decided not to record his academic performance, but rather to record data on his inattentiveness and his talking out of turn.

Procedure

Baseline. Both inattentiveness and the related behavior of talking out of turn, were recorded by a ten-second interval system, (Hawkins, McArthur, Rinaldi, Gray and Schaftenaar, 1967). For every ten seconds that went

---

reinforcement or punishment contingencies. Similarly, Madsen, *et al* (1968) found that the clear, repeated stating of classroom rules had little effect on children's behavior until appropriate consequences were made contingent.

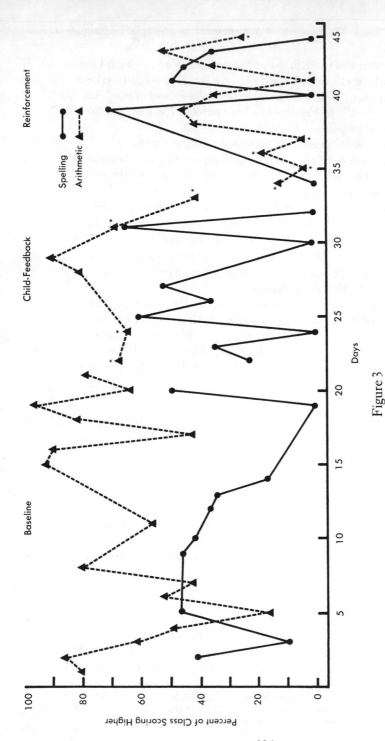

Figure 3

Dianne's relative performance in two academic areas under three experimental conditions; no specially programed feedback (Baseline), feedback to the child in the form of after-school notes about good achievement in arithmetic (Child-Feedback), and "backup reinforcement" for notes brought home (Reinforcement). No notes were given for good performance in spelling. If one of the activities did not occur, on any particular day, no data point is shown. Data were calculated by determining what percentage of her classmates (in attendance) achieved scores higher than hers on the day's written assignment.

by, the observer merely marked down on his paper a symbol to indicate whether Tim did or did not look away from his work (or the teacher, when she was giving instructions, or another child who was reciting) during that interval, and whether he did or did not talk out of turn. These data were recorded for 20 minutes each day, or 120 ten-second intervals. From the raw data were calculated in what percent of those intervals Tim was inattentive and in what percent of the intervals he talked out of turn. The observation was done during a social studies period early in the afternoon.

On ten occasions inter-observer reliability was checked in order to determine whether the regular observer was inadvertently biasing the data in any way. This was done by having a second observer record data independently of the regular observer and then calculating their agreement by dividing one observer's total, for a particular behavior, by the other observer's total (always dividing the smaller by the larger). When multiplied by 100, this ratio yields a percentage of agreement. On the ten reliability checks the two observers agreed an average of 90% on the frequency of inattention and 92% on talking out of turn (with ranges of 84% to 100% and 84% to 98%).

Child-Feedback. It was decided to provide the note consequences only for inattentiveness, but social approval was also provided intermittently for low rates of talking out of turn. During Child-Feedback Tim received a note (but no praise) after school whenever he was inattentive during fewer than 60 percent of the ten second intervals in the social studies period. The note said, "You did well today at paying attention during social studies." He was required to return it to the teacher before leaving school. If he did not meet the criterion for inattentiveness, but did show a low frequency of talking, the teacher would say after school, "You did well at not talking aloud today, but you didn't pay attention well enough to earn a note" (a procedure not intended by the experimenters, but, once begun, allowed to continue). Other than that, she was to make no evaluative comments to Tim about his inattentiveness or his talking.

Child-Parent Feedback. As in the first two studies, a condition was employed in which the subject was instructed to take home his notes, but his parents were given no instructions about providing backup reinforcement.

Reinforcement. Tim's parents were interviewed and agreed to extend his bedtime one half hour whenever he brought home a note. After bringing home three notes he was to receive a model car, and after eight notes, a baseball glove.

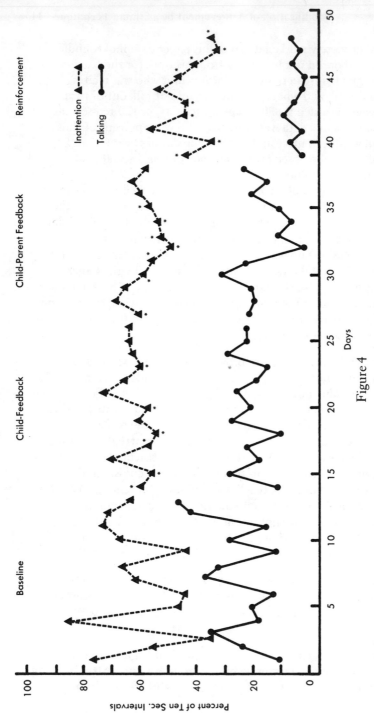

Figure 4

Tim's inappropriate behavior under four experimental conditions; no special consequences programed (Baseline), notes given Tim after school for relatively little inattentive behavior (Child-Feedback), notes to be taken home (Child-Parent Feedback), and "backup reinforcement" for notes brought home. No notes were given specifically for low rates of talking out. Each day's session was 20 minutes in length and occurred during social studies. Data indicate in what percentage of the 120 ten-second intervals Tim showed any amount of the behavior in question.

RESULTS AND DISCUSSION

The first experimental manipulation, the Child-Feedback condition, seemed to cause the two behaviors to become less variable but only talking out of turn showed any improvement. It declined from 26 percent to 20 percent, on the average, as a result of Tim's receiving a note after school that he had to return to the teacher before leaving school.

When Tim took the notes home, during Child-Parent Feedback, both response classes improved temporarily and then returned toward their previous level. At the outset of the following phase it was learned from the parents that when Tim first began bringing home notes they praised him, but that their consistency in doing this became less as the novelty of the notes wore off. This may account for the temporary improvement during this phase.

The Reinforcement condition produced an immediate improvement in both behaviors, though the note was actually contingent only upon low rates of inattentive behavior and the note was given nearly two hours after the behavior.

GENERAL DISCUSSION

Underachievement is a common problem in school children. If this problem can be reduced by such a simple technique as having his teacher give the child a note to take home when he does well and helping the child's parents provide apppropriate reinforcers at home, it would be well worth the effort. The modest experiments described here provide only a few guidelines, but certainly enough to suggest that school social workers, school psychologists, school principals, teachers, and the parents of an underachieving child would be wise to consider taking the initiative to set up this simple reinforcement system to modify behaviors related to underachievement.[8] So far it is apparent that even a delay of a few hours between the behavior and the token reinforcer (note) does not necessarily prevent the system from working. We also know that either one or more responses can be modified at once, that with some parents little guidance

---

[8] The general technique of daily feedback to parents and consequation at home has become a regular procedure utilized throughout the School Adjustment Program (Hawkins, 1971), a public school program for severely emotionally disturbed children in the Kalamazoo Valley Intermediate School District. Feedback procedures are often individually designed to solve specific individual problems, and they typically involve non-academic behaviors (e.g., talking out of turn, keeping hair combed or talking "baby talk") as well as academic (arithmetic, spelling, etc.).

from school personnel regarding reinforcement is needed, that the system can be effective with a wide range of ages, that intangible reinforcers (social reinforcers and privileges, as in Sherry's and Jim's cases) can be effective, and that tangible reinforcers, when they are used, need not be given daily (Dianne's case).

It will require further research and innovation to discover how long these effects last, how quickly the frequency and magnitude of the backup reinforcers can be reduced, what kinds of behaviors cannot be modified with such a system, what characteristics a child must have to make the system applicable, what kinds of reinforcers parents will readily dispense in exchange for tokens, and other such relevant questions.

References

Ayllon, J. and Azrin, N. H. Reinforcement and instructions with mental patients. *Journal of the Experimental Analysis of Behavior,* 1964, 7, 327–331.

Baer, D. M., Wolf, M. M. and Risley, T. R. Some current dimensions of applied behavior analysis. *Journal of Experimental Child Psychology.* 1967, 5, 463–479.

Hawkins, R. P. The School Adjustment Program: Individualized intervention for children with behavior disorders. Paper presented at the Second Annual Kansas Symposium on Behavior Analysis in Education, Lawrence, Kansas, May, 1971.

Madsen, C. H., Becker, W. C., and Thomas, D. R. Rules, praise and ignoring: elements of elementary classroom control. *Journal of Applied Behavior Analysis,* 1968, 2, 139–150.

McKenzie, H. S., Clark, Marilyn, Wolf, M. M., Kothera, R., and Benson, C. Behavior modification of children with learning disabilities using grades as tokens and allowances as back up reinforcers. *Exceptional Children,* 1968, 34, 745–752.

Schwarz, M. L., and Hawkins, R. P. Application of delayed reinforcement procedures to the behavior problems of an elementary school child. In R. Ulrich, T. Stachnick and J. Mabry (Eds.), *Control of human behavior, Vol. II: From cure to prevention.* Glenview, Illinois: Scott, Foresman, 1970.

Surratt, P. R., Ulrich, R. E., and Hawkins, R. P. An elementary student as a behavioral engineer. *Journal of Applied Behavior Analysis,* 1969, 2, 85–92.

Wolf, M. M., Giles, D. K., and Hall, R. V. Experiments with token reinforcement in a remedial classroom. *Behaviour Research and Therapy,* 1968, 6, 51-64.

The focus of this article is somewhat different from that of the majority of this book. First, it deals with college students, although there are very obvious possibilities for applying the same techniques to high school and junior high school students. Second, it focuses on the assignment of grades rather than on the social and tangible reinforcers discussed in most of the other articles. The Mastery approach may be a particularly unusual one for teachers who are used to grading on the curve and to having each student's grade reflect his relative position in the course. As an alternative, Biehler suggests permitting students two attempts to achieve a certain level of performance on each portion of the course; if he can do creditably on each part of the material, either on a first or a second attempt, then he earns a high grade. Biehler suggests using the B/C cutoff of the regular grade distribution as the "Mastery" level. Others have suggested using as a criterion the level of performance which would have earned an A on the tests given to the previous year's class which covered the same material. This means that if a score of 85 on a test was the A/B division the previous year, everyone who gets above an 85 this year would receive an A.

The use of a Mastery approach suggests, of course, that it would be possible for everyone in a class to earn an A (or F). It also suggests that everyone's grade depends solely on his own work and that the teacher can specify ahead of time exactly how much is the minimum he expects an A, B or C student to know, or to have done. The use of a contract system, in a Mastery approach, is suggested here by Biehler's description of pemitting students to choose which grade option they prefer. Much more specific contracts, which could be varied for each individual, could also be utilized. Advantages of this approach are that it permits a large degree of flexibility to the student, it assures that for a certain grade he must have a certain minimal level of mastery, and it reduces the tremendous pressures of test anxiety and intra-class competition. Disadvantages include the fact that students may do the minimal amount to get by and may be unwilling to do "superb" work if "good" work on everything is all that is required for an A. As you read the article, consider the effects such an approach might have on a typical high school class; would the students tend to slack off or would the knowledge that certain work would ensure a good grade cause an increase in their interest and productivity?

A First Attempt at a "Learning for Mastery" Approach

Robert F. Biehler*†

As I pondered a distribution of total scores for the purpose of assigning final grades in a course in educational psychology at the end of the Spring semester of 1969, I found myself recollecting opinions students had expressed in class discussion. During the semester, a significant number of students had voiced resentment against overemphasis of academic competition. I also found myself brooding about the sullen and apathetic reaction of students who were identified early in the semester as C students. These dissatisfactions with traditional grading procedures were increased when Benjamin Bloom's observations regarding "Learning for Mastery" came to my attention (in the May, 1968 issue of *Evaluation Comment* published by UCLA's Center for the Study of Instructional Programs). Bloom's analysis served to clarify my own perceptions of some of the limitations of the usual method of assigning grades. It seemed to me that there was much truth in the argument that a teacher begins a course with the expectation that only a minority of his students will learn at an acceptable level, and that this in turn leads to a self-fulfilling prophecy reaction which reduces aspirations and destroys the ego and self-concept of perhaps the majority of students in any course. Spurred by Bloom's statement that "Our basic task is to determine what we mean by mastery of the subject and to search for methods and materials which will enable the largest proportion of our students to attain such mastery," I made a first attempt at developing a "learning for mastery" approach within the framework of a traditional A to F grading system.

* Robert F. Biehler, "A First Attempt at a 'Learning Mastery' Approach," *Educational Psychologist* 7(1970): 7-9. Reprinted with permission.
† Chico State College

At the beginning of the Fall semester of 1969, students in two sections of a course in educational psychology were asked to help clarify the problem. We eventually came up with this statement: What might be done to reduce the pressure many students experience when they take exams, diminish the competitive aspects of higher learning, minimize the deflating impact of a low grade on a first test in a given course, maintain a respectable level of performance, and still assign grades within an A to F system?

After a considerable amount of discussion, a plan was developed which provided students with the opportunity to choose between two options: Letter Grade, or Mastery. The Letter Grade option was set up in the traditional way, i.e., the final grade was based on relative standing on a final distribution consisting of total scores of three exams. (Three short papers on journal articles, sections of books, observations, or personal analyses of problems in education were also required. At the suggestion of the students, these were graded "Pass" or "Redo.") The Mastery option was derived primarily from suggestions made by Bloom. First, a list of objectives was drawn up which consisted of brief descriptions of facts, classifications, experiments, concepts, principles and theories which were considered to be the most important points stressed in the text and lectures. (This outline of objectives was derived in part from Bloom's taxonomy and in part from Gagné's conditions of learning.) These lists were circulated early in the semester so that students would be provided with a reasonably precise description of what they were to be asked to master, and to serve as the basis for developing exams to determine if mastery had been achieved. (In Bloom's conception of learning for mastery, great stress is placed on arranging learning experiences in terms of a hierarchy of tasks. The student is then encouraged to learn these in sequence, and he achieves mastery when he reaches the top of the hierarchy. Because of the complexity of the subject matter of educational psychology—and/or my own limitations—I was unable to arrange subject matter in terms of such a hierarchy. Accordingly, the list of objectives developed was designed to assist students to grasp structure and inter-relationships, but not always in terms of a hierarchical frame of reference. As a consequence, mastery was determined on the basis of the degree to which a sample of the objectives was learned rather than how far the student progressed.)

An initial attempt to state the objectives in behavioral terms was deemed unsuccessful primarily because of the somewhat open-ended pedagogical approach used. Precisely stated objectives seemed to limit freedom for student and teacher alike, and some students argued that the use of such specific goals exacerbated the "memorize and regurgitate" aspect of education they wished to avoid. Accordingly, the final lists of objectives were stated in brief and general terms, e.g., "the Hawthorne effect, the experimenter bias effect, cognitive dissonance." (Perhaps the term "Key Points" would be more appropriate than "Objectives.") The lists of objectives served to alert students to what was considered important enough to be stressed on exams but also allowed for flexibility and a degree of freedom in interpretation. In addition, the fact that the student was assisted to grasp inter-relationships was seen as an advantage in the sense that it encouraged awareness of structure. Sets of ideas which were presented in terms of one frame of reference in the text and lecture were reorganized in a more global way on the lists of objectives. Exams were made up with reference to the lists, and students were encouraged to study by demonstrating to themselves (and/or fellow classmates) that they knew at least *something* about each point noted. Thus, the lists of points provided a frame of reference but still permitted freedom for individualistic interpretations of the data.

The exams (which consisted entirely of short-essay questions) were graded by assigning point values for each answer, and a distribution of scores was drawn. At the point on the distribution for each exam at which the dividing line was placed between B and C letter grades, a Mastery level was established. If a student failed to achieve at a point above the Mastery line, he was given the option of taking a retest on an alternate form of the exam. (Since two sections of the course were being taught, and each was given a different exam, the alternate form was already available.)

If a student achieved Mastery on all three exams (on the first or second try), handed in three short papers (graded Pass or Redo), and *also* handed in a more comprehensive paper which was considered to be equivalent to an A term paper, he qualified for an A. If a student achieved Mastery on all three exams (on the first or second try) and handed in three short papers (but no comprehensive paper) he qualified for a B. If a student either failed to achieve mastery on a second attempt on an exam, or chose not to make a second attempt he was given a C grade. If a student who originally chose the mastery option failed to achieve mastery on *more* than one exam, he was allowed to switch to the letter grade option, since it seemed pointless to force him to go through the motions of taking an exam a second time if he had no chance of improving his grade. (The fact that final grades had to be reported on an A to F system made it necessary to guarantee that a B grade on the Mastery option be equivalent to a regular letter grade of B.)

The opportunity to take any test a second time was intended to reduce the pressure many students experience when confronted with exams and also motivate students who got C's on a first exam to exert greater effort as opposed to more or less giving up on the course. The behavior of a student who gets a relatively low grade on a first exam often seems to corroborate Bloom's observations—a self-fulfilling prophecy reaction sets in. The student who is told he is average (or more accurately, *below* average, since a B seems to be the minimum acceptable grade in the minds of most students, teachers, administrators, and admissions officers), begins to act that way. He cuts class with increasing frequency, tends to become apathetic if not belligerent in class discussion, takes desultory notes and skims the text an hour or so before the exam. The line of reasoning seems to be, "As long as I'm going to get a C, I might as well get the lowest possible C." In the process, the self-concept of the student is degraded (both literally and figuratively) and the attitude of the student toward the subject being studied becomes neutral (at best) or negative. This in turn makes it highly unlikely that the student will retain or transfer much of what he has learned or do any subsequent outside reading in that area of study.

The extra paper to qualify for an A was introduced to try to give the student who wished to spend less time studying "what the teacher *forced* him to study" (to use the words of many students) the opportunity to have more time to devote to an analysis of a topic he considered to be "relevant" to his own interests. There is a degree of inconsistency involved in this aspect of the approach, since the teacher still makes a decision as to whether the personal interpretations of the student are of the appropriate "quality" or not, but most students were willing to accept this. Many who chose the Mastery option wanted to get away from exclusive emphasis on exams, but also accepted the fact that an A might be desirable to impress an admissions officer or personnel director.

The initial reaction of students to the two options was quite positive. The response of one coed was almost rewarding enough in itself to make the Mastery option seem worthwhile. She had been a C student all her life, but still clung to the faint hope that someday she might better herself. She was so enthused when the final plan was announced, she came up after class, exclaimed, "You're a *genius!*" and gave the impression that it was only through the exercise of considerable self-control that she prevented herself from embracing me. She had failed to achieve Mastery on the first exam, but she spent two full days restudying the material (according to her fiance, who lent moral and intellectual support) and scored well above the Mastery level on the retest. This was so reinforcing she studied just as diligently for the next two exams, passed them at the Mastery level, and earned the only "non-Mickey Mouse B of my career" (to use her words). The zest with which she came to class and the "tone" of her contributions to class discussion and the papers she wrote were taken as evidence that her self-concept had been given a much needed boost. This semester she took the trouble to come to me to report that she had signed up for her first elective in psychology. This was my prize pupil.

At the opposite extreme was another coed who was at the very bottom of the distribution on all three exams. She cut class frequently and probably spent no more than an hour cramming before each test. She exercised the option to retake all three exams and passed them just above the Mastery point. (There seemed to be grounds for suspecting that she had made arrangements with a sorority sister who was in the other section of the course so that she was provided with advance information about all of the questions which would be on the retest.) She handed in a paper to qualify for an A, but this was deemed unacceptable, and there was insufficient time for her to make a second effort. If there had been time, it seems probable she would have lifted an A paper out of the sorority file and had it retyped. The reaction of this girl suggests that some students will take advantage of the Mastery option, but it seems unwise to drop the approach because of this. Most of the students fell somewhere between the two extremes just described, but the general reaction was decidedly favorable.

This semester, the Mastery option is being used once again. A few changes have been made, however. The primary modification is to permit a student who wishes to try for an A grade on the Mastery option the chance to write six short papers (rather than the three required for a B). Many of the students who chose the letter grade option last semester reported that they did not want to expose themselves to the risk that the single comprehensive paper they wrote would be considered unacceptable, even though they had the opportunity to resubmit it. It seemed safer to concentrate on exams. The opportunity to write three extra short papers which is being offered this semester is an attempt to reduce the Russian Roulette aspects of the single paper. At the same time, the fact that the student will come to grips with ideas of his own choosing is seen as a way to permit a student to earn a legitimate A which reflects superior work, but without being restricted *only* to what the instructor stresses on exams. Short papers are also being used for reasons of transfer. It is hoped that the experience of reading and reporting on journal articles, sections of books, observations and experiences with teaching will lead to a tendency to continue to function in the same way once the course is finished.

The substitution of three short papers for a single comprehensive paper is also intended to encourage more students to take advantage of the

Mastery option. The initial plan for offering the two options was not perfected until after the first exam had been scored and returned last semester. This led to a situation where the top five or so students in each section elected the Letter Grade option. The reason for this seemed clear: they had achieved an A on the first exam and were confident they could do just as well on the remaining exams. This, in fact, is what happened. *Every* student who originally chose the Letter Grade option last semester earned an A. This semester, the plan was announced at the beginning of the course. Over 90 percent of the students indicated an initial preference for the Mastery option. In order to permit a maximum amount of flexibility (which seems desirable if pressure is to be held to a minimum), however, students are allowed to shift from one option to the other any time before the last three weeks of the semester. This has led to a surprising amount of scheming and maneuvering. Some students who did especially well on the first exam asked to shift to the Letter Grade option, even though they had originally indicated a preference for the Mastery idea. One hypothesis which might be advanced to account for this state of affairs centers around the possible impact of test anxiety. It appeared that anxiety about performing at a satisfactory level on the first exam led many students to over-react and to study more diligently than was necessary. (Even though they were invited to relax about exams, they were unable to do so.) When such bright but anxious students received a high grade as a reward for their efforts, they immediately began to think in terms of earning an A for the course by doing equally well on the remaining exams. This, in turn, caused them to lose all interest in learning for mastery. (The ten percent of students who selected the letter grade option at the very beginning of the semester were more cold-bloodedly calculating about the easiest way to earn an A.) The amount of plotting exhibited by some students who seek the line of least effort leads to a disappointingly cynical conclusion. It appears that quite a few students pay lip service to demands for less emphasis on tests and ask for greater opportunities for independent study. But when they are actually *given* a choice between these two alternatives, many prefer examinations. Perhaps they realize that "learning what someone else says is important" requires less effort than self-initiated learning.

The reactions of the better-than-average students lead to some doubts as to how effective a learning for mastery scheme will be with those who know they can do well on exams, or for those who are so anxious they are more or less "frightened" into doing well. Perhaps the sort of situation I have encountered would not be as likely to develop if learning experiences were arranged in hierarchical fashion as Bloom suggests. But even under Bloom's plan it seems likely that some students will worry about whether they will achieve mastery, or whether they are progressing as rapidly as they should. It will always be necessary to establish a Mastery level of some sort, either to guarantee that each stage in a hierarchy is achieved as a prelude to the next, or to assure a minimum standard of performance. As soon as this is done, it seems likely that some students are going to feel pressured. But perhaps this concern over already successful students—even anxious ones—is being over-emphasized. The primary target population of a learning for mastery approach consists of students who are identified as inadequate or below average. The reactions of such students to the Mastery option were quite encouraging.

It is apparent that the offering of a Mastery option requires a certain amount of extra work on the part of the instructor. However, the results so far indicate that the effort is well worth the trouble. While some calculating types will undoubtedly take advantage of the Mastery option in an effort to get an A with the least amount of effort, the compensating advantages are considerable. The attitude of most students, especially the perennial C types, seems much improved. Instead of acting rebuffed or fatalistic after the first exam many of those who find themselves toward the bottom of the distribution show acceptance if not a degree of enthusiasm. Attendance is better, class discussion more relaxed and lively. The median grade on exams has moved up a few points. The "quality" of papers suggests that they are not reacted to as busywork quite as much as formerly. While this is admittedly somewhat tenuous evidence, it does appear that the Mastery option described above has promise as a means for permitting more self-competition as opposed to exclusive competition *between* students for reducing pressure on exams, for expanding opportunities for students to study what they consider to be personally relevant, and for alleviating the negative impact on a C student's self-concept of the judgment that he is below average and likely always to remain that way. When a student responds to the Mastery option in an optimum way, it appears that he not only develops better feelings about himself, but also about the subject of study. If we hope to have prospective teachers leave their educational psychology course with a favorable attitude toward psychology, an inclination to want to use what they have learned, and a tendency to keep informed of new developments; the extra effort seems well worth the trouble.

A fourteen year old boy with abusive parents, brothers who shared his history of delinquency, and a reputation of being incorrigible at school since the second grade does not sound like an ideal subject for reading instruction, particularly when a probation officer was to serve as the teacher. Yet the program devised by Staats and administered by Butterfield proved to be successful in teaching the boy to read and in producing such side effects as better grades and behavior in school. No doubt the success of this program was heavily dependent on the very careful analysis of the general skill to be taught and on the use of reinforcement for various components of the skill—looking at the material, answering questions on it, reading aloud, recognizing new words on the first presentation, and correcting his own errors. The use of three types of token reinforcers, worth varying amounts of money, made it possible to give smaller rewards for less difficult tasks such as moving his eyes over the page, and larger rewards for more complex ones, such as correctly answering questions about the material read. That this procedure was successful is emphasized by their graphs showing increases in the amount read correctly, the number of words recognized correctly on first presentation and the improvement on a standardized reading achievement test.

Staats points out the importance of their study for the understanding of behavior deficits. The fact that a child or adult does not possess the ability to perform some behavior may not indicate that he is incapable of learning but rather that he has not been given the opportunity to learn when the reinforcement conditions were arranged to be motivating to him. Once the child has been treated aversively because he has not learned the behavior, he will tend to avoid the situation and thus become even less likely to learn it. Once labels such as "stupid" or "mentally retarded" are attached, the chances of the child's being given the opportunity to learn may be even further reduced. Staats and Butterfield have managed to reverse this procedure for a financial expenditure of $20.31. Although Butterfield in this case was a probation officer, there seems to be no reason why other people without teaching experience could not be used; in fact this seems to be an ideal procedure for utilizing teacher's aides or even volunteers. The success of the program with such a difficult subject would seem to warrant its consideration for teaching not only reading but a variety of other academic skills.

Treatment of Nonreading in a Culturally Deprived Juvenile Delinquent: An Application of Reinforcement Principles[1]

Arthur W. Staats
and
William Butterfield*

Staats has previously discussed behavior problems and their treatment in terms of learning principles (1964c, 1963). In doing so it was indicated that problem behaviors can arise in part (1) because behavior that is necessary for adjustment in our society is absent from the individual's repertoire, (2) because behaviors considered undesirable by the society are present in the individual's repertoire, or (3) because the individual's motivational (reinforcement) system was inappropriate in some respects.

Although a complete account is not relevant here, several points pertinent to the above conceptions will be made in introducing the present study. The notion that many behavior problems consist of deficits in behavior is important in the study of child development. Behaviorally speaking, a child is considered to be a problem when he does not acquire behaviors as other children do. It is conceivable that a deficit in behavior could arise because the child simply cannot acquire the

* Arthur Staats and William Butterfield, "Treatment of Nonreading in a Culturally Deprived Juvenile Delinquent: An Application of Reinforcement Principles," *Child Development* 36 (1965): 925-942. Reprinted with permission of The Society for Research in Child Development, Inc. Adapted by Dr. Staats for this edition.

[1] The present methods of reading training were formulated, and the present paper written, by the first author as part of a long term project applying learning principles and procedures to the experimental study of language-learning and reading. The methods were applied by the second author in his position as an officer of the Maricopa County Juvenile Probation Department. The second author also collected and tabulated the data. Appreciation is expressed to Chief Probation Officer John H. Walker for lending cooperation in the conduct of the study. In addition, Mary J. Butterfield made important contributions in the preparation of the reading materials used in the study.

behavior involved, even though the conditions of learning have been entirely adequate.

It would be expected, however, that behavioral deficits would also arise in cases where the conditions of learning have been defective. Learning conditions can be defective in different ways. For example, the child may never have received training in the behavior he must later exhibit. Or the training may be poor, even though the "trainers," parents, teachers, and so on, have the best intentions.

In addition, however, a child may be exposed to learning conditions that are appropriate for most children, but due to the particular child's past history of learning, are not appropriate for him. It is especially in these cases that people are most likely to conclude erroneously that since other children learn in the same circumstances, the child's deficit must be because of some personal defect. For example, in cases where the training is long term, adequate reinforcement must be available to maintain the attentional and work behaviors necessary for learning. As Staats has indicated (1964c, 1963, 1962), the reinforcers present in the traditional schoolroom are inadequate for many children. Their attentional behaviors are not maintained, and. they do not learn. Thus, a deficit in an individual's behavioral repertoire may arise although he has been presented with the "same" training circumstances from which other children profit. Learning does not take place because the child's previous experience has not provided, in this example, the necessary reinforcer (motivational) system to maintain good learning behaviors. It would seem that in such a circumstance the assumption that the child has a personal defect would be unwarranted and ineffective.

However, after a few years of school attendance where the conditions of learning are not appropriate for the child, he will not have acquired the behavioral repertoires acquired by more fortunate members of the class—whose previous experiences have established an adequate motivational system. Then, lack of skilled behavior is likely to be treated aversively. That is, in the present case the child with a reading deficit (or other evidence of underachievement) is likely to be gibed at and teased when he is still young, and ignored, avoided, and looked down upon when he is older. Although the individuals doing this may not intend to be aversive, such actions constitute the presentation of aversive stimuli. Furthermore, this presentation of aversive stimuli by other "successful" children, and perhaps by a teacher, would be expected to result in further learning, but learning of an undesirable nature. These successful children, teachers, academic materials, and the total school situation can in this way become learned negative reinforcers, which may be translated to say the child acquires negative attitudes toward school (see Staats, 1964b).

At this point, the child is likely to begin to escape the school situation in various ways (daydreaming, poor attendance, and so on) and to behave aversively in turn to the school and its inhabitants (vandalism, fighting, baiting teachers and students, and the like). Thus, a deficit in behavior, resulting from an inappropriate motivational system, can lead to the further development of inappropriate reinforcers and inappropriate behaviors.

The foregoing is by no means intended as a complete analysis of delinquency, dropouts, and the like. However, it does indicate some of the problems of learning that may occur in school. In addition, it does suggest that an analysis in terms of laboratory-established learning principles, when applied to problems such as in classroom learning of the above type, can yield new research and applied hypotheses. It was with this general strategy that the study of reading acquisition employing learning principles and reinforcement procedures was commenced (Staats, 1964a, 1964d, 1964e, 1962). The present study is a replication and an extension of these various findings to the development of a program for training non-readers to read. The program, which adapts standard reading materials, is based upon the principle of the token reinforcer system employed in the previous studies with younger children, thus testing the principles of reinforcement in the context of remedial reading training, as well as the feasibility of using this type of reinforcement system with a new type of subject. As such, the study has implications for the study of nonreading children of pre-adolescent, adolescent, and young adult ages. In the present case, the subject was also a culturally deprived delinquent child—and the study thus involves additional information and implications for the special problems associated with education in this population of children.

METHODS

THE SUBJECT

The subject was fourteen years and three months old. He was the fifth child in a Mexican-American family of eleven children and the mother and father. The parental techniques for controlling their children's behavior consisted of physical and verbal abuse. Both parents described their own childhood conditions as primitive. The father was taken out of school after completing the fifth grade to help with his father's work. Each of the subject's four older brothers had been referred to the juvenile court for misbehavior. The parents appeared to be at a loss as to how to provide effective control for family members.

The subject had a history of various miscreant behaviors, having been referred to the juvenile department nine times for such things as running away, burglary, incorrigibility, and truancy. During the course of the study the subject was again referred (with three other boys) on a complaint of malicious mischief for shooting light bulbs and windows in a school building with a BB gun. He associated with a group of boys who had been in marked difficulty with the law. The subject smoked and on occasion he drank excessively.

The study commenced when the subject was residing with his family. However, after the complaint on malicious mischief he was sent to a juvenile detention home. During his stay there he was allowed to attend school in the daytime. The study was finally concluded when he was committed to an industrial school for juvenile delinquent boys. This occurred because he baited the attendants at the detention home and caused disturbances which, although not serious, were very unpleasant and disruptive.

On the Wechsler Bellevue Form 1, given when the subject was 13-10, he received Verbal and Performance IQ's of 77 and 106, respectively, for a Full Scale IQ of 90. The examiner concluded that the subject was probably within the normal range for this test. On the basis of this test and HTP Projective Drawings, the subject was characterized as having a poor attention span and poorly integrated thought processes and as lacking intellectual ambitiousness. He was also described as seeking satisfaction in fantasy and as having good conventional judgment.

The subject had continually received failing grades in all subjects in school. He was described as having "been incorrigible since he came here in the second grade. He has no respect for teachers, steals and lies habitually and uses extremely foul language." The subject had been promoted throughout his school career simply to move him on or to "get rid of him." He was disliked by the teachers and administrators in grade school because of his troublesome behavior and was described by the principal as mentally retarded even though one of the tests taken there indicated a score within the normal range. Another test taken there gave him an IQ of 75. During the study the subject was attending a local high school and taking classes for low level students.

REINFORCER SYSTEM

In previous studies (Staats, 1966, 1964d, 1964e), a reinforcer system was demonstrated that was capable of maintaining attention and work behaviors for long term experimental studies. This system worked well with preschool children of ages 2 to 6 and with educable and trainable retardates of ages 8 to 11. The principle of the system was based upon token reinforcers. The tokens were presented contingent upon correct responses and could be exchanged for items the child could keep. In the previous studies toys of various values could be obtained when a sufficient number of tokens had been accrued in visible containers.

This system was adapted for use with the adolescent of the present study. In the adaptation there were three types of token, distinguished by color. The tokens were of different values in terms of the items for which the tokens could be exchanged. A blue token was valued at $1/10$ of one cent. A white token was valued at $1/5$ of a cent. A red token was worth ½ of a cent.

The child's acquisition of tokens was plotted so that visual evidence of the reinforcers was available. The tokens could be used to purchase a variety of items. These items, chosen by the subject, could range in value from pennies to whatever the subject wished to work for. Records were kept of the tokens earned by the subject and of the manner in which the tokens were used.

READING MATERIALS

The reading material used was taken from the Science Research Associates reading kit materials. The SRA kits consist of stories developed for and grouped into grade levels. Each story includes a series of questions which can be used to assess the reader's comprehension of the story. The reading training program was adapted from the materials as follows:

Vocabulary words. A running list was made of the new words that appeared in the series of stories. The list finally included each different word that appeared in the stories that were presented. From this list, the new vocabulary for each story was selected, and each word was typed on a separate 3×5 card.

Oral reading materials. Each paragraph in the stories was typed on a 5×8 card. Each story could thus be presented to the subject paragraph by paragraph.

Silent reading and comprehensive-question materials. Each story, with its comprehensive questions, was typed on an $8½ \times 13$ sheet of white paper.

PROCEDURE

Vocabulary presentation. The procedure for each story in the series commenced with the presentation of the new words introduced in that story. The words were presented individually on the cards, and the subject was asked to pronounce them. A correct response to a word-stimulus card was reinforced with a mid-value token. After a correct response to a word, the card was dropped from the group of cards yet to be presented. The subject was instructed to indicate words that he did not know the meaning of, and this information was provided in such cases.

When an incorrect response to a word stimulus occurred, or when the subject gave no response, the instructional technician gave the correct response. The subject then repeated the word while looking at the stimulus word. However, the word card involved was returned to the group of cards still to be presented. A card was not dropped from the group until it was read correctly without prompting. After an error on a word stimulus, only a low-value token was given on the next trial when the word was read correctly without prompting. The vocabulary-presentation phase of the training was continued until each word was read correctly without prompting.

Oral reading. Upon completion of the vocabulary materials, each paragraph was individually presented to the subject in the order in which the paragraph occurred in the story. When correct reading responses were made to each word in the paragraph, a high-value token was given upon completion of the paragraph. When a paragraph contained errors, the subject was corrected, and he repeated the word correctly while looking at the word. The paragraph was put aside, and when the other paragraphs had been completed, the paragraph containing errors was again presented. The paragraph was repeated until it was done correctly in its entirety—at which time a mid-value token was presented. When all paragraphs in a story had been completed correctly, the next phase of the training was begun.

Silent reading and comprehensive questions. Following the oral reading the subject was given the sheet containing the story and questions. He was instructed to read the story silently and to answer the questions beneath the story. He was also instructed that it was important to read to understand the story so that he could answer the questions.

Reinforcement was given on a variable interval schedule for attentive behavior during the silent-reading phase. That is, as long as he appropriately scanned the material he was given a low-value reinforcer an average of every fifteen seconds. The exact time for reinforcement was determined by a table of random numbers varying from one to thirty seconds. Whenever he did anything other than peruse the material, no reinforcement was given. The next interval was then timed from the moment he returned to the silent reading, with the stipulation that no reinforcement be given sooner than five seconds after he returned to the reading. If the interval was less than five seconds, a token was not given until the next interval had also occurred. Timing was done by a continuously running stop-watch. The subject was given an extra mid-value token at the end of the silently read story on those occasions when he read without moving his lips.

Upon completion of the story, the subject wrote his answers to the questions typed below the story and gave his answers to the technician. For each correct answer, the subject received a high-value token. For an answer with a spelling error, he was reinforced with a mid-value token when he had corrected the answer. For incorrect answers the subject had to reread the appropriate paragraph and correct his answer, and he then received a mid-value token.

Vocabulary review. Some of the vocabulary words presented to the subject in the first phase of training were words he already could read. Many others, however, were words that the procedure was set up to teach. The oral reading phase performance indicated the level of the subject's retention of the words he had learned—and also provided further training trials on the words not already learned. A further assessment of the subject's retention of the words that he did not know in the vocabulary training was made after each twenty stories of the SRA materials had been read. This test of individually presented words for each story was started about three days after completion of the twenty stories and constituted fairly long-term retention.

This test was also used as a review for the subject, and further training on the words was given. This was first done by reinforcing with a low-value token for every word he read correctly. However, the subject's attention was not well maintained by this reinforcement, and the procedure was changed to provide a mid-value token for correctly read words. When he could not read a word, or missed one, he was prompted and had to correctly repeat the name of the word while looking at the word. This word card was then put aside and presented later, at which time the subject was reinforced with a low-value token if he read it correctly. If not, the procedure was repeated until a correct unprompted trial occurred.

Achievement test. Prior to the commencement of the training, the subject was tested to assess his reading performance, and during the period of experimental training he was given two additional reading achievement tests. The first one given was the Developmental Reading Test. (At this time his vision and hearing were also tested and found to be normal.) After forty-five training sessions another reading test was given, this time the California Reading Test, Form BB, for grades 1, 2, 3, and L-4. Twenty-five sessions later, just before the termination of the study, the subject was given the California Reading Test, Form BB, for grades 4, 5, and 6. His performance on the three reading tests constituted one of the measures of his progress. The tests were given at the Arizona State University Reading Center.

Training sessions. The training sessions would ordinarily last for one hour or less, although a few sessions were as short as thirty minutes or as long as two hours. Not all of this time was spent in reading, however. A good deal of time was spent in arranging the materials, recording performance, keeping count of the reinforcers, plotting the reinforcers accrued, and so on. The time spent actually reading was tabulated. During the 4½-month

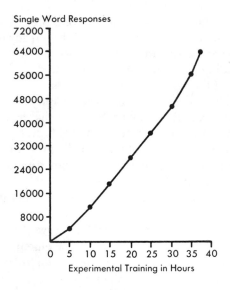

Figure 1

Number of single-word reading responses as a function of the time in experimental reading training.

experimental period seventy training sessions were conducted, with an average of about thirty-five minutes spent per session, or a total of forty hours of reading training.

During the period of training the subject made many reading responses. Figure 1 shows the number of single-word reading responses the subject made as a function of the hours of time spent in training. An estimate of the number of single-word reading responses was obtained from tabulating each presentation of a word card, the number of words in the stories, and the reading comprehension questions at the end of each story, as well as the words presented in the later single-word retention test. Actually, the number of words in the stories is an estimate obtained from the mean number of words in two out of each five stories. Thus, rather than giving the true absolute number of reading responses made, the figure gives an estimate. However, the most important aspect of the figure is to indicate the rate of this single-word reading-response measure as a function of time in experimental training. As can be seen, as the training progressed the subject covered the reading material at a slightly more rapid rate, as is shown by the slight positive acceleration in the curve. The importance of this result is to indicate that the child's behavior of attending to the task and making the appropriate reading responses did not diminish throughout the period of training. Thus, the reinforcement system employed was capable of maintaining the behavior for a long period of time. During this time the attentional and cooperative behaviors instigated resulted in many, many learning trials— *sine qua non* for the acquisition of achievement in any skill.

Before reading each story the subject was presented with individual cards for all the words included in that story which had not been presented in a previous story. When these words were presented, the subject would read a certain proportion correctly on first presentation, the other words being missed on the first presentation. The ones missed were considered to be new words, words that he had not previously learned. These words were tabulated separately. The cumulative number of these new words as a function of every five stories read is shown by the top curve of Figure 2. (The data for the first ten stories are not presented since they were not available for all three curves.) As this curve indicates, 761 new words were presented during the training.

Thus, the subject missed 761 words when they were first presented to him. However, he was given training trials on these words, and then he read them again in the oral reading of the paragraph. The number of these words that he missed in this oral reading phase is plotted in the bottom curve of Figure 2. This curve then indicates the number of errors made on the second reading test of the words that had been previously learned. Thus, only 176 words out of 761 (about 23 percent) were missed in the oral reading phase—showing retention for 585 words. The results indicate that the criterion of one correct unprompted reading trial in the original vocabulary-learning phase produced considerable learning when the words were read in context.

The middle curve in Figure 2 involves a measure of long term retention of the words that had been learned. This measure was obtained by testing the subject on the words, presented singly, that had been learned in the preceding twenty stories. This test was given 10 to 15 days after the training occurred. The training thus included the previous single-word presentations of the words, as well as those same words read orally and silently. In addition, however, the subject had also learned a considerable number of other words by the time of this test. As the middle curve shows, when tested 10 to 15 days later, he read 430 of the 761 words correctly, or, conversely, 331 words (about 43 percent) were missed. Thus, the procedures produced retention when the words were later presented out of context after a considerable intervening period.

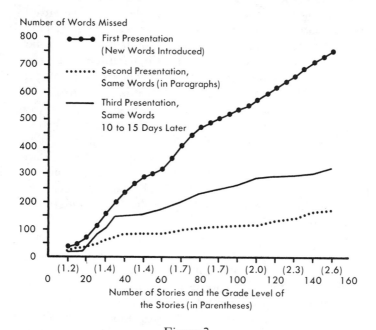

Figure 2

Number of words missed on first, second, and third presentations for the 150 stories.

The results appearing in Figure 2 indicate that the child covered a considerable amount of reading material, that he learned to read a number of new words when presented individually or in context, and that he retained a good proportion of what he had learned. The results also indicate that the child improved during the training in his retention. That is, his rate of getting new words in the first-presentation phase continued at a high rate throughout the study. (This supports the results shown in Figure 1 indicating that the child's behavior did not weaken during the training.) However, his "rate" of missing the new words on the second and third presentations decreased; that is, he retained more of the words he had learned. Thus, tabulation indicated that for the first thirty-five stories only about 33 percent of the words learned were retained 10 to 15 days later, whereas the subject's subsequent retention increased to about 55 percent. It should be noted that this improvement occurred even though the difficulty of the words (as shown in Figure 2 by the numbers in parentheses) became progressively greater during the training, moving from the 1.2 grade level of difficulty to the 2.6 grade level.

These results receive support from the data presented in Figure 3. As already indicated, on the first presentation of the vocabulary of a story, some words were missed out of the total presented—and the subject was then presented with training on these words. Figure 3 shows the number of the words presented and missed in ratio to the total number presented as this ratio is related to the number and difficulty of the stories presented. A smaller ratio indicates that the subject missed fewer of the total vocabulary words when they were presented for the first time. As can be seen in Figure 3, as the child read more stories in his training (even though they became more difficult), he missed fewer and fewer words that were presented to him. It should be stressed that he was thus improving in the extent to which he correctly responded to new words on *first* presentation. This improvement appeared to be correlated with other observations that indicated that the subject was also beginning to learn to sound out words as a function of the training. For example, he remarked that when in the judge's office he thought a sign said "information" because he could read the "in" and the "for" and the "mation." In addition, he reported a number of times that the training was helping him in school, that reading was getting easier for him in school, that he liked the reading training better as he went along, and so on. It would be expected (as will be supported by other data) that as the reading training improved his reading in school, the things he learned in school would also improve his performance in the reading training. It is this effect that may also be reflected in his increasing ability to read the new words presented to him.

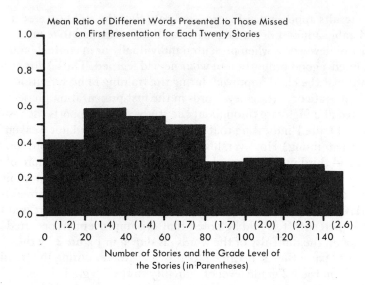

Figure 3

Ratio of words presented to those missed on first presentation
for the 150 stories.

In addition to this direct evidence of the child's progress in reading
training, and the foregoing indirect evidence that the reading training
was having general effects upon the child's behavior, the study was
formulated to obtain other sources of information concerning the child's
progress. One means of doing this was to give the child reading
achievement tests before beginning the reading training as well as during
the training. The results of these tests are shown in Figure 4. The first
point on the curve is a measurement obtained by use of the
Developmental Reading Test giving a total score of reading achievement
showing that the subject was performing at the grade 2 level. After forty-
five reading-training sessions, the subject's performance on the California
Reading Test showed a gain to the 3.8 grade level. By the end of the
training, after twenty-five more training sessions, he had advanced to the
4.3 grade level on the California Reading Test.

Another indication of the general effect of the reading training came
from the child's performance in school, both in school achievement and
deportment. The period of reading training coincided with a school term.
The boy received passing grades in all subjects: C in Physical Education,
D in General Shop, D in English, and D in Mathematics. It should be

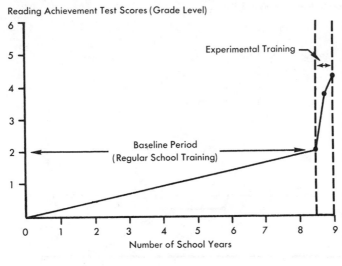

Reading Achievement Test Scores (Grade Level)

Figure 4

Reading-achievement test scores as a function of 8½ years
of school training and 4½ months of experimental training.

emphasized that these grades represent the first courses that this child
had ever passed, and thus his finest academic performance.

Furthermore, the subject began to behave better while in school. The
boy had always been a behavior problem in schools, and this continued
into the period during which he received reading training. As Figure 5
shows, during the first month of the training he committed ten
misbehaviors that resulted in the receipt of demerits. The behaviors were
as follows: disturbance in class (two times), disobedience in class (five
times), loitering (two times), and tardiness. In the second month he was
given demerits for scuffling on the school grounds and also for creating a
disturbance. In the third month he was given demerits for cutting a math
class and for profanity in class. As the figure shows, however, no
misbehaviors occurred in the fourth month or in the half-month before
the conclusion of the school term.

The subject requested that the tokens be exchanged for items that he
wanted in sessions 12, 17, 25, 31, 35, 43, 49, 55, and in the last session he
was given the value of the remaining tokens in cash. Items included were
a pair of "Beatle" shoes, hair pomade, a phonograph record, an ice cream
sundae, a ticket to a school function, money for his brother who was
going to reform school, and so on. Further information regarding the

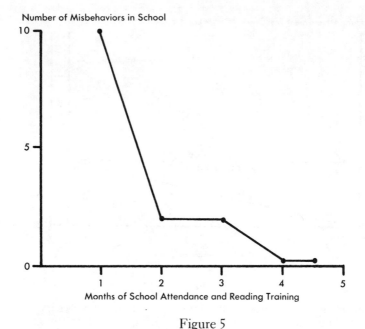

Number of Misbehaviors in School

Months of School Attendance and Reading Training

Figure 5

Number of official misbehaviors in school as a function of
time in the experimental training.

reinforcement system is given in Figure 6. The vertical axis of the graph
represents the ratio of the number of tokens obtained by the subject
relative to the number of single-word reading responses which he emitted.
Lesser ratios thus indicate more reading responses per reinforcer. This
ratio was plotted as a function of the progress made in the training
program, as given by the number of SRA stories he had completed. As
the training progressed the subject gradually made an increasingly greater
number of reading responses per reinforcer. This effect was not
accomplished by changing the rules by which the reinforcers were
administered. The effect, which was planned in the training program,
resulted from the fact that the stories became longer as the grade level
was raised. Since, for example, paragraph reading was reinforced by the
paragraph, the longer the paragraph, the greater the number of reading
responses that had to be emitted before reinforcement was obtained.
Thus, at the end of training the subject was getting about half as much
reinforcement per response as at the beginning of training. It should also
be indicated that the stories were more difficult as the training

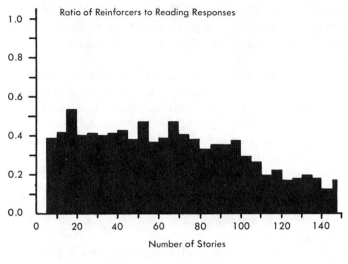

Figure 6

Ratio of the number of tokens received divided by the number of reading responses made as a function of the number of stories read.

progressed, so the effort involved in reading was increasing—although reinforcement for the reading was decreasing.

During the 4½ months of training, which involved forty hours of reading training and the emission of an estimated 64,307 single-word reading responses, the subject received $20.31.

DISCUSSION

In this section the various aspects of the reading training procedures will first be discussed. Then the implications of the results and analysis will be outlined both for further studies of remedial reading training as well as for a learning conception of certain aspects of cultural deprivation and delinquency.

The method of reading training used in the present study was supported by previous studies (Staats, 1964a; 1962) with preschool children in which words were first presented singly, then in sentences, and finally in short stories. The present study indicated that SRA materials can be adapted for a similar type of presentation in conjunction with the type of reinforcer system previously developed. From the SRA materials it was possible to present single-word training trials and oral reading training and to develop a silent reading training procedure, all involving reinforcement.

When the training of reading, at least in part, is considered as instrumental (operant) discrimination learning, the learning task consists of having the subject emit the correct speech response while looking at the verbal stimulus—this process being followed by reinforcement. This basic procedure was elaborated in the present study to include two levels of reinforcement. An unprompted reading response on the first trial was reinforced more heavily than one that had been previously missed. This procedure appeared to produce learning that was retained very well when the child later read the words orally in a paragraph, with considerable retention also occurring when the child was tested on the individual words 10 to 15 days later.

It may seem incongruous at first to attempt to reinforce silent reading since this behavior is not observable. However, it should be remembered that the subject actually has two types of behavior in the silent reading act. He looks at the verbal stimuli—that is, attends—and he makes "reading" verbal responses to the verbal stimuli. While the reading responses cannot be monitored when they are covert, the attending behavior can be. Of course, there is a danger involved in reinforcing the behavior of just looking at something. Perhaps the child will do nothing else. If he is heavily reinforced for sitting and looking at a page, and the actual reading responses are effortful, he may not emit the reading responses. The present procedure was set up to eliminate this possibility by using a double contingency. The child was reinforced for simple attention, but the reinforcement was low in value. The opportunity for a greater amount of reinforcement came during the answering of the questions. Thus, although simple attention was reinforced lightly, attention and reading responses were reinforced much more heavily. In this way it was possible to use reinforcement in a procedure designed to maintain reading for understanding, in addition to simple "word naming." (These results could be generalized to other types of learning.) Furthermore, this procedure provided an opportunity to train the subject to read silently. Although he had a tendency to make vocal or lip responses while reading, it was possible to strengthen reading without these other responses through differentially reinforcing the correct silent reading.

Thus, it may be concluded that the reading program increased the child's reading vocabulary as shown by the various measures of retention used in the study, the tests of reading achievement, as well as the child's improved school performance and his verbal description of improved attitude toward and performance in reading in school. There were also suggestions that the child was acquiring a "unit reading repertoire," that is, the general ability to sound out words through making the correct response to single letters and syllables. Thus, for example, the child made errors on fewer and fewer of the new words presented as the training progressed, even though the words were of greater difficulty. In addition, he retained a greater proportion of the words he learned as he went on. Further research of the present type must be conducted to test the possibilities for using a more phonic system of remedial reading training with the present type of subject.

A final point should be made concerning the training procedures used in the present study. The procedures are very specific and relatively simple. Thus it was not necessary to have a person highly trained in education to administer the training. In the present case the instructional technician was a probation officer. It might also be suggested that anyone with a high school education and the ability to read could have administered the training. This has implications for the practical application of the present methods, since one of the questions that arises in this context concerns the economy of the procedures. The procedures as described involved a ratio of one trainer to one student, as many remedial teaching procedures do. But the simplicity of the procedures used in this case suggests the possibility that savings may be effected because the instructional technician need not be so highly trained. Thus, the procedures could be widely applied or adapted by various professionals; for example, social workers, prison officials, remedial teachers, tutors, and so on. In an even more economical application, helpers of professionals could be used to actually administer the procedures; for example, selected delinquents (or prisoners) could administer the procedures to other delinquents. Thus, the procedures could be utilized in various situations, such as settlement houses, homes for juvenile delinquents, prison training programs, parts of adult education, and so on. All that is needed is a suitable system of reinforcers to back up the tokens.

It is relevant to add here that the type of token reinforcer system employed in the present study was first developed by Staats in 1959 in the context of an exploratory study of remedial reading. He communicated the efficacy of the token reinforcer system to Jack Michael at the University of Houston, who with Lee Meyerson began to work with mentally retarded children employing a similar system. The possibilities for use of the token-reinforcer system were also discussed with Teodoro Ayllon who, with Nathan Azrin, developed its use in the psychiatric hospital (Ayllon and Azrin, 1969). Montrose Wolf, who as a graduate student had contributed to the present author's studies extending the token reinforcer system to young children, helped introduce the system to the child research program at the University of Washington. On the basis of such personal dissemination along with publication of token-reinforcement studies, behavior modification work then began to employ the reinforcement system widely, as have a number of later education and special education studies.

Furthermore, additional studies have been conducted in the present project to further substantiate the general efficacy of the reinforcer system and the reading procedures, with various types of subjects. Thus, the present training procedures have been employed successfully in a study involving eighteen additional children (including seven educable retardates as well as several emotionally disturbed children) of junior high school age in Madison, Wisconsin. The instructional-technicians were nine average high school students and nine adult volunteers (Staats, et al. 1967).

In a later study (now being prepared for publication) with Karl A. Minke, thirty-two Negro ghetto children with behavior problems were given the treatment in Milwaukee. The instructional-technicians were literate Negro high school children from ghetto schools and two formerly unemployed Negro adults employed on the project in full-time positions. The treatment was conducted for a semester, and the results were again successful. Increases were shown in achievement tests, grades, attendance, and deportment, in comparison to a control group of thirty-two children. In addition Staats (1968) has conducted a long term project with young children in the study and treatment of cognitive deficits in such areas as first reading acquisition, number skill learning, and writing acquisition. The present methods and principles receive strong support as being generally applicable from these various studies.

In the present study, it may be worth pointing out that the results indicated that the child advanced as many years in reading achievement, as measured by the tests, during the experimental training as he had in his previous school history. A comparison of the relative costs—in the present case about forty hours of time of a person not necessarily trained in teaching and $20.31 for the reinforcers versus 8½ years of trained teachers' time, albeit in a group situation—suggests that the procedure introduced in the present study may not be uneconomical, even without improvements in the method. And, as will be further described, the child's failure in school may in many cases be considered as a contributer to the child's delinquency—which also carries a high cost to society. The present results, in suggesting that the training procedures may also effect general improvements in behavior, including misbehaviors in school, thus have further implications concerning the economy of the procedures.

The present study, among other things, tests the feasibility of using the type of reinforcing system formerly applied successfully to younger children to the study of learning in older children—in this case a fourteen-year-old juvenile delinquent. The reinforcer system worked very well with the present subject, maintaining his attention and working behaviors in good strength for a long period of time. And there was every reason to expect that the study could have been continued for a much longer period, probably as long as it would have taken to train the child to read normally.

It should be noted that although the amount of reinforcement given decreases during the training, as shown in Figure 6, the reading behavior is maintained in good strength throughout the study, as shown in Figures 1 and 2; thus, less and less reinforcement is needed to maintain the behavior even though the material increases in difficulty. As already described, this occurred because a progressively greater number of reading responses was necessary per reinforcer. This is analogous to gradually raising the ratio of responses to the reinforcers as considered in terms of ratio schedules of reinforcement. Staats has suggested that this type of gradual increase must occur to produce good work behaviors in humans (Staats, 1963).

This result in the present study is in part an answer to the question of whether the use of extrinsic reinforcers in training will produce a child who is dependent upon these reinforcers. It is not possible to discuss this topic fully now. However, it may be said that the extrinsic reinforcement can be gradually decreased until, as was happening with the present child, reading becomes reinforcing itself, or other sources of reinforcement maintain the behavior.

A word should be said concerning the relevance of reinforcement variables in the treatment of non-learning in culturally deprived children. Typically, as in the present case, such children do not, as a result of their home experiences, acquire "reinforcer systems" appropriate for maintaining learning in the traditional classroom. Rosen (1956) has shown that, in the present terminology, lower class children do not have experiences that make school involvement and learning itself positively reinforcing. This deficit, among others that affect the reinforcer system, can be expected to lead to poor school learning and other behavioral deficits. In such cases, there are increased opportunities for other poor social attitudes and undesirable behaviors to develop, as suggested in the introduction and exemplified in the present case.

The present study suggests that these conditions can be reversed through the application of learning principles and reinforcement variables to the task of repairing the child's behavioral-achievement deficit. There were indications that this treatment resulted in improvement in the reinforcement value of (attitudes toward) school for this child and consequently in the decrease in incidence of misbehaviors in school. The results thus suggest that under appropriate conditions the deficit in behavior stemming from the child's inadequate reinforcing system may be, at least in part, repaired by a properly administered, effective reinforcement system, resulting in a decrease in undesirable behaviors.

A comment should be made about the possibility of a Hawthorne effect; that is, that the social reinforcement provided by the instructional technician and possible extra-experimental reinforcement contributed to the results in the present study. It would be expected that such reinforcers could contribute to the overall effect—and in the present case the expenditure for the material reinforcers was small. In general, it can be expected that individuals will vary in the extent to which social reinforcers will be effective. For example, in preschool children social reinforcement is ineffective for long term training (Staats, 1964c, 1962), and the same would be expected for many individuals with behavior problems. Ordinarily, it might be expected that the weaker other sources of reinforcement are for the individual, the stronger must be the reinforcer system of the treatment procedure.

In conclusion, the present study helps support and replicate the previous findings and extends the general procedures and principles to the study of an adolescent child who is culturally deprived and is also a juvenile delinquent. The various sources of data used suggest that the present procedures and principles are applicable to this population also. Based upon these suggestions, further studies will be conducted on culturally deprived children, delinquent and nondelinquent, as well as studies of other types of nonachieving or underachieving readers.

It should also be indicated that the present study indicates the possibility for developing procedures for the objective application and testing of laboratory-derived learning principles within the context of an actual problem of behavior. As previously indicated (Staats, 1968, 1964a), verification of learning principles in the context of a problem of human behavior constitutes one way to further the generality of the principles themselves. It may thus be suggested that such studies have two types of implication: they have implications for people interested in dealing with the problems of human behavior, as well as for those interested in the extension and verification of the basic science.

References

Ellson D. G., Barber, L., Engle, T. L., and Kampaerth, L. "Programmed Tutoring: A Teaching Aid and a Research Tool," *Reading Research Quarterly*, 1965, 1.

Rosen, B. C. "The Achievement Syndrome: A Psychocultural Dimension of Social Stratification," *American Sociological Review*, 1956, 21: 203-211.

Staats, A. W. "A Case in and a Strategy for the Extension of Learning Principles to Problems of Human Behavior," in A. W. Staats (ed.), *Human Learning*. New York: Holt, Rinehart and Winston, 1964.(a)

Staats, A. W. "Conditioned Stimuli, Conditioned Reinforcers, and Word Meaning," in A. W. Staats (ed.), *Human Learning*. New York: Holt, Rinehart and Winston, 1964. (b)

Staats, A. W. (ed.) *Human Learning*. New York: Holt, Rinehart and Winston, 1964. (c)

Staats, A. W. "An Integrated-functional Learning Approach to Complex Human Behavior," in B. Kleinmuntz (ed.), *Problem Solving: Research, Method and Theory*. New York: Wiley, 1966.

Staats, A. W. *Learning, Language, and Cognition*. New York: Holt, Rinehart and Winston, 1968.

Staats, A. W., Finley, J. R., Minke, K. A., and Wolf, M. "Reinforcement Variables in the Control of Unit Reading Responses," *Journal of the Experimental Analysis of Behavior*, 1964, 7: 139-149. (d)

Staats, A. W., Minke, K. A., Finley, J. R., Wolf, M., and Brooks, L. O. "A Reinforcer System and Experimental Procedure for the Laboratory Study of Reading Acquisition," *Child Development*, 1964, 35: 209-231. (c)

Staats, A. W., Minke, K. A., Goodwin, W., and Landeen, J. "Cognitive Behavior Modification: 'Motivated Learning' Reading Treatment with Subprofessional Therapy-Technicians, *Behavior Research and Therapy*, 1967, 5:283-299.

Staats, A. W. (with contributions by Staats, C. K.) *Complex Human Behavior*. New York: Holt, Rinehart and Winston, 1963.

Staats, A. W., Staats, C. K., Schutz, R. E., and Wolf, M. "The Conditioning of Textual Responses Utilizing 'Extrinsic' Reinforcers," *Journal of the Experimental Analysis of Behavior*, 1962, 5:33-40.

Most studies using behavior modification techniques have focused on conditioning methods rather than modeling. Most of the research on the effects of observing a model, on the other hand, has been concerned with emotional behaviors like aggression and altruism, rather than cognitive ones like language. In this study, we found that exposure to a model who spoke in passive sentences was necessary to increase the child's usage of passives but that reinforcement and a problem-solving set were enough to increase his use of prepositional phrases. In other words, reinforcement does not appear adequate, let alone efficient, for increasing the use of a rare response which doesn't occur often enough to receive many reinforcements.

The use of a model may be a very effective way to teach children about grammar, without having to go through the dreary business of memorizing rules and examples. Children and adults often use correctly a lot of grammatical rules without being able to verbalize them. In the context of a problem-solving task, the children in this study were able to change their grammatical usage without any formal knowledge of grammar. One might suspect that labeling their own syntactic changes for them would be more effective and much more fun than teaching them the terminology first. A more recent study I did with Wendy Hassemer showed that exposure to a model could increase the complexity of children's sentence structure without any instructions to imitate or suggestions that some responses were better than others; this was true for boys and girls, second-graders and fourth-graders, monolingual children and bilingual children hearing English or Spanish sentences. The generality of this modeling effect on syntax suggests that teachers might be able to deliberately modify other aspects of language behavior such as pronunciation and vocabulary. As you read the Bandura and Harris study and see the kinds of changes that occurred in only a thirty minute session, consider the ways in which the same techniques might be used both with individuals and in a group to teach both English usage and possibly that of other languages.

Modification of Syntactic Style[1]

Albert Bandura
and
Mary B. Harris[2][*][†]

ABSTRACT

The present experiment was conducted to determine the role of appropriate modeling cues, reinforcement variables, and strong attentional responses in altering children's syntactic style. For an extremely infrequent response such as the passive construction, neither reinforcement nor modeling alone was effective in increasing the use of passives in sentences constructed by children in response to a set of simple nouns. However, children generated significantly more passives when verbal modeling cues were combined with attentional and reinforcement variables designed to increase syntactic discriminability.

[*] Albert Bandura and Mary Bierman Harris, "Modification of Syntactic Style," *Journal of Experimental Child Psychology* 4(1966): 341–352. Reprinted with permission.

[†] Stanford University

[1] This investigation was supported by Research Grant M-5162 from the National Institutes of Health, United States Public Health Service.

[2] The authors are indebted to Nicholas Anastasiow, Palo Alto Unified School District, for his aid in arranging the research facilities.

On the other hand, in the case of a
syntactic category as common as
prepositional phrases, reinforcement
combined with an active attentional
set increased children's usage of
prepositions, but modeling cues
were not a significant contributory
factor. These findings indicate that
syntactic responsivity which depends
upon the acquisition of general rules
rather than isolated responses can be
accounted for in terms of social-
learning principles.

Much of the research in psycholinguistics has been concerned with
formulating categories of syntactic structures and determining usage of
grammatical categories in language development under naturalistic
conditions (Menyuk, 1963, 1964; Miller and Ervin, 1964; Templin, 1957).
Although these approaches have provided systems for describing the basic
rules used to generate sentences, they have furnished little information
about the variables governing the acquisition and alteration of syntactic
structures which might form the basis for an adequate theory of language
learning.

Research conducted within the framework of social-learning theory
(Bandura, 1967; Bandura and Walters, 1963) provides substantial
evidence that modeling variables play a highly influential role in the
development of social response patterns, and their position with respect
to language seems almost unique. Since children cannot acquire words
and grammatical structures without exposure to verbalizing models, it is
obvious that some amount of modeling is indispensable for language
acquisition.

Because of the highly generative character of linguistic behavior, it is
generally assumed in psycholinguistic theories that modeling variables
cannot possibly play much of a part in language development and
production. The main reasoning, which is based on the mimicry view of
imitation (Brown and Bellugi, 1964; Menyuk, 1964) is as follows:
Children can obviously construct an almost infinite variety of sentences
that they have never heard; consequently, instead of imitating and
memorizing specific utterances that they may have heard at one time or
another, children learn sets of rules which enable them to generate an
unlimited variety of grammatical sentences. The limitations typically
attributed to modeling processes are largely due, however, to the

erroneous assumption that exposure to the verbal behavior of others can produce at the most mimicry of specific responses that are modeled.

Results of recent experiments (Bandura and McDonald, 1963; Bandura and Mischel, 1965) demonstrate that generalized behavioral orientations, judgmental standards, and principles for generating novel combinations of responses can be transmitted to observers through exposure to modeling cues. In these experiments the models and observers respond to entirely different sets of stimuli in the social-influence setting, and subsequent tests for generalized effects are conducted by different experimenters in different settings with the models absent, and with different stimulus items.

It seems extremely unlikely that rules about grammatical relations between words could ever be learned if they were not exemplified in the verbal behavior of models. An important question therefore concerns the conditions that facilitate abstraction or generalization of rules from verbal modeling cues. The principle underlying a model's specific responses can be abstracted if its identifying characteristics are repeated in responses involving a variety of different stimuli (Bandura, 1966). Thus, for example, if one were to place a series of objects on tables, chairs, boxes, and a variety of other places and simultaneously verbalize the common prepositional relationship between objects, a child would eventually discern the grammatical rule. He could then easily generate a novel grammatical sentence if a toy hippopotamus were placed on a xylophone and the child were asked to describe the depicted stimulus event.

In addition to the existence of modeling variables that are indispensable for acquisition of highly complex response patterns, there is no doubt that some form of reinforcement is usually contingent upon grammatical speech and that language is extremely functional in controlling the social environment. The informative properties of differential reinforcement may enhance acquisition by facilitating discrimination, whereas its rewarding properties may function to strengthen and increase existing linguistic responses.

Unlike nonverbal behavior, which is often readily acquired, language learning is considerably more difficult because sentences represent complex stimulus patterns in which the identifying features of syntactic structures cannot be easily discriminated. The present experiment was designed to investigate the role of modeling, reinforcement, and discrimination processes in modifying the syntactic style of children who had no formal grammatical knowledge of the constructions that were manipulated.

The grammatical categories chosen to be modified were the passive voice and the prepositional phrase. These constructions were selected because they are both relatively unambiguous and because both appear relatively free of any semantic connotations. The primary difference between them is that the production of a passive requires the use of one of Chomsky's (1957) postulated transformational rules and thus a higher level of linguistic development and organization than the construction of a prepositional phrase. Another important difference for the purpose of this study is the fact that the passive voice is utilized far less frequently than the prepositional phrase.

Young children generated sentences in response to simple nouns prior to, during, and after experimental treatments designed to increase passive and prepositional constructions. In order to determine the relative contributions of several learning variables to the modification of different classes of linguistic behavior, three variables, applied singly and in combination, were chosen for study. These included exposure to an adult model who generated a high proportion of sentences containing the appropriate syntactic structure; informative feedback provided by positive reinforcement of correct utterances of the model and subjects; and induction of an attentional set to identify the characteristics of "correct" sentences.

It was assumed that contingent reinforcement would be necessary for syntactic discrimination, and that an attentional set would further facilitate recognition of the identifying properties of passive and prepositional constructions. For a syntactic category as common as prepositional phrases it was predicted that high occurrence of attending responses combined with differential reinforcement would be sufficient to increase prepositional constructions. On the other hand, it was expected that the latter conditions alone would have no significant effect upon passive grammatical productions, which have a very low probability of occurrence in young children. It was predicted that, in addition to factors that increase syntactic discriminability, appropriate modeling cues would be necessary in order to create passive features in children's speech productions.

METHOD

SUBJECTS

The Ss were 50 boys and 50 girls drawn from second-grade classrooms in schools serving a middle-class community.

VERBAL STIMULI

The basic stimulus words selected for the children were 65 simple nouns commonly known at the first or second grade level and printed on index cards.

Two additional sets of 28 nouns were chosen as stimuli for the adult model. In the model's *passive* set, 21 of the 28 words (75%) had short sentences containing passives but no prepositional phrases written lightly upon them (e.g., "The *bird* was fed some worms"), and the other seven words had simple sentences containing no passives nor prepositional phrases. The *prepositional phrases* set of items had 21 simple sentences containing prepositions but no passives and seven containing neither construction.

The model's sentences were prepared in advance in order to ensure comparability of verbal modeling cues between subjects and across treatment conditions. If all of a model's linguistic performances contain only the syntactic structure to be manipulated in a given phase, an observer is provided with little or no basis for distinguishing, within the complex verbal pattern, the identifying characteristics of the desired syntax. Therefore, in order to increase syntactic discriminability, particularly in conditions employing selective reinforcement, seven of the model's sentences, which contained neither passives nor prepositional phrases, were interspersed among the experimental items, primarily in the first half of the set.

PROCEDURE

For all children the basic paradigm was the same. They were told that the experimenter was interested in how people make up sentences and that they would be shown a card with a word written on it and asked to make up a sentence using the word. For conditions involving the model, the children were informed that the *E* was interested in both adults and children and that he and the model would be taking turns in making up sentences. The model and the child were then introduced to each other, and instructions were given to them both. Children were instructed to tell the *E* if they could not read a particular word, and that she would identify it for them. The children were also told that any sentence at all was acceptable as long as it contained the word on the card. The 65 stimulus cards for the subject were shuffled and a random 60 were used; if a child did not know the meaning of one of the words or could not use it in a sentence after a reasonable length of time, one of the five remaining words was substituted.

Base rate measure. All children were first presented 20 words, one at a time, with no reinforcement given except mild encouragement for the first sentence or two for those *S*s who had difficulty in composing sentences at the outset. The *S*'s sentences were recorded verbatim and later scored for the frequency of passives and prepositional phrases.

Experimental treatments. Immediately following the base-rate assessment, *S*s were again presented 20 words and one construction was manipulated. In the conditions involving modeling procedures, the model first completed 13 sentences and then the *S* and the model alternated generating sentences in five-trial blocks. After a short break, another set of words was presented in which the second construction was manipulated. The modeled performances were interspersed among the children's trials in the same manner as in the preceding experimental phase.

Subjects in each condition were counterbalanced for sex and order of construction (i.e., half the boys and half the girls received the passive treatment first and prepositional condition second; the other half of the *S*s were administered the experimental treatments in reversed order).

Five different conditions were used, with 20 *S*s, equally divided between boys and girls, in each group. The *control* condition consisted of having the *S*s continue to make up sentences to the stimulus words, without any attempt being made to modify the syntactic properties of their sentence construction. For the purpose of the analysis only, however, one half of the children of each sex in the control condition were randomly assigned to each order and treated as if one construction had been influenced in each period, although no manipulation was actually done.

In the *reinforcement + set* condition, children were given both reinforcement and a problem-solving set. It was decided to have no group exposed to only reinforcement because results of a previous investigation (Bierman, 1964) as well as preliminary studies indicated that reinforcement alone was not effective in altering linguistic structure.

Reinforcement consisted of telling the child that for some of his sentences the *E* would give him a star to paste on a card and that he would have to figure out what kind of sentence would gain a star. After the experiment was over, he was told, he would receive a present, with the particular present dependent upon the number of stars he earned. For every correct construction uttered, the child was given a colored star accompanied by social reinforcing comments such as "very good," "right," etc. Problem-solving set consisted of telling the S to pay close attention to the sentences which did and did not gain stars and try to figure out just what it was about a sentence that earned a star. Throughout the procedure, he was urged to try to earn as many stars as possible, and asked occasionally to repeat sentences which were rewarded.

In the *modeling* condition an adult male model was introduced to the child, and they were told that he and the child would be taking turns in making up sentences. The model read his sentences in a clear voice, pausing to make it appear that he was inventing them on the spot. The model and the children alternated in constructing sentences in the order described previously.

In the *modeling + reinforcement* condition, modeling cues and positive reinforcement of syntactic structure were combined. Both the model and the child were rewarded for all the correct constructions; however, no instructions designed to produce strong attentional responses were given.

In the *modeling + reinforcement + set* condition, the factor of set was added to the experimental procedures described above. The children were instructed to pay close attention to the sentences that earned stars, and both children and the model were rewarded for correct constructions.

The frequency of passives and prepositional phrases in each block of 20 sentences was scored by the E. Use of the appropriate grammatical structure in the sentence was considered: the stimulus word did not have to be included as part of the critical phrase. A set of 600 sentences, drawn at random from the various groups, was also scored independently by a second judge to provide an estimate of interscorer reliability. The two judges were in virtually perfect agreement (99.7%).

RESULTS

The results for the linguistic constructions were analyzed separately, as the frequency of passives in several of the treatment conditions was extremely low and could not be evaluated by parametric techniques.

Passives. Table 1 presents the mean number of passives and the percentage of children constructing at least one sentence in the passive voice in different phases and conditions of the experiment. A Kruskal-Wallis test of the base-rate passive constructions by Ss in the five conditions showed no significant differences. Although more boys (30%) than girls (8%) produced at least one passive sentence in the base-rate measurement ($X^2 = 6.50$; $p < .02$), no significant sex difference in frequency of passive constructions was obtained within the experimental phase of the study.

A Kruskal-Wallis one-way analysis of variance computed on change scores between the base-rate level and the frequency of passive constructions in the manipulated phase of the experiment disclosed a highly significant treatment effect ($H = 20.3$; $p < .001$). Comparisons between pairs of conditions, evaluated by the Mann-Whitney U test, showed that children who had the benefit of modeling cues, reinforcement feedback, and an active attentional set generated

Table 1

Mean Number of Passives and Percentage of Children Constructing at Least One Passive Sentence in Different Phases and Experimental Conditions

| | Experimental conditions | | | | | | | | | |
| | Control | | Reinf. + Set | | Model | | Model + Reinf. | | Model + Reinf. + Set | |
Phase of experiment	Mean	%	Mean	%	Mean	%	Mean	%	Mean	%
Base rate	.20	15	.05	5	.80	40	.35	20	.25	15
Manipulated	.60	25	.10	10	.75	35	.80	50	2.80	75
Non-manipulated										
PP-P order	.30	20	.20	20	.40	40	.60	40	.20	20
P-PP order	.40	20	.20	20	.30	20	1.20	60	1.40	70

significantly more passives than either the controls ($U = 82$; $p < .001$), or children who were provided reinforcement ($U = 87$; $p < .001$), modeling cues ($U = 76.5$; $p < .001$), or modeling combined with reinforcement ($U = 94.5$; $p < .01$). The latter three groups, however, did not differ significantly from each other.

Within-group analyses by means of the Wilcoxon matched-pairs signed-ranks test provide additional evidence for the relative efficacy of the different experimental treatments. Children in the model + reinforcement + set condition displayed a highly significant increase in passive responses in the manipulated phase compared to their base-rate performances ($T = 2.5$; $p < .005$). The model + reinforcement condition also produced an increase in passive constructions at a borderline level of significance ($p = .07$), as evaluated by the sign test.

It will be recalled that half of the Ss within each condition were administered their respective experimental treatments in the passives-prepositional phrase order. For this subgroup of children, any induced change in linguistic responses could persist, at least temporarily, in the succeeding period during which the passive construction was no longer being manipulated. Comparison of the frequencies of passive sentences in the combined manipulated and non-manipulated phases relative to base-rate scores disclosed significant increases in the model + reinforcement $(T=5; p<.05)$, and the model + reinforcement + set $(T=0; p<.005)$ conditions. These findings suggest that extensive changes in syntactic style could have been achieved had the experimental treatments been continued over a longer period of time.

When the above subgroup data are combined with changes in passive constructions achieved during the manipulated phase by children who had received the prepositional-passive order, significant increases are obtained within both the model + reinforcement $(T=11; p<.025)$ and the model + reinforcement + set $(T=3; p<.005)$ groups. On the other hand, neither the control, reinforcement + set nor modeling conditions produced any significant increases in passive constructions.

Prepositional phrases. The mean numbers of prepositional phrases generated by children in the different phases and conditions of the experiment are presented in Table 2. Results of an analysis of variance

Table 2

Mean Number of Prepositional Phrases Constructed by Children in Different Phases and Experimental Conditions

Phase of experiment	Experimental conditions				
	Control	Reinf. + Set	Model	Model + Reinf.	Model + Reinf. + Set
Base rate	9.40	8.45	8.95	8.40	8.05
Manipulated	9.60	11.85	8.45	10.25	12.00
Non-manipulated					
P-PP Order	8.60	8.70	7.20	8.30	7.90
PP-P Order	11.30	14.10	7.50	9.20	7.40

computed on the base-rate scores disclosed no significant sex difference $(F=1.34)$, nor did Ss assigned to the various experimental conditions differ $(F=0.26)$ in this respect.

A $5 \times 2 \times 2 \times 2$ analysis of variance was performed on the difference scores with the main factors representing the 5 conditions, 2 treatment phases, 2 orders of grammatical constructions, and the sex difference. This analysis, summarized in Table 3, yielded a highly significant condition effect $(F=3.92; p<.01)$. As might be expected, children constructed more sentences containing prepositional phrases in the manipulated phase than in the non-manipulated period $(F=13.73; p<.01)$; they also generated more prepositional phrases when the experimental treatments were administered in the prepositional-passives order than in the reversed sequence $(F=4.12; p<.05)$.

Table 3

Analysis of Variance of Prepositional Phrases

Source	df	MS	F
Condition (C)	4	98.73	3.92**
Order (O)	1	103.70	4.12*
Sex (S)	1	3.90	<1
C×O	4	79.43	3.16*
C×S	4	18.25	<1
O×S	1	12.50	<1
C×O×S	4	32.53	1.29
Error (b)	80	25.17	
Treatment phase (P)	1	98.00	13.73**
P×C	4	31.18	4.37**
P×O	1	44.10	6.18*
P×S	1	3.40	<1
P×C×O	4	22.43	3.14*
P×C×S	4	12.28	1.72
P×O×S	1	26.00	3.64
P×C×O×S	4	5.95	<1
Error (w)	80	7.14	

* $p<.05$.
** $p<.01$.

The highly significant interaction between phases and experimental conditions $(F=4.37; p<.01)$ indicates that the various treatment variables were differentially effective in increasing children's use of prepositional phrases primarily in the manipulated period. The specific differences contributing to the treatment effect were therefore investigated by comparison of pairs of conditions. These analyses revealed that the reinforcement+ set and the model+ reinforcement+ set groups, which did not differ from each other, were superior at the .05 level of significance or better to the control and the model conditions.

Additional evidence of the relative efficacy of the different variables in augmenting prepositional constructions is furnished by within-group analyses of the increase from base rate to the manipulated phase of each condition separately. The increase was found to be highly significant for children in both the reinforcement + set ($t = 3.03$; $p < .01$), and the model + reinforcement + set groups ($t = 3.47$; $p < .01$), and of borderline significance for the model + reinforcement treatment ($t = 1.65$; $.10 > p > .05$). The control and the model conditions, on the other hand, did not display increments in prepositional constructions.

The significant phases × order interaction effect shows that children in both syntactic orders achieved comparable increases in prepositional phrases in the manipulated phase of the study; however, Ss receiving the prepositional-passive sequence generated significantly more prepositional phrases than children assigned to the passive-prepositional order.

The analysis of variance also yielded a significant triple interaction between treatment phases, experimental conditions, and construction order ($F = 3.14$; $p < .05$). This interaction primarily reflects the differential production of prepositional phrases by children in the reinforcement + set and the model + reinforcement + set groups during the second phase of the experiment in which the construction was no longer appropriate. Children in the reinforcement + set group continued to generate prepositional phrases above their base rate level ($t = 2.58$; $p < .02$) after the contingency was switched to passives, whereas Ss in the model + reinforcement + set condition showed no such perseverative effect ($t = 0.36$).

DISCUSSION

The results of this study provide evidence supporting the proposition that syntactic style, although difficult to modify, can nevertheless be significantly altered by appropriate social-learning variables.

As predicted, reinforcement procedures, even when combined with a strong attentional set, were ineffective in increasing the use of passives in sentences freely generated by children. The majority of Ss did not produce a single passive phrase and consequently, there were no responses that could be reinforced. Nor were the children able to discern, within the relatively brief exposure period, the critical syntactic category simply from observing a model construct a series of passive sentences. On the other hand, children were able to generate passives when verbal modeling cues were combined with procedures designed to increase syntactic discriminability. The most powerful treatment condition was one in which the attentional set was induced, modeled passive constructions were interspersed with some sentences in the active voice so as to enhance differentiation of relevant grammatical properites, and both the model and the children were rewarded for all passive constructions.

Although the actual content of the constructions was not analyzed, the passive sentences generated by the children were varied, and only rarely duplicated the models's verbal productions. Indeed, some of the sentences reflected notable inventiveness (e.g., "The tea was dranked" ... " Ice are put in boxes sometimes"). These findings thus provide further evidence that people can acquire observationally principles exemplified in a model's behavior and use them for generating novel combinations of responses.

In the case of the syntactic category of prepositional phrases, which has a relatively high base rate of occurrence, reinforcement combined with an active attentional set was sufficient for increasing children's usage of prepositions, but modeling cues were not an important contributory factor. However, the fact that Ss in the reinforcement + set condition continued to produce prepositional phrases when this construction was no longer appropriate, whereas children in the model + reinforcement + set group showed no such perseverative effect, suggests that the modeling cues mainly served a discriminative function signifying the change in reinforcement contingencies. These data would seem to indicate that under conditions where the desired patterns of behavior are already well established, modeling cues may facilitate flexibly adaptive behavior.

In the present experiment the model merely generated sentences with the appropriate grammatical structure while the experimenter controlled both the informative feedback and the administration of reinforcement. On the other hand, in naturalistic situations the model not only exemplifies the behavior, but also conducts any necessary discrimination training and serves as the reinforcing agent. The traditional training practice usually takes the form of parental repetitions of modeled verbal behavior accenting the elements that may have been omitted or inaccurately reproduced by the child (Brown and Bellugi, 1964).

The results clearly indicate that brief exposure (i.e., 20 observational trials) to verbal modeling cues alone has no demonstrable effect upon children's syntactic style. It would be interesting to determine whether children could eventually acquire implicit rules of syntax from repeatedly hearing the grammatical utterances of adult models over an extended period of time without the benefit of selective reinforcement or other forms of corrective feedback.

There is some recent corroboratory evidence (Lovaas, 1967) from studies designed to establish complex functions of speech in mute schizophrenic children that the social-learning variables manipulated in the present experiment govern syntactic learning as well as performance. After children acquire verbal responses and an adequate labeling vocabulary through a combined modeling-reinforcement procedure, grammatical speech is developed by rewarding discriminative responsivity in children to events that are modeled either verbally or behaviorally. In prepositional training, for example, the model gives a verbal instruction involving a preposition (e.g., "Put the block inside the box"), and the child is positively reinforced for performing the motor response appropriate to the verbal stimulus. Objects are then arranged in a particular way and the child verbally describes the relationships between the objects using the proper prepositions. For the third step, the child gives grammatical responses to sentences spoken by the model. As in the present experiment, children are gradually taught to abstract or generalize the linguistic rule by modeling a variety of objects in a variety of prepositional relationships.

References

Bandura, A. Social-learning theory of identificatory processes. In D. A. Goslin and D. C. Glass (Eds.), *Handbook of socialization theory and research.* Chicago: Rand McNally, 1967.

Bandura, A., and McDonald, F. J. The influence of social reinforcement and the behavior of models in shaping children's moral judgments. *J. abnorm. Soc. Psychol.* 1963, 67, 274–281.

Bandura, and Mischel, W. Modification of self-imposed delay of reward through exposure to live and symbolic models. *J. Pers. soc. Psychol.* 1965, 2, 698–705.

Bandura, A., and Walters, R. H. *Social learning and personality development.* New York: Holt, Rinehart and Winston, 1963.

Bierman, Mary. The operant conditioning of verbal behavior and its relevance to syntax. Unpublished B. A. Thesis, Harvard University, 1964.

Brown, R., and Bellugi, Ursula. Three processes in the child's acquisition of syntax. *Harvard Educ. Rev.,* 1964, 34, 133–151.

Chomsky, N. *Syntactic structures.* The Netherlands: Mouton, 1957.

Lovaas, O. I. A program for the establishment of speech in psychotic children. In J. K. King (Ed.), *Childhood autism.* Oxford: Pergamon Press, 1967 (in press).

Menyuk, Paula. Syntactic rules used by children from preschool through first grade. *Child Developm.*, 1963, 34, 407-422.

Menyuk, Paula. Alteration of rules in children's grammer. *J. ver. Learn. verb. Behav.*, 1964, 3, 480-488.

Miller, W., and Ervin, Susan. The development of grammar in child language. In Ursula Bellugi and R. Brown (Eds.), the acquisition of language. *Monogr. Soc. Res. child Developm.*, 1964, 29, No. 1 (Serial No. 92).

Templin, Mildred C. *Certain language skills in children.* Minneapolis: Univer. Minnesota Press, 1957.

PART 4

Studies Attempting to Decrease Certain Behaviors

In contrast to the great number of techniques which have been developed for increasing the frequency of desirable behaviors, relatively few techniques have been used to decrease the amount of misbehavior. Although punishment in the form of electric shock or nausea has been widely used in therapy situations, it is clearly inappropriate for the problems found in the classroom. Isolation, usually consisting of putting the child in a room by himself, has also been used in the therapy situation and in the home, but it is usually impractical for the classroom situation. The techniques recommended by experts in behavior modification for use in a classroom have generally focused on teacher comments or lack of comments and on a teacher's promise of reward if the students do not misbehave.

The articles by Madsen, Becker, Thomas, Koser and Plager and by Brown and Elliott show that praising children for appropriate behavior and ignoring their disruptive behavior results in a decrease in disruptive behavior. O'Leary and Becker confirm this result but demonstrate also that private reprimands for misbehavior can also serve to reduce its frequency, completely opposite to the rewarding effects of public comments. McAllister, Stachowiak, Baer and Conderman found, on the other hand, that public reprimands to high school students were effective in controlling their disruptive behavior when combined with varying amounts of praise for appropriate behaviors. Osborne, working with a deaf population of young adolescent girls, found that a different technique, that of giving free-time if no disruptive behavior occurred during a specified period, also reduced the incidence of misbehavior. Finally, Ward and Baker provide some evidence that focusing on the misbehavior of a few students in a classroom does not appear to affect the behavior of the other students in the class, although the total amount of attention paid to them may decrease slightly. The absence of ill-effects of these programs and their demonstrated success at ages from nursery school to high school suggests that these techniques should be part of the repertoire of the well-trained teacher.

*What usually happens in a classroom or at home when a child
does something which annoys his teacher or parent? Surely a
very common response consists of telling the child to stop it or
to do something else. For most normal, fairly obedient, children
this technique is effective in the short run; they do as they are
told. Thus in the classroom discussed in this paper as well as in
the typical elementary school classroom, the teacher's response
to seeing her students standing and out of their seats was to tell
them to sit down. As the authors report, the children obeyed;
yet the number of children standing remained too high for the
teacher's liking. As the study demonstrated, making a
determined attempt to publicly reprimand the children every
time they were standing served to actually increase the number
of children standing at any one time. Clearly, paying attention
to the child in the form of public criticism serves as a positive
reinforcer, contrary to many people's expectations. (Another
study in this book, by O'Leary and Becker, showed that private
reprimands, on the other hand, may have a punishing effect.)*

*The implications of this study extend far beyond the
relatively unimportant behavior of standing up. These results
and those of other research by the authors suggest very strongly
that teachers should ignore children's misbehavior and reward
them intermittently by attention in the form of praise for being
good. The combination of extinction of the unwanted behavior
and positive reinforcement for desired behavior (both direct and
vicarious) has been shown to be effective at various grade levels
and with various problem behaviors. As the authors suggest, the
crucial trick is to "catch the child being good." Once this
becomes natural for the teacher, it simply becomes part of the
way the classroom is administered; no artificial assistance of
staff, time or money is needed.*

An Analysis of the Reinforcing Function of "Sit-Down" Commands[1]

Charles H. Madsen, Jr.,
Wesley C. Becker,
Don R. Thomas,
Linda Koser
and
Elaine Plager*

Classroom control depends on teachers being aware of how their *specific* behaviors affect students in the classroom. A growing body of experimental evidence illustrates that problem behaviors of pre-school children such as *crying* (Hart, Allen, Buell, Harris, and Wolf, 1964) *autistic behavior* (Brawley, Harris, Peterson, Allen, and Fleming, 1966; Wolf, Risley and Mees, 1964), *regressive crawling*[2] (Harris, Johnston, Kelley, and Wolf, 1964), *non-cooperative behaviors* (Hart, Reynolds, Brawley, Harris, and Baer, 1966), *isolate play* (Allen, Hart, Buell, Harris, and Wolf, 1964), *self-mutilative scratching* (Allen and Harris, 1966), *hyperactivity* (Allen, Henke, Harris, Baer, and Reynolds, 1967), *talking* (Kerr, Meyerson, and Michael, 1965), *passivity* (Johnston, Kelley, Harris, and Wolf, 1966), and *classroom disruptiveness* (Allen, Reynolds, Harris, and Baer, 1966) have been successfully controlled through the contingent use of *social reinforcement*. Similar procedures also have been effective in controlling a wide range of *classroom behavioral problems* on the elementary level (Becker, Madsen, Arnold, and Thomas, 1967; Zimmerman and Zimmerman, 1962). *Attention, praise, proximity,* and

* Charles H. Madsen, Jr., Wesley C. Becker, Don R. Thomas, Linda Koser and Elaine Plager, "An Analysis of the Reinforcing Function of 'Sit-Down' Commands," in *Readings in Educational Psychology*, ed. Ronald Parker. (Boston: Allyn and Bacon, 1968), pp. 265–278. Reprinted with permission.

[1] Portions of this paper were presented at the South Eastern Psychological Association Convention. April 4–6, Roanoke, Virginia. The authors are indebted to the administration of Urbana, Illinois School District and acknowledge the pupils who made the study possible. This study was supported in part by grant HD-00881-05 from the National Institute of Child Health and Human Development.

[2] Reproduced in *Readings in Educational Psychology*, ed. Ronald Parker.

other social stimuli have also been found to maintain *inappropriate* as well as pro-social behavior in an institutional setting (Ayllon and Michael, 1959).

Some experimenters have trained mothers in the systematic use of social techniques. The mothers were then able to modify the behavior problems of their own children (Hawkins, Peterson, Schweid, and Bijou, 1966; Wahler, Winkel, Peterson, and Morrison, 1967). This is a very promising and constructive approach; however, clinical and school workers realize it is often difficult to achieve the cooperation necessary to use home training. If social agencies such as the school can not "give their problems back to the home," the alternatives are to train teachers in effective behavioral management procedures or to use professionals (school psychologists, social workers, etc.) to provide treatment for each child. Traditional approaches to individual treatment of problem children in schools have not produced convincing data concerning effectiveness. Often when changes are reported in therapy sessions there is still little change in classroom behavior. One preliminary attack on this issue indicates that the effectiveness of therapy for school problems (independently observed) was directly related to the amount of praise given pro-social behavior by the teacher (Madsen, Saudargas, Hammond, Dokterman, Luey, and Thomas, 1968). It appears that it is necessary to reward and praise new pro-social behaviors when they occur in the real-life situation or else the child does not maintain the behavioral patterns "learned" in therapy.

Becker and his group have taken the teacher training approach. The attempt was made to produce systematic data to show what teachers themselves can do to eliminate various kinds of problem behaviors (Becker, *et al.*, 1967). The evidence thus far when comparing the two approaches appears to indicate that teachers trained to use contingent social reinforcement in the classroom diminish behavioral problems to a greater extent than individual treatment (even though the teacher is teaching 26-30 other children at the same time).

The Becker *et al.*, (1967) study was completed in a public school with teachers who referred problem children in their own classrooms. Behavioral rating categories, reliability checks, and observational procedures were developed and teachers were trained in a seminar workshop. Teachers were taught to use social reinforcement as a reward for pro-social behavior. They were trained in the use of explicit rules, ignoring of inappropriate behavior and using praise and attention for behaviors which facilitate learning (Becker *et al.*, 1967). The results in five separate classrooms indicated a dramatic reduction in inappropriate behaviors with an attendant increase in pro-social behaviors as teacher praise and recognition were made contingent on appropriate behaviors.

A replication and extension of Becker's study (Madsen, Becker, and Thomas, 1967) indicated that the combination of rules, ignoring, and praise were effective, but rules alone, or ignoring plus rules, produced either no change or increased inappropriate behavior. A subsequent study (Thomas, Becker, and Armstrong, 1967) investigated effects of teacher's behaviors by systematically varying approving and disapproving behaviors. Approving behaviors such as praise, smiles, and physical contact maintained appropriate classroom behavior and inappropriate behaviors increased when approving behaviors were withdrawn. When the teacher tripled disapproving behavior significant increases in motor and noisemaking aspects of inappropriate behavior were observed.

The present study seeks to extend the knowledge of some of the ways in which a teacher's behavior can influence the behavior of the children in her classroom by examining the possible positive reinforcing effects of a teacher behavior that would usually be thought of as punishment.

Children standing up when they are supposed to be working has bothered elementary teachers for years. The generally preferred method for dealing with this problem has been for the teacher to instruct the offenders to sit down and do their work. The teacher's comments are delivered at various levels of intensity depending on the teacher and the situation. Most teachers are prone to *pay attention* to violations. The teacher may think that she is punishing the inappropriate behavior; however, the attention may serve as a reinforcer for the very behavior that the attention is intended to diminish. An interpretation that teacher disapproval is reinforcing for all classes of inappropriate behavior is not warranted from prior work in elementary schools (Thomas, Becker, and Armstrong, 1967); however, under some conditions there is good reason to expect such an effect. The present experiment was designed to show that giving disapproval to inappropriate behavior (standing up during individual seat work) serves to increase the very behavior that the teacher desires to eliminate.

BACKGROUND

STUDENTS

A "team" first grade room was comprised of 48 children (age 6-2 to 7-2; half boys, half girls) from a variety of socioeconomic backgrounds, and with a wide range of intellectual abilities. All students had attended kindergarten.

THE TEACHERS AND THE TEAM APPROACH

Both teachers had previous teaching experience. Observations showed the room to be generally well-controlled. The physical setting was a modern elementary school, with many two-room complexes joined by folding walls. The wall made it possible to transform two normal sized rooms into one large room or vice versa. One-half of the experimental room was designated as a desk-study area. The remaining space provided two reading instruction centers, a science area including pets and an aquarium, an art corner, an enclosed library area with child size benches and book cases (carpeted), a free play and activity center, and extensive space for special projects (with tables).

Responsibility for teaching was divided. The teachers shared reading and math, one teacher conducted all physical education, the other conducted music, and they took turns in other subject matter areas (science, art, etc.). They attempted to provide as much individual academic activity as possible. One teacher was generally free to circulate around the room and help children on an individual basis. In addition, reading groups were reformulated weekly and math almost daily. When experimental procedures began (middle of January) the reading program for thirty children was completely individualized with the rest of the class in small groups of comparable reading ability.

TEACHER'S PROGRAM

During the first three weeks of the school year the teachers helped the students to make the transition from the more unstructured program of kindergarten to the more formal approach used in the first grade. They taught individual and group activities, and provided a structure for discipline.

When reading began, the table-like desks were formed into six tables of eight desks each. The close proximity and large number of students provided more opportunity for talking, visiting, and standing up to reach across a table or visit someone at another table than in a regular room. Talking and getting out of seat were behaviors which interfered most with reading instruction. Both teachers were busy teaching separate reading groups while the rest of the class should have been working independently at their desks. Many times they were not. Reprimands by the teachers appeared ineffectual.

Prior to beginning the experiment the teachers had wanted to establish a quiet classroom during the valuable morning hours, and still keep the children's desks in the physically ideal formation. Therefore, a system of "class leader" was tried. Each table was assigned a number from one to six. A letter was sent to the parents explaining the system, and the reasons for starting it. A large weekly chart served to record points which could be earned by a table with good workers. Every Monday morning each member of the winning table was presented with a "class leader" badge and a note for parents. The leaders were given special privileges such as leading class lines, watering plants, taking down attendance slips, running errands, starting the Pledge of Allegiance, and marking the calendar. The class leader system rewarded appropriate behavior by marks on the chart, and a special badge. However, the reward was not immediate and the behavior of the table as a whole was noted rather than that of an individual child. The plan was in effect from November 1 to Christmas and seemed to be fairly effective. However, as the novelty wore off, the room became more difficult to control and the system was discontinued. The "warning system" was then inaugurated. A first warning was given children who behaved inappropriately and their names were written on the chalkboard. A second warning and the child was required to move his desk against a wall and his name was transferred to a "list" taped on the chalkboard. Listed children were deprived of the daily special afternoon activity (art, music, movies, story-time, etc.) and were sent to the desk half of the room to sit with heads down. However, as reading groups increased it became difficult for the teacher to teach and at the same time note children causing disturbances in the desk area. Getting up and writing names on the chalkboard was discontinued. After two weeks each child was made responsible for remembering whether or not he'd received a warning. This caused "forgetfulness' on the part of many. On some days there were more talkers with second warnings than "isolation spots" to put them in. At this point the experiment began.

EXPERIMENTAL PROCEDURES

OBSERVATIONS

The observers counted all children in the room who were noticeably up from their seats (including kneeling on seat, standing on one foot, etc.) during each ten-second interval. The average number of children standing per ten-second interval was tabulated. There are some times during individual study when a first grader stands appropriately, but to ensure accuracy and limit the number of judgments made by our observers only one exception was allowed. Whenever a child was going to or coming from a reading group and had a chair in his hands he was not tabulated. Any other time a child's bottom left his chair he was counted. Observers had previously been trained in the observational procedures (Becker, *et al*, 1967) and initial observer reliability was over 95% (average reliability including child and teacher categories for ten observations of 54 was 94.7 with a range from 90.4 to 99.2). One hundred 10-second intervals were observed daily (or 20 minutes, with a 10 second rest in each minute).

Teachers were observed at the same time as the children. Two types of verbal behaviors were recorded: (1) The number of times that either of the teachers reprimanded a child for standing or told anyone to sit down, and (2) the number of times that either teacher praised a child for sitting. The class was observed following the morning routine and immediately after class instructions concerning individual papers. That was the problem period when both teachers were engaged in reading instructions to small groups (except for two special observations when the regular routine was disrupted). The students were completing individual work-sheets at their desks. The time of observation was approximately 9:40 A.M. with very little variation. Baseline observations began January 24, 1967. Final observations were made in June, 1967.

RULES

Prior to the beginning of baseline observations it was determined that the rules for classroom conduct should be made explicit. Earlier experimental work (Madsen, Becker, and Thomas, 1967) provided evidence that rules alone caused very little change in the amount of inappropriate behavior. However, it was desirable to preclude the possibility that the children did not "know" that they were to be seated during the individual work period. The room remained under the teachers' warning system and explicit rules were added one week prior to baseline.

The teachers were instructed to formulate specific rules and go over them with the class four to six times per day. Rules were to be short and to the point and phrased in a positive manner. The teachers recorded the number of times the rules were reviewed on a daily basis and reminded the class of rules at times other than when someone was misbehaving. With the children's help they composed four rules which they posted on a large bulletin board:

1. We should work quietly.
2. We should keep our hands to ourselves.

3. We should stay in our seats when we are working.
4. We should keep our eyes on our own work.

The teachers went over the rules daily before morning work periods and stopped periodically during the morning to, "refresh our memory."

EXPERIMENTAL PHASES

The experimental program included, first, a baseline (Baseline I) during which observers counted the number of times children were standing and the verbal attention paid to standing (number of times children were told to sit down). No instructions were given teachers. Baseline recordings made it possible to assess later changes in standing as a function of differential teacher attention.

The second phase (Sit-Down I) approximately tripled the frequency of "sit down" commands. It was predicted that "sit down" commands would serve as a reinforcer for the behavior the commands were designed to eliminate, and that more children would stand up. Prior observations in this room had shown that the immediate effect of telling a child who was standing to "sit down," was compliance. However, it was predicted that the *"longer term"* effect would be an increase in standing. The teachers gave "sit down" commands only when children were standing when it was against the rules. To demonstrate effects conclusively, i.e., to show that "sit down" commands were controlling standing, a return to baseline (Baseline II) was included. Teachers were instructed to give "sit down commands at approximately the same rate as during Baseline I. It was predicted that the rate of children standing up would decrease to approximately the same rate as Baseline I.

The next phase (Sit-Down II) reinstated the high frequency of "sit down" commands, again to increase confidence in the results. The procedure of recording baseline observations, increasing "sit down" commands, returning to baseline, and once again increasing "sit down" commands would demonstrate whether or not "sit down" commands actually functioned as a positive reinforcer.

The final experimental phase tried to reduce standing behavior by instructing teachers to praise incompatible with standing behavior, such as sitting and working. Prior research had indicated the effectiveness of an approach based upon rules, ignoring inappropriate behavior, and praising appropriate behavior. Rules had already been started and maintained; praising incompatible behavior and ignoring standing were begun during the final phase.

Instructions similar to those given teachers in other studies (Becker, Madsen, Arnold and Thomas, 1967; Madsen, Becker and Thomas, 1967) were revised to read as follows:

> This phase is primarily directed toward *increasing* appropriate behaviors incompatible with inappropriate classroom behaviors by using praise and attention. Teachers are generally inclined to take good behavior for granted and pay attention only when a child acts up or misbehaves. During the last phases of this program you have deliberately been increasing your attention to standing by catching the child in misbehavior and commanding him to "sit down." You are now asked to use a procedure characterized as, "catching the child being good." Give the praise, attention, or smile when the child is seated and doing what is expected during individual study. Of course, you are free to use this same approach all day long. When one child begins to stand up or is walking around the room unnecessarily, praise the child next to him for sitting down and paying attention to his work. This will generally bring the offender to an awareness of what he is doing without giving any attention to the misbehavior. It is then important to watch for the next opportunity to praise the offender for his good behavior after he has been seated for a few seconds. Remember, however, not to praise immediately upon getting back to work or else you may well be teaching the child to stand up so he can sit down and be praised. This is why it is important to "catch the children being good" as regularly as possible. We are, of course, assuming that your commendation and praise is important to the child. This is generally the case, but sometimes it takes a while for the praise to become effective. Persistence in catching children being good and delivering praise and attention eventually pays off in better classroom management (this is true whether or not classroom management is now a problem). The procedure outlined will insure the ignoring of most standing behavior while paying attention and praising good individual work. In general, it will also be effective to praise for other things as well, such as concentrating on individual work, raising hand when appropriate, paying attention to directions and following through, sitting in desk and studying, sitting quietly, and keeping eyes on own paper. Try to use variety and expression in your comments. Stay away from sarcasm. Attempt to become spontaneous in your praise and smile when delivering praise. At first you will probably get the feeling that you are praising a great deal and it sounds a little phony to your ears. This is a typical reaction and it becomes more natural with the passage of time. Spread your praise and attention around. If comments sometimes interfere with the ongoing class activities then use facial attention and smiles. At times other than reading groups, walk around the room and pat or place your hand on the back of a child who is

doing a good job. Praise quietly spoken to the children has been found effective in combination with some physical sign of approval.

General rule: Give *praise* and *attention* to behaviors which facilitate learning. Tell the child what he is being praised for. Try to reinforce behaviors incompatible with those you wish to decrease (praise: sitting in seat and working properly, sitting with feet on floor and facing front, etc.).

In summary the experimental conditions were as follows:

Baseline I: No instructions given teachers, standing behavior and teachers' "sit down" and praise comments recorded. *Sit Down I:* Attention to standing was increased by teachers. Children were told to sit down when they stood up. *Baseline II:* Teachers returned to same level of "sit down" commands as initially observed, standing and teachers' comments recorded. *Sit Down II:* Attention to standing behavior was again increased by similar instructions to teachers as during Sit Down I, standing and teachers' comments recorded. *Praise:* During the final phase teachers instructed to praise behaviors incompatible with standing up, recordings continued.

RESULTS

The results of the study clearly substantiate the contention that teacher attention to the inappropriate behavior of standing served to increase the behavior in the classroom. Figure 1 shows that effects which are surprising to most teachers are produced by varying teacher frequency of "sit down" commands. Each time the teachers increased their frequency of admonitions to "sit down," the over-all level of standing-up increased. When the teachers praised incompatible "studying" behavior the frequency of standing decreased.

During Baseline I, the number of children standing per 10 second interval averaged (all six observations) 2.91, and the number of sit down commands during the same observations averaged 6.8. During the second phase (Sit Down I), when the teachers increased "sit down" commands (average 27.5), the number of children standing increased to an average of 4.07 per 10 second interval. Return to baseline (Baseline II) decreased the average number of children standing (average 2.95), paralleling the reduction in "sit down" responses by the teachers (average 5.6). Sit Down II produced another change upward. As the teachers said, "sit down" more frequently (average 28.3), more children stood up (average 3.86). During the final phase, when the teachers were praising sitting (average

21.1) and other behaviors incompatible with standing, the level of standing dropped to the lowest level (average 1.89).

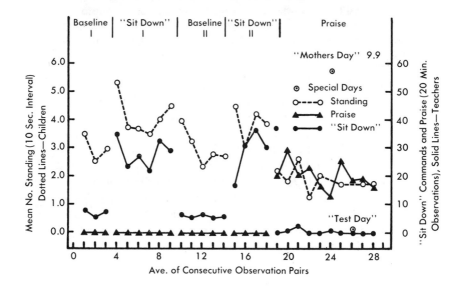

Figure 1

Standing-up by first graders as a function of "sit-down" commands and praise given by teachers.

(N = 45 children, 2 teachers)

Figure explanation:

Left side indicates the scale for children's standing behavior. Average number of children standing per one ten-second interval represents the scale values and applies only to the dotted lines. The observation period covered intervals (approximately 20 minutes). The total number of children counted during the 100 intervals was divided by 100 to arrive at the values to be plotted. Each point connected by dotted lines represents the average of two observation days (two 100 interval observations). Thus, Baseline I represents 6 days of observations. Two exceptions are the special days which were plotted separately and not averaged. Right side of the graph indicates the scale values for the teachers' attention to standing. The teacher code indicates the number of teacher comments of a "sit-down" (circles connected by solid lines) or a praise for sitting and studying (triangles connected by solid lines) variety. Contrasted with the child points which represent an average per one interval of observation the teacher points represent the total number of comments recorded during the entire 100 interval observation. The teacher points also represent averages of two consecutive observations with two exceptions. The special days are plotted as single points in the same line as the student points to maintain clarity.

Measures of teacher behavior and child behavior were taken concurrently. The observation points in the graph in all cases represent data collected during the same observation period.

DISCUSSION

The magnitude of the experimental effect, whether going from Baseline to "Sit Down" or from Baseline to Praise was approximately 1.0 child per 10 second interval. Stated a little differently, this means that during an average twenty-minute observation there was a total difference of approximately 100 children. A difference of approximately 100 who stay sitting down in a twenty-minute period could make any first-grade teacher happy. For any interpretation of the results it should be remembered that there were times (constant across conditions) when the children stood up when it was appropriate but they were still counted. For example: Children were allowed to go to the bathroom as long as they put their names on the board and only two were gone at any one time. When papers were completely finished, they were allowed to pass them in. Counting devices were encouraged for math, and the children had to take them to and from the cupboard. Children could sharpen pencils if absolutely necessary. Finally as every first-grade teacher knows, special emergencies sometimes occur. The observers counted everyone that moved off a chair, either above or below the chair level, unless a chair was being carried. Having two children up per interval in a first-grade class of 48 was considered good.

Since the recording procedure counted any child not in seat during a 10 second interval, it is possible that the experimental effects could be attributed to a few children staying out of their seats for longer periods of time. The observers and teachers indicate that this was clearly not the case. The children would sit down on being told to "sit down." There were no children in this class who stood out as being primarily responsible for the changes. Nevertheless, a recording procedure which permitted specification of effects on individual children would be very desirable in a future study. A video tape recording using a wide angle lens would permit a more refined analysis.

Mention should be made of two special points which dramatically illustrate situational differences in the behavior studied (Figure 1, observations 24 and 26). Fifty-two observations were taken at approximately the same time and under quite similar conditions, but within two weeks in May the observers ran into a special Friday when the children were preparing Mother's Day gifts and a "test day." In spite of a fairly high level of praise on "Mother's Day," the standing level rose to an average of 9.9 per 10 second interval when the children were engaged in an art activity. The two observers (a reliability check day) stated that trying to count all the children standing before the 10 seconds expired was like a very wild game (in spite of this, reliability was still 94%). Contrasted to "Mother's Day" was "test day," when achievement tests were administered. Standing averaged only 0.12 per 10 second interval. Clearly, standing behavior can be influenced by stimuli other than teacher's praise or criticism.

The focus of the study was on standing behavior; however, periodic observations of inappropriate verbalizations were recorded by individual table. One important conclusion comes from these results. The limited observations follow exactly the same pattern as the more extensive results on standing. Verbalization observations were available for the three last phases of the experimental program (four observations per condition). The number of verbalizations noted per twenty minute observation period during Baseline II was 37.6. There was an increase to an average of 71.0 during the Sit Down II phase and a subsequent decrease to an average of 25.0 during the praise phase of the experiment. This gives some indication that other behaviors in addition to standing were affected by the teachers' attention.

The warning system was continued throughout the experimental procedures and it is interesting to note the changes in the lengths of the lists for loss of privileges. Baseline lists averaged 10.8, Sit Down lists averaged 7.8, and praise lists averaged 3.8. The length of the lists changed somewhat over the time, but no dramatic reduction was apparent until the praise phase was inaugurated, giving more support to the contention that contingent praise enhances effective classroom behavior.

IMPLICATIONS

The "good teaching and learning situation" often alluded to by many writers, educators, and administrators is at best too abstract to be useful to the teacher who is actually involved with the instruction of children. Classroom control concerns very *specific* behaviors on the part of the teacher constantly interacting with the children. When separate behaviors, as opposed to generalized feelings, or attitudes are used as specific reinforcers (e.g. praise and attention) to control behavior, more positive "discipline" accrues. The present study demonstrates the effective use of specific behaviors in controlling one aspect of classroom activity, that is, standing up. If teachers will avail themselves of the general behavioral techniques and use these techniques to shape specific desirable behaviors, perhaps the "good teaching and learning situation" will become a reality.

References

Allen, K. E., and Harris, F. R. Elimination of a child's excessive scratching by training the mother in reinforcement procedures. *Behavior Research and Therapy*, 1966, 4, 79–84.

Allen, K. E., Hart, B. M., Buell, J. S., Harris, F. R., and Wolf, M. M. Effects of social reinforcement on isolate behavior of a nursery school child. *Child Development*, 1964, 35, 511–518.

Allen, K. E., Henke, L. B., Harris, F. R., Baer, D. M., Reynolds, N. J. Control of hyperactivity by social reinforcement of attending behavior. *Journal of Educational Psychology*, 1967, 58, 231–237.

Allen, K. E., Reynolds, N. J., Harris, F. R., and Baer, D. M. Elimination of disruptive classroom behaviors of a pair of preschool boys through systematic control of adult social reinforcement. Unpublished manuscript, University of Washington, 1966.

Ayllon, T. and Michael, J. The psychiatric nurse as a behavioral engineer. *Journal of the Experimental Analysis of Behavior*, 1959, 2, 323–334.

Becker, W. C., Madsen, C. H., Arnold, Carole R., and Thomas, D. R. The contingent use of teacher attention and praise in reducing classroom behavior problems. *Journal of Special Education*, 1967, 1, 287–307.

Brawley, E. R., Harris, F. R., Peterson, R. F., Allen, K. E., and Fleming, R. E. Behavior modification of an autistic child. Unpublished manuscript, University of Washington, 1966.

Harris, F. R., Johnston, M. K., Kelley, C. S., and Wolf, M. M. Effects of positive social reinforcement on regressed crawling in a preschool child. *Journal of Educational Psychology*, 1964, 55, 35–41.

Hart, B. M., Allen, K. E., Buell, J. S., Harris, F. R., and Wolf, M. M. Effects of social reinforcement on operant crying. *Journal of Experimental Child Psychology*, 1964, 1, 145–153.

Hart, B. M., Reynolds, N. J., Brawley, E. R., Harris, F. R., and Baer, D. M. Effects of contingent and non-contingent social reinforcement of the isolate behavior of a nursery school girl. Unpublished manuscript, University of Washington, 1966.

Hawkins, R. P., Peterson, R. F., Schweid, E., and Bijou, S. W. Behavior therapy in the home: Amelioration of problem parent-child relations with the parent in a therapeutic role. *Journal of Experimental Child Psychology*, 1966, 4, 99-107.

Johnston, M. K., Kelley, C. S., Harris, F. R., and Wolf, M. M. An application of reinforcement principles to development of motor skills of a young child. *Child Development*, 1966, 37, 379-387.

Kerr, Nancy, Meyerson, L., and Michael, J. A procedure for shaping vocalizations in a mute child. Ullmann, L. P., & Krasner, L. (Eds.), *Case studies in behavior modification*. New York: Holt, Rinehart, & Winston, Inc., 1965. Pp. 366-370.

Madsen, C. H., Jr., Becker, W. C., and Thomas, D. R. Praise, rules and ignoring as aspects of contingent teacher attention in reducing classroom behavior problems. Unpublished manuscript, University of Illinois, 1967.

Madsen, C. H., Jr., Saudargas, R., Hammond, R., Dokterman, C., Luey, M; and Thomas, D. R. Non-professional therapists and classroom problems: A comparison of therapeutic techniques. Paper presented at South Eastern Psychological Association Convention, April 4-6, 1968, Roanoke, Virginia. Mimeo—Florida State University.

Thomas, D. R., Becker, W. C., and Armstrong, M. Production and elimination of disruptive classroom behavior by systematically varying teacher's behavior. Unpublished manuscript, Univ. of Ill., 1967.

Wahler, R. G., Winkel, G. H., Peterson, R. E., and Morrison, D. C. Mothers as behavior therapists for their own children. *Behavioral Research and Therapy*, 1965, 3, 2, 113-124.

Wolf, M. M., Risley, T., and Mees, H. Application of operant procedures to the behavior problems of an autistic child. *Behavior Research and Therapy*, 1964, 1, 305-312.

Zimmerman, Elaine H., and Zimmerman, J. The alteration of behavior in a special classroom situation. *Journal of Experimental Analysis of Behavior*, 1962, 5, 59-60.

Physical and verbal aggression are very common among nursery school boys, often to the distress of their teachers. As the authors mention, ignoring the aggressive behavior of their students may be very difficult for nursery school teachers. The authors' speculation that the attention paid to the aggressive behavior by the teacher was the very factor maintaining it appears to be supported by their results: When the teachers were instructed to ignore aggressive behavior and praise the children for being good, the amount of aggressive behavior they displayed decreased significantly. These results, of course, are very similar to those of Madsen et al., who found that ignoring standing and praising children for sitting extinguished the behavior of standing.

Unfortunately, Brown and Elliott did not report any measures of the teachers' behavior other than anecdotal comments. Although they suggest that the teachers attended more to physical than to verbal aggression, particularly during the second baseline phase, no evidence of this is presented. If there were records of the teachers' actual behavior, the relationship of their behavior to that of the students could be more adequately assessed. It is possible, although unlikely, that the Hawthorne effect of knowing that an experiment was in progress either affected other aspects of the teachers' behavior than their responsiveness to aggression and attention to good behavior or affected the children's behavior directly. Even were this possibility true, however, the simplicity and effectiveness of their procedure should recommend it to teachers of nursery school and older children.

Control of Aggression in a Nursery School Class[1,2]

Paul Brown[3]
and
Rogers Elliott*†

ABSTRACT

The rate of emission of aggressive responses of 27, 3- and 4-year-old boys in a nursery school class was successfully manipulated by teachers systematically ignoring aggression and attending to acts incompatible with aggression.

The aim of the present study was to add to the data of the field of social learning theory (Bandura and Walters, 1963), at several points. First, among the techniques of controlling operant social behavior, simple extinction (Williams, 1959), simple reinforcement (Azrin and Lindsley, 1956), or both of them in combination (Zimmerman and Zimmerman, 1962; Ayllon and Michael, 1960; Baer, Harris, and Wolf, 1963) have been employed frequently with children. Second, the use of explicit learning techniques has been shown effective in young nursery school subjects (Ss)

* Paul Brown and Rogers Elliott, "Control of Aggression in a Nursery School Class," *Journal of Experimental Child Psychology* 2(1965): 103–107. Reprinted with permission.
† Dartmouth College
[1] This is a report of work done by the first author, under the direction of the second, in partial fulfillment of the requirements of the senior courses in independent research at Dartmouth.
[2] The authors thank Edith Hazard, director, and the members of the staff of the Hanover Nursery School. Not only did they make this study possible, they made it very enjoyable.
[3] Now at MacMaster University.

in two recent papers (Baer *et al.*, 1963; Homme, de Baca, Devine, Steinhorst, and Rickert, 1963). Finally, antisocial acts of the assertive-aggressive kind are known to have operant components which are extinguishable (Williams, 1959) and reinforcible (Cowan and Walters, 1963).

With the above as background, we took seriously the following:

> Theorizing and experimentation on the inhibition of aggression have focused exclusively on the inhibitory influence of anxiety or guilt, on the assumption that response inhibition is necessarily a consequence of pairing responses with some form of aversive stimulation. The development of aggression inhibition through the strengthening of incompatible positive responses, on the other hand, has been entirely ignored, despite the fact that the social control of aggression is probably achieved to a greater extent on this basis than by means of aversive stimulation (Bandura and Walters, 1963, p. 130).

We set out to control the aggressive behavior of all of the boys in an entire nursery school class, by using as techniques the removal of positive generalized reinforcement (attention) for aggressive acts, while giving attention to cooperative acts.

METHOD

SUBJECTS

The subjects were the 27 males in the younger (3- to 4-year-old) of the two groups at the Hanover Nursery School. Observation and teachers' reports made it clear that the younger boys were more aggressive than any other age-sex subgroup.

RATINGS

Aggressive responses were defined by enumeration of the categories of the scale devised by Walters, Pearce, and Dahms (1957). The scale has two major subcategories—physical aggression and verbal aggression. Each of these is subdivided into more concrete categories; e.g., under physical aggression are categories labeled "pushes, pulls, holds"; "hits, strikes"; "annoys, teases, interferes"; and there are similar specific descriptions (e.g., "disparages"; "threatens") under the verbal category.

The observations of the behavior were made by two raters, both undergraduates at Dartmouth.[4] They were trained in the use of the scale, and

[4] We thank James Miller and James Markworth for their assistance.

given practice in observing the class during the free-play hour from 9:20 to 10:20 in the morning. Such observation was possible because the rater could stand in a large opening connecting the two spacious play areas. The rating scale had the categories of aggressive behavior as its rows and 12 five-minute intervals as its columns. The raters simply checked any occurrence of a defined behavior in the appropriate cell.

One rater observed on Monday, Wednesday, and Friday mornings; the other observed on Tuesday and Thursday. On two of the four observed Wednesday sessions, both raters observed, so that interrater reliability could be estimated. At the conclusion of the study, the raters were interviewed to determine what changes, if any, they had observed in the behavior of teachers and children, and whether they had surmised the research hypothesis.

PROCEDURE

The pre-treatment period was simply a one-week set of observations of aggressive responses by the younger boys, to furnish a reference response rate. Two weeks later the first treatment period was initiated by the teachers and the first author (see below) and it lasted for two weeks. Ratings were taken during the second week of this period. The teachers were then told that the experiment was over, and that they were no longer constrained in their behavior toward aggressive acts. Three weeks after this another set of ratings was taken to assess the durability of the treatment effect. Finally, two weeks after this follow-up observation, the treatment was reinstituted for two weeks, and, again, observations were made in the second of these weeks.

The teachers were the agents of treatment (along with the first author) and they were instructed verbally, with reference to a typed handout, which read in part as follows:

> There are many theories which try to explain aggression in young children. Probably most are partly true and perhaps the simplest is the best. One simple one is that many fights, etc. occur because they bring with them a great deal of fuss and attention from some adult. If we remember that just 3 or 4 short years ago these children would have literally died if they were not able to command (usually by crying) attentive responses from some adult, we can see how just attending to a child could be rewarding. On the other hand, when a child is playing quietly most parents are thankful for the peace and leave well enough alone. Unfortunately, if attention and praise is really rewarding, the child is not rewarded when he should be. Thus, many parents unwittingly encourage aggressive, attention-getting behavior since this is the only way the child gets some form of reward. Of course this is an

extreme example but it would be interesting to see if this matter of attention is really the issue, and the important issue especially in a setting where punishment of behavior is not a real option.

At the school I have noticed that whenever it has been possible cooperative and non-aggressive acts are attended to and praised by teachers. During the intervening week we would like to exaggerate this behavior and play down the attention given to aggressive acts. I hope to concentrate on the boys, but if a boy and girl are concerned that is perfectly all right.

Briefly, we will try to ignore aggression and reward cooperative and peaceful behavior. Of course if someone is using a hammer on another's head we would step in but just to separate the two and leave. It will be difficult at first because we tend to watch and be quiet when nothing bad is happening, and now our attention will as *much as possible* be directed toward cooperative, or non-aggressive behavior. It would be good to let the most aggressive boys see that the others are getting the attention if it is possible. A pat on the head, 'That's good Mike,' 'Hello Chris and Mark, how are you today?' 'Look what Eric made,' etc. may have more rewarding power than we think. On the other hand, it is just as important during this week to have no reprimands, no 'Say you're sorry,' 'Aren't you sorry?' Not that these aren't useful ways of teaching proper behavior, but they will only cloud the effects of our other manner of treatment. It would be best not even to look at a shove or small fight if we are sure no harm is being done; as I mentioned before, if it is necessary we should just separate the children and leave.

RESULTS AND DISCUSSION

THE RATERS

The correlation between the raters of total aggressive responses checked in each of 24 five-minute periods was 0.97. This is higher than the average interrater correlation of 0.85 reported by Walters, *et al.* (1957), but their raters were working with a one-minute, rather than a five-minute observation period.

When interviewed, one rater said that the only change he saw in the children was in the two "most troublesome" boys, who at the end (the fourth-rating period) seemed less troublesome. The other noticed no change in any of the children, even though his ratings described the changes shown in Table 1. One rater had noticed, again during the fourth-rating period, that the first author was being "especially complimentary" to one of the troublesome boys, and the other rater did not notice any change in the behavior of any adult.

Table 1

Average Number of Responses in the Various Rated Categories of Aggression

	Categories of Aggression		
Times of observation	Physical	Verbal	Total
Pre-treatment	41.2	22.8	64.0
First treatment	26.0	17.4	43.4
Follow-up	37.8	13.8	51.6
Second treatment	21.0	4.6	25.6

AGGRESSIVE RESPONSES

Table 1 presents the average daily number of physical, verbal, and overall aggressive responses in each of the four periods of observations. Analyses of variance of the daily scores as a function of treatments yielded F ratios ($df = 3, 16$) of 6.16 for physical aggression ($p < 0.01$), 5.71 for verbal aggression ($p < 0.01$), and 25.43 for overall aggression.

There seems little doubt that ignoring aggressive responses and attending cooperative ones had reliable and significant effects upon the behavior of the children.

Verbal aggression did not recover after the first treatment, while physical aggression did. Since we were rating children, not teachers, we offer the following speculation with only casual evidence. We believe the teachers find it harder to ignore fighting than to ignore verbal threats or insults. It is certainly true that the teachers (all females) found aggression in any form fairly difficult to ignore. During treatment periods they would frequently look to the first author as if asking whether they should step in and stop a fight, and they often had the expression and behavior of conflict when aggressive, especially physically aggressive behavior occurred—i.e., they would often, almost automatically, move slightly toward the disturbance, then check themselves, then look at the first author. The more raucous scenes were tense, with the teachers waiting, alert and ready for the first bit of calm and cooperative behavior to appear and allow them to administer attention. The teachers, incidentally, were skeptical of the success of the method when it was first proposed, though they came ultimately to be convinced of it. What made its success dramatic to them was the effect upon two very aggressive boys, both of whom became friendly and cooperative to a degree not thought possible. The most aggressive boys tended to be reinforced for cooperative acts on a lower variable ratio than the others, because teachers were especially watchful of any sign of cooperation on their parts.

CONCLUSION

As Allen, Hart, Buell, Harris, and Wolf (1964) have pointed out recently, the principles involved in the present application of controlling techniques are simple. What makes this and other demonstrations of them successful in a real-life setting is systematic observation, systematic application, and systematic evaluation.

References

Allen, Eileen K., Hart, Betty, Buell, Joan S., Harris, Florence R., and Wolf, M. M. Effects of social reinforcement on the isolate behavior of a nursery school child. *Child Develpm.*, 1964, 35, 511–518.

Ayllon, T., and Michael, J. The psychiatric nurse as a behavioral engineer. *J. exp. anal. Behav.*, 1959, 2, 323–334.

Azrin, N. H., and Lindsley, O. R. The reinforcement of cooperation between children. *J. abnorm. soc. Psychol.*, 1956, 52, 100–102.

Baer, D. M., Harris, Florence R., and Wolf, M. M. Control of nursery school children's behavior by programming social reinforcement from their teachers. *Amer. Psychologist*, 1963, 18, 343 (Abstract).

Bandura, A., and Walters, R. H. *Social learning and personality development.* New York: Holt, 1963.

Cowan, P. A., and Walters, R. H. Studies of reinforcement aggression. I. Effects of scheduling. *Child Develpm.*, 1963, 34, 543–551.

Homme, L. E., C.de Baca, P., Devine, J. V., Steinhorst, R., and Rickert, E. J. Use of the Premack principle in controlling the behavior of nursery school children. *J. exp. anal. Behav.*, 1963, 6, 544.

Walters, J. C., Pearce, Doris, and Dahms, Lucille. Affectional and aggressive behavior of preschool children. *Child Develpm.*, 1957, 28, 15–26.

Williams, C. D. The elimination of tantrum behavior by extinction procedures. *J. abnorm. soc. Psychol.*, 1959, 59, 269.

Zimmerman, Elaine H., and Zimmerman, J. The alteration of behavior in a special classroom situation. *J. exp. anal. Behav.*, 1962, 5, 59–60.

Once it has been established that a teacher's reprimands or other comments can affect the child's behavior, a logical next step is to investigate the effects of different parameters of these comments. In the study by O'Leary and Becker, the authors kept the number of comments administered by the teacher constant at about twelve during a ten to fifteen minute rest period and varied only the intensity of the teacher's commands. Both during a base rate period and during an experimental period in which the teacher was asked to comment on a student's misbehavior in a voice loud enough to be audible to the whole class, the amount of disruptive behavior was higher than in either a period in which the teacher ignored disruptive behavior and praised appropriate behavior or a period in which the teacher commented on a child's misbehavior so quietly that only he could hear the comments.

O'Leary and Becker interpret their findings as suggesting that the quality of the teacher's reprimand directly affects its reinforcing properties. Another possibility is that the teacher's reprimand is not directly positively reinforcing and may in fact be punishing, but that the admiration or sympathy provided by peers who hear someone being scolded may serve to reinforce the student's misbehavior. When the peers no longer hear a person being criticized by the teacher, they may cease to reward him by their attention.

Regardless of which interpretation is correct, the technique of quietly reprimanding a student for misbehavior may be preferred by some teachers to that of ignoring misbehavior. If a teacher finds it almost impossible to ignore disruptive behavior, as many do, the use of private reprimands for this behavior may be as effective as ignoring it. And as the authors suggest, praising appropriate behavior in combination with private reprimands for disruptive behavior may be the most effective way of reducing a child's misbehavior.

The Effects of the Intensity of a Teacher's Reprimands on Children's Behavior[1]

K. Daniel O'Leary[2]
and
Wesley C. Becker*†

ABSTRACT

Summary: Relative frequency of disruptive behaviors displayed by first grade children during "rest time" was recorded by observers and related to experimentally controlled variations in teacher's behavior. Disruptive behaviors were measured by observing individual children sequentially for five 10-second time intervals each, using a coding system developed earlier. During baseline disruptive behaviors occurred on the average in 54% of the time intervals. When appropriate behaviors were praised and disruptive behaviors were ignored, disruptive behaviors averaged 32%. In the next phase,

* K. Daniel O'Leary and Wesley C. Becker, "The Effects of the Intensity of a Teacher's Reprimands on Children's Behavior," *Journal of School Psychology* 7(1968) 8–11. Reprinted with permission.

† University of Illinois

[1] This study was supported by Research Grant HD 00881-05 from the National Institutes of Health. The authors are indebted to the classroom teacher, Mrs. Alice K. Cutler, and principal, Mr. Richard A. Sturgeon, for their generous cooperation.

[2] Now at the State University of New York at Stony Brook, Long Island.

quiet reprimands were found to
function similarly to praise (39%
disruptive). Loud reprimands
increased disruptive behaviors to
53%. In the final phase, the praise
and ignore procedure reduced
disruptive behaviors again to 35% of
the time intervals.

The teacher's "personality" has long been felt to be one of the most
important determinants of classroom atmosphere as well as of children's
learning. Anderson & Brewer (1946) conducted a series of related studies
concerning integrative vs. dominating teachers in which they maintained
that dominating or hostile teachers would affect children's adjustment
adversely. They considered dominative behaviors to be the use of force,
commands, threats, shame, and blame; integrative behaviors included
approval, sympathy, and questioning the child about his interests. The
children of a dominating teacher showed significantly higher frequencies
of nonconforming behavior than children of an integrative teacher: they
paid less attention to their work and engaged more in activities such as
looking around and whispering to their companions.

The intensity of a teacher's reprimands is probably one of the most
important aspects of the behavior of a teacher who is labeled hostile or
dominating. This pilot study was designed to examine the effects of
commands and reprimands made to be audible to the whole class vs.
reprimands made very quietly. The five conditions of this study were: (I)
base period, (II) praise appropriate behavior, ignore disruptive behavior,
(III) reprimand disruptive behavior quietly, (IV) reprimand disruptive
behavior in a manner audible to the whole class, (V) praise appropriate
behavior, ignore disruptive behavior.

METHOD

SUBJECTS

A first grade class of 19 children were the subjects in this study. The 17
children in the class who were tested by the school had a mean IQ score
of 103 (CTMM).

OBSERVATIONS

Two college students observed a sample of children in varying order for
50 seconds each per day during the children's rest period. The disruptive

behaviors of selected children were rated for their occurrence or non-occurrence during five consecutive ten-second intervals. The rest period lasted 10 to 15 minutes so that about half of the children were observed each day. The children to be observed each day were chosen at random before the observers entered the classroom. The disruptive behavior schedule developed by Becker, Madsen, Arnold, & Thomas (1967) was used to record behavior. In general these behaviors consisted of talking, walking around the room, playing with objects in their desks, and turning to look at their neighbors. The reliability of observations was calculated by dividing the total number of agreements by the total number of agreements plus disagreements. An agreement was scored if both observers recorded the same behavior within the same ten second interval. A disagreement was scored if one observer recorded a behavior and the other observer did not. The average of six reliability checks made throughout the study was 82%. The overall level of disruptive behavior was represented by the percentage of intervals in which one or more of the disruptive behaviors occurred.

PROCEDURE

The base period lasted ten days and reflected the frequency of disruptive pupil behavior during rest period under usual classroom procedures. The teacher was asked to handle the children as she normally did. The observers were in the classroom for one month before any baseline data were recorded.[3] The initial attention-seeking behaviors of the children were effectively eliminated by this time.

Observations during the base period indicated that the teacher responded to the children with praise or reprimands approximately 12 times during each rest period. Consequently, for the remainder of the study the teacher was asked to respond to the children approximately 12 times during rest periods.

The second phase consisted of the use of praise for appropriate behavior and ignoring disruptive behavior. There were eight observations during phase two. The teacher was asked to praise appropriate behavior and ignore disruptive behavior throughout the day for the remainder of the study, except during the experimental manipulations of her behavior at rest period to be discussed next.

---

[3] Prior to the investigation of teacher reprimands, a procedure was initiated in which children received points and candy for academic and social achievement. Repeated measurements of the children's behavior during the base period indicated that this procedure did not reduce deviant behavior during the rest period. Consequently, the present study was performed during the children's rest period even though the children continued to receive points and candy for appropriate behavior at other times during the day.

During phase three the teacher was instructed to reprimand the children for disruptive behavior in a way which would be audible only to the reprimanded child. In contrast, during phase four, reprimands were to be audible to all children in the room. There were seven days of observation during phase three and five days of observation during phase four. Phase five consisted of four days of praising appropriate behavior and ignoring deviant behavior. Throughout these last three phases the teacher attempted to praise or reprimand about 12 times during the 10 minute rest period.

RESULTS

During the base period there was an average of 54% deviant behavior. The children talked incessantly. They would look at each other and make faces. They would play with things in their desks, and a few children would even walk around the room when they were supposed to be resting. Repeated reports by observers indicated that there was little use of a praise and frequent use of reprimands. During phase II deviant behavior dropped to 32%: there were approximately 12 praise comments per period and only two instances of reprimands. The average percentage of deviant behavior during phase III was 39%, which was not significantly different from phase II. The teacher reprimanded the children approximately 11 times per day during phase III and no praise comments were recorded. Reprimands audible to the whole class during phase IV resulted in a significant increase in deviant behavior (53%) when compared to phase II. The teacher reprimanded the children approximately 14 times per day during phase IV, and no praise comments were recorded. A return to praising appropriate behavior and ignoring deviant behavior during the four days of phase V was again associated with a reduction in deviant behavior (35%). The teacher praised the children approximately 10 times per day during phase V. On the fifth day of observations in phase V the teacher told the children that they could get a surprise if they were good resters. She praised the children lavishly and not one deviant behavior was observed.

DISCUSSION

This study confirmed the results of Becker et al. (1967) who found that praising appropriate behavior and ignoring disruptive behavior resulted in a decrease in disruptive behavior. The results also suggest that not all

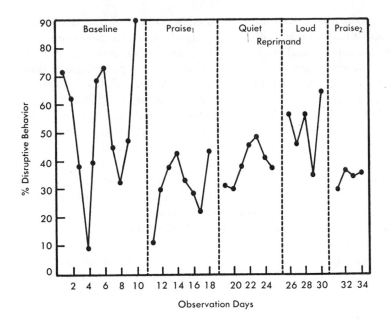

Figure 1

Percentage of disruptive behavior during rest period as a function of experimental phases. Each datum point is based on a sample of 8 to 15 children observed for 50 seconds each.

responses to disruptive behavior lead to an increase in the rate of deviant behavior. Although there are experiments which demonstrate that "attention" to disruptive behavior was associated with an increase in the frequency of disruptive behavior (Allen, Hart, Buell, Harris, & Wolf, 1964; Harris, Wolf, & Baer, 1964), the particular make-up of the attentional response to disruptive behavior is obviously important. A teacher who calmly walks over to a child and asks him to put his head down on his desk affects a child differently than does a teacher who yells, "Johnny, put your head down!"

The manner in which a teacher responds to disruptive behavior is of special importance because it is not easy for a teacher to ignore many disruptive behaviors. Even if a teacher did ignore disruptive behavior, peers often reinforce such behavior by laughing and watching the child who misbehaves. Some attempts by teachers to praise appropriate· behavior and ignore disruptive behavior result in pandemonium (O'Leary, Evans, & Becker, 1967). Children who are behavior problems in school probably have been subject to a great deal of punitive control at home, and a teacher who yells and commands her children may elicit undesirable conditioned emotional reactions which provide the stimuli for many inappropriate behaviors. In addition, the repeated use of verbal reprimands which are not backed up by punishment will lead to a lessening of their effectiveness. As Anderson and Brewer (1946) concluded, the dominating teacher incites resistance and defeats her own purpose. Praise for appropriate behavior and calm but firm reprimands are probably the most useful combination of social stimuli for maintaining appropriate behavior for most young children.

This pilot study suggests the importance of further investigation of the functional properties of various ways of administering reprimands. Time limitations restricted the experimental variations possible within the present study. To demonstrate more clearly the effects of quiet reprimands, it would have been desirable to return to baseline conditions between the first praise and quiet reprimands conditions. However, the facts that quiet reprimands were as effective as praise and that loud reprimands were not effective provide fairly convincing evidence on the difference in function of these two forms of reprimands.

References

Allen, K. E., Hart, B., Buell, J. S., Harris, F. R., & Wolf, M. M. Effects of social reinforcement on isolate behavior of a nursery school child. *Child Development,* 1964, *35,* 511–518.

Anderson, H. H., & Brewer, J. E. Studies of teacher's classroom personalities. II. Effects of teachers' dominative and integrative contacts on children's classroom behavior. *Applied Psychological Monographs,* No. 8. 1946.

Becker, W. C., Madsen, C. H., Arnold, C. T., & Thomas, D. R. The contingent use of teacher attention and praise in reducing classroom behavior problems. *Journal of Special Education,* 1967, *1,* 287–307.

Harris, F. R., Wolf, M. M., & Baer, D. M. Effects of social reinforcement on child behavior. *Young Children,* 1964, *20,* 8–17.

O'Leary, K. D., Evans, M., & Becker, W. C. Token reinforcement in a public school: A replication and systematic analysis. Unpublished manuscript, University of Illinois, 1967.

Although this study does not involve any unusual techniques, it illustrates clearly some of the practical issues that are involved in conducting a behavior modification project. The study was performed with high school students in a normal classroom, a group still rare as subjects for behavior modification projects. The inappropriate behaviors which the teacher wanted to reduce were talking out of turn and turning around in one's seat. The authors utilized a multiple baseline approach to avoid the necessity for a reversal phase. Therefore they first initiated the procedures to affect talking and only later applied the same procedures to reduce the amount of turning around. The fact that each behavior decreased only after the procedures which were predicted to reduce its frequency were instituted suggests that the teacher's behavior was indeed the factor affecting the students rather than simply maturation. The use of a control classroom taught by the same teacher lends further credence to this belief.

An interesting aspect of this program is that verbal criticism was used for inappropriate talking or turning around as well as praise for appropriate behavior. The articles in this book by Madsen et al. and O'Leary and Becker found that public verbal disapproval was actually a positive reinforcer for the elementary school children in their studies who were constantly getting out of their seats or misbehaving during a rest period. McAllister and his colleagues seemed to find just the opposite, since the frequency of inappropriate talking continued to be very low after praise for being quiet during the first two minutes of class was discontinued. Whether this difference was due to the age level of the students, to the fact that the majority of students in the present study were from lower-class families and thus might be more used to aversive control, or to the personality of the teacher cannot be ascertained. As the authors point out, the informational aspects of the comments may have been as important as the motivational ones.

One final thing to notice about the article is its description of the teacher's reactions to the practical difficulties in administering the procedures. As they point out, "the overall judgment of the teacher was that the procedures of recording and dispensing contingent consequences did, indeed, interfere with her teaching but that the results obtained more than compensated for this."

The Application of Operant Conditioning Techniques in a Secondary School Classroom[1]

Loring W. McAllister,
James G. Stachowiak,
Donald M. Baer,
and
Linda Conderman*†

ABSTRACT

The effects of teacher praise and disapproval on two target behaviors, inappropriate talking and turning around, were investigated in a high school English class of 25 students. The contingencies were applied to all students in the experimental class utilizing a multiple baseline experimental design in which the contingencies were aimed first at decreasing inappropriate talking behavior and then at decreasing inappropriate turning behavior. Observations were made of both

* Loring W. McAllister, James G. Stachowiak, Donald M. Baer and Linda Conderman, "The Application of Operant Conditioning Techniques in a Secondary School Classroom," *Journal of Applied Behavior Analysis* 2(1969): 277–285. Reprinted with permission. Copyright 1969 by the Society for the Experimental Analysis of Behavior, Inc.

† University of Kansas and Lawrence High School

[1] This study is based upon a dissertation submitted by the senior author to the Department of Psychology, University of Kansas in partial fulfillment of the requirements for the degree of doctor of philosophy. The authors express appreciation to Mr. William Medley, Principal, and Mr. Max Stalcup, Head Guidance Counselor, at Lawrence (Kansas) Senior High School for their assistance and cooperation in the conduct of the study. Reprints may be obtained from Loring W. McAllister, Western Mental Health Center, Inc., 438 West Main Street, Marshall, Minnesota 56258.

student and teacher behavior. The results demonstrated that the combination of disapproval for the target behaviors and praise for appropriate, incompatible behaviors substantially reduced the incidence of the target behaviors in the experimental class. Observations of these behaviors in a control class of 26 students taught by the same teacher revealed no particular changes. The findings emphasize the importance of teacher-supplied social contingencies at the secondary school level.

Numerous studies have reported the effectiveness of operant conditioning techniques in modifying the behavior of children in various situations. Harris, Wolf, and Baer (1964), in a series of studies on pre-school children, described the effectiveness of contingent teacher attention in modifying inappropriate behavior. Hall and Broden (1967), Patterson (1965), Rabb and Hewett (1967), and Zimmerman and Zimmerman (1962) have demonstrated the usefulness of teacher-supplied contingent social reinforcement in reducing problem behaviors and increasing appropriate behaviors of young children in special classrooms. Becker, Madsen, Arnold, and Thomas (1967); Hall, Lund, and Jackson (1968); and Madsen, Becker, and Thomas (1968) extended these techniques into the regular primary school classroom and demonstrated their effectiveness there. In all of the above studies, only a limited number of children were studied in each situation, usually one or two per classroom.

Thomas, Becker, and Armstrong (1968) studied the effects of varying teachers' social behaviors on the classroom behaviors of an entire elementary school classroom of 28 students. By observing 10 children per session, one at a time, they demonstrated the effectiveness of approving teacher responses in maintaining appropriate classroom behaviors. Bushell, Wrobel, and Michaelis (1968) also applied group contingencies (special events contingent on earning tokens for study behaviors) to an entire class of 12 preschool children.

There has been an effort to extend the study of teacher-supplied consequences to larger groups of preschool and elementary school subjects in regular classrooms, but no systematic research investigating these procedures has yet been undertaken in the secondary school classroom. Cohen, Filipczak, and Bis (1967) reported the application of various non-social contingencies (earning points, being "correct," and taking advanced educational courses) in modifying attitudinal and academic behaviors of adolescent inmates in a penal institution. But there is no record of investigations into the effects of teacher-supplied social consequences on the classroom behavior of secondary school students in regular classrooms.

At present, the usefulness of contingent teacher social reinforcement in the management of student classroom behaviors is well documented on the preschool and primary elementary school levels, particularly when the investigation focuses on a limited number of children in the classroom. Systematic replication now requires that these procedures be extended to larger groups of students in the classroom and to students in the upper elementary and secondary grades. The present study sought to investigate the effects of teacher-supplied social consequences on the classroom behaviors of an entire class of secondary school students.

METHOD

SUBJECTS

Students

The experimental group was a low-track, junior-senior English class containing 25 students (12 boys and 13 girls). At the beginning of the study the ages ranged from 16 to 19 yr (mean 17.11 yr); I.Q.s ranged from 77 to 114 (mean 94.43). Approximately 80% of the students were from lower-class families; the remainder were from middle-class families. The control group was also a low-track, junior-senior English class of 26 students (13 boys and 13 girls). The ages ranged from 16 to 19 yr (mean 17.04 yr); I.Q.s ranged from 73 to 111 (mean 91.04). About 76% of these students were from lower-class families, 16% were from middle-class families and 4% were from upper-middle to upper-class families. The experimental class met in the mornings for a 70-min period and the control class met in the afternoons for a 60-min period.

Teacher

The teacher was 23 yr old, female, middle class, and held a Bachelor's degree in education. She had had one year's experience in teaching secondary level students, which included a low-track English class. She taught both the experimental and control classes in the same classroom and utilized the same curriculum content for both. She stated that she had been having some difficulties in controlling classroom behavior in both classes and volunteered to cooperate in the experiment in the interest of improving her teaching-management skills. She stated that she had been able to achieve some rapport with these students during the two months that school had been in session. She described the students, generally, as performing poorly in academic work and ascribed whatever academic behaviors she was able to observe in them as being the result of her rapport with them. She stated that she was afraid that she would destroy this rapport if she attempted to exercise discipline over inappropriate classroom behaviors.

PROCEDURES

The basic design utilized was the common pretest-posttest control group design combined with the use of a multiple baseline technique (Baer, Wolf, and Risley, 1968) in the experimental class.

Target Behaviors

Both classes were observed for two weeks to ascertain general occurrence rates of various problem behaviors that had been described by the teacher. Inappropriate talking and turning around were selected as target behaviors because of their relatively high rate of occurrence. Inappropriate talking was defined as any audible vocal behavior engaged in by a student without the teacher's permission. Students were required to raise their hands to obtain permission to talk, either to the teacher or to other students, except when general classroom discussions were taking place, in which cases a student was not required to obtain permission to talk if his statements were addressed to the class and/or teacher and were made within the context of the discussion. Inappropriate turning was defined as any turning-around behavior engaged in by any student while seated in which he turned more than 90 degrees in either direction from the position of facing the front of the room. Two exceptions to this definition were made: turning behavior observed while in the process of transferring material to or from the book holder in the bottom of the desk was considered appropriate, as was any turning that took place when a student had directly implied permission to turn around. Examples of the latter exception would be when the class was asked to pass papers up or down the rows of desks, or when students turned to look at another student who was talking appropriately in the context of a recitation or discussion.

Observation and Recording

Behavior record forms were made up for recording observed target behaviors in both classes. A portion of the form is illustrated in Fig. 1. The forms for the experimental class contained 70 sequentially numbered boxes for each behavior; the forms for the control class contained 60 sequentially numbered boxes for each behavior (covering the 70- and 60-min class periods, respectively). The occurrence of a target behavior during any minute interval of time (*e.g.*, during the twenty-fifth minute of class time) was recorded by placing a check mark in the appropriate box for that interval (*e.g.*, box 25) beside the behavior listed. Further occurrences of that behavior during that particular interval were not recorded. Thus, each time interval represented a dichotomy with respect to each behavior: the behavior had or had not occurred during that interval of time. A daily quantified measurement of each behavior was obtained by dividing the number of intervals that were checked by the total number of intervals in the class period, yielding a percentage of intervals in which the behavior occurred at least once. Time was kept by referral to a large, easily readable wall clock whose minute hand moved 1 min at a time.

Behaviors were recorded daily during all conditions by the teacher. Reliability of observation was checked by using from one to two additional observers (student teachers and the senior author) who visited the classes twice per week. Students in this particular school were thought to be quite accustomed to observers, due to the large amount of classroom observation done there by student teachers from a nearby university. Except for the senior author and teacher, other observers were not made aware of changes in experimental conditions. Reliability was assessed by comparing the behavior record forms of the teacher and observers after each class period in which both teacher and observers recorded behavior. A percentage of agreement for each target behavior was computed, based on a ratio of the number of intervals on which all recorders agreed (*i.e.*, that the behavior had or had not occurred) to the total number of intervals in the period. Average reliability for talking behavior was 90.49% in the experimental class (range 74 to 98%) and 89.49% in the control class (range 78 to 96%). Average reliability for turning behavior was 94.27% in the experimental class (range 87 to 98%) and 90.98% in the control class (range 85 to 96%).

In addition, two aspects of the teacher's behavior were recorded during all conditions by the observers when present: (a) the number of inappropriate talking or turning instances that occasioned a verbal reprimand from the teacher, and (b) the number of direct statements of praise dispensed by the teacher for appropriate behaviors. These behaviors were recorded by simply tallying the number of instances in which they were observed on the reverse side of the observer's form. Reliability between observers was checked by computing a percentage of agreement between them on the number of instances of each type of behavior observed. Average reliability for reprimand behavior was 92.78% in the experimental class (range 84 to 100%) and 94.84% in the control class (range 82 to 100%). Average reliability for praise behavior was 98.85% in the experimental class (range 83 to 100%) and 97.65% in the control class (range 81 to 100%).

Baseline Condition

During the Baseline Condition, the two target behaviors and teacher behaviors were recorded in both the experimental and control classes. The teacher was asked to behave in her usual manner in both classrooms and no restrictions were placed on any disciplinary techniques she wished to use. The Baseline Condition in the experimental class was continued for 27 class days (approximately five weeks) to obtain as clear a picture as possible of the student and teacher behaviors occurring.

Experimental Condition I

This first experimental condition began in the experimental class on the twenty-eighth day when the teacher initiated various social consequences contingent on inappropriate talking behavior aimed at lowering the amount of this behavior taking place. The procedures agreed upon with the teacher for the application of social consequences were as follows:

1. The teacher was to attempt to disapprove of all instances of inappropriate talking behavior whenever they occurred with a direct, verbal, sternly given

Minute No.	1	2	3	4	5	6	7	8	9	10	11	12	13	14	15	16	17	18	19	20	21
Talking																					
Turning																					

Figure 1

Portion of behavior record form used to record incidence of target behavior.

reproof. Whenever possible, the teacher was to use students' names when correcting them. The teacher was instructed not to mention any other inappropriate behavior (*e.g.*, turning around) that might also be occurring at the time. Examples of reprimands given were: "John, be quiet!," "Jane, stop talking!," "Phil, shut up!," "You people, be quiet!." It was hypothesized that these consequences constituted an aversive social consequence for inappropriate talking.

2. The teacher was asked not to threaten students with or apply other consequences, such as keeping them after school, exclusion from class, sending them to the Assistant Principal, *etc.* for inappropriate talking or for any other inappropriate behavior.

3. The teacher was to praise the entire class in the form of remarks like: "Thank you for being quiet!," "Thank you for not talking!," or "I'm delighted to see you so quiet today!" according to the following contingencies: (a) During the first 2 min of class, praise at the end of approximately each 30-sec period in which there had been no inappropriate talking. (b) During the time in which a lecture, recitation, or class discussion was taking place, praise the class at the end of approximately each 15-min period in which no inappropriate talking had occurred. (c) When silent seatwork had been assigned, do not interrupt the period to praise, but praise the class at the end of the period if no inappropriate talking had occurred during the period. (d) At the end of each class make a summary statement concerning talking behavior, such as: "Thank you all for being so quiet today!," or "There has been entirely too much talking today, I'm disappointed in you!," or, "You have done pretty well in keeping quiet today, let's see if you can do better tomorrow!"

The concentration of praising instances during the first 2-min of class was scheduled because the baseline data revealed inappropriate talking as particularly frequent at this time.

Although the teacher continued to record instances of turning behavior, she was instructed to ignore this behavior in the experimental class during Experimental Condition I. In effect, baseline recording of turning behavior continued during this Condition. No changes were made in the teacher's behavior in the control class.

Experimental Condition II

After Experimental Condition I had been in effect in the experimental class for 26 class days and had markedly reduced talking behavior (see Results), Experimental Condition II was put into effect on the fifty-fourth day of the study. In this condition, the contingent social consequences for talking behavior in the experimental class were continued and, in addition, the teacher initiated the same system of contingent social consequences for turning behavior, with the aim of reducing the amount of this behavior occurring. This subsequent provision of similar consequences, first for one behavior and then for another, constitutes the multiple baseline technique.

The procedures agreed upon for providing reprimands for inappropriate turning behavior were the same as those for talking behaviors, except that the teacher referred to "turning" instead of "talking" in her reproofs. She could now also mention both behaviors in her reproof if a student happened to be doing both. The procedures regarding the application of praise contingent on not turning around were also the same as before, except that the higher frequency of praising during the first 2 min of class was not used. Also, the teacher could now combine her positive remarks about not talking and not turning if such were appropriate to existing conditions. Finally, since inappropriate talking behavior had been reduced considerably by this time, the procedure of praising every 30 sec during the first 2 min of class was dropped. As before, no changes were made in the teacher's behavior in the control class.

RESULTS

Because data were not collected on individual students, it is not possible to specify exactly how many students were involved in either inappropriate talking or turning behavior. The observers and teacher agreed that over one-half of the students in both classes were involved in inappropriate talking behavior and that about one-third of the students in both classes were involved in inappropriate turning behavior.

TALKING BEHAVIOR

Figure 2 indicates the daily percentages of intervals of inappropriate talking behavior in the experimental and control classes throughout the study. During the Baseline Condition in the experimental class and the equivalent period in the control class (Days 1 through 27), the average daily percentage of inappropriate talking intervals was 25.33% in the experimental class and 22.81% in the control class. The two classes were thus approximately equivalent with respect to the amount of inappropriate talking behavior in each before the experimental interventions were made in the experimental class. As can be seen, the introduction of the contingencies in Experimental Condition I on Day 28 immediately reduced the percentage of intervals of inappropriate talking behavior in the experimental class. From this point on, the amount of inappropriate talking behavior in the experimental class continued to decrease and finally stabilized at a level below 5%. Meanwhile, the control class continued to manifest its previous level of inappropriate talking behavior. In the period from Day 28 through Day 62, when the study was concluded, the average daily percentage of inappropriate talking intervals in the control class was 21.51%, compared with an average of 5.34% in the experimental class.

TURNING BEHAVIOR

The results obtained with the second target behavior, inappropriate turning around, can be seen in Fig. 3, which indicates the daily percentages of intervals of inappropriate turning behavior in both classes during the study. During the Baseline Condition in the experimental class and the equivalent period in the control class (Days 1 through 53), the level of inappropriate turning behavior was slowly increasing in both classes. The average daily percentage of inappropriate turning intervals during this time was 15.13% in the experimental class and 14.45% in the control class. As with talking behavior, the two classes were roughly equivalent in the amount of inappropriate turning behavior observed before experimental interventions were made. The introduction of Experimental Condition II contingencies on Day 54 again immediately reduced the percentage of inappropriate turning intervals in the experimental class. This behavior continued to decrease during the remaining days of the study. In the control class, the level of inappropriate turning behavior remained essentially the same. In the period from Day 54 through Day 62, the average daily percentage of inappropriate turning intervals in the control class was 17.22% and in the experimental class was 4.11%.

TEACHER BEHAVIOR

During the Baseline period on talking behavior, the average number of instances of inappropriate talking per class period that received some type of verbal reprimand from the teacher was 25.76% in the experimental class and 22.23% in the control class. The majority of these verbal responses took the form of saying, "Shhh!". On occasion, observers noted that the teacher corrected students directly, using their names. On several occasions she made general threats, stating that she would keep people after school if talking did not subside; however, she was never observed to carry out this kind of threat. During this period there were no observations of the teacher's dispensing any praise for not talking. During Experimental Condition I, the teacher disapproved of an average of 93.33% of inappropriate talking instances per class period in the experimental class. In the control class during this time, she disapproved of an average of 21.38% of inappropriate talking instances per class period. She also praised on an average of 6.07 occasions per experimental class period, contingent on not talking, during this time. With two exceptions, she was not observed directly to praise not talking in the control class.

During the Baseline period on inappropriate turning behavior, the average percentage of inappropriate turning instances per class period that received verbal reprimands from the teacher was 12,84% in the experimental class and 13.09% in the control class. Most of these were simple instructions, like, "Turn around!", and she used the student's

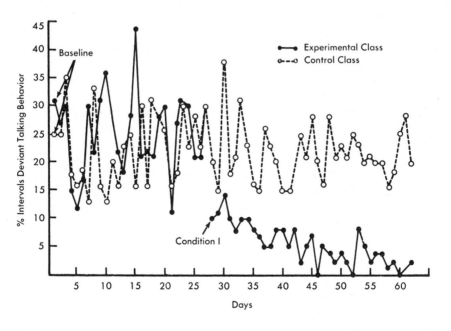

Figure 2

Daily percentages of intervals of inappropriate talking behavior in experimental and control classes during Baseline and Experimental Condition I periods.

name in most cases. During Experimental Condition II, the average percentage of inappropriate turning instances per class period that occasioned disapproving responses from the teacher was 95.50% in the experimental class and 18.50% in the control class. In addition, she praised on an average of 5.75 occasions per experimental class period, contingent on not turning. In the control class she was not observed to provide any such praise for not turning.

DISCUSSION

The results indicate quite clearly that the statements of praise and disapproval by the teacher had consistent effects on the two target behaviors observed in the experimental class. Both behaviors decreased. That the statements were, in fact, responsible for the observed modifications in behavior was demonstrated through the multiple baseline procedure in which the target behaviors changed maximally only

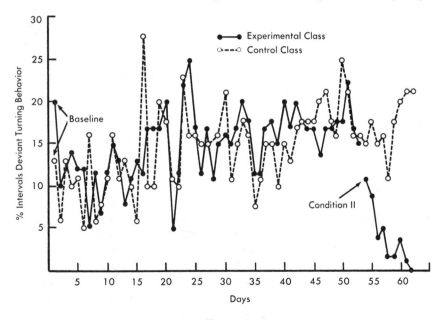

Figure 3

Daily percentages of intervals of inappropriate turning behavior in experimental and control classes during Baseline and Experimental Condition II periods.

when the statements were applied. The use of the control class data further substantiates this contention. The observations of teacher behavior in the study provide evidence that the program was being carried out as specified in the two classrooms.

The design of the study does not make it possible to isolate the separate effects of the teacher's statements of praise and disapproval on the students' behaviors. It is possible that one or the other of these was more potent in achieving the observed results. In addition to the possibility that statements of praise or disapproval, in themselves, might have differed in their effectiveness in modifying behavior, the different manner in which these two types of statements were delivered may have resulted in differing effects. The design, it will be remembered, called for disapproving statements to be delivered to individual students, while praise was delivered to the class as a whole. This resulted in a sudden onset of numerous disapproving statements delivered to individual students when Experimental Condition I was put into effect. The observers agreed that the students seemed "stunned" when this essentially radical shift in stimulus conditions took place. The immediate and marked decrease in inappropriate talking behavior at this point may have resulted because of this shift. The phenomenon can be compared to the sudden response rate reductions observed in animals when stimulus conditions are shifted suddenly. The decrease in inappropriate turning behavior observed when Experimental Condition II was put into effect, while immediate, was not of the same magnitude as that observed previously. Perhaps some measure of adaptation to this type of stimulus shift had taken place. Regardless of the possible reasons for the immediate effects observed when the experimental conditions were put into effect, it is also true that the direction of these effects was maintained thereafter in both experimental conditions. The combination of praise and disapproval undoubtedly was responsible for this.

Assuming that praise statements were functioning as positive reinforcers for a majority of the experimental class, they may have operated not only directly to reinforce behaviors incompatible with inappropriate talking and turning but also to generate peer-group pressure to reduce inappropriate behavior because such statements were contingent on the entire class' behavior. Further studies are needed to investigate the effects of peer-group contingencies on individual behavior.

Although it appears that the statements of praise and disapproval by the teacher functioned as positive reinforcers and punishers, respectively, an alternative possibility exists. These statements may have been operating primarily as instructions that the students complied with. It is conceivable that had praise statements, for example, been delivered as instructions independent of the occurrence of inappropriate behavior the same results might have been obtained. Also, it should be noted that results obtained in other studies (Lovaas, Freitag, Kinder, Rubenstein, Schaeffer, and Simmons, 1964; Thomas, Becker, and Armstrong, 1968) indicate that disapproving adult behaviors do not have a unitary effect on children's behavior. What would appear to be punishing types of statements are sometimes found to function as positive reinforcers. Informal observations indicated that this seemed to be the case in this study, at least as far as one student was concerned.

Several comments may be made regarding the practical aspects of the present approach. The study further exemplifies the usefulness of the multiple baseline technique, which makes it unnecessary to reverse variables in order to demonstrate the specific effectiveness of the experimental variables. Many teachers and school administrators will undoubtedly find this approach more acceptable in their schools. The notion of reversing variables to reinstitute what is considered to be maladaptive or inappropriate behavior is extremely repugnant to many educators who are more interested in "getting results" than in experimental verification of the results obtained.

The study differs from most previous operant research in classrooms in that the focus was on recording and modifying target behaviors without specific regard to the individual students involved. Most earlier studies have focused on observing the behavior of one student at a time. With this approach, it takes considerable time to extend observations to an entire class and usually this is not done. While observations of an entire class are not always necessary from a practical point of view (i.e., only a few students are involved in inappropriate behaviors), the present approach does seem feasible when the number of students involved in one or more classes of inappropriate behavior is large. From an experimental point of view, this study was deficient in not providing more exact information as to the number of students actually involved in the target behaviors. Once this facet is determined, however, the essential approach seems quite feasible and practical.

It might be argued that a group-oriented approach will not function in the same way with all members of the group. This is potentially possible, if not probable. However, two practical aspects should be considered. In the first place, such an approach could conceivably remediate the total situation enough to allow the teacher to concentrate on those students who either have not responded or who have become worse. Secondly, perhaps a general reduction in inappropriate behavior is all the teacher desires. In this study, for example, the results obtained were, according to the teacher, more than enough to satisfy her. She did not, in other words, set a criterion of eliminating the target behaviors.

A significant practical aspect of this study was the amount of difficulty encountered by the teacher in recording behavior and delivering contingent praise and disapproval. It might be asked how she found time to teach when she was involved in these activities. Perhaps the best judge of the amount of difficulty involved with these techniques is the teacher herself. She reported that, initially, recording behaviors was difficult. The task did take considerable time and did interrupt her on-going teaching. On the other hand, the large amount of talking and other inappropriate behaviors occurring at the beginning of the study also interrupted her teaching. She felt that as the study went on she became more accustomed to recording and it became easier for her to accomplish. She pointed out that the fact that she usually positioned herself at her desk or rostrum also made recording somewhat easier because the forms were readily available. This was her usual position in the classroom; she did not change to make recording easier. Considerable time was required to deliver contingent praise and disapproval at the beginning of the experimental conditions. This also tended to interrupt teaching tasks as far as the teacher was concerned. However, she felt that this state of affairs did not last long because the target behaviors declined so immediately and rapidly. The overall judgment of the teacher was that the procedures of recording and dispensing contingent consequences did, indeed, interfere with her teaching but that the results obtained more than compensated for this. When the levels of inappropriate behavior had been lowered she felt she could carry out her teaching responsibilities much more efficiently and effectively than before. She felt strongly enough about the practicality and effectiveness of the techniques to present information and data on the study to her fellow teachers and to offer her services as a consultant to those who wanted to try similar approaches in their classrooms.

The senior author held frequent conferences with the teacher after class periods. The aim was to provide her with feedback regarding her performance in class. She was actively praised for appropriate modifications in her classroom behavior and for record-keeping behavior. Likewise, she was criticized for mistakes in her application of program contingencies.

Finally, the data of this experiment are considered significant by reason of the strong implication that teacher praise and disapproval can function to modify the behavior of high-school level students. This potentially extends the implications of earlier research accomplished on the pre-school and elementary levels.

References

Baer, D. M., Wolf, M. M., and Risley, T. R. Some current dimensions of applied behavior analysis. *Journal of Applied Behavior Analysis*, 1968, 1. 91–97.

Becker, W. C., Madsen, C. H., Jr. Arnold, C. R., and Thomas, D. R. The contingent use of teacher attention and praise in reducing classroom behavior problems. *Journal of Special Education*, 1967, 1, 287–307.

Bushell, D., Jr., Wrobel, P. A., and Michaelis, M. L. Applying "group" contingencies to the classroom study behavior of preschool children. *Journal of Applied Behavior Analysis*, 1968, 1, 55–61.

Cohen, H. L., Filipczak, J., and Bis, J. S. *Case I: an initial study of contingencies applicable to special education.* Silver Spring, Md.: Educational Facility Press—Institute for Behavioral Research, 1967.

Hall, R. V. and Broden, M. Behavior changes in brain-injured children through social reinforcement. *Journal of Experimental Child Psychology*, 1967, 5, 463–479.

Hall, R. V., Lund, D., and Jackson, D. Effects of teacher attention on study behavior. *Journal of Applied Behavior Analysis*, 1968, 1, 1–12.

Harris, F. R., Wolf, M. M., and Baer, D. M. Effects of adult social reinforcement on child behavior. *Young Children*, 1964, 20, 8–17.

Lövaas, O. I., Freitag, G., Kinder, M. I., Rubenstein, D. B., Schaeffer, B., and Simmons, J. B. *Experimental studies in childhood schizophrenia— establishment of social reinforcers.* Paper read at Western Psychological Assn., Portland, April, 1964.

Madsen, C. H., Becker, W. C., and Thomas, D. R. Rules, praise and ignoring: elements of elementary classroom control. *Journal of Applied Behavior Analysis*, 1968, 1, 139–150.

Patterson, G. R. An application of conditioning techniques to the control of a hyperactive child. In L. P. Ullman and L. Krasner (Eds.), *Case studies in behavior modification.* New York: Holt, Rinehart & Winston, 1966. Pp. 370–375.

Rabb, E. and Hewett, F. M. Developing appropriate classroom behaviors in a severely disturbed group of institutionalized kindergarten-primary children utilizing a behavior modification model. *American Journal of Orthopsychiatry*, 1967, 37, 313–314.

Thomas, D. R., Becker, W. C., and Armstrong, M. Production and elimination of disruptive classroom behavior by systematically varying teacher's behavior. *Journal of Applied Behavior Analysis*, 1968, I, 35–45.

Zimmerman, E. H. and Zimmerman, J. The alteration of behavior in a special classroom situation. *Journal of the Experimental Analysis of Behavior*, 1962, 5, 59–60.

Although Osborne's study was done with pre-teenaged students at a school for the deaf, the techniques he used should be applicable to a wide variety of students in many situations. Like the study by Madsen, Becker, Thomas, Koser, and Plager, this project had as its aim to reduce the amount of time that students spent out of their seats. The technique used by Osborne was very different, however. Students were permitted to have five minutes of free time if they were able to stay in their seats for a fifteen-minute period. Although technically this procedure was supposed to utilize positive reinforcement for an alternative behavior to standing, similar to the praise for sitting used in the Madsen study, it is likely that being required to remain in their seats while others had free time was viewed by those girls who had been standing as a mild punishment. In actual fact, as Osborne points out, it is not clear whether the free time periods constituted negative reinforcement in the form of escape from the unpleasant classroom situation or positive reinforcement, since the acts engaged in during the brief recesses were enjoyable.

One feature of this study is its demonstration that one can gradually increase the amount of good behavior to be expected without losing control over the children's behavior. Thus, increasing the amount of time during which the girls had to sit in their seats to earn free time had no disruptive effect on their behavior. As expected, reversing the contingencies so that the girls earned a break only if they stood up at least once drastically increased the amount of standing; however it is a little surprising that a period of noncontingent reinforcement did not also increase the amount of standing. It is possible, therefore, that maturation or some other change in the school situation may have been partially responsible for their improved behavior; however, the technique of using free time as a reward is certainly worth trying.

Free-Time as a Reinforcer in the Management of Classroom Behavior[1]

J. Grayson Osborne*†

ABSTRACT

Six subjects, comprising one class at a school for the deaf, were given reinforcement consisting of time free from school work for remaining seated in the classroom. As a result, the frequency of leaving their chairs was sharply reduced. A second procedure presented free-time not contingent on remaining seated. Little change was seen in the already lowered response rate. An extension of the time required to be seated with corresponding reduction in the number of daily free-time periods did not reduce the effectiveness of the procedure. A one-day observation after six weeks indicated that the procedure was still effective. A one-day

* J. Grayson Osborne, "Free-Time as a Reinforcer in the Management of Classroom Behavior," *Journal of Applied Behavior Analysis* 2(1969): 113–118. Reprinted with permission. Copyright 1969 by the Society for the Experimental Analysis of Behavior, Inc.
† New Mexico School for the Deaf
[1] Reprints may be obtained from the author, New Mexico School for the Deaf, 1060 Cerrillos Road, Santa Fe, New Mexico 87501.

contingency reversal, requiring
subjects to leave their chairs at least
once during each seated period in
order to receive free-time,
substantially raised the frequency of
out-of-seat responses.

Recent studies have indicated that classroom behavior of humans can be
successfully manipulated given proper application of the controlling
environmental contingencies. Homme, C. de Baca, Devine, Steinhorst,
and Rickert (1963) reported that preschool nursery children would
engage in the low-probability behaviors of sitting quietly and looking at a
blackboard if those behaviors were intermittently followed by the
opportunity to engage in higher-probability behaviors such as running or
shouting. Thomas, Becker, and Armstrong (1968) showed that disruptive
behavior in the classroom can be manipulated as a function of teacher's
behavior. They further suggested that one important classroom
management device is the use of approval for appropriate behavior.

The usefulness of the token economy has also been proven in the
classroom. Wolf, Giles, and Hall (1968) demonstrated that overall
achievement gains could be nearly doubled in a remedial classroom, using
a token reinforcement system, over what was achieved in the regular
classroom without the token system. Wolf *et al.* (1968) estimated the
average cost of their token system at $250 for each of the 16 students for
a year. Other investigators have produced gains in specific academic areas
utilizing token systems. For example, Staats and Butterfield (1965)
produced a large number of reading responses in a non-reading juvenile
delinquent. The cost for that subject was $20.31 over 40 hr of work.
Staats, Minke, Goodwin, and Landeen (1968) extended Staats' earlier
work to 18 junior-high aged subjects. Reading responses were
strengthened over 38.2 hr of training at a cost of approximately $22 per
subject. In both studies, significant achievement gains in reading resulted.

Birnbrauer, Bijou, Wolf, and Kidder (1965) in their work with
institutionalized retardates showed that the token economy need not be
expensive to be effective. Extrapolation from their data, which indicate
an average payoff of 5¢ per week per student for a regular school year,
would suggest a financial cost of less than $20 for back-up reinforcers. In
an extension of their earlier work, these same investigators were able to
strengthen academic behavior within a similar token system. The costs
averaged approximately $7 per student for the 15 students in the class
over 1 yr (Birnbrauer, Wolf, Kidder, and Tague, 1965).

Studies utilizing the token economy have demonstrated its usefulness in education. However, in many cases the cost of providing back-up reinforcers is outside the financial ability of most institutions without special funding. In addition, most school administrations oppose paying their students for learning. The classroom management techniques propounded by Homme and Becker indicate that much behavior can be modified in the classroom without a token economy and its cost.

The present study illustrates a behavior management technique that can be used to control behavior in the classroom with no financial cost to the institution involved.

METHOD

A teacher approached the experimenter regarding her class's behavior. She was experiencing problems in maintaining students' attention. Discussion indicated that a major difficulty was the occurrence of behavior incompatible with academic behavior: students were often out of their chairs while the teacher was teaching. The teacher reported that this was disruptive to the entire class. Attempts to reseat students meant interruption of the teacher's presentation until calm was restored. The strong possibility existed that the behavior of students leaving their seats was being maintained by the time away from school work it provided.

SUBJECTS

Six girls at the New Mexico School for the Deaf ranged in age from 11 yr 8 months to 13 yr 8 months; they were grouped in one class because of poor school achievement and less than average intelligence.

Table 1

Subjects	Age	Achievement*	I.Q.**	Hearing Loss
1	12–10	2.1	74***	Severe
2	13–8	2.0	63	Severe-Profound
3	13–3	2.5	62	Severe-Profound
4	11–8	2.4	65	Profound
5	13–4	2.1	53	Profound
6	12–10	2.1	53	Severe

* Stanford Achievement Test (Elementary).
** Leiter International Performance Scale (1948 revision) except as noted.
*** Wechsler Intelligence Scale for Children (Performance Scale).

Table 1 contains a complete description of the subjects. None of the girls was described by the staff as a behavior problem.

The class was in session in the same room from 8:05 A.M. until 12:10 P.M. Monday through Friday with no scheduled recess. A once-weekly session in the school library provided the only regular occasion on which a scholastic activity took place outside the classroom. Physical education, home economics, and other activities took place in the afternoon elsewhere on campus.

PROCEDURES

Baseline Measurement

The overall procedure followed the standard single-organism, ABA design where each subject was her own control. Before instituting modification procedures, the frequency of occurrence of students leaving their seats was measured over five days. All data were recorded by the teacher on special data sheets, divided by subject, into successive time periods from 8:05 A.M. to 12:00 noon. The length of these periods was arbitrarily established at 15 min with each period separated from the former one by 5 min.

Response Definition

The response was easily defined. A subject attaining an upright position without teacher permission constituted an out-of-seat response. Construction of the one-piece chair-desks made it impossible to assume this position within the plane of the chair-desk. Hence, a subject was literally out of her seat before the response criterion was met. (Without the help of elaborate timing apparatus, it was not feasible to measure the time spent seated; hence, the use of an easily definable response, the converse of remaining seated.) In "emergencies," an out-of-seat response was allowed with teacher permission. Sharpening pencils, getting a drink of water, going to the restroom and the like were allowed only on "free" time.

The teacher continued her usual policy with respect to all other negative behavior throughout the study. Generally, this involved verbal reprimands, turning a student's chair-desk toward the wall, or taking the student to the principal's office. These consequences generally followed severe disobedience, foul language, or temper outbursts.

Reliability

Responses were also recorded by the experimenter and a supervising teacher on separate occasions. The supervisor was largely unaware of the nature of the project. She was given a chart identical to the teacher's, told how the response was defined, and asked to note instances of the behavior when she visited the classroom during her regular observation periods. Generally, the length of the supervisor's stay was for one or two of the seated segments. The experimenter also occasionally recorded response occurrences. A total of 15 seated segments over the course of the study was observed by the supervisor or the experimenter in which the six subjects were present. Over these 90 observations the teacher's record was compared with the supervisor's or the experimenter's. Reliability was computed by dividing the sum of agreements and disagreements between teacher and observer into total agreements. In this way, reliability was checked in each phase of the study on approximately 18% of the days the study was in effect. On none of the 90 observations did the teacher's record differ from that of the supervisor or the experimenter.

First Free-Time Contingent Period

To begin the modification, the teacher presented the following instructions to the class at 8:05 A.M.: "From now on we will be doing something new. I want you all to sit in your chairs. You must not leave them without asking me. If you can do that, you will be given five minutes of your own time at 8:20."

The teacher announced each successive free-time period as it occurred. If the teacher was engaging in a formal presentation to the class, this presentation was halted during the free-time period. If a student left her seat during a seated segment, the teacher said: "You forgot, no break." Otherwise, her presentation of the ongoing seat work was continued.

Free-time was restricted to the interior of the classroom with the exception of trips to the restroom or water fountain. The subjects were not forced to get up during free-time periods if they did not want to. Those who had not earned the free-time were required to remain seated and working and not allowed to interact with their peers during that period. At the end of a free-time period, the teacher indicated that it was time to begin again and when the next free-time period would come. Five days were completed under this condition.

Free-Time Non-Contingent Period

To start this period the teacher presented the following instructions at 8:05 A.M. of the eleventh day: "I want you all to sit in your chairs. You must not leave them without asking me; but if you forget, you will still be given your break." In this section of the study if a student left her seat during a seated segment, the response was noted but the teacher said nothing and the class activity continued.

Five days were allowed under this condition.

Second Free-Time Contingent Period

The second modification period began immediately after the non-contingent free-time condition was terminated. To reinstate modification conditions the teacher repeated the set of instructions delivered in the first modification period. Thirty-five days were recorded under these conditions.

Pursuant to another modification in the class, a point system for completion of academic work was introduced on Day 28. Within this system, the subjects could earn check marks and gummed stars on a chart, and were occasionally given a field trip outside of school time. In all other respects the class was conducted as usual.

Third Free-Time Contingent Period

The teacher noted that the students did not always use all of their free-time periods. That is, for one or two of these periods each day some students would remain seated and perhaps working. Thus, it was thought likely that an increase in seated time and a corresponding decrease in the number of free-time periods would not lessen the effectiveness of the procedure. Beginning on the fifty-first day of the study at 8:05 A.M., the teacher presented the following instructions to the class: "Starting today we will work until 8:30 before we take our break. Remember you must not leave your chairs without asking me. If you can do that, you will be given five minutes of your own time at 8:30."

For the remainder of the study seated segments were 25 min in length. Free-time periods remained 5-min long; however, lengthening each seated segment by 10 min reduced the number of free-time periods per morning from 12 to 8.

Post-Check

Approximately six weeks after the termination of data collection, a single day's post-check was made. The contingencies of the third free-time contingent period had been left in effect by the teacher throughout the intervening time.

Contingency Reversal

In the week following the post-check the teacher was asked to reverse the response requirement for a single day. At 8:05 A.M. that day she presented the following instructions to the class: "Today we will do something different. If you remain seated, you will not be allowed to take your break. You must get out of your seat at least once each period in order to have your break."

RESULTS

Figure 1 shows the rate of out-of-seat responses for each subject under the different procedures. The different procedures are separated by the vertical dashed lines. Omitted data points comprise days when a given subject was absent.

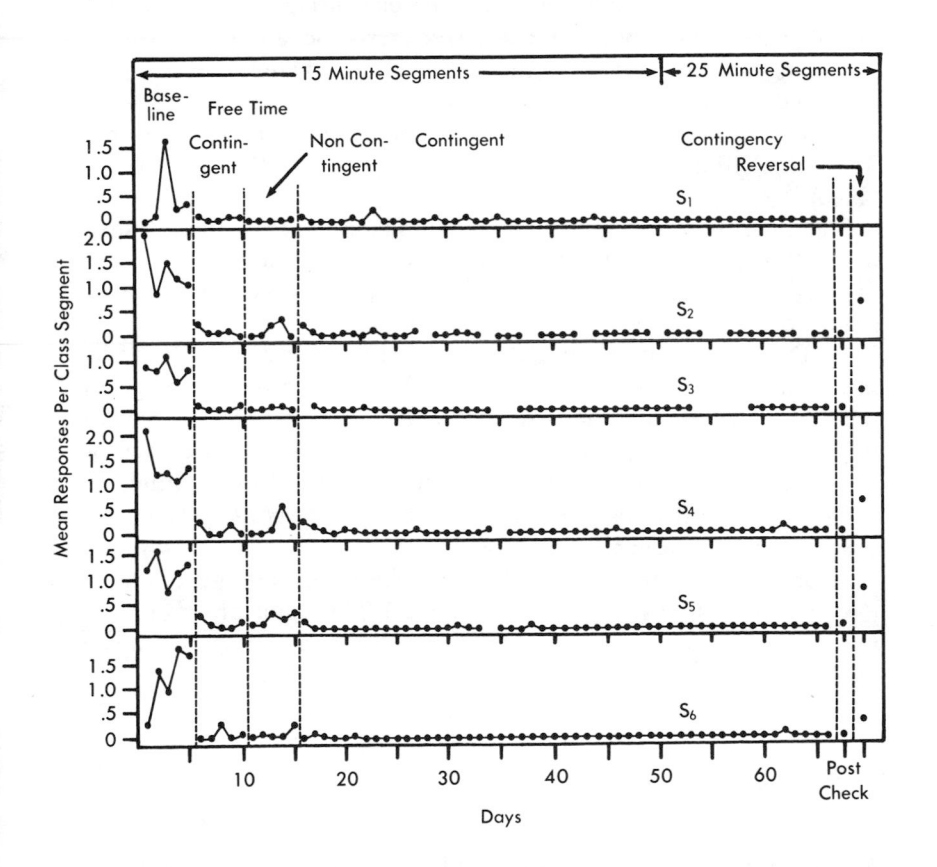

Figure 1

The average number of out-of-seat responses for each subject per class segment for each day of the study.

Before the reinforcement contingency was introduced (Days 1 to 5) the students engaged in slightly more than one out-of-seat response per 15-min segment. After the modification procedure was introduced, responding decreased sharply (Days 6 to 10). During the first free-time contingent period, only 0.08 responses took place per student in the average 15-min period. That is, a response occurred approximately once each 30 min. The difference between baseline and first modification periods was highly significant ($t = 47.35$; $p < 0.001$ one-tailed).

While the shapes of premodification base-lines were dissimilar for the six subjects, Fig. 1 shows that the effect of the procedure, a sharply reduced response rate, was similar for all.

When free-time periods were awarded non-contingently (Days 11 to 15), little change was noted in the lowered response rate (Fig. 1).

Making free-time periods again contingent on remaining seated produced another decrease in the frequency of the response. The difference between the free-time non-contingent period and the second free-time contingent period was significant ($t = 1.86$; $p < 0.05$ one-tailed).

Free-time periods contingent on remaining seated for 15-min segments were left in effect through Day 50. Inspection of the individual performances (Fig. 1) indicates that fewer responses occurred as that point was approached.

On Day 51 the seated segments were lengthened to 25 min. It can be seen that no responses occurred on 15 of the 16 days recorded under this procedure. On Day 62 (points "a" in Fig. 1), one student told two others that it was time for a break, when in fact it was not. These two responses were the only instances of out-of-seat behavior during this condition.

On the day of the post-check six weeks later, no responses were observed during the entire morning.

Approximately one week after the post-check the contingency was reversed. On that day, 25 responses occurred. This was a rate of one response approximately every 8 min, as compared to no responses for the entire morning during the post-check.

DISCUSSION

Reinforcing behavior that is compatible with learning would seem possible by offering brief periods of free-time from the learning environment. In this study, the amount of in-seat behavior was increased by making time away from school work contingent on remaining seated for specified periods of time.

Several alternative explanations could account for the effectiveness of the free-time periods as reinforcers in this study. No experimental manipulations were made which would favor one explanation over another.

If the aversiveness of the regular classroom environment is granted (Skinner, 1968), the presentation of free-time may have constituted an escape conditioning procedure. That is, by remaining seated for a given period of time, the subjects could escape seat work and the teacher's formal presentation for a 5-min period, while those who had been out of their seats in the preceding segment had to continue working.

On the other hand, the free-time periods afforded the subjects the opportunity to engage in positively reinforcing activities such as obtaining a drink of water, talking with classmates, or talking with the teacher about favored subjects; the free-time periods may, therefore, have been positive reinforcers. If that was in fact the case, the present procedure constituted operant conditioning of desirable classroom behavior by positive reinforcement.

Finally, the present results can be explained in terms of the Premack reinforcement principle. That principle states that one event is capable of reinforcing another event if the reinforcing event has a higher probability of occurrence and its occurrence is made contingent upon emission of a lower-probability behavior (Premack, 1959). In the present study, the high-probability behavior (*i.e.*, reinforcing event) was non-academic behavior which could be emitted during the free-time period contingent upon prior emission of the lower-probability behavior of remaining seated for a given time.

The possibility exists that the students came under instructional control when procedural changes were instituted. This is unlikely, however, in view of the fact that instructions were presented only once at the beginning of each procedural change. Hence, long-term maintenance of the behavior was probably due to the modification procedures.

The lack of clear change in the response rate when free-time (*i.e.*, reinforcement) was presented non-contingently may have been due to "adventitious" reinforcement. At the start of that procedure (Day 11), all subjects had attained nearly perfect performances in remaining seated to obtain free-time. That is, more in-seat behavior was occurring than its converse, out-of-seat behavior. Hence, at free-time presentation the behavior most likely to be occurring was in-seat behavior and, therefore, remaining seated may have been adventitiously maintained in strength by the subsequent presentation of the non-contingent free-time. The literature presents a similar case with pigeons (Herrnstein, 1966).

The use of the point system to increase academic output that began on Day 28 may have contributed to keeping the subjects seated. However, inspection of Fig. 1 shows that in the 10 days before Day 28, nearly 80% of the 60 subject-days in that period contained no out-of-seat responses.

In terms of financial outlay, the study provided a "cost-free" technique for managing classroom behavior available to most teachers. At the end of the study, total free-time per day equalled 40 min—a time approximately double a standard recess in the public school—but seemingly a reasonable payment to maintain the behavior of a special population. Although not attempted in the present study, it is conceivable that a further lengthening of the time required to be seated, and consequent reduction in the number and total daily duration of free-time periods, could have been successfully implemented.

References

Birnbrauer, J. S., Wolf, M. M., Kidder, J. D., and Tague, C. E. Classroom behavior of retarded pupils with token reinforcement. *Journal of Experimental Child Psychology.* 1965, 2, 219–235.

Birnbrauer, J. S., Bijou, S. W., Wolf, M. M., and Kidder, J. D. Programmed instruction in the classroom. In L. Ullmann and L. Krasner (Eds.), *Case studies in behavior modification.* New York: Holt, Rinehart & Winston, 1965. Pp. 358–363.

Herrnstein, R. J. Superstition: a corollary of the principles of operant conditioning. In W. K. Honig (Ed.), *Operant behavior: areas of research and application.* New York: Appleton-Century-Crofts, 1966. Pp. 33–51.

Homme, L. E., C. de Baca, P., Devine, J. V., Steinhorst, R., and Rickert, E. J. Use of the Premack principle in controlling the behavior of nursery school children. *Journal of the Experimental Analysis of Behavior,* 1963, 6, 544.

Premack, D. Toward empirical behavior laws: I. Positive reinforcement. *Psychological Review,* 1959, 66, 219–233.

Skinner, B. F. *The technology of teaching.* New York: Appleton-Century-Crofts, 1968.

Staats, A. W. and Butterfield, W. H. Treatment of non-reading in a culturally deprived juvenile delinquent: an application of reinforcement principles. *Child Development,* 1965, 36, 925–942.

Staats, A. W., Minke, K. A., Goodwin, W., and Landeen, J. Cognitive behavior modification: 'motivated learning' reading treatment with subprofessional therapy-technicians. *Behaviour Research and Therapy*, 1965, 5, 283–299.

Thomas, D. R., Becker, W. C., and Armstrong, M. Production and elimination of disruptive classroom behavior by systematically varying teacher's behavior. *Journal of Applied Behavior Analysis*, 1968, I, 35–45.

Wolf, M. M., Giles, D. K., and Hall, R. V. Experiments with token reinforcement in a remedial classroom. *Behaviour Research and Therapy*, 1968, 6, 51–64.

What are the implications of the use of contingent teacher attention to change the disruptive behavior of a few children upon the other children in the classroom? Ward and Baker observed the effects of the use of behavior modification techniques upon other children in the classroom as well as the experimental children. The results should be reassuring to those who worry about what happens to those who are not the subjects of the experiment: The control students did not significantly increase their disruptive behaviors and although there was a nonsignificant drop in the amount of attention paid by the teacher to these children, the proportion of the teacher's attention devoted to task-relevant behavior did not change. On a variety of psychological tests, no change in performance was found for either control or experimental children. It seems reasonable to conclude that teachers need not be concerned about neglecting the other children in the class if they decide to systematically alter the attention paid to some of the children.

Ward and Baker did not find dramatic changes in the experimental children, although the decrease in the proportion ⌐f deviant behavior and the increase in the proportion of teacher attention directed to task relevant behaviors were significant. They felt that the great decrease in the amount of disruptive behavior shown during special training sessions with the teachers and the target children should have generalized more strongly to the regular classroom setting. More detailed training of the teachers and monitoring of their classroom behaviors in the form of feedback might prove effective in facilitating this transfer. Whether or not some changes in test performance would have occurred had the behavior changes been greater is another unanswered question. One final point to consider is the author's suggestion that the percentage of disruptive behavior might have been expected to increase, since the experiment was done at the end of the school year. Their use of control children in four other first-grade classrooms should have provided data relevant to this hypothesis; however, no mention of the behavior of this second group of control children is given.

Reinforcement Therapy in the Classroom[1]

Michael H. Ward
and
Bruce L. Baker*†

ABSTRACT

Teachers were trained in the systematic use of attention and praise to reduce the disruptive classroom behavior of four first-grade children. Observation measures showed a significant improvement from baseline to treatment for these children and no significant changes

* Michael H. Ward and Bruce L. Baker, "Reinforcement Therapy in the Classroom," *Journal of Applied Behavior Analysis* (1968): 323–328. Reprinted with permission. Copyright 1968 by the Society for the Experimental Analysis of Behavior, Inc.
† Harvard University
[1] This research was supported in part by National Institute of Mental Health Grant No. 1-F1-MH-36, 634-01 (MTLH), and Harvard University Faculty Science Research Grant No. 33-493-68-1718. The authors wish to acknowledge the cooperation and assistance of Assistant Superintendent William Cannon of the Boston Public Schools, and Principal Gladys Wood and Assistant Principal Mary Lynch of the Aaron Davis School. Appreciation is expressed to the teachers, Carol Baumgardt, Sandra Napier, and Elaine Schivek, whose collaboration made this study possible. Our sincere thanks to Virginia Worcholick, Susan Hole, and Janet Ward, who served as observers, and to Sally Sanford, who did the testing. Reprints may be obtained from Michael H. Ward, Psychology Services, Menlo Park Division, Palo Alto VAH, Miranda Drive, Palo Alto, California 94204.

for same-class controls. While the amount of teacher attention to target children remained the same from baseline to treatment, the proportion of attention to task-relevant behavior of these children increased. Psychological tests revealed no adverse changes after treatment.

Reinforcement techniques have been demonstrated to be quite effective in altering behavior in the laboratory situation (Krasner and Ullmann, 1965), and recently there have been increasing attempts to extend these methods to treatment in "real-life" situations. Of considerable importance is the potential usefulness of reinforcement therapy in the school classroom (*e.g.*, Clarizo and Yelon, 1967; Hall, Lund, and Jackson, 1968; Woody, 1966).

Zimmerman and Zimmerman (1962) eliminated disruptive classroom behavior in two emotionally disturbed boys by removing the social consequences of maladaptive behavior. Quay, Werry, McQueen, and Sprague (1966) reported on the use of conditioning techniques in a small special class with conduct problem children. A program in which public school teachers were trained to manage classroom behavior problems by the contingent use of teacher attention and praise has been described by Becker, Madsen, Arnold, and Thomas (1967).

While these applications of reinforcement methods are certainly encouraging, several legitimate questions are often raised by psychologists and teachers concerned with treating disruptive classroom behavior. One critical area of concern is the generalization of treatment effects. First, when a child's disruptive behavior is successfully reduced, what are the effects on other aspects of his observable behavior and on his psychological test functioning? Second, how are other pupils in the class affected when the teacher concentrates on treating deviant behavior in one or two specific children?

The present study further explored the effectiveness of the teacher as a therapeutic agent, but it also attempted to assess the generalized effects of reinforcement therapy. Thus, teachers were trained to eliminate deviant behavior by differentially reinforcing the target children's desirable and undesirable classroom behavior. Control procedures were instituted to ascertain the effects of the reinforcement therapy procedures on the psychological adjustment of target and non-target children.

METHOD

SUBJECTS

Twelve first-grade Negro children in an urban public school were assigned to three groups.

The Experimental Group (Group E) consisted of four behavior problem children. Three boys presented a high frequency of disruptive classroom behaviors, such as inappropriate talking and running around; one girl was highly withdrawn and inattentive. These target children were selected from three separate classrooms, on the basis of teachers' referrals and direct observations.

Control Group CI (Group CI) consisted of four children, matched for sex with the Group E children and selected at random from the three teachers' class lists. Thus, for each target child, a control child in the same classroom was also studied.

Control Group CII (Group CII) consisted of three boys and one girl, selected randomly from the classroom of a fourth first-grade teacher. These pupils provided a baseline for test-retest changes in psychological test performance, independent of any experimental manipulations.

APPARATUS

All treatment was carried out in the classroom. For two of the experimental subjects, two small (4-in.) electrically operated signal lights were used in six special-treatment sessions (after Patterson, 1965).

PROCEDURE

For five weeks, the frequency of various deviant classroom behaviors of Group E and Group CI children was coded by trained observers. Deviant behavior was calculated as the percentage of 30-sec intervals in which the child exhibited any behavior which was not task-relevant. These observations constituted the baseline measure of deviant behavior.

At week six, the experimental treatment phase was instituted and continued for seven weeks (until the end of the school year). In the treatment phase, teachers systematically ignored deviant behavior and reinforced, with attention and praise, task-relevant productive behavior. Regular classroom observations of the Group E and Group CI children were continued throughout the study; the Group CII children were not observed at any time.

All three groups were administered a battery of psychological tests, both during baseline and at the conclusion of the seven-week experimental treatment phase.

Observers and Observations

Three female undergraduates were trained to observe and record classroom behavior. The observers sat in the rear of the classroom; they did not interact with or respond to the children. Each Group E child was observed for four 15-min periods per week; each Group CI child was observed for two 15-min periods per week. During the observation period, the child was watched for the first 20 sec of each 30-sec interval of time; in the remaining 10 sec, the observers recorded the behaviors that had occurred. The observation periods were randomized throughout the school day to assure an adequate time-sampling. Inter-observer reliability checks were made periodically.

Table 1 shows the categories of behavior rated. These included gross and fine motor behaviors, aggression, deviant talking, non-attending, and disobeying, thumbsucking, and relevant appropriate behaviors such as hand-raising, task-oriented behavior, and so forth. In addition, the teacher's attention to children, as well as the nature of her comments, was coded.

Teachers and Training Sessions

Three female teachers were initially informed that their behavior problem children would be observed for five weeks, at which time the investigators would again meet with them to discuss some techniques for modifying these behavior problems. None of the teachers was given any further information at this time. At no point were the teachers told that the same-class control children were being observed.

After baseline measurements had been completed, the investigators began a series of four weekly seminar-discussions with the three teachers. These sessions were devoted to discussions of behavior modification and the progress of the target children. The seminars included a general introduction to operant conditioning, reinforcement and punishment procedures, schedules of reinforcement, and selected aspects of the experimental literature relating to these and other topics (*e.g.*, Ullmann and Krasner, 1965).

It was first necessary to help teachers identify and specify deviant behaviors. Throughout the treatment phase of the study, the investigators visited the classrooms and pointed out behavior problems. Thus, rather than: "He's always bad," teachers soon learned to define

Table 1

Classroom Behavior Rating Schedule (after Becker *et al.*, 1967)

Motor Behaviors (at seat)	*Thumb Sucking (and other objects)*
Rocking in chair; moving chair in place; sitting out of position; standing while *touching* chair or desk.	Thumb or finger sucking; sucking such objects as a pencil, *etc.*
Gross Motor Behaviors (not at desk)	*Relevant Behavior*
Getting out of seat; running; jumping; skipping; *not touching* desk or chair.	Time-on-task; answering question; listening; following directions. Important; *Must* include *entire* 20-sec interval, except orienting response of less than 4-sec duration.
Aggression	*Hand Raising*
Hitting; punching; kicking; slapping; striking with object; throwing object at another person; pulling hair; disturbing another's books, desk, etc.; destroying another's property. Do *not* rate unless act is committed.	Raises hand to ask or answer question; do *not* rate if child blurts out without being acknowledged. *Note:* may be rated with task-relevant behavior.
Deviant Talking	*Teacher Attention*
Carrying on conversation with other children; blurts out answer without being called upon; making comments or remarks; crying; screaming; laughing loudly; coughing loudly, singing, whistling; any vocal noise.	Teacher attends to the Subject *during* the 20-sec interval.
	Positive Comments
	"Good," "fine," "nice job" are said by teacher to Subject during the 20-sec interval.
Non-Attending and Disobeying	*General Reprimand*
Does something different from that which he has been directed to do or is supposed to do; includes "daydreaming"; *Note:* the above to be rated *only* when other classes are inappropriate (no other symbol may appear in interval). Note: Ignoring teacher's *direct* question or command may be rated in addition to other categories.	*Teacher* issues a *general* reprimand to the class or a group of students.
	Negative Comments
	"Shut up," "sit in your seat," "you're a bad boy," etc. are said by teacher to Subject during the 20-sec interval.

inappropriate behavior in more specific terms: "He is frequently out of his seat and he blurts out without being called on." It was also necessary to indicate to teachers which behaviors were to be reinforced when. Thus, for two of the behavior problem boys, six special 30-min treatment periods were conducted, in which an experimenter-controlled signal light on the child's desk was used as a reinforcer for sustained task-relevant behavior. The main purpose of this procedure was to bring the child's behavior under experimental control and allow the experimenter to indicate to the teacher the types of behaviors to be reinforced.

The principal therapeutic tool was the contingent use of teacher attention. The teachers were instructed to extinguish deviant behaviors by ignoring them, and to strengthen task-relevant behaviors by attending to and praising them. The need for immediacy, consistency, and contingency in reinforcement therapy was stressed. That is, the teacher was instructed to give *immediate* attention in a *consistent* manner, *contingent* upon the child's exhibiting task-relevant behavior.

A fourth female teacher, from whose classroom Group CII was chosen, did not participate in the seminar-discussions; at no time was she informed of the nature of the study.

Tests and Measures

The measure of deviant classroom behavior was the direct observations described above; these included both the target behaviors and other types of deviant behavior.

In the baseline period, and again at the conclusion of the seven-week treatment period, each of the 12 children was tested individually by an independent examiner on the following battery of tests: four subtests of the WISC, the Draw-A-Person Test, and a projective questionnaire designed to measure attitudes toward school and feelings about self.

The Comprehension, Mazes, Digit Span, and Block Design subtests of the WISC were used to reflect the child's ability to pay attention to a task, and his general scholastic functioning. In the DAP Test, the child was asked to draw a picture of a person, using standard art paper and crayons provided by the tester. Such drawings have been used as measures of a child's adjustment, maturity, and self-image. Finally, the child was shown a photograph of a Negro child of the same sex and comparable age; the facial expressions in these pictures were judged by the authors to be "neutral." Twenty questions were asked about this child's feelings toward himself and toward school (e.g., "Is his teacher nice to him?" "Do the other kids in school like him?" "Does he like school?").

All children were given both sets of tests by the same examiner, who was not informed of experimental conditions.

RESULTS

CLASSROOM BEHAVIOR

Reliability of Observations

Inter-observer reliability of the observation periods was determined by the percentage of intervals in which the observers agreed perfectly as to whether deviant behavior had occurred. The mean percentage perfect agreement of the 31 reliability checks was 81% (SD = 21.6).

Behavior Observations

Figure 1 shows the amount of deviant behavior in the behavior problem children and their same-class controls during baseline and during treatment. In the five-week baseline period, the Group E children showed 74% deviant behavior, while the Group CI children showed 37% deviant behavior, a difference significant at p = 0.002 (t = 5.14; df = 6).[2] There was no overlap among subjects in the two groups.

For the last five weeks of treatment, Group E showed 57% deviant behavior, a decrease from baseline significant at p = 0.03 (t = 3.91; df = 3). During this same period, Group CI showed 41% deviant behavior, a

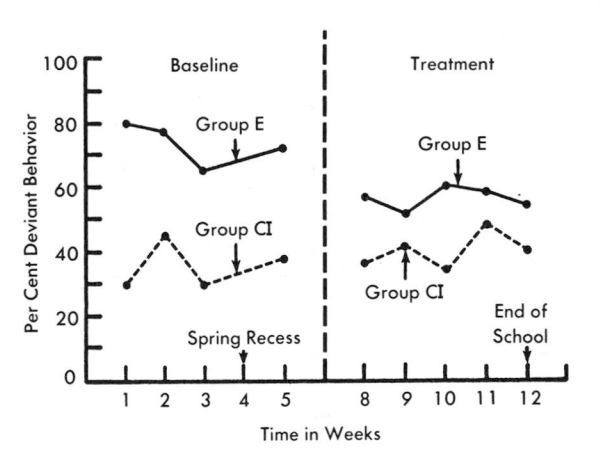

Figure 1

Deviant behavior of Group E and Group CI.

---

[2] All statistical tests of significance are two-tailed.

slight, though not significant increase from baseline (t = 0.32; df = 3).
The groups no longer differed significantly, although the deviant
behavior in the target children was not decreased to the level of their
controls by the end of school.

None of the specific categories of deviant behavior showed an increase
in either Group E or Group CI, nor did teachers report any new behavior
problems. Hence, the reduction in the target disruptive behavior was not
followed by an increase in other classroom deviance.

Teacher Attention

The principal therapeutic intervention used in the experiment was
teacher attention to task-relevant behavior. However, as shown in Fig. 2,
the observed improvement in the experimental children cannot be
attributed simply to increased teacher attention, since there was no

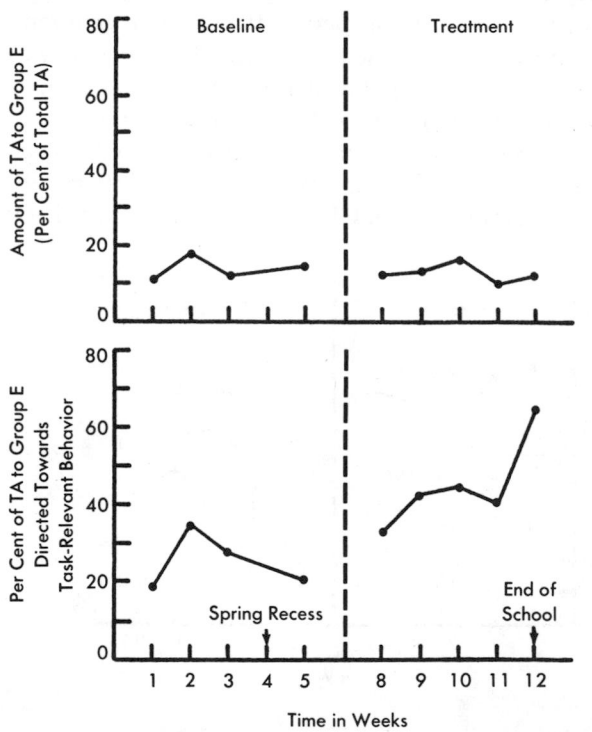

Figure 2

Teacher attention to Group E: Amount of TA directed
towards Group E and per cent of attention to Group E
directed towards task-relevant behavior.

significant change from baseline to treatment in the *amount* of attention to target children (t = 0.07; df = 3). Teachers did increase significantly from baseline to treatment in the *proportion* of their attention to target children that was directed towards task-relevant behavior (t = 3.46; df = 3; p = 0.04).

Nevertheless, it appears that the teachers did not thoroughly master the contingent use of their attention to task-relevant behavior, and that further improvement in the target children might have been possible. For instance, the change in deviant behavior for Group E reported above did not include observations taken during the special treatment sessions with two children. For these two experimental children, the deviant behavior during the special signal-light reinforcement periods decreased dramatically to an average of 18%. Yet there was apparently little generalization to other times.

Although the teachers did not increase their attention to target children, the data suggested that they decreased their attention somewhat to Group CI children; there was a slight, but not significant decrease in the amount of teacher attention from baseline to treatment (t = 2.49; df = 3, p = 0.09). The proportion of teachers' attention directed toward task-relevant behavior did not change from baseline to treatment for Group CI (t = 0.11; df = 3).

PSYCHOLOGICAL TESTS

On the pre-treatment WISC, the behavior problem children were significantly lower than the controls on the Mazes subtest (t = 2.71; df = 10; p < 0.03); the groups did not differ on the other sub-scales. The changes in WISC scores after treatment were minimal and did not significantly differentiate the groups, although Group E tended to decrease on the Comprehension subtest relative to Group CII (t = 2.14; df = 6, p = 0.08).

The pre-treatment DAP drawings of the behavior problem children were generally like those of the control children, except that the Group E drawings were significantly smaller in size (t = 2.85; df = 10, p < 0.02). This variable has been considered an indicator of anxiety (Ward, 1968).

The pre and post-treatment drawings were scored on all those variables considered in the drawing literature to be suggestive of adjustment or maturity. No significant differences between groups in change scores were found on any single variable or on a combination score. Emotional adjustment, rated by two judges uninformed as to the order and conditions in which the drawings were produced, showed no consistent effects. Similarly, changes on the projective questionnaire did not differentiate the groups.

DISCUSSION

One focus of the present study was to ascertain the generalized effects on the target child of treating a specific behavior; especially studied were the deleterious effects on the child's classroom behavior and psychological test functioning. The data provide no evidence for adverse changes in the children as a consequence of teachers' employing reinforcement techniques or as a result of specific deviant behaviors being reduced.

On the other hand, the target children did not show the generalized improvement in psychological test functioning found by Baker (1968) with enuretic children treated by conditioning. Yet, the present treatment did not produce the distinctive cure which results with enuretics. Also, enuresis is usually an "involuntary" behavior, the alleviation of which is a considerable relief for the child. Deviant classroom behavior is in some sense "voluntary"; it is emitted for environmental gains, such as the teacher's attention, and may be more a discomfort to others than to the child himself. If attention is withdrawn from such an operant, the child will attempt other behaviors to regain attention. Whether the end result is new maladaptive behavior or generalized improvement may depend on what the teacher now reinforces.

A second focus was the generalized effects of reinforcement therapy on the class. No support was found for the argument that behavior of other pupils in a class deteriorates when the teacher's attention is somehow diverted from them in treating behavior problem children. Although teachers did slightly decrease the amount of attention given to control children, there was no significant increase in the control children's deviant behavior. This is particularly encouraging since the treatment was carried out in the last weeks of the school year when, according to teachers, disruption in the classroom typically rises. It appears, nonetheless, that in future treatment programs, more stress should be placed on the teacher maintaining normal relations with nontarget children.

The principal reinforcer employed was contingent teacher attention. It is assumed that the decrease in deviant behavior in the target children resulted from the greater proportion of attention that teachers paid to these children's task-relevant behavior. It is recognized that the observed relationship between an increase in the proportion of teacher's attention to task-relevant behavior and an increase in such task-relevant behavior may have been artifactual; that is, if task-relevant behavior increased for some other undetermined reason and amount of teacher attention remained the same, then an increase in proportion of attention to task-relevant behavior would have also been found. Yet, it seems most likely that modified use of teacher attention was primary, especially in view of other reports indicating the functional role of teacher praise in increasing appropriate behavior in the classroom (Madsen, Becker, and Thomas, 1968).

The treatment procedures were not uniformly successful with all target children. Most notably, the withdrawn and inattentive behavior of one child changed very little. This behavior seems less under the control of teacher attention than more acting out behaviors; also, the latter are easier for the teacher to define, to notice, and to respond to correctly. Treating withdrawn behaviors may require better training in behavior shaping. In general it seems possible that more behavioral improvement could have been effected in all of the target children if the teachers had been more thoroughly trained. It is clear from the results of the special treatment sessions, in which the deviant behavior of two of the children dropped to 18%, that the full effectiveness of the reinforcement techniques was not realized at all times. It is likewise possible that a longer treatment period would have provided more time for the teachers' therapeutic skills to take effect.

Yet, the significant decrease in disruptive behavior in the target children, and the absence of adverse changes in these or other pupils, indicate that teachers can be trained as effective "therapists," using reinforcement techniques in the classroom. This finding, consistent with the conclusion reached by Becker et al. (1967), has important implications for in-classroom management of behavior problems. First, the availability to teachers of a set of techniques for controlling the disruptive behavior of students is of obvious advantage in terms of smoother classroom functioning. In addition, being taught to manifest productive task-relevant classroom behavior is worthwhile to the child himself. A child who is hyperactive or otherwise deviant in school necessarily misses many of the learning experiences which normally accrue to an attentive, actively participating pupil. A final consideration is that in situ amelioration of maladaptive behavior somewhat obviates the educational and financial disadvantages involved in removing a child from the classroom in order to attempt therapeutic rehabilitation.

While the results of this limited study are themselves encouraging, future research should continue to look beyond the specific behaviors being treated, and consider the generalized effects of reinforcement therapy.

References

Baker, B. L., Symptom treatment and symptom substitution in enuresis. *Journal of Abnormal Psychology*, in press.

Becker, W. C., Madsen, C. H. Jr., Arnold, Carol, and Thomas, D. R. The contingent use of teacher attention and praise in reducing classroom behavior problems. *Journal of Special Education*, 1967, 1, 287–307.

Clarizo, H. F. and Yelon, S. L. Learning theory approaches to classroom management: rationale and intervention techniques. *Journal of Special Education*, 1967, 1, 267–274.

Hall, R. V., Lund, Diane, and Jackson, Deloris. Effects of teacher attention on study behavior. *Journal of Applied Behavior Analysis*, 1968, 1, 1–12.

Krasner, L. and Ullmann, L. P. (Eds.) *Research in behavior modification*. New York: Holt, Rinehart & Winston, 1965.

Madsen, C. H. Jr., Becker, W. C., and Thomas, D. R. Rules, praise, and ignoring: elements of elementary classroom control. *Journal of Applied Behavior Analysis*, 1968, 1, 139–150.

Patterson, G. R. An application of conditioning techniques to the control of a hyperactive child. In L. P. Ullmann and L. Krasner (Eds.), *Case studies in behavior modification*. New York: Holt, Rinehart & Winston, 1965. Pp. 370–375.

Quay, H. C., Werry, J. S., McQueen, Marjorie, and Sprague, R. L. Remediation of the conduct problem child in the special class setting. *Exceptional Children*, 1966, 32, 509–515.

Ullmann, L. P. and Krasner, L. *Case studies in behavior modification*. New York: Holt, Rinehart & Winston, 1965.

Ward, Janet. *Integration and racial identification: a study of Negro children's drawings*. Unpublished bachelor honor's thesis, Radcliffe College, 1968.

Woody, R. H. Behavior therapy and school psychology. *Journal of Social Psychology*, 1966, 4, 1–14.

Zimmerman, Elaine H. and Zimmerman, J. The alteration of behavior in a special classroom situation. *Journal of Experimental Analysis of Behavior*, 1962, 5, 59–60.

PART 5

More Complex Studies

The articles in the previous two sections tended to focus on relatively few behaviors to be changed and to use simple reinforcement or extinction to affect these behaviors. The studies in this section differ from the preceding ones in the scope of the problems attacked or surveyed and in the range and complexity of the techniques used. The first three studies deal with token reinforcement programs and discuss possibilities for their use in some detail. Axelrod summarizes their use in "special" classrooms and concludes that they have been effective with a wide variety of teachers, children, and problems. Glynn reports the use of a token reward system in a normal high school classroom. When students were permitted to determine how many tokens their own performance earned, performance improved over a base rate period and over that of students in a control group. At the same time fewer tokens were taken than in a group in which the experimenter determined the contingencies. Contrasting with Glynn's self-control system is the system utilizing peer influence instituted by Graubard, in which the academic and social behaviors of the delinquent boys who served as subjects could earn rewards for the whole group. In his article, Graubard suggests that the influence of the peer group may be necessary for delinquent children, since praise from the teacher is probably not rewarding to them. Although not all of the students in the studies described by Clark and Walberg were delinquent, all of them did attend schools in a lower-class, poverty stricken area of the city. In contrast to Graubard's prediction, however, Clark and Walberg found that praise and attention from the teacher were effective in changing both academic behaviors and attitudes.

A third approach to dealing with delinquent children is that of Cantrell, Cantrell, Huddleston, and Wooldridge, who utilized a written contract system involving the adolescent and his parents and/or teacher. They suggest that this procedure is particularly useful when there is no professional nearby who can monitor the behavior in person.

The last two articles in this section deal not with delinquents but with normal college students taking introductory courses. Although similar to Biehler's mastery approach, both of these studies go far beyond his work in the complexity of the program and contingencies they specify. Keller's article discusses such innovations as the use of several levels of instructors in the course and the requirement of demonstrating mastery to earn the privilege of attending lectures or demonstrations. Myers went a step beyond Keller in permitting students only the option of an A or an incomplete and in eliminating lectures entirely. Both courses involved a programmed sequencing of the material and the requirement of mastery at each level before proceeding to the next. Many of the facets of these studies could, of course, be utilized with younger students as well.

One important advantage of token reinforcement is its great versatility; the technique can be used in a large number of situations to change a great variety of responses with many different kinds of students. This review by Axelrod looks at the many studies which have been done outside the traditional classroom. Judicious use of token systems appears to have been effective with students as diverse as the mentally retarded, the urban underachievers and the hyperactive, suggesting their broad applicability to educational problems. However, as Axelrod points out, many studies have used extra personnel and equipment and have depended on reinforcers not usually available in the classroom. For schools which have fewer staff, space and financial resources, more emphasis may have to be placed on back-up reinforcers readily available in the classroom—praise, privileges, and other activities suggested by the students.

Many approaches to understanding the child in special education classes have focused on his personality, his feelings about himself and school, and the reactions of others to his handicaps. Often the implicit message of such approaches is that the child cannot be expected to change his behaviors, academic or social, until his emotional problems are understood and dealt with. The consistent success of token reinforcement programs, which focus not on inner problems but on behavior, suggests that perhaps the more traditional approach is not the most appropriate one for changing behavior, although it may (or may not) lead to greater self-understanding and happiness for the student. Certainly the use of a token system should be considered by the special education teacher, particularly when he can specify the behaviors he would like to see changed.

Token Reinforcement Programs in Special Classes

Saul Axelrod *†

ABSTRACT

A review of token reinforcement programs in the special education classroom indicates that positive results were almost invariably obtained, even with different types of target behaviors and various kinds of populations. It is suggested that future studies concentrate on devising means of withdrawing tokens without interruption of progress and that greater use be made of reinforcers already existing in the classroom.

A recent extension of the principles of operant conditioning includes the use of token reinforcement as a means of modifying behavior in the special education classroom. Token reinforcers are objects or symbols

* Saul Axelrod, "Token Reinforcement Programs in Special Classes," *Exceptional Children* 37(1971): 3710379. Reprinted with permission.
† Saul Axelrod is Assistant Professor, Department of Educational Psychology, University of Connecticut, Storrs.

which in and of themselves probably have little or no reinforcing value (Birnbrauer, Wolf, Kidder, & Tague, 1965). However, they may be exchanged for a variety of objects or privileges which are reinforcing. For example, an individual might use his tokens to purchase several different kinds of candies, toys, or a trip to the zoo. As a result of this association with different types of reinforcement, the tokens should become generalized reinforcers which are independent of any particular state of deprivation or satiation which an individual is experiencing. The superiority of the token reinforcement system over other systems employing a particular primary reinforcer is considerable. For example, if food is used to reinforce a certain behavior, the effectiveness of the reinforcement procedure is greatly dependent upon the state of deprivation of the individual. Tokens, on the other hand, are not so limited, since they can be used to purchase several different types of reinforcers or can be saved until a later time when a particular state of deprivation does exist. In addition, several tokens can be accumulated and exchanged for some item that has more reinforcing value for an individual than a single piece of candy.

A significant advantage of token reinforcers over the use of grades in maintaining appropriate behavior in the classroom was reported by McKenzie, Clark, Wolf, Kothera, and Benson (1968). These investigators pointed out that grades have traditionally been the token reinforcement system of schools. However, the effectiveness of grades is often minimal since the amount of time between behavior and reinforcement is frequently between 6 and 9 weeks. As a result, an association between responding and reinforcement is unlikely. In accordance with this notion, Clark, Lachowitz, and Wolf (1968) pointed out that a major benefit of a token program is that the token can be used as an immediate reinforcer of a response and thus can close the time lapse between the appropriate response and the backup reinforcer. For example, it would be difficult to provide a trip to the circus as an immediate reinforcer for completing a difficult reading assignment. However, it would be quite easy to administer a sufficient number of tokens for this trip immediately following the appropriate behavior.

Token reinforcement programs have generally been employed in classroom situations in which teacher attention has been ineffective in controlling the students' behavior (Kuypers, Becker, & O'Leary, 1968). The administration of a token is usually preceded by some type of approval (e.g., "good boy") so that teacher praise will eventually become a conditioned reinforcer. It is often intended (Kuypers et al., 1968) that control over student behavior will be transferred from the tokens to the teacher through this conditioned reinforcement procedure.

INCREASING ACADEMIC PERFORMANCE

MENTALLY RETARDED POPULATIONS

Severely Retarded Class

A study by Birnbrauer and Lawler (1964) appears to be the first published investigation of the use of a token reinforcement system in a special education classroom. Subjects for this experiment were 37 severely retarded children who were divided into classes of 6 to 13 pupils. Each teacher conducted his class without the help of teaching assistants. Of the 36 subjects, 14 had never attended school before, three had been dropped from school due to "incorrigibility," and four were "severe behavior problems." All had IQ's of 40 or less. The children were gradually introduced to a token reinforcement program using poker chips which could be exchanged for a variety of backup reinforcers. Chips were awarded for clearly defined behaviors. At the end of the school year, 33 of the 37 pupils hung up their coats upon entering the classroom, sat down quietly, and waited for their assignments. In addition, 11 worked without assistance on programed reading material which required 10 to 30 minutes to complete. It was found, however, that many of the children did not change their behavior outside the classroom.

Programed Material

Birnbrauer, Bijou, Wolf, and Kidder (1965) discussed a special education classroom in which a token reinforcement system was combined with programed instructional material (PI) to teach various school subjects (reading, writing, and arithmetic) and related practical skills (e.g., telling time). Subjects for the study were eight boys ranging in chronological age (CA) from 9 to 13 and in mental age (MA) from 5-5 to 7-3 (Peabody Picture Vocabulary Test: PPVT). Their clinical diagnoses included brain damage and familial retardation. A token reinforcement system was instituted after the discovery that the pupils would not work effectively for approval and knowledge of results. The student to teacher ratio was frequently one to one. The authors reported that within 5 months, seven of the eight pupils were "good students." It was claimed that the subjects studied longer, accomplished more work, and exhibited a minimal number of disruptive behaviors.

Tokens vs Teacher Attention

The question of whether the reinforcement program or the greater attention paid to students' problems is responsible for producing increased student output is frequently raised. A study by Birnbrauer, Wolf, Kidder, and Tague (1965) shed some light on this matter. The purpose of this investigation was to determine the effectiveness of the reinforcers in maintaining appropriate behavior on the Sight Vocabulary Program by systematically withdrawing and reapplying the reinforcers. Of the 17 mentally retarded children who took part in this study, two were mongoloid, three were familial, nine were brain damaged, and three had no available diagnosis. IQ's ranged from 50 to 72 (PPVT). The study consisted of three conditions: The first (B) paired social approval with tokens; the second (NT) used teacher approval but no tokens; the third condition (B₂) was the same as the first. The study used one male certified teacher and three female assistants. The results indicated that five children showed no decrement in performance during NT. Six children made more errors during NT, but completed the same or a greater number of items and presented no greater number of behavior problems. Four children made more errors, did less work, and presented serious disciplinary problems during NT. After tokens were reinstated all subjects returned to the original level or better. It appeared, therefore, that the token reinforcement procedures rather than teacher attention accounted for the behavioral changes.

Bijou, Birnbrauer, Kidder, and Tague (1966) reported on 3 years of research in which a token reinforcement system was applied to teaching reading, writing, and arithmetic to retarded children. Subjects consisted of 27 boys and girls ranging in CA from 8-7 to 14-9. The average IQ (PPVT) for the group was 63. Eleven of the subjects were diagnosed as brain damaged, three as mongoloid, four as cultural-familial, and nine as uncertain or unknown. Although no mention was made of the number of teachers who were involved, the classroom situation was structured so that a newly admitted student would receive almost constant attention from a teacher. The authors implied that the results of this study were quite favorable, but failed to include objective data.

OTHER POPULATIONS

Multiply Handicapped Teenagers

Nolen, Kunzelman, and Haring (1967) performed a study which was directed toward improving the academic and social behavior of junior high age children with a variety of disorders. Subjects ranged in age from 12 to 16 years and in achievement levels from preschool to sixth grade. Etiologies included a variety of emotional and learning disorders, as well as mental retardation. The authors stressed, however, that their program centered on the diagnosis of skill problems rather than on physical or psychological deficits. Following the development of skill sequences and the determination of the students' functioning levels within these sequences, individual programs were devised. The teacher allotted points, which were exchangeable for reinforcers appropriate to teenagers, for each of a number of academic tasks. After 100 days, a median of 2.7 years gain in arithmetic and 2.05 years gain in reading was found. To test the effectiveness of the reinforcement, the experimenters administered rewards on a noncontingent basis for a period of time. This technique produced a significant decrease in appropriate academic behavior which was quickly resumed once reinforcement was reinstituted on a contingent basis. Followup studies of three students who were transferred from this classroom indicated that their performances were lower in the traditional classroom than in the experimental classroom. However, their productivity was still superior to other students' in their new class.

Urban Underachievers

In accordance with current national problems, Wolf, Giles, and Hall (1968) conducted a program which was intended to improve the academic performance of low achieving children from an urban poverty area. Fifteen of the subjects for this study were from the sixth grade while the sixteenth was from the fifth grade. All subjects scored at least 2 years below their grade level on the reading portion of the *Stanford Achievement Test* (SAT). According to school records, IQ's ranged from 73 to 104. Classes, which were conducted by one teacher with two teaching assistants, were held after school hours and during summer months. In addition, students attended regular classes during school hours. A token reinforcement program which included a wide range of backup reinforcers was instituted. The first of two experiments concerned two subjects and attempted to determine whether the rate of reading certain material was a function of the distribution of points. It was found that manipulation of the number of points earned by reading significantly affected the reading rate of both children. In one case, doubling the number of points the child could receive produced a significant level of response even though he had not responded at all under the original conditions. In the second experiment, subjects were given their choice of types of academic materials with which to work. However, the number of points which could be earned for completing various units was changed periodically. For example, at one time reading units were worth 5 points, while arithmetic and English units were worth 2 points. At another time, reading was worth 8 points, arithmetic was worth 2 points, and English was worth one-half a point. The material a child chose varied according to the number of points that could be earned. At the end of the year the data indicated that the control group, which only attended regular classes, gained a median of .8 year on the SAT, while the experimental group showed a median gain of 1.5 years. These results were significant at the .01 level of confidence. In addition, subjective teacher remarks indicated that the children from the experimental group performed better while in the regular school classroom than they had previously.

Dropouts

A study by Clark and his colleagues (1968) also employed a population representative of contemporary problems. This investigation was directed toward improving the academic skills of school dropouts by means of a token reinforcement program. Subjects for the study were two groups of five girls matched according to differences between their number of years of formal education and their scores on the *California Achievement Test* (CAT). All the girls were between 16 and 21 years old. One group was termed the classroom group and received the token reinforcement program. The second group was designated the job group and received job placement. The classroom group subjects were given their choice of a variety of instructional materials. Points, which were exchangeable for money, were awarded on the basis of performance on these materials.

As the study progressed, the distribution of points was shifted to increase the probability of a student's working in an area in which she was deficient. For example, if a girl were deficient in arithmetic, more points would be awarded for appropriate arithmetic performance. One, and often two teachers were in the classroom. Four girls in the classroom group attended class for 8 weeks and 4 days while the fifth attended 24 days. According to the CAT pretest and posttest scores, the classroom subjects gained a median of 1.3 years while the job group gained only .2 year.

Learning Disabled

In order to improve the level of academic achievement in a learning disabilities class, McKenzie and his coworkers (1968) introduced a token reinforcement system. Subjects for this study were ten students ranging in age from 10 to 13 years. Although their ability levels did not indicate mental retardation, their achievement levels were retarded by at least 2 years in one or more academic areas. All were diagnosed as having minimal brain damage and emotional disturbance. Based on their academic performance, the children were reinforced with recess, special privileges, weekly grades, et cetera. Achievement under these conditions was judged to be less than optimal. A program conducted by a teacher and teacher aides was then instituted in which the amount of allowance a child would receive from his parents was determined by his weekly grades. Since the parents were already accustomed to giving their children allowances, a burden was not added to the parents' budgets. A significant increase in arithmetic and reading achievement was observed while using weekly allowances as backup reinforcers. Due to the risk involved, no reversal of reinforcement conditions was attempted.

Reading Disabled

Haring and Hauck (1969) did a study concerned with improving the reading achievement level of four elementary school boys through a combination of PI material and token reinforcement. Subjects for this investigation were disabled in reading, but average or above in intelligence. According to the *Gates-McKillop Diagnostic Reading Tests*, reading development showed a lag of from one to 5 years. Several experimental conditions were employed. During condition A the material was presented without the answers. During the second condition (B), correct answers were provided following a response by the subject. Condition C included a counter which tallied the number of correct responses. This count was available both to the boys and the experimenters. Condition D provided continuous token reinforcement for correct responding, whereas condition E programed reinforcement on a variable ratio schedule (e.g., an average of every five correct responses was reinforced). A transfer from PI material to work lists, basal readers, and library books was involved in condition F. The teacher's role in this program was minimal since much of the material was automated. The study consisted of 91 sessions of 65 minutes each. The data showed that the later conditions produced higher rates of correct responding than conditions A and B. In addition, it was found that the boys gained from 1.5 to 4.0 years in reading achievement during the 5 months of the study, according to the *Sullivan Placement Test*. Transition to the more traditional situation in condition F was reported as successful, but definitive data were lacking.

Emotionally Disturbed

Hewett, Taylor, and Artuso (1969) used an engineered classroom design with "emotionally disturbed" students. A total of 54 children were assigned to six classrooms with nine students in each. Each class had a teacher and a teacher aide. Children ranged in CA from 8-0 to 11-11

years with Full Scale WISC IQ scores between 85 and 113. Nearly all
showed academic retardation. The experimental condition involved the
use of checkmarks and backup reinforcers for appropriate behavior. Any
instructional approach which the teacher chose to follow except the use
of tangible or token rewards was used in the control condition. Class 1
(E) stayed in the experimental condition for 32 weeks. Class 2 (C) stayed
in the control condition for 32 weeks. Classes 3 and 4 (CE) and classes 5
and 6 (EC) were in the control condition for 16 weeks and the
experiment condition for 16 weeks. The dependent variables were
reading and arithmetic achievement measured by the CAT and task
attention. A comparison of classes E and C indicated that the
experimental condition produced superior task attention and arithmetic
achievement but not reading achievement. The data of class C and
classes CE verified these findings. The data of classes EC indicated that
removal of the experimental condition resulted in improved task
attention and did not affect reading or arithmetic achievement levels. To
account for these surprising observations, Hewett and his associates
(1969) hypothesized that (a) the teachers became more effective
secondary social reinforcers, and (b) the competence of group EC
increased as a result of the experimental condition.

REDUCING DISRUPTIVE BEHAVIORS

MENTALLY RETARDED POPULATIONS

Hyperactivity

The purpose of a study by Patterson, Jones, Whittier, and Wright (1965)
was to condition the attending behavior of a hyperacitve child in a
classroom situation. In addition, it was intended that the effect
generalize to situations in which the conditioning apparatus was not
being used. An experimental subject (ES) and a control subject (CS) were
employed. ES was a brain injured, mentally retarded boy with a WISC
IQ of 65. CS was a brain injured boy with a range in IQ scores from the
eighties to the low nineties according to the PPVT and *Raven Matrices
Test*. During conditioning trials ES wore an earphone into which a signal
was passed for each 10 seconds during which ES attended properly. Later
a variable interval schedule was used. Each buzz indicated that a piece of
candy or a penny was accumulated toward a total which was to be shared
by the entire class. Following conditioning, the apparatus was removed
and a 4 week extinction period was begun. Differences between ES and

CS were insignificant during baseline. However, after conditioning sessions were started, it was found that ES performed significantly more attending behaviors than did CS. These measurements were taken during the period prior to which ES would wear the conditioning apparatus for that day. During extinction, ES maintained a significantly higher rate of attending than did CS. Patterson therefore obtained generalization of the conditioning effect.

Obscene Conduct

Sulzbacher and Houser (1968) used a group contingency procedure to eliminate a disruptive behavior in a classroom. This design was constructed so that the rewards of each depended upon the behavior of the group as a whole. Subjects for this study were 14 educable mentally retarded children, seven of whom were boys. Ages ranged from 6-7 to 10-5. The problem behavior was the frequent occurrence of an obscene gesture. The children were informed that there would be a 10 minute recess at the end of the day. However, each display or reference to the obscene gesture by any member of the class decreased recess time by one minute for the entire class. The program was designed so that one teacher could carry out the entire procedure without assistance. The frequency of undesirable behaviors decreased from a mean of 16 per day to 2.11 per day. After removal of the contingency, the behavior increased, but to a lower level than the baseline level.

Maladaptive Behaviors

Perline and Levinsky (1968) attempted to determine the effect of token reinforcement on the maladaptive behaviors of severely retarded children in a residential preschool setting. Subjects ranged in age from 8 to 10 years and in social quotient from 22 to 38. Five maladaptive behaviors were defined including aggression toward peers and throwing objects. Two experimental conditions were applied concurrently for 10 days. All children were given tokens for lack of maladaptive behaviors and lost a token if they misbehaved. However, for half the children, each deviant behavior led to a timeout period consisting of 5 to 15 minutes during which the child was not allowed to move from a certain area. For the other half of the children, no additional contingencies were used. The data indicated that a decrease in maladaptive behaviors for each of the five categories occurred. However, there were no appreciable differences between using token reinforcement and token reinforcement with time-out.

OTHER POPULATIONS

Hyperactivity

Patterson (1965) devised a token reinforcement program to control the disruptive behaviors of a child in a classroom setting. The subject was a 9 year old boy in the second grade, who demonstrated hyperactive behavior and academic retardation. Neurological signs indicated minimal brain damage while IQ scores were in the borderline range. After observing the boy for several hours, it was decided that the greater part of his hyperactivity could be broken down into talking, pushing, and hitting. A small box with a flashlight bulb and an electric counter was then placed on the boy's desk. If he did not perform any disruptive behaviors for a period of time (which increased as trials progressed) the light flashed and the counter clicked. At the end of each session, all members of the class divided up the amount of candy or pennies corresponding to the number of points on the electric counter. This program required the presence of the teacher and an experimenter. The data indicated that 8.4 fewer disruptive responses per minute occurred during conditioning.
This result was at the .01 level of significance. After the experiment was completed, the teacher reported that the boy was less disruptive and played more with other children.

Emotionally Disturbed

An extension of the Patterson (1965) study was performed by Quay, Werry, McQueen, and Sprague (1966). Although an explicit description of the children was not given, it appears that the children were emotionally disturbed. Each student was given a box containing a light which could be flashed following attending behaviors of a fixed duration. The children were later given a piece of candy for each light flash. The program, which was conducted by one teacher and an experimenter, increased attending from 41 percent during baseline to 71 percent during the last 20 days of reinforcement. A return to baseline conditions was not attempted.

O'Leary and Becker (1967) attempted to devise a token reinforcement system which could be used by one teacher in an average size classroom. In addition, the authors were interested in the possibility of gradually withdrawing the tokens without an increase in deviant behavior by transferring control to teacher attention and grades. Subjects for this study were 17 nine year old children described as "emotionally disturbed." Kuhlmann-Anderson IQ scores ranged from 80 to 107. After the baseline period, the experimenter placed the following instructions on the blackboard: "In Seat, Face Front, Raise Hand. . . ." The children were told that they would receive points (which were determined by the experimenter) depending on how well they followed instructions. These points could be exchanged for a variety of backup reinforcers. The number of ratings made each day gradually decreased and the number of points required to obtain a prize gradually increased. By requiring more appropriate behavior to receive a reward and increasing the delay of reinforcement, it was hoped that transfer of control from tokens to teacher praise and attention would occur. During baseline, the daily mean of deviant behaviors varied between 66 and 91 percent. This decreased to a range of 3 to 32 percent during the token procedure. This result was significant at the .001 level. A return to baseline conditions during school sessions during the following fall was planned. However, extensive changes in the pupil population prevented this possibility. Anecdotal evidence, however, indicated that after the procedure was put into effect, the students behaved better during class sessions in which tokens were not used than they had previously.

Out-of-Seat Behavior

A group contingency procedure was utilized by Gallagher, Sulzbacher, and Shores (1967) to reduce disruptive behaviors in a classroom. The subjects were five boys who were enrolled in an intermediate class for emotionally disturbed children. The boys ranged in age from 7-11 to 11-8 [sic]. It was hypothesized that more deviant behaviors occurred when at least one member of the class was out of his seat. Hence, an attempt was made to eliminate out-of-seat behavior. The children were informed that they could have a 24 minute coke break at the end of the day if they did not leave their seats without permission. A chart was posted which displayed 2 minute segments from 24 to 0. Each child's name was assigned a different color chalk. When a child left his seat without permission, the teacher marked off 2 minutes with the designated color from the entire class's coke time. The frequency of the boys' being out of their seats decreased from an average of 69.5 to 1.0 times per day. In addition, an overall decline in disruptive classroom behaviors was reported. Although the program used one master and three student teachers, it would appear that it could have been conducted by one teacher without assistance.

Socially Maladjusted

Kuypers, Becker, and O'Leary (1968) performed an experiment to reduce the number of disruptive behaviors in an adjustment class through the use of a token reinforcement program. Subjects for this study were six third grade and six fourth grade children who were described as socially maladjusted. Data were collected on only the six most disruptive children. They were given tokens (which could be used to purchase various items) for staying in their seats, facing front, and other attending behaviors. During baseline, deviant behavior occurred 54 percent of the time. This decreased to 27.8 percent during the token period and then increased to 41.5 percent when the tokens were removed. Generalization to other situations was minimal. The authors admitted that these results were less impressive than those obtained by O'Leary and Becker (1967). Kuypers attributed the limited success to the following: (a) the tokens were awarded on an absolute basis rather than for individual improvement, (b) the teacher was not trained in the use of operant conditioning techniques, and (c) the observers tended to be a disturbance to the class.

CRITICISMS

Although the studies reviewed above are almost unanimous in revealing the ability of token reinforcement to produce favorable changes in the special education classroom, the area has not been free of methodological and engineering difficulties. A frequent problem with many of the studies has been the failure of the experimenters to clearly demonstrate that contingent token reinforcement was responsible for the academic changes which occurred.

In an operant conditioning experiment, the researcher typically notes the frequency of the behavior of interest under normal or baseline conditions. He then applies some consequence to the behavior in an attempt to alter its rate of occurrence. If the rate changes in the predicted direction, the experimenter still cannot be certain that this change was due to the consequence which was applied to the behavior. It is possible that the alteration of the rate was due to the passage of time, maturation of the subjects, increased teacher effectiveness, or many other ongoing factors. To circumvent this difficulty, the experimenter will frequently return the subjects to the conditions which existed before the reinforcement techniques were applied. A return of the behavior to the original baserate lends credence to the idea that it was the contingent reinforcement or punishment which accounted for the behavioral change.

Nevertheless, many of the token studies have failed to include a reversal to baseline conditions (e.g., Birnbrauer & Lawler, 1964; Perline &

Levinsky, 1968). It might be argued that the ability of operant principles to alter behavior has been demonstrated in a sufficient number of cases that a reversal phase is unnecessary, especially in a purely therapeutic situation. As Sidman (1960) noted however, "An investigator may, on the basis of experience, have great confidence in the adequacy of his methodology, but other experimenters cannot be expected to share his confidence without convincing evidence [p. 75]" (cited by O'Leary & Becker, 1967).

The manner in which many of the studies were conducted raises questions as to their usefulness in the special education classroom. One problem has been the use of a large number of personnel in order to execute the programs. Birnbrauer's (1965) study used three teachers in a classroom of eight boys, whereas the Patterson (1965) study required the presence of a teacher and an experimenter. Although it is desirable that such a personnel-teacher ratio exist ordinarily, it is unrealistic to expect this situation in many special education classrooms. A somewhat promising solution to this problem is given in the group contingency design used by Gallagher's group (1967) and by Sulzbacher and Houser (1968). These studies treated the entire class as a unit and thus simplified the administration of reinforcement and the bookkeeping procedures.

Another limitation of some of the above studies is that electronic equipment was required for their execution (e.g., Patterson, 1965; Patterson et al., 1965). Although it could be argued that this equipment is not complex, it is doubtful that the necessary apparatus would be installed by many special education teachers without the assistance and encouragement of a researcher. The availability of the appropriate researcher is often limited.

FUTURE RESEARCH

The Kuypers (1968) study stated that "a general goal of token systems is to transfer control of responding from token systems to other conditioned reinforcers such as teacher praise and grades [p. 101]." If this is an accepted aim of token reinforcement programs, future research must be conducted in this direction. The most frequently stated suggestion (e.g., Kuypers et al., 1968) for achieving transfer from the token system to the more traditional classroom situation is to precede the delivery of tokens with praise. This arrangement is intended to eventually establish social events as conditioned reinforcers and to allow a teacher to maintain student behavior with social reinforcement alone.

Another proposal concerning the removal of tokens was given by O'Leary and Becker (1967). By requiring progressively more behavior to receive a prize and by increasingly delaying reinforcement, the authors claimed that a transfer from tokens to teacher praise could be achieved eventually.

Which, if either, of these proposals will be fruitful will be determined by future investigation. The question seems an important one, since it is unlikely that a token system would be applied indefinitely in any school setting.

In the present author's opinion, future token experiments should employ reinforcers already available in the classroom. Studies which are dependent on the introduction of candies and toys into the classroom can only be applied for a limited period of time because of the strain eventually placed on the school's or teacher's budget. Most special education teachers permit their students to have free play time, field trips, and games. Rather than permitting the students to engage in such activities independent of classroom performance, the privileges could be used as reinforcers in the token program. This approach has been successfully employed by Sulzbacher and Houser (1968) and offers the most economical and easily transferred system of behavior modification.

References

Bijou, S. W., Birnbrauer, J. S., Kidder, J. D., & Tague, C. E. Programmed instruction as an approach to the teaching of reading, writing, and arithmetic to retarded children. *Psychological Record*, 1966, 16, 505–522.

Birnbrauer, J. S., Bijou, S. W., Wolf, M. M., & Kidder, J. D. Programmed instruction in the classroom. In L. P. Ullmann and L. Krasner (Eds.), *Case studies in behavior modification*. New York: Holt, Rinehart & Winston, 1965. Pp. 358–363.

Birnbrauer, J. S., & Lawler, J. Token reinforcement for learning. *Mental Retardation*, 1964, 2, 275–279.

Birnbrauer, J. S., Wolf, M. M., Kidder, J. D., & Tague, C. Classroom behavior of retarded pupils with token reinforcement. *Journal of Experimental Child Psychology*, 1965, 2, 219–235.

Clark, M., Lachowitz, J., & Wolf, M. A pilot basic education program for school dropouts incorporating a token reinforcement system. *Behavior Research and Therapy*, 1968, 6, 183–188.

Gallagher, P., Sulzbacher, S. I., & Shores, R. E. A group contingency for classroom management of emotionally disturbed children. Paper read to Kansas Chapter, The Council for Exceptional Children, Wichita, March, 1967.

Haring, N. G., & Hauck, M. Improved learning conditions in the establishment of reading skills with disabled readers. *Exceptional Children*, 1969, 35, 341–352.

Hewett, F., Taylor, F., & Artuso, A. The Santa Monica project: Evaluation of an engineered classroom design with emotionally disturbed children. *Exceptional Children*, 1969, 35, 523–529.

Kuypers, D. S., Becker, W. C., & O'Leary, K. D. How to make a token system fail. *Exceptional Children*, 1968, 35, 101–109.

McKenzie, H. S., Clark M., Wolf, M. M., Kothera, R., & Benson, C. Behavior modification of children with learning disabilities using grades as tokens and allowances as back up reinforcers. *Exceptional Children*, 1968, 34, 745–752.

Nolen, P., Kunzelmann, H. P., & Haring, N. G. Behavioral modification in a junior high learning disabilities classroom. *Exceptional Children*, 1967, 34, 163–168.

O'Leary, K. D., & Becker, W. C. Behavioral modification of an adjustment class. A token reinforcement program. *Exceptional Children*, 1967, 33, 637–642.

Patterson, G. R. An application of conditioning techniques to the control of a hyperactive child. In L. P. Ullmann and L. Krasner (Eds.), *Case studies in behavior modification*. New York: Holt, Rinehart & Winston, 1965. Pp. 370–375.

Patterson, G. R., Jones, R., Whittier, J., & Wright, M. A. A behavior modification technique for the hyperactive child. *Behavior Research and Therapy*, 1965, 2, 217–226.

Perline, I. H., & Levinsky, D. Controlling behavior in the severely retarded. *American Journal of Mental Deficiency*, 1968, 73, 74–78.

Quay, H. C., Werry, J. S., McQueen, M., & Sprague, R. L. Remediation of the conduct problem child in the special class setting. *Exceptional Children*, 1966, 32, 509–515.

Sidman, M. *Tactics of scientific research*. New York: Basic Books, 1960.

Sulzbacher, S. I., & Houser, J. E. A tactic to eliminate disruptive behaviors in the classroom: Group contingent consequences. *American Journal of Mental Deficiency*, 1968, 73, 88–90.

Wolf, M. M., Giles, D. K., & Hall, R. V. Experiments with token reinforcement in a remedial classroom. *Behavior Research and Therapy*, 1968, 6, 51–64.

Many teachers who have attempted to institute token reinforcement programs in their classrooms have encountered a variety of objections. Glynn suggests in this article that one of the major objections, the dislike of external control, is based on a faulty equation of external control and extrinsic reinforcement. In his study, he compared a group of students who received tokens contingent on their performance on a ratio schedule determined by the experimenter, a group which was allowed to select for themselves as many tokens as they felt their work merited, and a group receiving noncontingent tokens, as well as a no-token control group. All groups later were exposed to a self-reinforcement period following a second baseline phase. Although the groups did not differ significantly in the first base rate period, both contingently reinforced groups performed better in the experimental phase than did the noncontingent-reward and no-token groups. Moreover, students in the self-reinforcement groups set higher standards for themselves in the second and third token periods and on a review test than did those in the other two token groups.

These successful results of letting students determine the amount of reward their work had earned might be due at least in part to the fact that all of the girls who served as subjects were already well-motivated to learn. With younger children or those who do not see any merit in learning academic material, it is unlikely that a self-reinforcement procedure would be immediately effective. Perhaps the influence of the peer group, as Graubard's article would suggest, could be elicited to assist in setting and maintaining standards. Alternatively, the students could be trained in evaluating their own performance by a combination of modeling and shaping; they could be asked to evaluate their own work, and those who rewarded themselves appropriately could be given bonus tokens. By the use of such preliminary training, not only the self-determination of the amount of reward earned and the self-administration of the reward used by Glynn but also self-control of the behaviors to be changed and goals to work towards might also be implemented.

One relatively minor problem Glynn discusses is the use of back-up reinforcers. Because he was not permitted to control access to reinforcements within the school, he was forced to rely on material rewards. Evidently the trinkets which he selected as prizes because of their relevance to the material covered were not very durable as rewards, and satiation appeared to occur. Although the typical secondary school may not permit the teacher much control over the use of preferred behaviors as reinforcers, Glynn's discussion suggests that a careful analysis of the durability of the back-up reinforcers to be used should be carried out before the beginning of the actual program.

Classroom Applications of Self-Determined Reinforcement[1]

E. L. Glynn *†

ABSTRACT

Self-determined, experimenter-determined, and chance determined token reinforcement treatments were compared with a no-token treatment, in terms of effect on the learning of history and geography material in the classroom. Each treatment was assigned to one of four heterogeneous classes of Grade nine girls. An initial baseline period preceded the differential reinforcement period, and a token withdrawal period followed. Subsequently, the self-determined treatment was employed in all three token reinforcement classes, before a

* E. L. Glynn, "Classroom Applications of Self-Determined Reinforcement," *Journal of Applied Behavior Analysis* 3(1970): 123–132. Reprinted with permission. Copyright 1970 by the Society for the Experimental Analysis of Behavior, Inc.

† University of Toronto

[1] Reprints may be obtained from the author. Department of Education, University of Auckland, Box 2175, Auckland, New Zealand. Research reported in this paper was carried out in partial fulfillment of the Ph.D. degree at the Ontario Institute for Studies in Education (University of Toronto). The author is indebted to his chairman, Dr. S. B. K. Henderson for his valued support and encouragement.

final baseline period occurred.
Findings included a similarity of
initial baseline performance for all
classes, an equal superiority of self-
determined and experimenter-
determined treatments to chance-
determined and no-token
treatments, and significant
improvement from initial baseline
to final baseline for self-determined
and experimenter-determined
treatments, but not chance-
determined and no-token
treatments. Differential token
reinforcement experience was found
to influence subsequent rate of self-
determined token reinforcement.

There is confusion in the thinking of educators on the use of extrinsic
reinforcers in the control of children's classroom learning.

Clearly, educators do not object to extrinsic reinforcers *per se*, since
grades, promotions, degrees, diplomas, and medals appear to enjoy the
same widespread usage that Skinner noted in 1953. Moreover, it is
difficult to imagine a classroom where teacher praise and reprimand are
not used in an attempt to control children's behavior. Despite this
widespread use of extrinsic reinforcement, there is objection to the
employment of certain forms (such as candy and tokens) on the grounds
that the student will become dependent on them and will be unable to
perform without them. (Anderson, 1967.) Yet, surely, the same objection
should hold against all forms of extrinsic reinforcement, including teacher
praise and reprimand.

Perhaps an explanation for this confusion is that the operation of a
token reinforcement system, more than the generally inconsistent
operation of teacher praise and reprimand, emphasizes the extent to
which children's behavior is under the control of an external agent.
External control of behavior is distasteful to many educators who would
agree with R. M. Gagné, that ". . . the student must be progressively
weaned from dependence on the teacher or other agent external to
himself." (Gagné 1965, p. 213.)

It is suggested that some of the confusion has resulted from equating
extrinsic reinforcement with external control of behavior. The two terms
are not interchangeable. Skinner (1953), in discussing self-control,

suggests the individual may be capable of controlling his own behavior by means of dispensing his own reinforcement contingent upon making certain classes of responses. Various studies of self-reinforcement (Kanfer, Bradley, and Marston, 1962; Bandura and Kupers, 1964; and Bandura and Perloff, 1967), have permitted human subjects to take over the reinforcing function of the experimenter, by signalling correct responses, or rewarding themselves from a supply of tokens. Such self-administered reinforcing systems do seem to possess behavior maintenance capabilities, at least for simple responses—cranking a wheel (Bandura and Perloff, 1967), and visual discrimination (Kanfer and Duerfeldt, 1967).

The present study attempted to apply self-administered reinforcement procedures to classroom learning. If these procedures were to prove effective, they may be more acceptable to educators because they suggest a way to wean children from dependence on an external agent, and at the same time, would permit the use of effective extrinsic reinforcers.

Three major purposes of the study were: (1) to compare the effectiveness of self-determined and experimenter-determined token reinforcement treatments in the classroom setting; (2) to examine the effects of token withdrawal following these treatments; and (3) to examine the effect of differential token reinforcement experience on the amount of subsequent self-determined token reinforcement. A distinction is made here between *determination* and *administration* of reinforcement. All token reinforcement in this study was self-administered, but the amount of reinforcement was experimenter-determined, chance-determined, or self-determined (within the limits imposed by the experimental procedure).

METHOD

EXPERIMENTAL SITUATION

The study was planned to require a minimum of accommodation on the part of teacher and children, since it was intended to test the practicability of token reinforcement within the regular classroom program. The study did not require the teacher to alter subject content or teaching methods. Four intact class groups were used, which meant that no changes in timetable were requested, and children were never removed from their usual class setting. The subject matter, history and geography, was taught to all four classes, in the same topical order, by the one teacher. The token reinforcement treatments were administered by one experimenter in all four classes.

SUBJECTS

One hundred and twenty-eight ninth-grade girls, in four classes in a Toronto Separate School, served as subjects. Class size ranged from 30 to 34. Girls had been assigned to classes from an alphabetic list, which was divided into four sections. While not truly random, this procedure at least precluded deliberate stratification of classes according to ability.

None of the children presented any problem to the teacher with regard to disruptive behavior. The teacher considered all children "well-motivated" to learn, and interested in the subject matter. Having been present for a portion of the history and geography lessons of all four classes for the baseline period, the experimenter shared these opinions with the teacher.

DEPENDENT VARIABLES

1. Test Performance

Working from a list of history and geography topics supplied by the teacher, the experimenter prepared 40 reading sheets, each of approximately 500 words. The class history and geography texts provided source material. Accompanying each reading sheet was a sheet of 20 five-option multiple-choice questions, based on the factual content of the reading sheets. Hence, the major dependent variable for each of the five phases of the study was the average number of test items correctly answered by each girl.

An attempt was made to match the readings and tests closely with the teacher's program. This was not always achieved because of the occasional need for the teacher to revise a topic before going on to the next, and because the experimenter was requested to produce several readings on New Zealand, at a time when the teacher had almost completed her coverage of the topic. The four classes received all readings and tests, in the same order, with each phase of the study containing approximately five history and five geography readings.

2. Performance-Token Ratios

The tokens were slips of paper, 2 by 1 in. (5 by 2.5 cm) bearing a star and the words "one credit." Tokens were exchanged for a variety of inexpensive prizes at the end of the first token phase, and at the end of the study. After each token reinforcement phase, a performance-token ratio was obtained for every girl. This ratio was formed by computing the total number of correct test items obtained in a particular phase, and dividing this number by the total number of tokens received in that phase.

Originally, it was planned to make the tokens exchangeable for the potentially reinforcing events available within the school program, and selected by children according to preference. Examples of such potentially reinforcing events are: time off a particular activity, library time, free time, homework exemptions, punishment exemptions, and the right to perform special duties. However, it was discovered that control of such events was out of the hands of the teacher concerned. Secondary school teachers do not have the same freedom in manipulating timetables and reinforcing events as do elementary school teachers, where one teacher handles one class for almost all the academic program.

In view of this difficulty, it was decided to provide a series of prizes, which could be obtained by turning in credits. An opportunity was taken to make the prizes relevant to some of the history and geography material, by using numerous inexpensive New Zealand souvenir items. When turning in their tokens, the girls were allowed to select a prize from the many items displayed, according to their rank order in number of tokens earned. There was a sufficient range of prizes for even the last-ranked child to have some choice.

3. Inter-class Communication

An attempt was made to measure the extent of inter-class communication that occurred during the study, since it was realized that performance of one class could also be influenced by the knowledge that other classes were receiving different treatments. A set of three open-ended questions was administered to all children at the end of the study, asking them whether the treatment given their own class differed from that given the other classes, and if so, to state how.

PROCEDURE

1. First Baseline Phase (Baseline I)

This was a two-week period that served to establish basal measures of test performance in each of the four classes, and to accustom the children to the presence of the experimenter and the testing procedures. No tokens were issued.

Each day, the children were given a passage to read for 3 min, immediately after which the passage was collected, and a further 3 min were allowed for the multiple-choice test. (In considering these short time limits, it should be noted that the material encountered on the reading sheets would also have been covered by current teacher lessons). When the 3-min test session was over, immediate feedback of results was given, by means of the experimenter reading out the letter code for correct answers. The children then counted the number of test items correct, and entered this on a slip of paper in individual envelopes supplied for the purpose. Finally, test sheets and envelopes were collected by the experimenter. Instructions stressed that information in the envelopes would not be made available to anyone other than the experimenter.

2. First Token Phase (Token I)

This was the only period in which token reinforcement procedures differed across classes. The procedures employed were:

(a)   Experimenter-determined token reinforcement. Under this treatment, children received tokens according to an explicit rate of one token per four correct answers. During the token reinforcement periods, five tokens were placed in each envelope each day. The children were instructed to calculate the numbers of tokens earned by dividing their test score by four. An arbitrary rule permitted the taking of an additional token for a fractional number. (Thus a child would take four tokens if the number earned were 3¼, 3½, or 3¾.)

(b)   Self-determined token reinforcement treatment. Under this treatment, children were invited to: "decide how many tokens you think you should award yourself. You can decide on any number from zero to five." No rules or suggestions were made concerning bases for decision making. The use of envelopes was intended to minimize the effect of social cues from peers, and of modeling peer standards, both of which are known to influence the rate of self-reinforcement (Marston, 1964; Bandura and Whalen, 1966; McMains and Liebert, 1968).

(c)   Chance-determined token reinforcement. This was, in effect, an incentive-control treatment. Throughout the first token phase, the total number of tokens received by this class was kept identical with that of the self-reinforced class. Each day, chance-reinforced children were randomly assigned a "partner" from among the self-reinforced children. Ragardless of performance of the chance-reinforced child, she found in her envelope the number of tokens that her self-reinforced "partner" for the day had taken. As well as providing an incentive control treatment, this procedure enabled the examination of the effect of such inconsistent experience of amount of reinforcement on extent of subsequent self-reinforcement.

(d)   No-token reinforcement treatment. No token reinforcement was given under this treatment. The procedure was exactly the same as during Baseline I.

3. First Token Withdrawal Phase (Withdrawal I)

During this phase, token reinforcement was withdrawn from experimenter-reinforced, self-reinforced, and chance-reinforced classes.

4. Second Token Phase (Token II)

Tokens were reintroduced for the experimenter-reinforced, self-reinforced, and chance-reinforced classes, but all three classes were now permitted to operate the self-reinforced procedure. The major question asked was whether the children previously reinforced according to an externally imposed standard (experimenter-reinforced) would subsequently display a rate of self-reinforcement close to this standard.

5. Second Baseline Phase (Baseline II)

During this phase, the baseline readings and tests were readministered, in order to compare increase in performance on re-learning among the four classes. Tokens were withdrawn for the first half (Withdrawal II), but included for the second half (Token III).

6. Review Test

A review test was constructed of items from each of the tests administered during the first token phase, the token withdrawal, and the second token phase, in order to determine whether treatment effects were of a long-term nature. Since the test was administered after the repeat of baseline, the test-retest interval was 2 to 4 weeks for items from the second token phase (Sections C), 4 to 6 weeks for items from the token withdrawal phase (Section B), and 6 to 8 weeks for items from the first token phase (Section A). For the review test, seven tokens were provided in the envelopes of the experimenter-reinforced, self-reinforced, and chance-reinforced classes, and the self-reinforced procedure was applied in all three classes.

RESULTS

Daily test performance scores of all classes throughout the study are listed in Table 1. Also shown are the mean test performance scores for each phase of the study.

Table 1

Mean Performance Scores for all Sessions and Phases

		Class			
Session		Non-Reinforced	Chance-Reinforced	Experimenter-Reinforced	Self-Reinforced
Baseline I:	1	10.60*	9.57	9.88	9.66
	2	11.60*	10.54	11.13	11.47
	3	9.69*	8.80	8.70	8.35
	4	9.82	8.63	8.91	9.91*
	5	10.71*	10.19	9.47	8.70
	6	12.21*	10.87	9.81	10.69
	7	9.72*	6.97	8.39	9.25
	8	10.55*	9.32	9.81	9.70
	9	9.46*	6.55	7.44	7.25
	10	9.63	9.42	8.78	9.97*
	Mean:	10.38*	9.02	9.13	9.47
Token I:	11	7.44	7.14	8.33*	8.33*
	12	10.08	9.37	11.29*	10.15
	13	9.38	9.53	11.08	12.66*
	14	10.30	9.37	11.32	11.45*
	15	8.07	6.28	9.14	10.14*
	16	10.53	10.41	11.62	12.54*
	17	9.57	8.07	10.32*	10.07
	18	11.50	11.33	13.97*	13.27
	19	11.17	11.13	12.41	12.56*
	20	10.07	10.00	12.06*	11.61
	Mean:	9.71	9.13	11.12*	11.09
Withdrawal I:	21	11.25	9.20	11.61*	10.67
	22	10.53	8.75	10.52	11.10*
	23	12.83*	12.52	12.75	12.39
	24	13.31	13.79	13.63	14.48*
	25	11.29	10.86	10.94	12.73*
	26	8.44*	7.39	8.44*	7.40
	27	10.62*	9.46	9.74	10.23
	28	10.31*	8.87	10.13	8.80
	29	10.69	10.03	9.70	11.23*
	30	8.59*	6.83	8.55	8.32
	Mean:	10.44	9.72	10.53	10.87*
Token II:	31	11.12*	9.42	9.48	10.16
	32	11.97	10.55	11.84	12.28*
	33	9.89*	8.58	9.48	9.33
	34	11.47	10.42	11.63*	11.10
	35	9.17	8.10	9.52	9.87*

	36	11.50	9.46	11.28	13.22*
	37	8.36	7.52	8.76	9.13*
	38	9.63	8.83	11.03*	9.38
	39	9.83	10.34	11.10	12.16*
	40	12.30	11.45	12.65*	11.80
	Mean:	10.47	9.33	10.64*	10.59
Baseline II:					
(a) Withdrawal II:	41	10.90	11.42	12.42	12.70*
	42	13.64	12.55	13.84	14.09*
	43	10.36*	8.13	10.06	10.00
	44	8.36	9.97	10.91*	10.90
	45	11.57	10.40	11.25	11.07
	Mean:	10.74	10.49	11.79	11.87*
(b) Token III:	46	11.38	11.04	12.78	13.19*
	47	10.29	9.50	10.42*	10.10
	48	10.72	10.72	10.83	11.57*
	49	10.59*	8.93	9.37	9.83
	50	11.14	10.41	11.23	12.35*
	Mean:	10.48	9.78	10.89	10.96*

* Indicates highest scoring class.

It was considered that the performance of the non-reinforced class provided the best available estimate of variations due to fluctuations in test difficulty. Accordingly, Fig. 1 was produced by depicting the daily performance of the three treatment classes, in terms of difference from the non-reinforced class, so that variation due to fluctuating test difficulty might be removed.

BASELINE I

An analysis of variance performed on mean scores for Baseline I yielded a non-significant between-classes effect ($F3, 116 = 1.65$, $p > 0.05$), and Hartley's test for homogeneity of variance yielded an F max. of 1.40 which is not significant. The four classes were thus regarded as being similar in performance during Baseline I.

TOKEN I

An analysis of covariance was performed on Token I mean scores, using Baseline I mean scores as covariate. The between-classes effect was significant. ($F3, 115 = 16.69$, $p < 0.001$). An analysis of variance for repeated-measures on test scores in every alternate session of the Token I phase yielded an insignificant classes-by-sessions interaction. ($F 12, 464 =$

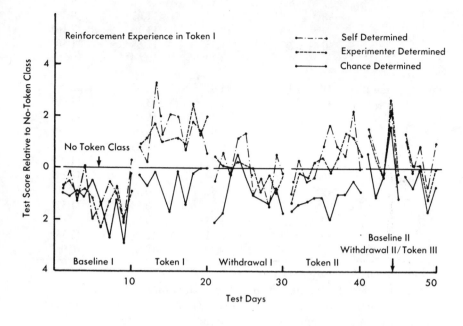

Figure 1

Daily test performance of the three token classes relative to the no-token class.

1.61, p > 0.05). Hence, analyses of mean Token I scores do not conceal any useful information about differential performance of classes across sessions.

The significant between-classes effect noted above is evident in Fig. 1. Token I mean scores were adjusted for the effect of the covariate (Baseline I performance), by the method suggested by Winer (1962, p. 592). Comparisons were made among the adjusted means by the Newman-Keuls procedure. The experimenter-reinforced and self-reinforced classes did not differ from one another, nor did the non-reinforced and chance-reinforced classes differ from one another. However, both the experimenter-reinforced and the self-reinforced classes differed significantly from the non-reinforced and chance-reinforced classes. The self-determined reinforcement procedure was equally as effective as the externally determined one, in producing an increase in performance.

WITHDRAWAL I

The analysis of covariance performed on Withdrawal I mean scores (using Baseline I mean scores as covariate), yielded a significant between-classes effect ($F\ 3, 115 = 3.24$, $p < 0.05$), though the effect was weaker than that of Token I. This was expected, since in Token I, performance was directly influenced by differences in treatment procedures. Again, a repeated-measures analysis of variance yielded a non-significant classes-by-sessions interaction ($F\ 12, 464 = 1.17$, $p > 0.05$) so that analyses of mean scores for Withdrawal I did not conceal information about differential performance of classes across sessions. The significant effect reported above suggests that there remained some effects of Token I treatments during Withdrawal I. This can be seen in Fig. 1. After the mean scores from Withdrawal I had been adjusted for the effect of the covariate, Newman-Keuls comparisons were made among them. It was found that the experimenter-reinforced and self-reinforced classes performed better than the non-reinforced class, but not better than the chance-reinforced class.

TOKEN II

The analysis of covariance performed on Token II mean scores (using Baseline I mean scores as covariate) yielded a significant, though weak, between-classes effect ($F\ 3, 115 = 2.85$, $p < 0.05$), but none of the possible comparisons among adjusted means yielded significant differences at the 0.05 level by Newman-Keuls tests. However, it can be seen from Fig. 1 that the experimenter-reinforced and self-reinforced classes were superior to the non-reinforced class for the greater part of Token II, while the chance-reinforced class always remained inferior to the non-reinforced class, suggesting some differences in performance between classes.

A repeated-measure analysis of variance of Token II data yielded a significant classes-by-sessions interaction ($F\ 12, 464 = 2.47$, $p < 0.01$). Hence, Token II mean scores obscure differential performance of classes across sessions. Figure 1 shows that the experimenter-reinforced and self-reinforced classes displayed a more obvious improvement in performance relative to the non-reinforced class than did the chance-reinforced class.

BASELINE II

As the readings and tests administered during Baseline II were the same as those for Baseline I, comparisons of performance gains over the two administrations were made across classes.

Highly significant phase effects were found, for both the Withdrawal II and Token III halves of the repeated-baseline tests, but these may be readily attributed to general practice effects. However, significant classes-by-phases interactions were also found: F 3, 116 = 4.23, p < 0.01 (for Withdrawal II), and F 3, 116 = 2.80, p < 0.05 (for Token III). Newman-Keuls comparison were carried out to examine these effects further. Table 2 shows that the interaction effect is attributable to significant increases on Baseline II administration for the experimenter-reinforced and self-reinforced classes. This increase is not significant in the case of the non-reinforced and chance-reinforced classes.

Table 2

Newman-Keuls qr Values for Differences between Baseline I and Baseline II Mean Test Performance Scores.

Test Days	Class	Baseline I	Baseline II	qr
1–5	NR	10.49	10.74	0.84
and	YR	9.43	10.49	3.53
41–45	ER	9.55	11.79	7.42**
	SR	9.49	11.87	7.86
6–10	NR	9.84	10.48	1.77
and	YR	8.58	9.78	3.32
16–50	ER	8.66	10.89	6.18**
	SR	8.81	10.96	5.96**

** p<0.01

REVIEW TEST

Analysis of variance performed on scores from each section of the Review Test yielded a significant between-classes effect (F 3, 108 = 4.47, p < 0.01) for Token I items (Section A). Newman-Keuls comparisons of class means revealed a pattern of significant results parallel to that of Token I performance. On Section A items, both the experimenter-reinforced and self-reinforced classes (x = 9.89 and 9.71) were slightly better than the non-reinforced and chance-reinforced classes (x = 8.21 and 8.00). There was no significant difference between the self-reinforced and experimenter-reinforced classes, nor between the non-reinforced and chance-reinforced classes. The performance increments resulting from differential reinforcement schedules evidently have some permanence. Sections B and C of the Review Test (Withdrawal I and Token II items) yielded no between-classes effects that reflected earlier treatments.

PERFORMANCE-TOKEN RATIOS

Table 3 presents data concerning number of tokens taken, and performance-token ratios of the three token classes throughout the study.

Analysis of variance indicated no significant differences in number of tokens taken by the three classes during Token I ($F\ 2, 90 = 0.453$, p >0.25). Hence, amount of token reinforcement can be regarded as similar across classes. Token I performance-token ratios were subjected to analysis by a median test for independent groups (Hays, 1962), since variances for the three groups departed widely from homogeniety (F max. $3, 30 = 9.05$, p < 0.01). The observed Chi-squared value for the median test was 35.1 (p < 0.001). Hence, despite similarity of amount of token reinforcement during the Token I phase, the performance-token ratio for the self-reinforced class was higher than those of the experimenter-reinforced and chance-reinforced classes, indicating that the self-reinforced class had "worked hardest" per token.

Table 3

Number of Tokens Taken and Performance-Token Ratios in all Token Phases

Phase	Chance-Reinforced Class		Experimenter-Reinforced Class		Self-Reinforced Class	
	Number	Ratio	Number	Ratio	Number	Ratio
Token I	2.87	3.26	3.10	3.60	2.90	3.99
Token II	2.63	3.54	3.13	3.43	2.76	3.92
Token III	2.83	3.71	3.29	3.33	2.95	3.89
Review Test	3.82	7.77	5.82	5.77	3.57	9.50

Similar results emerged in Token II. Again, no significant difference in amount of token reinforcement was found ($F\ 2, 90 = 2.37$, p > 0.05), but significant differences were found in performance-token ratios, ($F\ 2, 90 = 3.18$, p < 0.05), with that of the self-reinforced class being higher than those of the experimenter-reinforced or chance-reinforced classes.

In Token III, analysis of variance revealed that classes did differ in terms of amount of token reinforcement taken ($F\ 2, 90 = 4.19$, p < 0.05) with the self-reinforced class taking fewer tokens than the experimenter-reinforced class, though more than the chance-reinforced class. Yet, as Table 3 shows, the self-reinforced class again displayed the highest performance-token ratio.

The above pattern of results was also found in the data from the Review Test. There were significant differences both in amount of token reinforcement taken by the three classes (F 2, 81 = 62.59, p < 0.001), and in the performance token ratios (F 2, 81 = 9.20, p < 0.001). It can be seen from Table 3 that the self-reinforced class again took fewer tokens than the experimenter-reinforced and chance-reinforced classes, and displayed the highest performance-token ratio on the Review Test.

Table 4 supplies information on the variability in performance-token ratios for all token reinforcement phases. Clearly, the experimenter-reinforced class displayed the least variability throughout.

COMMUNICATION BETWEEN CLASSES

On the open-ended questions concerning knowledge of the treatment of other classes, the maximum "information score" was 3.0. Mean scores for the four classes were: non-reinforced, 0.74; chance-reinforced, 0.73; experimenter-reinforced, 0.44; and self-reinforced, 0.27. Newman-Keuls comparisons showed the self-reinforced class mean to be significantly lower than those of the chance-reinforced and non-reinforced classes. This could indicate that reported performance differences might be confounded by other factors arising from amount of information about other classes. However, a detailed examination of responses to the open-ended questions suggested that the extent of any such confounding was not great. Children made surprisingly few statements about how procedures in any of the classes had differed from their own.

DISCUSSION

1.   EFFECTIVENESS OF SELF-DETERMINED REINFORCEMENT

Restrictions must be placed on generalizing from the findings of this study, both in terms of the particular children involved, and in terms of the narrow range for self-determined reinforcement permitted by the procedure. It is an open question as to whether these results would be replicated with younger or underprivileged children, without some modification of procedure—for example, providing a wider variety of more meaningful prizes. It is also an open question as to whether similar results would have been obtained with these children, had there been

Table 4

Standard Deviations of Performance-Token Ratios

Phase	Chance Reinforced Class	Experimenter- Reinforced Class	Self- Reinforced Class
Token I	0.98	0.43	1.31
Token II	1.01	0.59	0.63
Token III	1.12	0.62	0.76
Review Test	3.86	1.86	3.69

wider limits allowed on amount of reinforcement, and had there been no check by the experimenter on the amount of reinforcement taken. Furthermore, these results would appear more convincing, had there been a further non-reinforced control class at another school. This would have yielded direct information about the effect on the non-reinforced class, of knowledge of reinforcement contingencies in the other classes. More accurately than the self-report measures used in this study, it would determine whether the performance of the non-reinforced class during token phases, was, in fact, only a reflection of test difficulty, or whether it was confounded with adverse motivational effects arising from knowledge of other treatments.

Nevertheless, the study does suggest that the concept of self-determined reinforcement is both applicable and appropriate for studies of academic performance in the classroom. Self-determined reinforcement, within the above-mentioned limits, proved to be at least as equally effective as experimenter-determined reinforcement, in terms of improving academic performance. Children were able to control successfully the token reinforcement for their classroom learning, when both social cues and specific instructions about extent of reinforcement were minimized. It would seem that the notion of systematic social reinforcement as a "critical component" of an effective token system (Kuypers, Becker, and O'Leary, 1968) may need to be qualified.

It is clear that token reinforcement procedures were less effective in Token II and Token III than in Token I. Since tokens were exchanged for prizes for the first time at the end of Token I, and since identical sets of prizes were available at the end of Token III, it is thought that the tokens dropped much of their value as reinforcers. There is a need for future studies to ensure a sufficiently varied set of reinforcing events to back up the tokens. The particular prizes used in this study were nevertheless effective during Token I, possibly because of their novelty.

2. PERFORMANCE OF THE CHANCE-REINFORCED TREATMENT CLASS

This class performed at a level generally below that of the non-reinforced class throughout the study. The inconsistent experience of this class in terms of amount of reinforcement during the Token I phase, seems to have not only precluded performance increments during this phase, but also to have prevented subsequent self-determined reinforcement procedures from having any incremental effect. This is certainly an indication that the ability to apply self-determined reinforcement is strongly influenced by the standards of externally determined reinforcement previously experienced. Hence, inconsistency of reinforcement can occur not only in terms of interspersing reinforcement with non-reinforcement as consequences of a given behavior, but also in terms of unpredictable amounts of reinforcement for a given behavior. These results suggest that parents and teachers, who function as major external reinforcing agents for children's behavior, should be aware that one consequence of maintaining such inconsistent standards of reinforcement may be impairment of the child's ability to apply self-determined reinforcement procedures effectively. If such an ability is considered as one component of self-control, as Marston and Kanfer (1963) suggest, then inconsistent experiences of amount of reinforcement would have a debilitating effect on the development of an individual's ability to control his own behavior.

3. WITHDRAWAL OF TOKENS

Findings suggest that after token withdrawal, the four classes did not revert to the similarity of performance displayed during the baseline. Token reinforcement classes experimenter-reinforced and self-reinforced remained slightly superior to the non-reinforced class. There seems little evidence to justify the fear that children would become dependent upon token reinforcement so as to be unable to perform without it.

4. PERFORMANCE-TOKEN RATIOS

Data on performance-token ratios provide further support that the operation of self-determined reinforcement is influenced by standards of externally determined reinforcement previously experienced. Table 3 shows that the experimenter-reinforced class adhered more closely to the performance-token ratio experienced during the Token I phase than did either the self-reinforced or chance-reinforced class. The experimenter-reinforced class had been supplied with an explicit ratio, whereas the self-reinforced and chance-reinforced classes had not. Yet, the self-reinforced and chance-reinforced classes moved towards a much higher performance-token ratio, especially on the Review Test. Table 4 indicates that the experimenter-reinforced class displayed the least variability in ratios throughout the study. This would be expected if members of this class were adhering to a common standard. The striking finding is that the children who had the greatest opportunity for leniency in taking tokens (self-reinforced class), actually imposed the strictest ratio on themselves.

The performance-token ratios observed in this study imply that an alternative to a teacher laying down explicit acceptable standards of performance for classroom learning, might be the provision of access to reinforcement on the basis of standards determined by individual children.

5. APPLICABILITY OF PROCEDURES

The token-reinforcement procedures employed proved to be well suited to classroom use. Tokens did not have to be paid out individually to each child (a saving of time and energy for the teacher). Handing out the envelopes took about 1 min each day, and children took about the same time to take their tokens and return the envelopes. Since envelopes contained a slip bearing daily performance scores, a continuous record was available showing performance and number of tokens taken. For experimental purposes, it can be noted that by including differential instructions in envelopes, several reinforcement procedures might be operated simultaneously.

References

Anderson, R. C. Educational Psychology. *Annual Review of Psychology*, 1967, 18, 129–164.

Bandura, A. and Kupers, C. J. Transmission of self-reinforcement through modeling. *Journal of Abnormal and Social Psychology*, 1964, 69, 1–9.

Bandura, A. and Whalen, C. K. The influence of antecedent reinforcement and divergent modeling cues on patterns of self reward. *Journal of Personality and Social Psychology*, 1966, 3, 373–382.

Bandura, A. and Perloff, B. Relative efficiency of self-monitored and externally imposed reinforcement systems. *Journal of Personality and Social Psychology*, 1967, 7, 111–116.

Gagné, R. M. *The conditions of learning*. New York: Holt, Rinehart & Winston, 1965.

Kanfer, F. H., Bradley, M. M., and Marston, A. R. Self-reinforcement as a function of degree of learning. *Psychological Reports*, 1962, 10, 885–886.

Kanfer, F. H. and Duerfeldt, P. H. Motivational properties of self-reinforcement. *Perceptual and Motor Skills*, 1967, 25, 237–246.

Kuypers, D. S., Becker, W. C., and O'Leary, K. D. How to make a token system fail. *Exceptional Children*, October 1968, 101–117.

Marston, A. R. Variables affecting incidence of self-reinforcement. *Psychological Reports*, 1964, 14, 879–884.

Marston, A. R. and Kanfer, F. H. Human reinforcement: experimenter and subject controlled. *Journal of Experimental Psychology*, 1963, 66, 91–94.

McMains, M. J. and Liebert, R. M. Influence of discrepancies between successively modeled self-reward criteria on the adoption of a self-imposed standard. *Journal of Personality and Social Psychology*, 1968, 8, 166–171.

Skinner, B. F. *Science and human behavior*. New York: Macmillan, 1953.

Winer, B. J. Statistical principles in experimental design. New York: McGraw-Hill, 1962.

A common observation made by teachers of delinquents is that they do not seem motivated to learn the usual classroom skills in the same way that the typical "socialized, achievement-oriented" middle-class child does. Graubard mentions that one reason for this may be that the conventional rewards of praise and attention from the teacher may not be particularly rewarding to a delinquent child, who is much more affected by the pressures of his peer group. Instead of opposing these pressures, Graubard attempted to utilize them in this study by making rewards for the group contingent upon the good behavior of all the students. In addition to this condition and a non-contingent reward control condition, the author also examined the effect of a combined condition, in which an individual could earn both rewards for the group and additional rewards for himself. The amount of appropriate behavior was greatest in the group plus individual condition, smaller in the group reward condition and smallest in the noncontingent reward condition; the opposite was true for inappropriate behavior. Although academic performance measures were not reported for each period, all eight boys gained roughly two grades in reading level during the one month period.

The boys in this study were allowed to select the rewards for which they wanted to work and to police each other's adherence to the rules formulated by the teacher. Her role was to teach, to ring a bonus bell signalling that extra points could be earned, and to dispense rewards. In the course of the study, the amount of work and good behavior necessary to earn points was increased as was the value of academic behavior relative to deportment. This combination of standards set arbitrarily by the teacher with the choice of adherence left up to the class appeared to be successful.

Graubard's interpretation suggests that permitting the group to select the behaviors to be rewarded would have been inappropriate at the beginning of the study, when the peer group pressures were very opposed to academic work. By the end of the project, however, academic work and proper deportment within the classroom appeared to be sanctioned by the peer group, even when the boys were working partly for individual rewards. If the program had lasted longer, it eventually might have been possible to let the boys participate in the selection and recording of the behaviors to be reinforced and the dispensing of the rewards. It may also be true that attention and praise from the teacher would become rewarding as the classroom situation loses its aversiveness and her attention is paired with material rewards and social rewards from peers. Although this project was carried out in a summer school program, it appears very feasible for a regular classroom. Certainly, the cost of the reinforcers would be less than that of the delinquents' vandalism and the counselors usually provided for them.

Utilizing the Group in Teaching Disturbed Delinquents to Learn

Paul S. Graubard*†

ABSTRACT

A group of disturbed, delinquent children were taught under 3 conditions. The group acted as its own control. Dependent variables were reading gains and appropriate classroom behaviors. Making rewards for all subjects contingent on each subject's behaving appropriately proved superior to giving rewards on a noncontingent basis. Giving group reinforcers for appropriate classroom behavior plus individual reinforcers for academic achievement proved to be the most efficacious. The group can be a powerful instrument in teaching disturbed delinquents.

It has been demonstrated that the use of teacher praise and attention can effectively modify the behavior of low achieving and obstreperous children (Hall, Lund & Jackson, 1968). Other studies report that token

---

*Paul S. Graubard, "Utilizing the Group in Teaching Disturbed Delinquents to Learn," *Exceptional Children* 36(1969): 267-272. Reprinted with permission.

† Paul S. Graubard is Associate Professor, Department of Special Education, Ferkauf Graduate School of Humanities and Social Sciences, Yeshiva University, New York.

reinforcement productively changes behavior with the emotionally disturbed (O'Leary & Becker, 1967), the retarded (Bijou, 1966), the culturally deprived (Wolf, Giles, & Hall, 1968), and with a culturally deprived juvenile delinquent (Staats & Butterfield, 1965).

The Staats and Butterfield study was limited in that only a single subject was worked with and the teacher did not have to contend with antisocial behavior being reinforced by peers. Peers are, however, present in school situations. A study by Zimmerman and Zimmerman (1962) in a special education class found, in contrast to the Hall study, that teacher praise acted to decrease academic performance. Peer reinforcement might account for the different results of the two studies, for in certain subcultures the peer group can be a more powerful reinforcer than the teacher. Nevertheless, the effect of the peer group is largely unexplored in the educational literature, and clinical experience and sociological theory suggest that many learners are caught up in the battle between peer and school values. These students probably comprise a sizable proportion of the educational casualties in schools. Enough theory has been generated to warrant attacking this problem directly.

THE CULTURE OF THE DELINQUENT

Cloward and Ohlin (1960) suggested that the school represents a value system and a way of life that is unacceptable to urban delinquents. Thus, a delinquent who is successful in school according to school norms risks losing status in his group. Cloward and Ohlin also argued that because of differential opportunities, certain rewards of society are denied to many youngsters. These individuals then band together to form a delinquent subculture which is capable of developing its own reward system. Parsons (1954) maintained that school and academic learning are perceived as unmasculine by delinquents and predelinquents. The group is formed to consolidate a masculine front as imposing as the demands of the schools. Parsons maintained that this is particularly true in urban areas where the female centered household is more common.

In the face of this, the general pattern of schools is to attempt to win individual students over to the traditional social values of success and reward. This has been called the "artichoke technique," because the teacher attempts to peel the child away from the group just as one peels the artichoke leaves off the stem. This technique is not universally successful because of the limited battery of rewards available to the teacher, as well as the relatively low power and status of the school when compared with the peer group. Clinical evidence has been found

(Minuchin, Chamberlain, & Graubard, 1967) that with disturbed delinquents, rewards and teaching coming from peers are more effective than rewards and teaching associated with authority figures, such as teachers.

The primary purpose of this project was to ascertain whether the delinquent peer culture could explicitly be enlisted in the acquisition of academic skills and the diminution of antischool behavior, and to determine if children could learn more effectively and efficiently by utilizing the peer group as the reinforcing agent rather than the teacher. Another purpose of the study was to examine the process of managing and teaching disruptive groups by a clearly explicated teaching method.

METHOD

Subjects

The subjects were eight boys in residential treatment through court order for antisocial behaviors. They formed a natural group in that they comprised the residential population of an agency and made up a delinquent subculture within the agency. The boys had lived together for approximately one year. They ranged in age from 10 to 12. Their psychiatric diagnoses varied although the label "undifferentiated" is the most descriptive (Auerswald, 1964). IQ scores ranged from 74 to 112. Reading levels ranged from third to sixth grade. The referring agency was asked to select their most aggressive children for inclusion in the experimental classroom. Each subject had an extensive history of disruptive behavior in school situations.

Setting

Sessions were held at a university classroom 4 days a week for a one month period during the summer. The room, which was similar to public school classrooms in New York City, was a self contained unit equipped with a one way vision mirror and closed circuit television.

Instructional Program

The teaching day was divided into several segments: a reading period in which SRA and Sullivan materials were used, an arithmetic period in which teacher-made worksheets were completed, a dramatics period, a social studies discussion period, and free time if work had been completed and no antisocial conduct had been displayed during the school day. During this free time the boys were allowed to play games, but the children generally elected to bring their own records and phonograph and dance.

Data Recording

Subjects were observed directly. Observers, stationed behind the one way mirror, observed the class for two 24-minute periods each hour. The subjects did not know when they were being observed although they were fully aware that there was an observer. The observer checked off the behavior of each subject by going down the list of names every 10 seconds for a 3 minute period. Each boy was observed approximately 36 times per hour, or 108 times per school morning. Using an observation schema adapted from Becker (1967), the subjects were given an "A" for appropriate behavior, which was defined as following directions, eyes on work, writing, speaking to the teacher or to peers about school matters, or following school routines and/or teacher instruction. The boy received an "I" for inappropriate behavior, which was defined as disrupting the class, cursing, throwing objects, hitting, being out of seat without permission, or talking without permission. The subjects received an "E" for excused absence, which was defined as going to the bathroom with permission, going for a drink with permission, etc. A finer breakdown of both appropriate and inappropriate behaviors was kept to help plan programs for individual boys, but these different behaviors can be subsumed under "A" or "I" for this report. The only school rules which were put into effect were that (a) attendance was mandatory (an agency requirement), (b) subjects could not destroy property, and (c) subjects could not use physical force. Infraction of these rules meant that the boys had to leave school for the day.

The observer ratings were checked by two other judges at least three times each week and agreement never fell below 92 percent. Reliability was calculated by total numbers of agreement over total numbers of observations times 100.

DESIGN

The class was taught under three different conditions. In each case the teacher's performance was continually monitored by two judges to make sure that she followed the required, predetermined teaching conditions. In the first condition (A) a group consensus determined reinforcers. The subjects selected kits, goldfish, shirts, baseball bats, marbles, and money. Points were assigned to each of these given items and the acquisition of these reinforcers was contingent upon *each* subject in the group achieving a minimum number of points. Points could be earned for following school rules and achieving specified outputs of academic work explicitly defined for each subject area. Rules dealing with attendance, destruction of property, and use of physical force in the classroom were given to the subjects and not open to discussion. Other rules dealing with talking out, standards for work, rules for discussions, procedures for working with the teacher, etc., were evolved by the teacher and pupils. The teacher then explained that she would not insist that children follow the rules, but would instead devote all her energy to assisting with academic work keeping records, and giving out points for appropriate behavior. If the class engaged in inappropriate behavior the teacher would tolerate it, but the subjects would not receive their reinforcers.

Management of the class was then given to the subjects. No formal structure was established for this. Instead, the subjects would spontaneously remind transgressors that inappropriate behavior affected them all. A frequency count showed that these reminders usually came from the children who scored highest on a class sociometric device and were judged by the adults to be the group leaders.

The teacher did not react to inappropriate behavior (except when it involved destruction of property or use of physical force). To achieve appropriate behavior she rang a bonus bell at which time she would dispense bonus points. The bonus bell was rung at variable intervals; at first it was rung frequently (once every 4 minutes or less) on a random schedule, and later at longer intervals. If everyone were behaving appropriately when the bell rang, each subject earned 10 bonus points.

The bonus bell was based on the assumption that the more that the subjects displayed appropriate behavior the more likely they were to be rewarded. This assumption was predicated on the fact that since the boys could never be sure when the bonus bell would ring, and since acting appropriately when the bell rang resulted in achieving desired rewards, it was to their own advantage to act appropriately most of the time to increase the probability of being "caught" acting appropriately. The bonus bell was used for each contingency period although it was used less and less as the project progressed.

The group consensus period was followed by the noncontingent (B) reward condition. During this condition the same academic routines and work were followed as in the A period but points were given at the beginning of the day and thus were not contingent on the subjects' behaviors. Teacher praise, grades, and exhortation were used to help the boys complete academic tasks and follow school regulations. In addition, the teacher intervened during periods of obstreperous behavior, whereas under group consensus, obstreperous and inappropriate behaviors were ignored and left for the group to handle.

After the noncontingent teaching condition, the A group consensus condition was reinstated. (See A¹ in Figure 1 and Table 1.) Then the last condition (C) was initiated. During this condition (group and individual contingencies), each subject still had to achieve minimum behavior and academic points to win group prizes, but the prizes were changed to snacks such as chicken, cake, and pizza. Individuals were then allowed to work for self selected prizes which were again made contingent upon achieving additional specified numbers of academic points. During the beginning of the project, behavior points were worth twice as much as academic points, but as the sessions progressed, these procedures were reversed.

RESULTS

The dependent variables in this study were appropriate and inappropriate classroom behaviors and reading levels. Reading gains were measured by progression from lower level SRA material to SRA material of a higher grade level. Each subject was able to read and comprehend material at least two color cards above his own entry point or baseline during the course of the 20 session project. SRA programs are divided into different levels of difficulty which are shown by a color code. These levels of difficulty roughly correspond to grade level.

Table 1

Probability Levels of Change in Behavior During Different Teaching Conditions

Conditions		Appropriate	Excused	In-appropriate
Noncontingent (B) vs. Group Consensus	(A¹)	.04	NS	.02
(A¹) Group Consensus vs. Group + Individual	(C)	.01	NS	.01
(C) Group + Individual vs. Noncontingent	(B)	.005	.02	.005

Note:—Due to the small number of days during A, significance between A and B is not possible to obtain by the median test and therefore no statistical analysis was made, but inspection of Figure 1 shows the trend of the direction of the changes.

Figure 1 shows how subjects performed during each condition. Since conditions were run for different lengths of time and since subjects were absent for varying lengths of time because of dental visits, etc., the most meaningful comparison seemed to be percent of behaviors based on total number of observations for each teaching condition.

The probability values of the changes in behavior have been calculated by the median test (Siegal, 1956) and are shown in Table 1.

Two things must be said about the results:

1. As the sessions progressed, the subjects had to complete increasingly longer assignments to achieve the same number of points and the behavior points decreased in value.
2. For purposes of this study, cursing was considered an inappropriate behavior. During the group conditions the majority of "I's" were received for cursing, an act which appeared to receive tremendous group reinforcement. Given a teacher with a high tolerance level for vulgar words, the "I" behaviors would have decreased to practically zero.

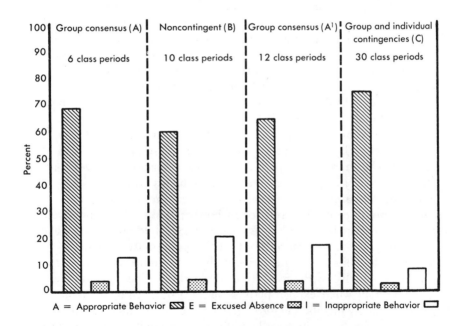

Figure 1

Subjects' behaviors during different teaching conditions.

In addition the subjects had to leave school for infraction of rules regarding destruction of property and/or using physical force four times during the B condition, one time during the A condition, and no time during C.

DISCUSSION

The data show that the procedures used in this classroom were effective, in increasing academic output of the group, in shaping appropriate classroom behaviors, and in eliminating disruptive behaviors. In fact, during the individual reward condition, for 3 days of the 6 day period, there were only two or fewer disruptive incidents observed in students who had been especially picked for aggressive behavior and who had a long history of failure in and expulsion from public schools. The group was able to move from a 24 percent inappropriate behavior level (approximately once in every 4 minutes) to 10 percent (once in 10 minutes), a much more tolerable level. In addition, subjects showed substantial progress in reading achievement as measured by completed frames of programed instruction and completion of teacher produced arithmetic worksheets. While the design of this study does not allow us to gauge the relative efficiency of this method compared to other approaches, such as going directly from noncontingent to individual rewards, the fact that this group was able to learn and behave in school is important in and of itself.

The process by which this occurred is worth analyzing, albeit speculatively. The fact that the group gave its consensus for rewards appears to be an important part of the process. Academic prowess and classroom conformity are not values that are highly admired by this population (Brown, 1965; Parsons, 1954). Great pressure is put on children not to conform to rules of authority (Polsky, 1962), and severe punishment is meted out by their peers to those children who do violate peer values. It is felt by the author that the group must consciously legitimize learning so that the individuals in the group do not have to concern themselves with loss of status for learning. This is not unlike family therapy where explicit permission must be given by the more powerful family members before a given topic can be discussed by individuals. In the group reward condition, learning is reinforced by the group since the group benefits from the performance of the individual. While there is no direct evidence from this study, it is doubtful if many individuals are strong enough to resist the mores of the delinquent group regarding school achievement, and this might help to explain the low achievement of so many delinquent youth (Prentice & Kelley, 1963).

Once the group had sanctioned learning there was a sudden shift in the performance of individuals and disruptions began to decrease. While group rewards appear to be considerably better than noncontingent payoff, Condition C, group and individual rewards, was introduced because the eventual goal was to bring these subjects into the mainstream of education and to have them work with only minimal dependence on the group. In addition, there was a concern about a least effort effect where subjects would only work to achieve the group minimum.

Individual rewards were then introduced so the subjects could receive rewards in excess of those achieved by the group, contingent on the subject's own effort. Under this condition, after they had received the group's permission to learn, a dramatic increase in learning was noted with a simultaneous decrease of disruptive behavior.

The fact that the group took responsibility for itself, gave individual members permission to learn, and could concretely achieve its own goals and rewards appears to have been the paramount factor in the success of this project.

The group's managing itself is not unlike aspects of the civil rights struggle in which groups and communities manage themselves, but will not be told what to do. It is recognized that this study was of short duration, used a small number of subjects, and took place in a laboratory setting rather than a public school. In other settings and over longer periods of time the boys might have reverted to former patterns of behavior or been more intractable regarding change. Only longer term studies which are now underway in public school settings can answer these questions. Nevertheless, the subjects were capable of shifting behavior when the environment shifted so that the teacher was able to teach and guide academic learning for most of the school day, and the group appeared to be instrumental in this process. To date, there has been little consonance between the world of disturbed delinquent children and the school. Instead of being cognizant of, negotiating with, and enlisting the support of the group, educators have traditionally ignored it and usually this has been done at the expense of the teacher and especially the children.

References

Auerswald, E. Developmental effects of poverty in children of hard core urban families: Implications for nosology and treatment. Paper presented at the American Orthopsychiatric Association, Chicago, 1964.

Becker, W. C., Madsen, C. H., Jr., Arnold, C. R., and Thomas D. R. The contingent use of teacher attention and praise in reducing classroom behavior problems. *Journal of Special Education*, 1967, I, 287-307.

Bijou, S. W. Functional analysis of retarded development. In N. R. Ellis (Ed.), *International review of research in mental retardation.* Vol. 1. New York: Academic Press, 1966, Pp. 1-19.

Brown C. *Manchild in the promised land.* New York: MacMillan, 1965.

Cloward, R., & Ohlin, L. *Delinquency and opportunity: A theory of delinquent gangs.* Glencoe, Ill.: Free Press, 1960.

Hall, V., Lund, D., & Jackson, D. Effects of teacher attention on study behavior. *Journal of Applied Behavior Analysis*, 1968, I, 1-12.

Minuchin, S., Chamberlain, P., & Graubard, P. A project to teach learning skills to disturbed delinquent children. *American Journal of Orthopsychiatry,* 1967, 37, 558-567.

O'Leary, K. D., & Becker, W. C. Behavior modification of an adjustment class: A token reinforcement system. *Exceptional children.* 1967, 33, 637-642. 1967, 33, 737-642.

Parsons, T. *Essays in sociological theory* (Rev. ed.). Glencoe, Ill.: Free Press, 1954.

Polsky, H. *Cottage six—The social system of delinquent boys in residential treatment.* New York: Russell Sage Foundation, 1962.

Prentice, N., & Kelley, F. J. Intelligence and delinquency: A reconsideration. *Journal of Social Psychology*, 1963, 60, 327-339.

Siegal, S. *Non-parametric statistics in the behavioral sciences.* New York: McGraw-Hill, 1956.

Staats, A., & Butterfield, W. Treatment of nonreading in a culturally deprived juvenile delinquent: An application of reinforcement principles. *Child Development*, 1965, 36, 925-942.

Wolf, M., Giles, D., & Hall, V. Experiments with token reinforcement in a remedial classroom. *Behavior Research and Therapy*, 1968, 1, 51-64.

Zimmerman, E., & Zimmerman, J. The alteration of behavior in a special classroom. *Journal of Experimental Analysis of Behavior*, 1962, 5, 159-160.

In this article Clark and Walberg report a series of seven experiments, all using children from schools in poverty areas and most involving children who previously had been doing very poorly in school. Although some authors have suggested that lower socioeconomic status children might be less sensitive to praise from a teacher since they are less likely than middle class children to share the teacher's values and perhaps to admire him, this opinion would not be borne out by these authors' results. Consistently, they found positive effects of giving children extra praise or social rewards for good performance: Improvement was found for such diverse behaviors as spelling, level of aspiration in several areas, a word-making task, liking for teachers, and reading. Moreover the amount of praise received from teachers was significantly related to both students' attitudes toward their parents and teachers' attitudes toward their students. Although these latter results cannot be said to prove that receiving or giving increased praise caused these attitude changes, they are supportive of such an interpretation.

If the social rewards used by the authors have been so uniformly successful, particularly with those children from a poverty area who have been classified by the school system as "educable mentally handicapped," one might conclude, as the authors suggest, that "all teachers need to be trained in the systematic application of rewards." One obstacle in working with these children is the tendency to give them very little praise, since their performance is so far below that of middle-class "normal" children. Another problem is the alternative tendency to give them much noncontingent warmth and affection without relating your reactions to their performance. In view of the authors' successful results and the many anecdotal reports of classes in lower socioeconomic status areas being run almost totally by aversive control, their suggestion for training teachers to use praise appropriately deserves to be taken seriously.

The Use of Secondary Reinforcement in Teaching Inner-City School Children

Carl A. Clark
and
Herbert J. Walberg*†

ABSTRACT

For a number of years we have been experimenting with the effects of rewards on classroom learning. We have found the classroom to be a satisfactory laboratory, particularly with slow-learning and mentally retarded pupils. It is our belief that when there is greater recognition that the classroom can be an excellent place for experimentation, and when rigorous experimental conditions are permitted and encouraged, the progress of psychological research and educational practice will be accelerated, and there will be less reliance on pedagogical philosophies and methods which are subjectively based upon authority or fad.

* Carl A. Clark and Herbert J. Walberg, "The Use of Secondary Reinforcement in Teaching Inner-City School Children," *The Journal of Special Education* 3(1969): 177–185. Reprinted with permission.
† Chicago State College and Harvard University

A number of studies will be reported here which illustrate the thesis that the classroom can serve as an educational laboratory. These studies concern the school achievement of retarded and culturally-deprived students.[1]

STUDY 1: COMPETITION AS MOTIVATION

Harris (1958) carried out one of our first experiments in the controlled use of secondary reinforcement in classroom learning. The independent variable was the learning of spelling. The motivation was competition, certainly one of the most important of learned human drives. The children in the experiment had been classified as "mentally handicapped." The motivation of competition has not often been used with such children in academic situations, since it is often assumed that they have had their learned competitive drives for scholastic success extinguished, or have found competition to have negative effects.

Five classrooms of educable mentally-handicapped (EMH) children in the Chicago Public Schools took part in this study. Ten children were selected at random from each classroom. Five of these ten were chosen at random from each class to receive the experimental treatment, the other five making up a control group. Subjects were assigned entirely at random, and the ages and IQs for the experimental and control groups were very similar: The mean age for the experimental group was 13 years 6 months; IQ, 70; and the average number of semesters in EMH classrooms was 5.44. The mean age for the control group was 13 years 7 months; IQ, 69; and the number of semesters in EMH classes, 5.92. Twice a week the experimental subjects took part in a spell-down, while the control subjects had regular spelling lessons, consisting of routine drill and copying.

The reinforcement of winning in the spell-down was controlled, so that every child in the experimental group had at least several successes. To

---

[1] Dr. Concetta V. Romanow participated in guiding Studies 1, 2, and 3, which were conducted by Jo Ahn Brown, Grace J. G. Dawson, and Leola G. Harris, respectively. We conducted studies 4, 5, 6, and 7 within the Chicago Project of the Great Cities School Improvement Program, which was sponsored by the Ford Foundation and administered by the Chicago Public Schools. Some of the findings reported here were presented at the American Association for the Advancement of Science annual meeting in Berkeley, California, 1965, and at the American Psychological Association annual meeting in New York, 1966.

assure distribution of rewards, easier words were occasionally given to poorer spellers and harder words to better spellers.

The experimental group gained over twice as much as the control group in number of words correctly spelled on a post-test given at the end of the semester (significant at the .05 level). The design for the experiment was a Lindquist (1953) Type III analysis of variance, in which the principal experimental variable was a within-groups effect, implying that the experimental effect would not be accounted for by individual differences.

This study illustrates the use of a particular type of reward (success in competition) based on aroused competitive motivation—a strong secondary drive. It indicates that competition should be considered a useful motivation for even so-called mentally retarded pupils, provided all can experience frequent success.

STUDY 2: PRAISE

Dawson (1961) studied the effects of praise given by a teacher to mentally-handicapped pupils. The principal idea was to control amount and distribution of praise given to the children, in order to determine its effect on verbal learning.

Both a primary and an advanced EMH classroom were used, with 16 pupils in each. For four weeks the teacher gave increased praise to a random half of each class. There was no indication to any of the children that they were participants in an experiment, and no changes apparent to the children were made in the regular classroom procedure. The teacher praised all the children at least as much as usual and gave extra praise to the experimental subjects in ways that would make detection of this extra rewarding by any of the children—experimental or control—unlikely. A usual classroom practice for these children was that they were frequently excused from the room for special instruction, errands, or counseling. During the experiment, these occasions were used by the teacher to give additional praise to the experimental subjects. She also praised the children by writing comments on test papers and homework.

After four weeks, the post-test was given, and the gain in the number of words correctly spelled by the control groups, primary and advanced, was found to average between seven and eight. The highly-praised children, however, gained an average of 16 words, a significantly greater gain ($p < .01$). There was no significant interaction of initial ability, or primary or advanced classification, with conditions of praise. The design for the experiment was a Lindquist (1953) Type I analysis of variance with the crucial variable being "praise."

STUDY 3: CONCOMITANT LEARNING

Rigorous secondary reinforcement of classroom verbal responses may result not only in the direct learning of these responses, but also in the learning of other (often internal) responses that occur at the same time. Some of these are "attitude," "level of aspiration," responses to the teacher and to the on-going classroom procedure, and, very generally, whatever responses occur frequently and coincidentally with the specific dependent variable. The cues produced by some of these responses might, in turn, operate as secondary drives and thus provide further bases for secondary reinforcement in classroom learning situations.

In a study of several of these attitudinal variables (Brown, 1964), 64 children in two fourth grade classrooms were randomly assigned to experimental and control groups within each class. The ages were eight to 11; average, 9.4 years. The average Kuhlmann-Anderson IQ for all children was 95.5. All lived in a low-rent public housing community on Chicago's South Side, where the median family income was $2,920 per year, and 43 percent of the families received public welfare assistance.

The experimental variable was praise administered by the teacher. All children got at least the same amount of praise they had been receiving, but the experimental subjects received a much greater amount. Half of each group (randomly assigned) were of the same sex.

There were five dependent variables. One was vocational level of aspiration, defined by a specially-constructed test with separate, comparable test forms for boys and girls. A second dependent variable was a word-making test, in which the subjects were to form as many words as possible from each of a given set of longer words. A level of aspiration score was also obtained for performance on this task. A fourth set of scores was obtained for dart-throwing at a target, with a level of aspiration score for this task as another dependent variable. All of these variables were measured before and after the experimental period.

School work was conducted as usual, but increased praise was administered to the experimental group. The children were unaware that an experiment was taking place, and they had no reason to expect that the dependent variable tasks would be administered again.

A Type III analysis of variance (Lindquist, 1953) showed that the high praise group gained significantly more than the control group in level of

Table 1
Level of Aspiration
Post-test minus Pre-test (Gains)

	High Praise	Low praise
Word-making	10.44	0.13 p<.01
Dart-throwing	6.88	1.72 p<.01
Vocational aspiration	12.97	0.72 p<.01

vocational aspiration ($p < .01$). In fact, there was practically no change in the control group, while children in the high praise group raised their sights much higher in their future vocational expectations. The boys gained about as much as the girls.

The same results were obtained concerning expressed aspirations for both the word-making and dart-throwing tasks. The highly-praised children significantly improved their scores on the word-making task as compared to the controls, and, again, there was practically no change for the control children. There was no significantly greater change for the experimental subjects on actual scores for dart-throwing, though the mean change for the experimental group was slightly greater. The latter result is no surprising, since there was no interpolated dart-throwing practice in the study and since this task is much less related to the interpolated classroom activities than are tasks such as word-making. There was a significant gain, however, in the level of aspiration for dart-throwing. The highly praised group predicted considerably higher scores for themselves than did the low-praised group.

The study, in summary, showed that the effects of reinforcement in a regular classroom situation will generalize to attitudes and to skills not usually studied in class. Rewarded success in regular classwork may therefore make for greater success in future vocational work, even though they may not be directly related. This factor may be generalized even for success in physical activity. More research, of course, is necessary to test the generality of the effects of teachers' praise on behavior outside the school.

STUDY 4: ATTITUDES TOWARD TEACHERS

Will increased rewards given outside the classroom, such as in the home, generalize to classroom work or to attitudes toward the teacher or the school? To study this question, we administered a teacher attitude scale (developed by Dr. Benjamin D. Wright and colleagues at the University of Chicago) to 200 children, 11 to 13 years of age, in special classes for slow learners. The teachers were asked not to be present when the scale was administered, and the pupils were assured that no teacher or school administrator would be given the results. The parents of the children were then contacted and asked if they would participate in a home quiz program with their children, for which we would furnish the materials.

Some 60 parents indicated initial interest, but only 40 followed through to the point of actual participation. These parents were assigned to experimental and control groups, using a table of random numbers. The control parents were told that since all who offered could not participate at once, they could take part in the study in the following semester.

The parents in the experimental group read the questions on the home quiz to their children and immediately informed them when they gave the right answer, which was given on the question sheet. The questions were designed to be of easy to moderate difficulty. Thus the children were frequently reinforced during the twice-weekly sessions with their parents. Each week the parents sent the two question sheets back, with check-marks indicating the responses of their children.

Occasionally some of the parents would fail to hold sessions with their children. When this happened, if they did not respond to a follow-up letter, they were visited by a counselor. The final count of those who participated fully to the end of the experiment was 14 in the experimental group. One pupil in the control group was not present for the final testing, leaving 19 in that group.

At the end of the fall term, all 200 pupils were given the teacher attitude scale again. The over-all result was a significantly less favorable attitude toward their teachers. The control group loss in teacher attitude score was very close to that of the total group.

The children of the experimental group, however, showed a large statistically significant gain ($p < .01$).

Reinforcement by parents in the home in connection with a school-like quiz session, therefore, apparently helps create a better attitude toward teachers. This study also indicates that in the absence of a stepped-up reward program by the parent or teacher, there may be a gradual deterioration of the pupil's attitude toward the teacher during the course of the school year.

Table 2
Actual Gains

	High Praise	Low praise
Dart-throwing	6.91	5.13 p>.05
		(not significant)
Word-making	13.13	1.41 p<.01

STUDY 5: ATTITUDES TOWARD PARENTS

A correlational study was done in six classrooms, of about 20 students each, at the same school used in Study 4. Students in a college educational psychology course observed and recorded rewards and reproofs given by the teachers throughout the semester. There was a low correlation (.16) between the children's ratings of their parents at the beginning of the semester and total rewards received by them during the semester. The correlation between total rewards and the children's ratings of their parents at the end of the semester was .41 (a difference between ratings significant at the .05 level). The more highly-rewarded children tended to have more favorable attitudes toward their parents. There is reason to believe, therefore, that children who receive individual praise from their teachers at school will improve their attitudes toward their parents. This complements the finding of the previous experiment that children working with their parents on school-related problems improve their attitudes toward their teachers.

STUDY 6: EFFECTS OF REWARDING ON TEACHERS

What effect will rewarding children have on the teachers who give the rewards? The study we made that has some bearing on this question gives an encouraging answer. Each of five teachers had two randomly-assigned classes in a summer reading program. Each teacher was asked to present extra rewards (praise and comments on papers) to one of the two classes— again randomly determined by the experimenters. The teachers also kept a daily tabulation of types of behavior of each pupil. The behaviors were classified as positive, e.g., "asks questions about class-work" and "volunteers answers to questions," and negative, e.g., "misbehaves" and "not working on assignment." The experiment continued for three weeks. The distribution in both groups of positive assessment, as compared to negative, deviated far from chance expectations (beyond the .01 level), using the Chi Square test. The experimental pupils had more than five times as many positive marks as the controls and only half as many negative.

This study indicates that teachers tend to rate those pupils highly whom they have rewarded. Possibly the rewarded pupils behaved better, thus contributing to a more favorable attitude toward the pupil; but it is also possible that rewarding improves the attitude of the rewarder to the subject, even apart from responses made by the subject.

STUDY 7: REWARDS SCORED

Perhaps the most important factor in the application of secondary reinforcement to classroom learning is the systematization of the distribution and measurement of the rewards. In the regular classroom, rewards are normally given to pupils continuously throughout the day. But often they are a response on the part of the teacher to reinforcement he receives from the pupils through their meeting teacher expectations of behavior. Thus a certain number of pupils meet the teacher's desires for achievement and are rewarded and therefore achieve more; while others, achieving less and being rewarded less, then achieve still less or not at all. The rewards these children get often come from the attention they get for misbehaving or from doing poor quality school work and these, therefore, are the behaviors that are actually being reinforced. Such children are being taught to misbehave and do poor school work.

It is necessary to break these vicious circles through carefully planned reward systems to be continuously applied throughout the school life of every child. One might think that such a planned reward system would make for a mechanical classroom situation lacking in spontaneity. In our experiments we have found the reverse to be the case. This was shown not only by the measurements of attitudes of pupils and teachers, but in the statements made by teachers participating in the experiments. They were, with very few exceptions, highly enthusiastic about the reward systems, and they often referred to an increased eagerness to participate in learning by the pupils. Such was the case even in one of our more mechanically contrived reward systems, used in an experiment now to be described (Clark & Walberg, 1968).

In this study, individual cards were given daily to each pupil. Each card contained sequentially-numbered squares which the pupil could circle as a reward when told to do so by the teacher. The cards were collected at the end of each period and the number of rewards for each pupil tallied. In order to help control the possibility that a pupil could mark his card when he was not receiving rewards, special blue pencils with blue-colored "leads" were given out. A pupil was to pick up and use this only when he was told to circle a number after being praised. Numbers circled with ordinary pencils would not count, and it would be fairly obvious if a pupil picked up and used the special blue pencil—obvious to both the teacher and the other pupils.

A special problem with the use of the blue pencil and card system was the possible "gadget effect." But as this effect in itself contributed a reward, it did not create much of a problem; we were more concerned with the fact of a reward than with the type of reward. We did two things, however, to lessen and control for the "gadget effect" and the so-called "Hawthorne effect" (Wallen & Travers, 1963). (The "Hawthorne effect" is a term often used to refer to the demonstration of an experimental effect, which is actually due to the fact that the subjects know they are in an experimental group, rather than to the effect of the experimental variable.) One of the two "Hawthorne effect" control methods was to have both the experimental and control groups use the cards for tallying rewards, and the other was to have both groups go through an identical control period of several weeks, during which time the novelty effect could wear off. The dependent variable in this experiment was reading achievement.

When pre-and post-tests are given over a comparatively short time interval, several problems are introduced into the analysis: regression toward the mean, item memory, and practice effects may confuse the results. It was decided, therefore, that the main analysis would be based on a single reading test given at the end of the experiment. Some control over initial individual differences would be attained by using IQ as a control variable in an analysis of covariance procedure.

The experiment took place in a Chicago school located on the southwest side of the inner city, an area consisting largely of slum dwellings and public housing apartments populated by Negroes, many of them fairly recent migrants from southern states. The neighborhood is characterized by low standards of living and high rates of unemployment, crime, delinquency, and school dropout.

The children in the experiment were from 10 to 14 years of age and were from one to three years behind the typical achievement grade levels. They were potential dropouts selected for special training in the Chicago Great Cities School Improvement Program. The children were assigned on a random basis to nine classes in an after-school remedial reading program with 10 to 15 in each class and a total of 110 in the experiment.

At the beginning of the experiment, all the teachers and children were asked to follow the same instructions. Each child received the specially-prepared tally card we have described, and the teachers were asked to distribute the praise rewards so that every child would receive several each day. At the end of each class session, each pupil wrote down the total number of tally marks (representing rewards) he had received. After each class, the teachers checked the card markings for accuracy and sent the cards to the experimenters.

After six sessions the reward rates per child and per teacher appeared to stabilize, and the five teachers (previously randomly determined) of the experimental groups (randomly constituted) were confidentially asked to double or triple the number of rewards, while the four teachers of the control groups were asked to "keep up the good work." After these requests were made, large increments appeared in the number of tally marks for the experimental group, while the numbers for the control group remained at approximately the same levels.

At the end of the second three-week period, the 62 children in the experimental groups and the 48 in the control groups took the first three sections of the Science Research Associates Reading Test (Form A, grades 4 to 6). The mean total score for the experimental groups was 31.62, with a standard deviation of 7.43, and the mean for the control groups was 26.86, with a standard deviation of 8.60. The analysis of variance for the unadjusted raw scores produced an F-ratio of 9.52 (significant at the .01 level).

In the covariance analysis with Kuhlmann-Anderson IQs as the control variable, the F-ratio was 7.90 (still significant at the .01 level). The smaller F-ratio for the adjusted scores, even though the error mean square was smaller, was the result of a slightly higher mean IQ for the experimental group. The mean IQ for this group was 92.05, and for the control group, 90.73. This difference was not statistically significant.

A scale designed to measure the pupils' attitudes toward their teachers was also administered with the teachers not present. The pupils of the experimental groups showed more favorable attitudes toward their teachers than those of the control groups. This result is in line with other reward studies we have conducted, which also show that highly-rewarded pupils have more favorable attitudes toward school and school materials, and that rewards tend to raise their levels of aspiration for future goals.

The teachers in the experiment were questioned about the reward system. All stated that their pupils were enthusiastic about it, though one teacher said, "At first they thought the idea of circles funny; later they were competing for circles." In response to the question concerning generation of enthusiasm, most of the teachers went beyond mere affirmation to say, "very much," "a great deal," "to the extent that we were late leaving at times."

The teachers did have reservations about the use of circling as a continual classroom method. Indeed, we are well aware of the need for investigation of possible satiation effects.

The main points here, however, are (1) the use of a systematic distribution of praise apparently will not lead to a dry classroom atmosphere devoid of enthusiasm, and (2) increased, distributed praise leads to increased achievement.

CONCLUSION

We have long known that rewards enhance learning, but that is not the issue. What is necessary is that our knowledge be applied systematically, continually, and consistently. A great deal of research is necessary to find out how to carry out such practices. We believe that we now have enough evidence of reward effects in classroom situations that secondary reinforcement principles should be systematically applied in all classrooms; however, when an experiment ends under the pressure of time, curriculum, and tradition, pupils and teachers usually revert to previous routines.

The implication is clear. All teachers need to be trained in the systematic application of rewards, and the ability to use this approach should be considered a basic professional skill subject to assessment. There is too much left to chance when we rely on those things that we often assure "just happen" in teachers—insight, empathy, warmth, knack, etc. It is necessary that an explicit system of reward applications be expected of all teachers in all school systems and for all types of children.

References

Brown, Jo Ahn. The effect of varying amounts of praise on aspiration level and achievement of elementary school children. Thesis, Chicago Teachers College, 1964.

Clark, C. A. & Walberg, H. J. The influence of massive rewards on reading achievement in potential urban school dropouts. *Amer. Educ. Res. J.*, 5 (3) 1968.

Dawson, Grace J. G. The effect of an exceptional amount of praise on the spelling habits of educable mentally handicapped children. Special Report, Chicago Teachers College, 1961.

Harris, Leola G. A study of competition in motivating achievement of educable mentally handicapped children. Thesis, Chicago Teachers College, 1958.

Lindquist, E. F. *Design and analysis of experiments in psychology and education.* Boston: Houghton Mifflin, 1953.

Wallen, N. E. & Travers, R. M. W. Analysis and investigation of teaching methods. In Gage, N. L. (Ed.), *Handbook of research on teaching.* Chicago: Rand McNally, 1963.

Sometimes professionals trained in behavior modification techniques are not available to administer directly a treatment program. Cantrell et al. suggest here a means for helping concerned parents and teachers deal with "problem" adolescents without the close supervision of a professional. By writing out a contract which spells out exactly the number of points an adolescent can earn for certain behaviors, and by getting the consent of both the student and his parents, the problem of adequate definition of the behaviors to be changed was minimized. As the authors point out, having the parents or teachers mail in completed record forms and receive feedback about them from the professional staff appeared to be a necessary part of the program. A minimum of direct observation and face-to-face consultations was also necessary, but generally the parents and teachers seemed capable of administering the program without close supervision.

One great advantage of using a contract system with adolescents is that spelling out the contingencies in writing and having a formal agreement may allay some of the suspiciousness sometimes present between parents and "problem" adolescents. Moreover it eliminates the feeling that something is being forced upon one or the other member of the family and provides a chance for them to discuss their complaints in specific, behavioral terms rather than general allegations. For teachers, too, having a list of the specific behaviors to be counted and the procedures to be followed might serve to alleviate some of the helplessness felt in dealing with recalcitrant adolescents who simply will not cooperate. Finally, the "fairness" of the plan, both as written and as carried out, may assist the adolescent and his parents or teacher in establishing some basic trust where it has been lacking previously. In general, then, contract systems may be particularly valuable both when the expert in behavior modification cannot provide firsthand supervision of a program and when the children to be involved are adolescents.

Contingency Contracting with School Problems

Robert P. Cantrell[1],
Mary Lynn Cantrell,
Clifton M. Huddleston,
and
Ralph L. Wooldridge*†

ABSTRACT

Contingency contracting procedures used in managing problems with school-age children involved analyzing teacher and/or parental reports of behavior problem situations, isolating the most probable contingencies then in effect, the range of reinforcers presently available, and the ways in which they were obtained. The authors prepared written contracts delineating remediative changes in reinforcement contingencies. These contracts specified ways in which the child could obtain existing individualized reinforcers contingent upon approximations to desired appropriate behaviors chosen as

* Robert P. Cantrell, Mary Lynn Cantrell, Clifton M. Huddleston and Ralph L. Wooldridge, "Contingency Contracting with School Problems," *Journal of Applied Behavior Analysis* 2(1969): 215–220. Reprinted with permission. Copyright 1969 by the Society for the Experimental Analysis of Behavior, Inc.
  † Louisiana Polytechnic Institute
  [1] Reprints may be obtained from Robert P. Cantrell, Center for Developmental and Learning Disorders, 1919 Seventh Avenue South, Birmingham, Alabama 35233.

incompatible with the referral problem behaviors. Contract procedures were administered by the natural contingency managers, parents and/or teachers, who kept daily records of contracted behaviors and reinforcers. These records were sent to the authors and provided feedback on the progress of the case. Initial results of this procedure have been sufficiently encouraging to warrant recommending an experimental analysis of contingency contracting as a clinical method.

This paper discusses our adaptation of operant methodology to deal with school children's problem behaviors in the setting of a diagnostic and remediation center. The methods described are based primarily on the structuring of available reinforcement contingencies to reinforce approximations to the desired appropriate school behaviors. The data presented are preliminary but suggest that systematic research in these methods might be very fruitful. The term "contingency contract" was borrowed from L. P. Homme (1966), who used written contracts with adolescent potential dropouts to spell out the reinforcers that were to follow completion of academic tasks. The present contract involved a somewhat different procedure. The contingency contract was a written explanation of the changes in contingencies to be used by the natural contingency managers, parents and/or teachers. It usually also contained: (1) a written schedule of desired behaviors (such as approximations to school attendance or behaviors involved in appropriate school achievement) with assigned point values, and (2) a written schedule of high probability behaviors (Premack, 1965) (individually defined rewards, privileges, preferred activities) with assigned exchange values.

The efficacy of structuring reinforcement contingencies to shape or maintain adaptive behavior in children is evident in a growing volume of behavior studies (Staats, Minke, Finley, Wolf, and Brooks, 1964; Ullmann and Krasner, 1965; Homme, 1966; Nolen, Kunzelmann, and Haring, 1967; O'Leary and Becker, 1967; Bushell, Wrobel, and Michaelis, 1968; Wolf, Giles, and Hall, 1968; McKenzie, Clark, Wolf, Kothera, and Benson, 1968; Hewett, Taylor, and Artuso, 1969). The present procedure was devised to see if viable changes in child behavior could be brought about by guiding parents and teachers in procedures of contingency control where frequency counting, direct observation, and direct manipulation by professionals were not immediately possible. Problems with which these procedures have been used have ranged from persistent school runaway behavior, school nonattendance, hyper-aggressivity, and stealing, to achievement motivation in underachieving students. Subjects were public school children, first through eleventh graders, from the seven parish areas served by the Louisiana Tech Special Education Center; all lived at a distance of 10 to 85 miles from the Center. The procedures described were initially the result of the need to deal with situational difficulties of sometimes near-crisis dimensions for the families and schools involved. Since most of these problems were of situational origin, the primary intervention procedures thought necessary were those of minimal prescriptive restructuring to alleviate the immediate problem.

Formulation of a contingency contract generally approximated the following pattern. Initially, referral information indicated if a problem might be largely one of motivation rather than academic programming. In considering the use of a contract, some sign was needed that the child could actually do or had done what was expected of him (such as inconsistent grades, intelligence test results, or adequate achievement test scores). If the child was badly in need of special academic programming, motivation by means of a contract might have been detrimental, unless that programming could have been provided in that setting. Also, if special programming would have been sufficient for motivation in and of itself, there would obviously have been no need for a contract.

After referral, the first step was to interview the child's adult agents. If the school appeared incapable of following the exigencies of a contract explicitly, only the parents and home were involved. If the home was unlikely to cooperate and the school would, only the school was involved. In most cases both agencies entered in, even though personal interviews might have been only with parents. Parents who had exhausted all available external sources of remediation and who were still concerned about their child's problems appeared to be the most willing to restructure their child-management contingencies.

Parents and teachers were told that it would be better not to attempt to write a contract unless they definitely wanted such help and were willing to involve their own personal effort in its success. This was done for at least two reasons: (1) If the system were to be attempted half-heartedly, it would not be enforced consistently and whatever extinction procedures were necessary would not occur. (2) If the agents were to give up on the system at the point where the child was testing it most severely, they would probably terminate with the maladaptive behavior at a higher peak and one even more resistant to change than before.

Initial interviews with the natural contingency managers were used to provide answers to the following questions:

1. What specifically were the key problem behaviors and how often did they occur? These primary behaviors were isolated and some provisions for counting their pre-intervention frequency were made to provide "baseline" data.
2. What was the typical or occasional consequence of these problem behaviors? Careful interviewing at this point provided a fairly complete list of usual consequences and some estimate of the schedules of their usage which appeared to be maintaining the maladaptive behavior.
3. What were the events, privileges, pastimes, foods, and material possessions which already served as reinforcements for this child? These were usually obtained by asking the parents or teachers what the child liked to do if he had the opportunity, what he spent the most time doing, what he would work for, and if any other consequence might possibly serve as a reinforcing event. Parents and teachers were usually able to provide a fairly complete list of reinforcers for their children in a roughly hierarchical arrangement of value to the child. For each reinforcer the parent was queried as to how the child at that time gained access to these reinforcers. In almost all cases, access to desired reinforcers was not being made contingent upon approximations to the desired behavior.
4. What might be used as a definite punishment or extinction consequence of an undesirable behavior if needed? This question was usually posed to the parents in the form of asking what the child would work to avoid, what seemed to be the most effective punishment if punishment were needed, and how easily might the parents or teachers be able to legislate specific punishing contingencies if they were found to be necessary. Here again, parents or teachers were usually able to identify a rough hierarchy of events which the child would work to avoid.

Once these basic questions were answered, the problem became one of how to change the contingencies in order to utilize reinforcers already available. The written contract had to be clear, complete, useful as ongoing data to judge its effectiveness, and simple enough to carry out that its demands did not make it aversive to the agents enforcing it. The child was presented with the record sheets and the new regimen by his parents or teacher. In most cases he took his weekly sheet of earned points to school where his teacher gave him points as earned and then brought it home where his parents gave him points earned at home. Points earned at school and home were spent on a daily and weekly basis. His weekly record sheet of points spent was kept at home for easy reference by the child.

Behavioral change was monitored by building into the contract methods of measuring the problem behavior before the contract went into effect, of graphing progress continually, and of measuring the problem behavior after intervention with the contract had been completed. Independent records from the schools (such as grades, attendance records, incidences of maladaptive behavior) were obtained in addition to parental report forms.

The contracts generally fell into two ways of arranging contingencies once the problem behaviors and available reinforcers had been delineated. In the first, receipt of the reinforcers was simply made contingent on adaptive behaviors that were incompatible with the problem behaviors. For example, R's parents and teachers complained that he did not complete homework or class assignments unless he did so very carelessly and that he did not work or listen to directions without constant reminders and "pushing." R's contract was formulated as follows:

Contingency Contract

This contract defines the ways in which R can earn points by doing specific things at school and at home that would be necessary for his academic growth (*i.e.*, completing class assignments and homework). He exchanges these points for preferred activities or money (*i.e.*, going places, watching television, Coke money, *etc.*). He can earn an approximate maximum of 50 points per day or 250 points per week under this schedule.

R's teacher marks his points earned each day on his weekly record sheet of points earned (Fig. 1) and sends home an average of one graded paper per day for which he gets additional points. His mother gives him points for homework done at home and keeps a record of points spent on the appropriate weekly sheet (Fig. 2). When R wants to spend his points, he is allowed to and given verbal praise for having worked well enough at school to have enough points. When he does not have sufficient points for something he wants, a simple statement that he does not yet have enough points is made. It is crucial that R receive these privileges only when he has the required number of points already on his chart.

It appears that R's non-working at school results in getting more attention from adults than his working ordinarily does. Switching the tables on him should result in increased effort on his part. Efforts should be made to give R attention and approval when he is working and behaving as we would hope. Inappropriate behavior or non-working should result in little attention (punishment, reminders, scolding included) given to him. Insofar as possible, R should learn that he will be ignored when he is not working or behaving appropriately, but when he does put forth effort and behave appropriately, people are proud of him and give him attention.

In comparing six weeks' grades for the report before intervention and the report after intervention, R's grades stayed the same in three subjects, improved one letter in two subjects, and improved two letters in one subject.

In the second general method of contract arrangement, the behavioral steps leading toward the desired terminal behavior were arranged in sequential, programmed fashion. Receipt of the reinforcers was then made contingent on these steps. In the case of S, a "school phobic" child, points were earned for approximations or steps toward full school attendance where she had previously had problems: getting out of bed (5 points); getting dressed (5 points); having breakfast (5 points); no crying

Week of: _____

R earned points for:	Mon.	Tues.	Wed.	Thurs.	Fri.	TOTALS
Homework:						
completed (3 points)						
well done* (5 additional)						
Class assignments:						
completed (1 point each)						
well done* (2 additional)						
with no more than 2 misspelled words						
or careless arithmetic errors						
(1 additional)						
Listening and complying to directions						
without reminder (1 point each time)						
Daily grades:						
A (10 points)						
B (6 points)						
C (3 points)						
D (1 point)						
Homework:						
started with no warnings (5 points)						
one warning (3 points)						
two warnings (2 points)						
three warnings (1 point)						
completed by supper time (2 additional)						
TOTALS						

*Bonus: Baseball glove as soon as R earns 75 points total in these two "well done" categories

Figure 1. Weekly record sheet of points earned.

before school (5 points); no illness before school (5 points); going to schoolbus (5 points); getting on schoolbus (5 points); going to class (5 points); going into classroom (5 points); staying in class (5 points per 15 min.); no crying at school (5 points); no illness at school (5 points); homework started with no reminders (15 points); with one reminder (10 points), with two reminders (5 points), completed (5 additional points). S exchanged points for: TV viewing, renting toys or books, helping mother in kitchen (25 points per 30 min.); outside play time (50 points per 30 min.); having friends over or going to visit friends (100 points); going out privilege (150 points); overnight visit with friend (200 points); spending money (1 point per penny); plus an additional bonus of one article of new clothing for going to school one full week. The terminal state desired in S's case, full school attendance without resistance, was attained on the eighth school day after the contract was initiated and maintained throughout the rest of that and the next school year.

An essential part of the program was the inclusion of a built-in feedback system. Most of the contracts provided for parents or teachers to mail completed record forms to us weekly. Upon their receipt, blank

Week of: _____

R exchanged his points for:	Mon.	Tues.	Wed.	Thurs.	Fri.	Sat.	Sun.	TOTALS
Outdoor time (5 points per ½ hour)								
Television viewing time (5 points per ½ hour)								
Kitchen time (cooking privileges) (5 points per ½ hour)								
Driving (as parents direct) (10 points per ½ hour)								
Going out privilege (10 points per event)								
Staying with friend all night or having one over for night (25 points per event)								
Money (up to limit set by parents) (5 cents per point)								
TOTALS								

Figure 2. Weekly record sheet of points spent.

forms were sent them for another week. Agents were initially given two weeks' worth of forms to allow for one week's transit in the mails. Parents and/or teachers were encouraged to write or call as problems or questions arose. The information gleaned from the obtained record forms was used to initiate telephone conference calls or visits to the agents or to clarify or change the contracts as behavior shifts occurred. This follow-up was crucial. Even if the contingency change as designed had "hit" upon the right combination of reinforcement schedules, consistent encouragement of the parents or agents of the contract was often necessary in order to maintain the behavior until new patterns of interaction had become more solidified.

In many cases, fading procedures from the contract were instituted at the child's request. A fading procedure was seldom needed to wean the child away from the contract system. In most cases, the children themselves gave agents clues as to when to cease the program or how to ease it back to a more natural set of contingencies. In others, external situations caused a natural change back to more natural behavior management, such as the end of the school year. Parents often indicated a reluctance to terminate the contract before the end of the school year. Only a few resumed use of the contract at the beginning of the subsequent school year.

Parents and school personnel have communicated to the contract writers their enthusiasm about the procedures and results, and have often referred other cases for similar treatment. The fact that the contracts use reinforcers already present in the child's environment, rather than introducing new ones, seems to have appeal to the natural contingency managers with whom we have worked. Training the natural contingency managers inductively through the prescriptive, precise procedures of the contracts seems to result in the principles being learned more completely than when we have attempted to teach the principles of modifying behavior before dealing specifically with the problem behavior at hand.

Optimally, the use of direct observation in the home or the school to ascertain the agent's compliance with the contract, plus the use of multiple baseline procedures to validate the efficacy of the contract on other problem behaviors for the same child, would have provided more data for the validity of the procedures beyond parent and school reportings. Even here, the establishment of a functional relationship between the instigation of the contract and the changes that accrue would be subject to the problems of indeterminacy and changes in expectation (Rosenthal and Jacobson, 1968). Relying on the agent's report of behavior alone also posed difficulties in determining the actual course of the behavior as it was occurring. On the one hand, if the contract was being consistently enforced and still was not working as expected, the possibility existed that the authors of the contract had not eliminated the salient reinforcers maintaining the problem behavior or had not provided strong enough reinforcers to change it to a more adaptive form. In this case, a new combination or revision of the old combination of reinforcers in the old contract was necessary. On the other hand, it appeared to be risky to assume that the system needed changing too soon. Many of the maladaptive behaviors were thought to have been shaped by the child's being able to "wait out" or "outlast" adult contingencies. If this were the case, the problem became one of encouraging the adult agents to maintain the newly initiated contingencies in order to break the control—counter-control cycle being tested by the child. Further studies are now in progress using multiple baseline and independent observation in the home and school to clarify further the processes involved.

A primary concern of professionals often is one of maximum efficiency in meeting the behavioral crises of individual cases while continuing their professional efforts in other endeavors. If experimentally verified, the "contingency contract" method offers one possible avenue to resolve in a clinical setting the perpetual "minimax" conflict of bringing about maximal behavioral change with minimal expenditure of professional time and money. The prospects of the natural contingency managers in the child's situation, teachers and parents, actually administering the new procedures may be one means of closing the gap between the availability of professional staff and the press of public demand for their services.

In summary, the application of reinforcement theory in the form of written contingency contracts as specific directions through which the natural contingency managers can change problem behaviors appears to be a potentially useful tool for professionals dealing with children's problems. The effect of such contracting appears to be largely dependent upon: (1) the capacity of the professionals who prepare the contingencies to derive from verbal information those contingencies that appear to be maintaining the problem behavior and then to change them, and (2) the relative ability of the adults involved to maintain the contingencies spelled out by the contract.

References

Bushell, D., Jr., Wrobel, Patricia A., and Michaelis, Mary L. Applying "group" contingencies to the classroom study behavior of preschool children. *Journal of Applied Behavior Analysis*, 1968, 1, 55–62.

Hewett, F. M., Taylor, F. D., and Artuso, A. A. The Santa Monica Project: Evaluation of an engineered classroom design with emotionally disturbed children. *Exceptional Children*, 1969, 35, 523–529.

Homme, L. Human motivation and the environment. In N. Haring and R. Whelan (Eds.), *The learning environment: relationship to behavior modification and implications for special education.* Lawrence: University of Kansas Press, 1966.

McKenzie, H. S., Clark, Marilyn; Wolf, M. M., Kothera, R. and Benson, C. Behavior modification of children with learning disabilities using grades as tokens and allowances as back-up reinforcers. *Exceptional Children*, 1968, 34, 745–752.

Nolen, Patricia A., Kunzelmann, H. P., and Haring, N. G. Behavioral modification in a junior high learning disabilities classroom. *Exceptional Children*, 1967, 33, 163–168.

O'Leary, K. D. and Becker, W. C. Behavior modification of an adjustment class: a token reinforcement program. *Exceptional Children*, 1967, 33, 637–642.

Premack, D. Reinforcement theory. In D. Levine (Ed.), *Nebraska symposium on motivation: 1965.* Lincoln: University of Nebraska Press, 1965. Pp. 123–180.

Rosenthal, R. and Jacobson, Lenore. *Pygmalion in the classroom: teacher expectation and pupils' intellectual development.* New York: Holt, Rinehart & Winston, 1968.

Staats, A. W., Minke, K. A., Finley, J. R., Wolf, M., and Brooks, L. A reinforcer system and experimental procedures for the laboratory study of reading acquisition. *Child Development*, 1964, 35, 209–231.

Ullman, L. P. and Krasner, L. (Eds.) *Case studies in behavior modification.* New York: Holt, Rinehart & Winston, 1965.

Wolf, M. M., Giles, D. K., and Hall, R. V. Experiments with token reinforcement in a remedial classroom. *Behaviour Research and Therapy*, 1968, 6, 51–64.

The course and methods which Keller describes in this paper have become very well-known among psychologists. Many aspects of the procedures for teaching this course differ sharply from the traditional introductory psychology course. The division of material into a large number of units and the requirement of mastery on one before proceeding to the next were rare at the college level before Keller's course. The idea of having to earn the right to attend a lecture or demonstration rather than being required to attend is still very unusual. Another distinctive feature of Keller's approach was the utilization of three levels of teaching personnel—an undergraduate proctor who provided individual and immediate assistance, a graduate classroom assistant who provided the material for the proctors and did the clerical work, and a faculty member who designed the material and tests and provided lectures and demonstrations, as well as making the final decisions about the course. As with most programmed learning sequences, the students took frequent tests, progressed at their own rates, and mastered the material as far as they went. In fact, most students finished all the material and received an A.

Keller defends his course against criticism that the program oversimplifies material by breaking it down into minute bits or makes learning cold and impersonal by having people just sit at their desks and work on their own exercises. Certainly both students and proctors appeared to find their participation very valuable, and academic measures seemed to indicate that the material was much better learned than it is in a traditional class. Keller also mentions some other approaches to teaching college courses which utilize some of the features of his course, such as the individualized instruction and immediate feedback and discusses the implications of such programs for the traditional role of the teacher.

Is such an approach either feasible or desirable at the high school or elementary school level? Certainly, some aspects of it have already been seen, such as working at individual exercises and the emphasizing teaching machines which provide immediate feedback. What about the possibilities of using older children as tutors for the younger, a method which has been tried occasionally, or of having students "earn" the right to attend special demonstrations by showing mastery of the material? Before we say goodbye either to teacher or to Keller, some of the implications of his article for education at younger levels should be explored.

"Good-Bye, Teacher . . ."[1]

Fred S. Keller[*][2]

When I was a boy, and school "let out" for the summer, we used to celebrate our freedom from educational control by chanting:

> Good-bye scholars, good-bye school; Good-bye teacher, darned old fool!

We really didn't think of our teacher as deficient in judgment, or as a clown or jester. We were simply escaping from restraint, dinner pail in one hand and shoes in the other, with all the delights of summer before us. At that moment, we might even have been well-disposed toward our teacher and might have felt a touch of compassion as we completed the rhyme.

"Teacher" was usually a woman, not always young and not always pretty. She was frequently demanding and sometimes sharp of tongue, ever ready to pounce when we got out of line. But, occasionally, if one did especially well in home-work or in recitation, he could detect a flicker of approval or affection that made the hour in class worthwhile. At such times, we loved our teacher and felt that school was fun.

It was not fun enough, however, to keep me there when I grew older. Then I turned to another kind of education, in which the reinforcements

*Fred S. Keller, " 'Good-Bye, Teacher . . .'," *Journal of Applied Behavior Analysis* 1(1968): 79–89. Reprinted with permission. Copyright by the Society for the Experimental Analysis of Behavior, Inc.

[1] President's Invited Address, Division 2, Amer. Psychol. Ass., Washington, D.C., Sept. 1967.

[2] Arizona State University. Currently on leave of absence at the Institute for Behavioral Research, 2426 Linden Lane, Silver Spring, Maryland. Reprints may be obtained from the author, 3229 Park View Road, Chevy Chase, Maryland.

were sometimes just as scarce as in the schoolroom. I became a Western Union messenger boy and, between deliveries of telegrams, I learned Morse code by memorizing dots and dashes from a sheet of paper and listening to a relay on the wall. As I look back on those days, I conclude that I am the only living reinforcement theorist who ever learned Morse code in the absence of reinforcement.

It was a long, frustrating job. It taught me that drop-out learning could be just as difficult as in-school learning and it led me to wonder about easier possible ways of mastering a skill. Years later, after returning to school and finishing my formal education, I came back to this classical learning problem, with the aim of making International Morse code less painful for beginners than American Morse had been for me (Keller, 1943).

During World War II, with the aid of a number of students and colleagues, I tried to apply the principle of immediate reinforcement to the early training of Signal Corps personnel in the reception of Morse-code signals. At the same time, I had a chance to observe, at close hand and for many months, the operation of a military training center. I learned something from both experiences, but I should have learned more. I should have seen many things that I didn't see at all, or saw very dimly.

I could have noted, for example, that instruction in such a center was highly individualized, in spite of large classes, sometimes permitting students to advance at their own speed throughout a course of study. I could have seen the clear specification of terminal skills for each course, together with the carefully graded steps leading to this end. I could have seen the demand for perfection at every level of training and for every student; the employment of classroom instructors who were little more than the successful graduates of earlier classes; the minimizing of the lecture as a teaching device and the maximizing of student participation. I could have seen, especially, an interesting division of labor in the educational process, wherein the non-commissioned, classroom teacher was restricted to duties of guiding, clarifying, demonstrating, testing, grading, and the like, while the commissioned teacher, the training officer, dealt with matters of course logistics, the interpretation of training manuals, the construction of lesson plans and guides, the evaluation of student progress, the selection of non-commissioned cadre, and the writing of reports for his superiors.

I did see these things, of course, in a sense, but they were embedded deeply within a special context, one of "training" rather than "education". I did not then appreciate that a set of reinforcement contingencies which were useful in building simple skills like those of the radio operator might also be useful in developing the verbal repertories, the conceptual behaviors, and the laboratory techniques of university education. It was not until a long time later, by a very different route, that I came to such a realization.

That story began in 1962, with the attempt on the part of two Brazilian and two North American psychologists, to establish a Department of Psychology at the University of Brasilia. The question of teaching method arose from the the very practical problem of getting a first course ready by a certain date for a certain number of students in the new university. We had almost complete freedom of action; we were dissatisfied with the conventional approaches; and we knew something about programmed instruction. We were also of the same theoretical persuasion. It was quite natural, I suppose, that we should look for fresh applications of reinforcement thinking to the teaching process (Keller, 1966).

The method that resulted from this collaborative effort was first used in a short-term laboratory course[3] at Columbia University in the winter of 1963, and the basic procedure of this pilot study was employed at Brasilia during the following year, by Professors Rodolfo Azzi and Carolina Martuscelli Bori, with 50 students in a one-term introductory course. Professor Azzi's report on this, at the 1965 meetings of the American Psychological Association and in personal correspondence, indicated a highly satisfactory outcome. The new procedure was received enthusiastically by the students and by the university administration. Mastery of the course material was judged excellent for all who completed the course. Objections were minor, centering around the relative absence of opportunity for discussion between students and staff.

Unfortunately, the Brasilia venture came to an abrupt end during the second semester of its operation, due to a general upheaval within the university that involved the resignation or dismissal of more than 200 teachers. Members of the original psychology staff have since taken positions elsewhere, and have reportedly begun to use the new method again, but I am unable at this time to report in detail on their efforts.

Concurrently with the early Brazilian development, Professor J. G. Sherman and I, in the spring of 1965, began a series of more or less independent applications of the same general method at Arizona State University. With various minor changes, this work has now been tried through five semesters with an increasing number of students per term (Keller, in press [a], in press [b], 1967; Sherman, 1967). The results have

---

[3] With the aid of (Dr.) Lanny Fields and the members of a senior seminar at Columbia College, during the fall term of 1963–64.

been more gratifying with each successive class, and there has been as yet no thought of a return to more conventional procedures. In addition, we have had the satisfaction of seeing our system used by a few other colleagues, in other courses and at other institutions.[4]

In describing this method to you, I will start with a quotation (Keller, 1967). It is from a hand-out given to all the students enrolled in the first-semester course in General Psychology (one of two introductions offered at Arizona State University) during the past year, and it describes the teaching method to which they will be exposed unless they elect to withdraw from the course.

> "*This is a course through which you may move, from start to finish, at your own pace. You will not be held back by other students or forced to go ahead until you are ready. At best, you may meet all the course requirements in less than one semester; at worst, you may not complete the job within that time. How fast you go is up to you.*
>
> "*The work of this course will be divided into 30 units of content, which correspond roughly to a series of home-work assignments and laboratory exercises. These units will come in a definite numerical order, and you must show your mastery of each unit (by passing a "readiness" test or carrying out an experiment) before moving on to the next.*
>
> "*A good share of your reading for this course may be done in the classroom, at those times when no lectures, demonstrations, or other activities are taking place. Your classroom, that is, will sometimes be a study hall.*
>
> "*The lectures and demonstrations in this course will have a different relation to the rest of your work than is usually the rule. They will be provided only when you have demonstrated your readiness to appreciate them; no examination will be based upon them; and you need not attend them if you do not wish. When a certain percentage of the class has reached a certain point in the course, a lecture or demonstration will be available at a stated time, but it will not be compulsory.*
>
> "*The teaching staff of your course will include proctors, assistants, and an instructor. A proctor is an undergraduate who has been chosen for his mastery of the course content and orientation, for his maturity of judgment, for his understanding of the special problems that confront you as a beginner, and for his willingness to assist. He will provide you with all your study materials except your textbooks. He will pass upon your readiness tests as satisfactory or unsatisfactory. His judgment will ordinarily be law, but if he is ever in serious doubt, he*

---

[4] For example, by J. L. Michael with high-school juniors on a National Science Foundation project at Grinnell College (Iowa), in 1965; and by J. Farmer and B. Cole at Queens College (New York) in a course similar to the one described here.

can appeal to the classroom assistant, or even the instructor, for a ruling. Failure to pass a test on the first try, the second, the third, or even later, will not be held against you. It is better that you get too much testing than not enough, if your final success in the course is to be assured.

"Your work in the laboratory will be carried out under the direct supervision of a graduate laboratory assistant, whose detailed duties cannot be listed here. There will also be a graduate classroom assistant, upon whom your proctor will depend for various course materials (assignments, study questions, special readings, and so on), and who will keep up to date all progress records for course members. The classroom assistant will confer with the instructor daily, aid the proctors on occasion, and act in a variety of ways to further the smooth operation of the course machinery.

"The instructor will have as his principal responsibilities: (a) the selection of all study material used in the course; (b) the organization and the mode of presenting this material; (c) the construction of tests and examinations; and (d) the final evaluation of each student's progress. It will be his duty, also, to provide lectures, demonstrations, and discussion opportunities for all students who have earned the privilege; to act as a clearing-house for requests and complaints; and to arbitrate in any case of disagreement between students and proctors or assistants. . . .

"All students in the course are expected to take a final examination, in which the entire term's work will be represented. With certain exceptions, this examination will come at the same time for all students, at the end of the term. . . The examination will consist of questions which, in large part, you have already answered on your readiness tests. Twenty-five percent of your course grade will be based on this examination; the remaining 75% will be based on the number of units of reading and laboratory work that you have successfully completed during the term."

(In my own sections of the course, these percentages were altered, during the last term, to a 30% weighting of the final examination, a 20% weighting of the 10 laboratory exercises, and a 50% weighting of the reading units.)

A picture of the way this method operates can best be obtained, perhaps, by sampling the activities of a hypothetical average student as he moves through the course. John Pilgrim is a freshman, drawn from the upper 75% of his high-school class. He has enrolled in PY 112 for unknown reasons and has been assigned to a section of about 100 students, men and women, most of whom are also in their beginning year. The class is scheduled to meet on Tuesdays and Thursdays, from 9:15 to 10:30 a.m., with a laboratory session to be arranged.

Together with the description from which I quoted a moment ago, John receives a few mimeographed instructions and some words of advice from his professor. He is told that he should cover two units of laboratory work or reading per week in order to be sure of taking an A-grade into his final examination; that he should withdraw from the course if he doesn't pass at least one readiness test within the first two weeks; and that a grade of Incomplete will not be given except in special cases. He is also advised that, in addition to the regular classroom hours on Tuesday and Thursday, readiness tests may be taken on Saturday forenoons and Wednesday afternoons of each week—periods in which he can catch up with, or move ahead of, the rest of the class.

He then receives his first assignment: an introductory chapter from a standard textbook and two "sets" from a programmed version of similar material. With this assignment, he receives a mimeographed list of "study questions", about 30 in number. He is told to seek out the answers to these questions in his reading, so as to prepare himself for the questions he will be asked in his readiness tests. He is free to study wherever he pleases, but he is strongly encouraged to use the study hall for at least part of the time. Conditions for work are optimal there, with other students doing the same thing and with an assistant or proctor on hand to clarify a confusing passage or a difficult concept.

This is on Tuesday. On Thursday, John comes to class again, having gone through the sets of programmed material and having decided to finish his study in the classroom, where he cannot but feel that the instructor really expects him. An assistant is in charge, about half the class is there, and some late registrants are reading the course description. John tries to study his regular text, but finds it difficult to concentrate and ends by deciding to work in his room. The assistant pays no attention when he leaves.

On the following Tuesday, he appears in study hall again, ready for testing, but anxious, since a whole week of the course has passed. He reports to the assistant, who sends him across the hall, without his books and notes, to the testing room, where the proctor in charge gives him a blue-book and one of the test forms for Unit 1. He takes a seat among about 20 other students and starts work. The test is composed of 10 fill-in questions and one short-answer essay question. It doesn't seem particularly difficult and, in about 10 min John returns his question sheet and is sent, with his blue-book, to the proctor's room for grading.

In the proctor's room, in one of the 10 small cubicles, John finds his special proctor, Anne Merit. Anne is a psychology major who passed the same course earlier with a grade of A. She receives two points of credit for about 4 hr of proctoring per week, 2 hr of required attendance at a weekly proctor's meeting, and occasional extra duty in the study hall or test room. She has nine other students besides John to look after, so she will not as a rule be able to spend much more than 5 or 10 min of class time with each.

Anne runs through John's answers quickly, checking two of them as incorrect and placing a question mark after his answer to the essay question. Then she asks him why he answered these three as he did. His replies show two misinterpretations of the question and one failure in written expression. A restatement of the fill-in questions and some probing with respect to the essay leads Anne to write an O.K. alongside each challenged answer. She congratulates John upon his performance and warns him that later units may be a little harder to master than the first.

John's success is then recorded on the wallchart in the proctors' room, he is given his next assignment and set of study questions, and sent happily on his way. The blue-book remains with Anne, to be given later to the assistant or the instructor for inspection, and used again when John is ready for testing on Unit 2. As he leaves the room, John notices the announcement of a 20-min lecture by his instructor, for all students who have passed Unit 3 by the following Friday, and he resolves that he will be there.

If John had failed in the defense of one or two of his answers, he would have been sent back for a minimal period of 30 min for further study, with advice as to material most needing attention. If he had made more than four errors on his test, the answers would not have been considered individually; he would simply have been told that he was not ready for examination. And, if he had made no errors at all, he would probably have been asked to explain one or two of his correct answers, as a way of getting acquainted and to make sure that he was the one who had really done the work.

John did fail his first test on Unit 2, and his first two tests on Unit 4 (which gave trouble to nearly everyone). He missed the first lecture, too, but qualified for the second. (There were seven such "shows" during the term, each attended by perhaps half of the students entitled to be there.) After getting through his first five units, he failed on one review test before earning the right to move on to Unit 6. On the average, for the remainder of the course, he required nearly two readiness tests per unit. Failing a test, of course, was not an unmixed evil, since it permitted more discussion with the proctor and often served to sharpen the concepts involved.

In spite of more than a week's absence from school, John was able, by using the Wednesday and Saturday testing sessions, to complete his course units successfully about a week before the final examination. Because of his cramming for other courses during this last week, he did not review for his psychology and received only a B on his final examination. His A for the course was not affected by this, but his pride was hurt.

Sometime before the term ended, John was asked to comment on certain aspects of the course, without revealing his identity. (Remember, John is a mythical figure.) Among other things, he said that, in comparison with courses taught more conventionally, this one demanded a much greater mastery of the work assignments, it required greater memorization of detail and much greater understanding of basic concepts, it generated a greater feeling of achievement, it gave much greater recognition of the student as a person, and it was enjoyed to a much greater extent (Keller, in press).

He mentioned also that his study habits had improved during the term, that his attitude towards testing had become more positive, that his worry about final grades had diminished, and that there had been an increase in his desire to hear lectures (this in spite of the fact that he attended only half of those for which he was qualified). When asked specifically about the use of proctors, he said that the discussions with his proctors had been very helpful, that the proctor's non-academic, personal relation was also important to him, and that the use of proctors generally in grading and discussing tests was highly desirable.

Anne Merit, when asked to comment on her own reactions to the system, had many things to say, mostly positive. She referred especially to the satisfaction of having the respect of her proctees, of seeing them do well, and of cementing the material of the course for herself. She noted that the method was one of "mutual reinforcement" for student, proctor, assistant, and instructor. She suggested that it ought to be used in other courses and at other levels of instruction. She wondered why it would not be possible for a student to enroll in a second course immediately upon completion of the first, if it were taught by the same method. She also listed several changes that might improve the efficiency of the course machinery, especially in the area of testing and grading, where delay may sometimes occur.

In an earlier account of this teaching method (Keller, 1967), I summarized those features which seem to distinguish it most clearly from conventional teaching procedures. They include the following:

"1. The go-at-your-own pace feature, *which permits a student to move through the course at a speed commensurate with his ability and other demands upon his time.*

"2. The unit-perfection requirement for advance, *which lets the student go ahead to new material only after demonstrating mastery of that which preceded.*
"3. The use of lectures and demonstrations as vehicles of motivation, *rather than sources of critical information.*
"4. *The related* stress upon the written word in *teacher-student communication: and, finally:*
"5. *The* use of proctors, *which permits repeated testing, immediate scoring, almost unavoidable tutoring, and a marked enhancement of the personal-social aspect of the educational process.*"

The similarity of our learning paradigm to that provided in the field of programmed instruction is obvious. There is the same stress upon analysis of the task, the same concern with terminal performance, the same opportunity for individualized progression, and so on. But the sphere of action here is different. The principal steps of advance are not "frames" in a "set", but are more like the conventional home-work assignment or laboratory exercise. "The 'response' is not simply the completion of a prepared statement through the insertion of a word or phrase. Rather, it may be thought of as the resultant of many such responses, better described as the understanding of a principle, a formula, or a concept, or the ability to use an experimental technique. Advance within the program depends on something more than the appearance of a confirming word or the presentation of a new frame; it involves a personal interaction between a student and his peer, or his better, in what may be a lively verbal interchange, of interest and importance to each participant. The use of a programmed text, a teaching machine, or some sort of computer aid within such a course is entirely possible and may be quite desirable, but it is not to be equated with the course itself." (Keller, 1967.)

Failure to recognize that our teaching units are not as simple as the response words in a programmed text, or the letter reactions to Morse-code signals, or other comparable atoms of behavior, can lead to confusion concerning our procedure. A well-known critic of education in America, after reading an account of our method, sent me a note confessing to "a grave apprehension about the effect of breaking up the subject matter into little packages." "I should suppose," he said, "it would prevent all but the strongest minds from ever possessing a synoptic view of a field, and I imagine that the coaching, and testing, and passing in bits would amount to efficient training rather than effectual teaching."

Our "little packages" or "bits" are no smaller than the basic conceptions of a science of behavior and cannot be delivered all at once in one large synoptic parcel. As for the teaching-training distinction, one needs only to note that it is always the instructor who decides what is to be taught, and to what degree, thus determining whether he will be called a trainer or a teacher. The method he uses, the basic reinforcement contingencies he employs, may be turned to either purpose.

Many things occur, some of them rather strange, when a student is taught by a method such as ours. With respect to everyday student behavior, even a casual visit to a class will provide some novel items. For example, all the students seated in the study hall may be seen studying, undistracted by the presence or movements of others. In the test room, a student will rarely be seen chewing on his pencil, looking at a neighbor's blue-book, or staring out the window. In the crowded proctors' room, 10 pairs of students can be found concurrently engaged in academic interaction, with no couple bothered by the conversation of another, no matter how close by. Upon passing his assistant or instructor, in the corridors or elsewhere, a student will typically be seen to react in a friendly and respectful manner—enough to excite a mild alarm.

More interesting than this is the fact that a student may be tested 40 or 50 times in the course of one semester, often standing in line for the privilege, without a complaint. In one extreme instance, a student required nearly two terms to complete the work of one (after which he applied for, and got, permission to serve as a proctor for the following year).

Another unusual feature of our testing and grading is the opportunity given to defend an "incorrect" answer. This defense, as I noted earlier, may sometimes produce changes in the proctor's evaluation, changes that are regularly checked by the assistant or the instructor. Occasionally, a proctor's O.K. will be rejected, compelling the student to take another test, and sensitizing the proctor to the dangers of leniency; more often, it produces a note of warning, a correction, or a query written by the instructor in the student's blue-book; but always it provides the instructor with feedback on the adequacy of the question he has constructed.

Especially important, in a course taught by such a method, is the fact that any differences in social, economic, cultural, and ethnic background are completely and repeatedly subordinated to a friendly intellectual relationship between two human beings throughout a period of 15 weeks or more. Also, in such a course, a lonesome, ill-favored underprivileged, badly schooled, or otherwise handicapped boy or girl can be assured at least a modicum of individual attention, approval, encouragement, and a chance to succeed. The only prerequisite for such treatment is a well-defined amount and quality of academic achievement.

Another oddity of the system is the production of a grade distribution that is upside down. In Fig. 1, are the results from a class of 208 students at Arizona State University during the past semester. Note the diminishing relative frequency as one moves from A to D. The category of E, indicating failure, is swollen by the presence of 18 students who failed to take up their option of W (withdrawal from the course). Grades of C and D were due to the failure of students to complete all the units of reading or laboratory before going into the final examination.

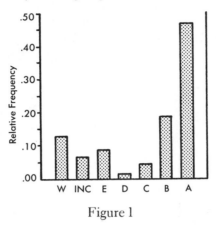

Figure 1

Figure 2 shows data from the class 1 yr earlier. Essentially the same distribution holds, except for the category of Incomplete, which was then too easily obtainable. Discouraging the use of the Incomplete, together

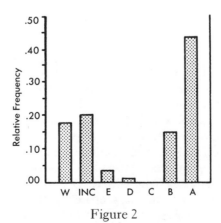

Figure 2

with the provision of more testing hours, apparently has the effect of regularizing study habits and equalizing the number of tests taken per week throughout the term.

In Fig. 3 (filled bars), the grade distribution is for a section of 25 students in an introductory course at Queens College (N.Y.) during the second semester of the past school year. The same method of teaching was employed as at Arizona State, but the work requirement was somewhat greater in amount. The distinctive feature here is the relative infrequency of low grades. Only four students received less than a B rating. Professor John Farmer, who provided me with these data, reports that the two students receiving F had dropped out of the course, for unknown reasons, after seven and eight units respectively.

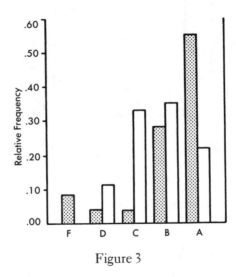

Figure 3

With this teaching method, students who are presumably inferior may show up better upon examination than presumably superior students taught by more conventional procedures. Figure 4 shows two distributions of grades on a mid-term examination. The empty bars represent the achievement of 161 students of an Ivy League College, mainly sophomores, in the first semester of a one-year lecture-and-laboratory course in elementary psychology. The filled bars represent the achievement of 66 Arizona State University students, mainly freshman, on an unannounced mid-term quiz prepared by the Ivy League instructor and from which 13% of the questions had to be eliminated on the grounds of differential course coverage.

Relevant to this comparison is that pictured in Fig. 3. The grade distribution obtained by Professor Farmer (and his associate, Brett Cole) is here compared with one obtained from a section of 46 students in the same course, taught in the conventional manner by a colleague who is described as "a very good instructor." The filled bars show the Farmer-Cole results; the empty ones are those from Professor Brandex.

Such comparisons are of some interest and may relieve the tedium of a lecture, but they raise many questions of interpretation, and their importance should not be over-emphasized. The kind of change needed in education today is not one that will be evaluated in terms of the percentage of A's in a grade distribution or of differences at the 0.01 (or 0.001) level of confidence. It is one that will produce a reinforcing state of affairs for everyone involved—a state of affairs that has heretofore been reached so rarely as to be the subject of eulogy in the world's literature,

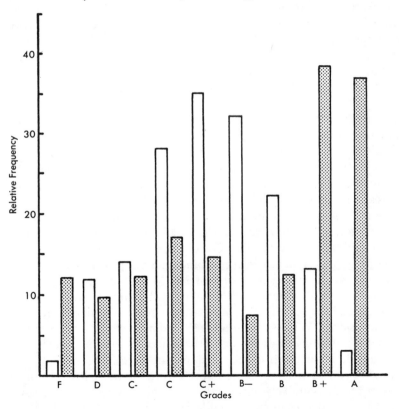

Figure 4

and which, unfortunately, has led to the mystique of the "great teacher" rather than a sober analysis of the critical contingencies in operation.

Our method has not yet required a grant-in-aid to keep it going. On one occasion we tried to get such help, in order to pay for mimeograph paper, the services of a clerk, and one or two additional assistants. Our request was rejected, quite properly, on the grounds that our project was "purely operational." Almost any member of a present-day fund-granting agency can recognize "research" when he sees it. I do think, however, that one should be freed, as I was, from other university demands while introducing a system like ours. And he should not be asked to teach more than two such courses regularly, each serving 100 students or less, unless he has highly qualified assistants upon whom he can depend.

Neither does the method require equipment and supplies that are not already available to almost every teacher in the country. Teaching machines, tape recorders, and computers could readily be fitted into the picture. Moving pictures and television could also be used in one or two ways without detriment to the basic educational process. But these are luxuries, based on only partial recognition of our problem, and they could divert us from more important considerations. (Proctors, like computers, may go wrong or break down, but they can often be repaired and they are easily replaced, at very little expense.)

The need for individualized instruction is widely recognized, and the most commonly suggested way of filling this need is automation. I think that this solution is incomplete, especially when applied to the young; and I'd like to mention a personal experience that bears upon the matter.

In the summer of 1966, I made numerous visits to a center for the care and treatment of autistic children.[5] One day, as I stood at the door of a classroom, I saw a boy get up from his chair at the end of a class period and give a soft pat to the object on the desk in front of him. At the same time, he said, with a slight smile, "Good-bye, Teaching Machine!"

This pseudo-social behavior in this fundamentally asocial child amused me at the time. It reminded me of Professor Moore's description of the three-year-old who became irritated when his "talking typewriter" made a mistake, called the device a "big bambam", requested its name, and ended by asking, "Who is your mother?" Today, however, I am not so sure that this is funny. It does suggest that affection may be generated within a child for an electromechanical instrument that has been essential to educational reinforcement. Unfortunately, such a machine, in its present form, is unlikely to generalize with human beings in the boy's world, giving to them a highly desirable reinforcing property. In fact, the

---

[5] At the Linwood Children's Center, Ellicott City, Maryland.

growth of this type of student-machine relation, if it were the only one, would be a poor substitute for a directly social interaction.

In an earlier report upon our method, I mentioned that it had been anticipated, partially or *in toto*, in earlier studies and I described one of these in some detail. As for current developments by other workers in our field, I have not made any systematic attempt to examine the offerings, even those that deal with college or university instruction. However, I have been impressed by several of them which seem to have points in common with ours, which have met with some success, and which will probably be increasingly heard from in the future.

One of these is the Audio-Tutorial Approach to the teaching of botany, developed by S. N. Postlethwait at Purdue University (Postlethwait and Novak, 1967). Another is the Socratic-Type Programming of general psychology by Harry C. Mahan (1967) and his associates at Palomar College, in California; and a third is the Interview Technique recently applied by C. B. Ferster and M. C. Perrott (1968) in teaching principles of behavior to graduate students in education at the University of Maryland.

Professor Postlethwait's method places great emphasis upon "independent study sessions" in which students carry out each individual work assignment in the course at their own pace, by means of the extensive use of tapes and films. Teaching assistants provide for oral quizzing on major concepts and help the students with difficult assignments. Weekly "small assembly sessions" are used primarily for recitation and the discussion of problems or small research projects; and "general assembly sessions" deal mainly with motivational materials. Postlethwait reports high student interest and greatly improved performance with the use of this technique. "Grades have risen from 6% A's under the conventional system to as high as 25% A's in some semesters. Failures have decreased from 20% in the conventional system to as few as 4%."

"Socratic-Type Programming" is described by Professor Mahan as "a philosophy and technology of instruction which emphasizes student response rather than presentations by the teacher. Its basic media consist of exercises made up of questions and short answers covering the content of a standard text, the text itself, tapes for recording the questions in the exercises, a classroom tape recorder for administering tests, tape duplicating facilities, a listening center in the college library, and student owned tape recorders for home use whenever possible. Classroom time is devoted largely to the discussion of points covered by the questions. All examinations are the short-answer type and are presented aurally on tape." Students must pass three periodic tests with a score of 85% or better before they are permitted to take a comprehensive final examination. The method does not yet permit "multiple exit" from the course, but Mahan says it is "tending very much in that direction." (1967).

The Interview Technique, as described by Ferster and Perrott, does permit students to complete the course at different times, and it also approximates the student-and-proctor feature. Progress through the course is possible by verbalizing successive units of course content in a lengthy series of short interviews. The interviews are conducted mainly between students currently enrolled in the course, and any student is free to leave the course when all of his reading assignments have been adequately covered. The interviewer may sometimes be a staff member, as at the beginning of the course, but generally he is a student who has already been interviewed by someone else on the topic in question. The interviews are highly formalized, with the interviewer playing the role of the listener, checker, appraiser, and summarizer. Each interview is an open-book affair, but of such short and sharply-defined duration (10 min, as a rule) that the student can do no more than cue himself by reference to the printed page.

The goal of this method is nothing less than fluency with respect to each main feature of the course. Lectures, group discussions, and demonstrations are available at certain times, contingent upon a given stage of advance. Inadequate interviews are rejected, in whole or part, without prejudice, and with suggestions for further study. A product of high quality is guaranteed through staff participation at critical points. A modification of this procedure, which is to include written tests and the employment of advanced-student proctors, is planned by Professor Ferster for the introductory course in psychology at Georgetown University during the coming semester.

In systems like these, and in the one I have centered on, the work of a teacher is at variance with that which has predominated in our time. His public appearances as classroom entertainer, expositor, critic, and debater no longer seem important. His principal job, as Frank Finger (1962) once defined it, is truly "the facilitation of learning in others." He becomes an educational engineer, a contingency manager, with the responsibility of serving the great majority, rather than the small minority, of young men and women who come to him for schooling in the area of his competence. The teacher of tomorrow will not, I think, continue to be satisfied with a 10% efficiency (at best) which makes him an object of contempt by some, commiseration by others, indifference by many, and love by a few. No longer will he need to hold his position by the exercise of functions that neither transmit culture, dignify his status, nor encourage respect for learning in others. No longer will he need to live, like Ichabod Crane, in a world that increasingly begrudges providing him room and lodging for a doubtful service to its young. A new kind of teacher is in the making. To the old kind, I, for one, will be glad to say, "Good-bye!"

I started this paper on a personal note and I would like to end it on one. Twenty-odd years ago, when white rats were first used as laboratory subjects in the introductory course, a student would sometimes complain about his animal's behavior. The beast couldn't learn, he was asleep, he wasn't hungry, he was sick, and so forth. With a little time and a handful of pellets, we could usually show that this was wrong. All that one needed to do was follow the rules. "The rat," we used to say, "is always right."

My days of teaching are over. After what I have said about efficiency, I cannot lay claim to any great success, but my schedule of rewards was enough to maintain my behavior, and I learned one very important thing: *the student is always right.* He is not asleep, not unmotivated, not sick, and he can learn a great deal if we provide the right contingencies of reinforcement. But if we don't provide them, and provide them soon, he too may be inspired to say, "Good-bye!" to formal education.

References

Ferster, C. B. and Perrott, M. C. *Behavior principles.* New York: Appleton-Century-Crofts, 1968, Pp. 542.

Finger, F. W. Psychologists in colleges and universities. In W. B. Webb (Ed.), *The profession of psychology.* New York: Holt, Rinehart and Winston, 1962, Pp. 50-73.

Keller, F. S. Studies in international morse code: 1. a new method of teaching code reception. *Journal of Applied Psychology,* 1943, 27, 407-415.

Keller, F. S. A personal course in psychology. In R. Ulrich, T. Stachnik, and J. Mabry (Eds.), *The control of behavior.* Glenview, Ill.: Scott, Foresman, 1966, Pp. 91-93.

Keller, F. S. Neglected rewards in the educational process. *Proc, 23rd Amer, Conf. Acad. Deans,* Los Angeles, Jan., 1967. Pp. 9-22.

Keller, F. S. New reinforcement contingencies in the classroom. In *Programmiertes lernen,* Wissenschaftliche Buchgesellschaft, Darmstadt, in press.

Keller, F. S. Engineering personalized instruction in the classroom. *Rev. Interamer de Psicol.,* 1967, 1, 189-197.

Keller, F. S. and Schoenfeld, W. N. The psychology curriculum at Columbia College. *American Psychologist*, 1949, 4, 165–172.

Mahan, H. C. The use of Socratic type programmed instruction in college courses in psychology. Paper read at West. Psychol. Ass., San Francisco, May, 1967.

Postlethwait, S. N. and Novak, J. D. The use of 8-mm loop films in individualized instruction. *Annals N.Y. Acad. Sci.*, Vol. 142, Art. 2, 464–470.

Sherman, J. G. Application of reinforcement principles to a college course. Paper read at Amer. Educ. Res. Ass., New York, Feb., 1967.

Certainly, the program devised by Myers seems very strange to someone who has taken a typical statistics course. Students in his study were not ordinarily permitted to take the textbook out of the classroom, they could not take an exam until they had done the written work on that unit, and they had to correct all errors on exams and retake an exam on which they made three or more errors. On the other hand, they were not required to attend class, could take each exam as often as necessary, could finish the course when they did the work and were assured of an A for completing the work or an incomplete if they did not. Since almost no students wanted lectures, none were given. What reactions might be expected to such a course? Myers students reported enjoyment of the course as taught, with particular appreciation for the chance to work at their own pace. Evidently they also had trouble in believing that they were really assured of an A if they did the work, but the fact that all but one student received an A should have reassured them.

Although it is hard to assess from Myers' account how the performance of the students in this class differed from those in most statistics courses, it seems hard to believe that the lack of any drop outs is not statistically significant when compared with most statistics courses. Certainly the students felt that they did more work than in a usual class and did not feel that the grading was lenient; and Myers mentions that many of them would have preferred to do less work and receive a lower grade, had that option been permitted.

An interesting sidelight of the program is the students' focus on the task in conversations with the instructor. Even at the college level, there appears to be a lot of feeling on the part of students that classes should not be cold and impersonal with contact between students and the instructor limited to formal settings. In this case, however, students chose to focus their conversations on the material at hand. Perhaps one effect of this mastery approach is to emphasize knowledge of the material to the exclusion of social interaction. Whether this type of relationship is considered lacking in warmth and value or the model of a good teaching-learning experience is a matter each teacher will have to decide for himself.

Operant Learning Principles Applied to Teaching Introductory Statistics[1]

William A. Myers*†[2]

ABSTRACT

A grade of A was given in an introductory statistics course for meeting a set of contingencies that included no work outside of class (except by request), near-perfect performance on exams following each unit of work in a programmed text, correction of all exam errors, self pacing of work, and the chance to finish the course early. A grade of incomplete was given otherwise. Correlations among performance measures failed to show any meaningful relationships between time taken to finish the course, errors made on exams, and errors made in the programmed text.

* William A. Myers, "Operant Learning Principles Applied to Teaching Introductory Statistics," *Journal of Applied Behavior Analysis* 3(1970): 191–197. Reprinted with permission. Copyright 1970 by the Society for the Experimental Analysis of Behavior.

† Wisconsin Regional Primate Research Center

[1] I am grateful to Barry Bragg (now Dr. Bragg) who, as teaching assistant in the course, worked harder than I had a right to expect.

[2] Now at the Minneapolis, Minnesota, Veterans' Hospital. Reprints may be obtained from the author, 2648 Humboldt Avenue South, Minneapolis, Minnesota 55408.

Responses to a five-part
questionnaire were overwhelmingly
favorable to the course, but did not
vary as a function of grade point
average, time taken to finish the
course, or number of errors made on
exams. The uniformly high level of
performance, the students' lack of
interest in social contact with the
instructor during class, and the
absence of drop-outs are all
attributed to the contingencies
employed, chief among which,
according to the instructor's
judgment and student rankings,
were self-pacing, frequent non-
punitive exams and a guaranteed
grade of A for near-perfect work at
every stage.

Persons interested in the application of operant methods to instruction
are familiar with such implied criticisms as: does the student feel
deprived of personal contact with the instructor? Does the student feel
he is being treated as an object or is not recognized as an individual? Was
the material so easy that a sense of excitement and adventure was totally
missing? Does the student think the grading system was fair? Would the
student voluntarily take another course taught by similar methods? Were
the bright students bored an appreciable part of the time? In addition to
these attitudinal questions, there is the question of the quality of
objectively measured performance in a course taught by operant
methods.

Answers to the above questions have so far been favorable for an
operant approach to instruction (Keller, 1968; McMichael and Corey,
1969), but additional data are needed, particularly from students.

There is another whole set of attitudinal questions which, since they
do not impugn operant techniques, are not asked by critics; namely, are
there features of the operant approach to instruction which students
actively like?

The main purpose of the introductory statistics course described here
was to arrange the conditions of learning so that a group of students with
varied background and ability would master the course content.
Performance and attitudinal data were collected to determine whether
that purpose was realized and to evaluate the set of learning conditions
employed.

The methods used were similar enough to those described by Keller (1967) to be considered as a partial replication of his methods. Certain departures from his methods were deliberately introduced in the hope that they would reduce the number of students failing to complete the course, the major flaw in Keller's approach.

The course was given at the University of Wisconsin in an eight-week summer session in 1968. Of the 38 students enrolled, there were seven sophomores, 15 juniors, 10 seniors, and six adult specials. Most were in the college of liberal arts, with a scattering from business, agriculture, and education.

METHOD

CONTINGENCIES

At the first class meeting, the instructor explained the rules of the course and gave a brief rationale for them. Students were told that they could work only in class; that the time allowed for work was continuous 2.5 hr period each weekday; that they could arrive and leave whenever they chose, but the text book (Elzey, 1968) could not be taken out of class; that each unit of the book and the exercises following it had to be completed in writing before taking the exam for that unit; that each exam must be passed with fewer than three errors before beginning the next unit; that all errors on exams had to be corrected whether the exam was passed or not; that a grade of A would be given for passing all 24 unit exams and a grade of Incomplete for anything less; that individual tutoring could be had anytime by raising a hand or while an exam was being graded, but it had to be initiated by the student himself; that the instructor and teaching assistant were to be considered equals insofar as grading exams was concerned, and that the course was over when the last unit exam in the book was passed.

Unit exams varied in length and type of question depending on the nature of the material covered in the corresponding unit of the text. An effort was made, however, to include a number of questions requiring calculation from each unit. Students moved freely between the classroom and another room containing desk calculators.

DAILY STUDY SESSIONS

A session began when the instructor unlocked the storeroom where the texts and exams were kept between sessions. Students found their own books and began work. When they were ready for an exam, they took it from a folder after showing the instructor or teaching assistant that the unit and the book exercises had been done. When they finished an exam, they had the option of bringing it either to the instructor or the teaching assistant for grading.

When they left for the day, books were left in the classroom, except in cases where the instructor gave the student the option of taking the book home for the weekend. This option was offered when a student needed more time to complete the work.

When asked on several occasions if they wanted lectures to supplement the text, only a handful said yes. Accordingly, no lectures were given.

RESULTS

PERFORMANCE

Figure 1 indicates that there were large individual differences in the time taken to complete the course, in the number of errors made on exams,

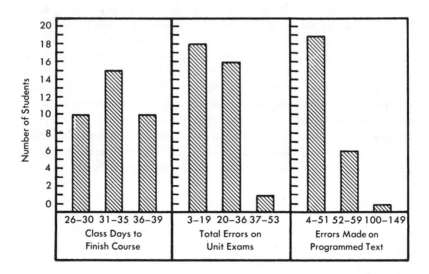

Figure 1

Performance among students in time taken to finish the course, number of errors made on unit exams, and number of errors made in the programmed text.

and in the number of errors made in working through the text. The Pearson Product-Moment correlation between number of days to finish the course and errors made on the exams was 0.414 ($P<0.05$); between number of days to finish and errors made in the book, $r=0.43$ ($P<0.05$); and between errors in the book and errors on exams, $r=0.04$ (n.s.).

Work done in class was generally intensive. Although it was not prohibited, there was virtually no eating, sleeping or magazine reading. When asked why they did not take advantage of the freedom to leave class for a break, most students said they were acutely conscious of a time pressure, even though, objectively, there was more than enough time.

QUESTIONNAIRE

There were five parts to the questionnaire. In the first part were 15 items comparing the course as taught against what they imagined it would have been under the lecture method. Each item was rated on a seven-point scale whose midpoint was "no difference between the course as it was given and a lecture course" and whose end points were "a lot more by the course as it was given" and "a lot less by the course as it was given." Since they did not actually take the course by the lecture method (except for four students who had previously failed or dropped the course when it was given by the lecture method), their judgments were necessarily between the course as it was taught and their impression of the lecture method from past experience.

Out of 18 items in Part I, 16 elicited relatively extreme judgments, all favoring the course as taught. Some of the judgments most favorable to the course were (1) "the amount of material fully understood" ($x=2.03$: the verbal equivalent lies between "a lot more" and "a moderate amount more" by the course as given); (2) confidence in solving statistical problems ($x=2.11$); (3) amount ot time bored in class ($x=6.62$: the verbal equivalent lies between "a lot" and "a moderate" amount less by the course as given); (4) the extent to which natural differences of ability among the students were taken into account ($x=2.00$); (5) the extent to which the course failed to recognize you as an individual ($x=6.22$). All of these findings agree with Keller's (1967).

In Part II, the students ranked a list of 13 features of the course in the order of "their importance to you." The fact that students have very different past histories of academic performance is reflected by the high variability of the rankings. The item receiving the highest mean rank ($x=2.65$) and the lowest variability was "Being able to work at your own pace." The item receiving the next highest rank ($x=4.89$) was "Taking an exam on each set," followed by "Not being penalized for mistakes on exams by lowering the grade (x= 5.54)."

Table 1 shows which features of the course received the first five ranks as a function of cumulative grade point average. All groups agree that self-pacing is most important. Although agreement is close on the remaining four items shown in the table, there are important differences. While all groups consider grading contingencies important, those who have been well rewarded in the past value means (Item 3) above ends (Items 11 and 12), whereas those who have been poorly rewarded in the past value ends (Items 11 and 12) above means (Item 3).

Section III asked for absolute judgments on a five-point scale concerning the difficulty of exams, amount of work required for exams, adequacy of book, and amount of vocal instruction. The mid-point was "about right" and the extremes were "much more than necessary" and "much less than necessary." The means of the judgments were all within half a scale point of the midpoint and the variability was very small (range of the Average Deviation was 0.05 to 0.63).

Section IV asked for personal evaluations of the teaching assistant and instructor on strictness of grading, extent to which they were helpful and encouraging, and their skill in explaining material. With one exception, the means of the judgments were close to but on the favorable side of the mid-point of a seven-point scale. The exception occurred on the item concerning the instructor's grading of exams. The mean judgment was

Table 1

Features of the course receiving the first five ranks as a function of students' cumulative grade point average (on a four-point grading scale).

	GPA	
3.0 and Above	2.5 and Above	Below 2.5
8	8	8
3	3	11
11	12	12
12	11	3
13	13	1

Note—The numbers designate the following items in the list of features to be ranked.

1. Being able to move around or take a break when you felt like it.
3. Taking an exam on each set.
8. Being able to work at your own pace.
11. Not being penalized for mistakes by lowering the grade.
12. Knowing you would get an A if you did everything asked of you.
13. Being asked to correct mistakes on exams.

Table 2

The number of students willing to take future courses taught by operant versus lecture method.

Question	Yes	No
Would you take another course like this one in statistics?	29	6
Would you take another course by the lecture method in statistics?	10	26
Would you take another course in psychology by the lecture method?	34	1
Would you take another course in psychology taught like this one?	27	6
Would you take another course like this one in subjects besides statistics and psychology?	29	6

Note—The responses do not add to the same total for each question due to several missing answers.

3.54, which deviates slightly from the midpoint towards the "too strict" end of the scale.

The results of Section V, which asked the students to predict their future choices between the type of course as given and the lecture method, are shown in Table 2. Their responses favored the operant method, but did not show a willingness to give up the lecture method entirely.

In answer to the question, "What did you like most about the course?," 19 of 37 mentioned self-pacing. Other frequent responses were "receiving positive reinforcement for each unit" and "having immediate knowledge of results." Only one of the students mentioned something other than a programmed contingency.

By contrast, many answers to the question, "What did you like least about the course?," were irrelevant to the teaching method used (e.g., "having to take the course in the psychology building, which is extremely ugly and sterile").

The final section, entitled simply "Comments," contained many remarks favorable to the course, the instructor, and the teaching assistant. The most frequent theme of these comments and also of conversations before class was the need for more courses taught by these methods. The enthusiasm of students for the method used, although it is not as easily interpreted as numerical data to specific questions, was astonishing in its volume and repetitiveness. One student asked three days in a row if he was really going to get an A for meeting the instructor's demands.

In order to answer questions concerning the effects of individual performance differences on attitudes towards the course, the students were divided into groups based on their cumulative grade point averages, the number of class days required to complete the course, and the number of errors made on the unit exams.

The data in Table 3 do not show any discernible effect of grade point average or number of class days to complete the course on questionnaire ratings. The number of errors made on exams is a different story. On most of the items in Part I, the groups (C2 and C3) that made the most errors on the exams had mean ratings more favorable to the course than the group (CI) that made the fewest errors on exams. To complete the symmetry of this relationship between number of errors and attitude towards the course, the group (C3) with the most errors gave ratings more favorable to the course than the group (C2) that made an intermediate number of errors on 11 of the 18 items of Part I.

Item 6 of Part I deserves special mention because of the high frequency with which boredom is ascribed to operant methods of instruction. The item asks ". . . what per cent of the time were you bored in class?" A rating of seven means "a lot less by the course as given." The group with the highest grade point average had a mean rating of 6.92 with an average deviation of 0.15 ($N = 12$). The middle and lowest groups had mean ratings of 6.38 (A.D. $= 0.95$) and 6.58 (A.D. $= 0.62$) respectively.

Of 38 students taking the course, 37 received As, one received a B[3], and no one received an Incomplete.

DISCUSSION

In Keller's course (1967) 20% of the students took Incompletes and another 19% failed or dropped the course. In McMichael and Corey's course (1969), 12% of the contingently-managed group dropped the course. The fact that there were no dropouts in the course described here is probably due in part to its being given in summer school when many students attempt to meet curriculum requirements.

Another reason may have been the contingencies used in grading. The over-all requirement for an A may be thought of as a second-order multiple schedule in which the student had to complete a fixed number

---

[3] Of 38 students, 37 received an A and one, who went through the course in his own way without consulting the instructor, received a B.

Table 3

Comparisons of mean ratings on Part I of the questionnaire as a function of grade-point average, time taken to complete course, and number of errors on exams. Entries are the number of items from a total of 18 on which the mean rating of one group favored the course more than the mean rating of another.

Grade-Point Average		Time to Finish Course		Errors on Exams		
$A_1 > A_2$	$A_1 > A_3$	$B_1 > B_2$	$B_1 > B_3$	$C_1 > C_2$	$C_1 > C_3$	$C_2 > C_3$
9	11	9	9	3	4	7

A_1—grade-point average of 3.0 or greater
A_2—grade-point average between 2.5 and 3.0
A_3—grade-point average less than 2.5
B_1—up to 35 days
B_2—between 36 and 40 days

B_3—between 41 and 45 days
C_1—between 4 and 15
C_2—between 16 and 25
C_3—between 26 and 53

of work units (24), each requiring a variable amount of work [FR24(VRx)]. The consequence of completing each unit may be a combination of events including (1) the satisfaction of passing the unit exams (2) the opportunity to proceed, (3) the confidence produced by near-perfect performance and (4) advancing faster than other students. Meeting the overall requirement produced three academic credits of A and, to judge from the questionnaires, various pleasant affective states. Failure to complete the course not only produced an undesirable grade, but it negated all the work done before quitting. Many students said they would have been satisfied with a grade lower than A, so the contingencies should thwart the option of mediocre performance, providing the instructor has chosen to require A-quality work and has made this clear in his work contract with the students. The perseverance usually seen in ratio schedules (Ferster and Skinner, 1957, pp. 39–41) coupled with an unwelcome event contingent on quitting may have been sufficient to prevent dropping-out in this course.

The frequently heard charge that programmed texts are boring, particularly to students, may or may not be true, but a distinction should be made between the boredom attributable to the text itself and that attributable to a set of contingencies that includes a programmed text. As a record of feelings about the set of contingencies used in this course, the questionnaire data indicate that no one was bored, least of all the students with the highest grade-point averages. A related criticism is the charge that programmed learning is too easy, but all three grade-point groups judged that they had done a moderate to a lot more work than they would have done in a lecture course, and none of the groups thought the grading of exams was lenient, so it is safe to conclude that none of the groups thought the course too easy. The questionnaire items dealing with (1) the amount of personal contact with the instructor, (2) the extent to which natural differences of ability was taken into account, and (3) the extent to which the student was treated as an individual all received highly favorable ratings regardless of grade point average, time taken to finish the course, or number of errors made on exams. The agreement among students, given these differences, was the most surprising finding in the questionnaire data. It seems highly likely that the favorable attitudes reported were a function of the success that all but one student experienced. Providing that the success is earned in a way that meets acceptable academic criteria, this would seem to be an uncontroversial outcome. The experience of success may also explain the paradoxical result recorded in Table 3. Those who made the most errors liked the course most; perhaps because they were successful in spite of their errors.

The behavior of the students in this course also bears on the much discussed issue of student-faculty contact. Although they were friendly and talkative (especially about the teaching method being used) outside of class hours, they chose to limit their contacts with the instructor during class hours to matters concerning the content of the course, in spite of the fact that they could have had conversation with the instructor at any time simply by raising their hand. The great majority refused the offer of supplementary lectures and most students cut short attempts by the instructor to talk about anything but the subject matter. As one student put it, "With the chance of finish-the course early, why should we waste time talking to you?" Keller (1965) also reported that lectures given as supplements to his course in introductory psychology were poorly attended. This raises the possibility that the amount and kind of contact that students seek from faculty is not some sort of behavioral invariant, but rather a function of the learning conditions operative in a given course. At the very least, this finding falsifies the generalization that social contact between student and instructor during class is a necessary condition for effective learning.

The correlations between performance measures were much smaller than would be expected on the view that these measures are largely determined by the students' personalities. Knowing how many errors a student made on the programmed text, for example, was not useful in predicting his rate of progress or his exam performance. The fact that planned contingencies can produce low correlations among performance measures shows that performance is not an invariant beyond the instructor's ability to change, but rather an outcome that can be made sensitive to classroom conditions. This implies that the instructor bears a good part of the responsibility for arranging the conditions that produce high-level performance.

The view that the student bears some responsibility for his own performance is equivocally supported by the present data. Table 1 shows that students can identify the major conditions of learning that led them to high levels of performance. Of 13 features of the course given to them for ranking, the students ranked them in nearly the same order of importance as the instructor. This finding is equivocal, however, because it is possible that students do not know how to put these conditions of learning into an effective combination. It is also an open question whether they would have identified the important contingencies at all without at least one exposure to their effectiveness.

There were, of course, sizable individual differences in performance, but these were not considered in assigning grades. Their value to the students is evident, however, in that the brighter and harder working students finished the course earlier. As part of the instructor's explanation to the students of the contingencies in the course, it was announced that performance differences were relevant to grades only if a student failed to do quality work even under optimal conditions. It could then be justifiably said that a student was not capable of earning an A. It was further explained, however, that (1) the conditions for this course were probably not optimal, and (2) given university entrance requirements, everyone present could do A-level work. In consequence of this rationale, it was decided that a grade of B or C would mean only that a student had not done the work, not that he could not do it. Under the conditions of the course, therefore, the practice of employing grades to designate ability levels could not be justified and was not used for that purpose. Instead, either a student did all the work required and received an A, or he failed to do some of the work and got an Incomplete.

The number and role of staff in this course with 38 students was very different from the staffing of similar efforts aimed at large groups. Both Keller (1967) and Malott (1969) employed a hierarchy of personnel while, in the present case, there were only two staff members and the hierarchical distinction between them was deliberately minimized. It would appear that staffing can take many forms, providing basic contingencies are met.

The most frequent argument in favor of operant methods in education is that with ever-increasing student populations they are a fiscal necessity. The fact that an operant approach worked well in a small group should help to highlight its educational value as well.

References

Elzey, F. F. *A programmed introduction to statistics*. Belmont, Calif.: Wadsworth, 1966.

Keller, F. S. "Goodbye Teacher . . ." *Journal of Applied Behavior Analysis*, 1968, 1, 79–89.

Keller, F. S. Neglected rewards in the educational process. Proceedings 23rd American Conference of Academic Deans, Los Angeles, Jan., 1967. Pp. 9-22.

Keller, F. S. In a talk given to the Center for Research in Human Learning at the University of Minnesota, 1965.

Ferster, C. B. and Skinner, B. F. *Schedules of reinforcement*. New York: Appleton-Century-Crofts, 1957.

Malott, R. W. and Svinicki, J. G. *Contingency management in an introductory psychology course for 1000 students*. Western Michigan University. Unpublished.

McMichael, J. S. and Corey, J. R. Contingency management in an introductory psychology course produces better learning. *Journal of Applied Behavior Analysis*, 1969, 2, 79–83.

Skinner, B. F. *The technology of teaching*. New-York: Appleton-Century-Crofts, 1968.

PART 6

Practical and Theoretical Issues

The articles in this last section of the book do not report research projects concerned directly with changing the classroom behavior of students. The first two articles, those by Andrews and Wetzel, are empirical studies reporting the methods and results of programs designed to train teachers and teacher's aides in utilizing behavior modification techniques with their students. Both articles indicate some success with such programs, although Andrews' paper focuses more on the results and Wetzel's more on the training methods used.

The next three papers discuss some of the issues in using behavior modification techniques. O'Leary discusses the practical problems which arise in instituting token reinforcement programs and suggests means of coping with them. Homme focuses on the use of high probability behaviors as rewards and suggests means for making their use more effective. Woody mentions the whole range of behavior modification and behavior therapy techniques available to the school psychologist and suggests that the training of school psychologists should be altered to enable them to become familiar with the use of these techniques.

One issue which Woody raises, that of the relative effectiveness of behavior therapy and traditional psychotherapy, is also dealt with by Bandura. In his paper Bandura discusses this question and other ethical issues involved in controlling human behavior and comes to the conclusion that behavior modification techniques are indeed ethical if properly used. Finally, Baer, Wolf and Risley summarize some of the major aspects of studies which attempt to analyze and modify behavior and suggest the characteristics which they consider to be indicative of a valuable report in this area.

Although these articles do not illustrate specific ways of modifying classroom behaviors, they dwell on the broader issues of training people to use these techniques, of making practical decisions about implementation, and of assessing their morality and validity. When one goes beyond the classroom to use these techniques on a much wider scale, such issues may become crucial. Today behavior modification is being used in mental hospitals, an Army training camp, and institutions for juvenile delinquents, as well as in the therapist's office and the schools. The reported success of such programs implies that their use may continue to expand. The day may come when familiarity with the principles of behavior modification will be expected not only of teachers and psychologists but of everyone.

Instead of working directly with the children whose behavior is to be changed, Andrews worked with a group of teachers to train them in using behavior modification techniques. The major behavioral data he reports, however, are not the teachers' behaviors but those of the students in their classroom. According to the teachers' second hand reports, problem behaviors ranging from one child's leaving her seat to another girl's soiling her pants were reduced by the teachers' manipulations. Moreover the attitudes of the participants toward Andrews' class appeared to be quite favorable.

As Andrews points out, the traditional model for using the services of professional psychologists in the schools involves individual treatment or consultation. A more efficient method might be the approach he used in having them train the teachers who could then deal directly with the behavior problems they encounter. The fact that his program concentrated primarily on simple behaviors is not an indication that such a training program need be limited to such, since the brief time allotted for Andrews' study could certainly be expanded. However, the fact that the teachers were all volunteers and generally enthusiastic should not be overlooked. The possibility of Hawthorne effects and of observer biases is very great, as well as the probability that teachers who are philosophically opposed to the use of such techniques would not choose to enroll in such a course. Of course, one might argue that those who do not volunteer for this kind of program would be unlikely to implement the techniques taught anyway. Although it cannot be concluded from Andrews' study that all teachers can or should be taught to use behavior modification techniques, it appears that a training program can indeed affect the teachers who volunteer to enroll in it and that these effects show up in the behavior of their students.

The Results of a Pilot Program to Train Teachers in the Classroom Application of Behavior Modification Techniques[1]

Joseph K. Andrews[*][†]

ABSTRACT

A four week inservice pilot program was carried out for the purpose of training a group of elementary teachers in the classroom application of behavior modification principles. The teachers were able to effect changes in classroom behavior as a consequence of their participation in the training program.

Many investigators have demonstrated that the systematic application of behavior modification principles can bring about behavior change in educational settings. Hart, Allen, Buell, Harris, & Wolf (1964) were able to reduce crying by manipulating its social consequences, and Zimmerman & Zimmerman (1962) eliminated tantrum behavior in a special class child by making teacher approval contingent upon appropriate social behavior. Other studies have shown that it is possible

---

[*] Joseph K. Andrews, "The Results of a Pilot Program to Train Teachers in the Classroom Application of Behavior Modification Techniques," *Journal of School Psychology* 8(1970): 37–42. Reprinted with permission.

[†] Havre de Grace, Maryland

[1] Appreciation is expressed to the following Harford County school personnel for making the necessary arrangements for the training program: Mrs. Violet Merrimen, Supervisor; Mr. Joseph Maley, Principal; Mr. James Wilson, Principal; and Mr. Paul Ouellette, Pupil Personnel Worker.

to reduce appreciably disruptive classroom behavior by applying operant principles (Thomas, Becker, & Armstrong, 1968; Madsen, Becker, & Thomas, 1968; Allen, Reynolds, Harris, & Baer, 1966). Other investigations have centered on increasing the amount of time spent in attending to a task (Allen, Henke, Harris, Baer, & Reynolds, 1967; Walker & Buckley, 1968), increasing the amount of time engaged in study behavior (Hall, Lund, & Jackson, 1968), establishing cooperative social behavior (Hart, Reynolds, Brawley, Harris, & Baer, 1966; Buell, Stoddard, Harris, & Baer, 1968), and the acquisition of speech in preschool disadvantaged children (Reynolds & Risley, 1968; Hart & Risley, 1968).

It has been demonstrated that parents can be trained to apply behavioral principles to cause change in their own problem children (Walder, Cohen, Breiter, Daston, Hirsch, & Leibowitz, 1967; Walder, Cohen, Daston, Breiter, & Hirsch, 1967; Walder, Breiter, Cohen, Daston, Forbes, & McIntire, 1966). In addition, there has been some emphasis on training teachers to apply behavioral principles in the classroom (Hall, Panyan, Rabon, & Broden, 1968; Ward & Baker, 1968). The training programs carried out by Hall et al. (1968) and Ward & Baker (1968) were very effective, but employed a number of relatively sophisticated procedures (e.g., one or two in-room observers to record behavior, and some electrically operated signal lights). These procedures should be carried out whenever and wherever possible; however, most school-oriented practitioners do not have the time, facilities, or personnel to employ them. Therefore, this project was undertaken to investigate the feasibility of a short-term teacher training program in the classroom application of behavioral principles.

METHOD

The idea for this project arose after a short explanation of behavioral techniques was presented to the teachers of two schools during a half-day in-service meeting. After the meeting a questionnaire was sent to these teachers to determine how many would be interested in participating in a series of sessions devoted to operant techniques.

Of the 40 teachers to whom the questionnaire was sent, 14 indicated interest. Three of the 14 could not participate in all of the training sessions because of year-end administrative duties.

The teachers represented kindergarten through grade four and ranged in experience from one to ten years. In addition to the regular class teachers, the group included two teachers of the educable mentally retarded, one teacher of the trainable mentally retarded, and one speech therapist.

PROCEDURE

The writer requested and obtained permission to conduct the training program, at least in part, during the regular school day. The schools permitted the teachers to leave early one day a week so that the schools contributed 50% of the time and the teachers contributed 50% of their time.

Although more sessions would have been desirable, the training program consisted of four one and one-half hour sessions. The "text" was *Living with children* (Patterson & Gullion, 1968). The book is written in programmed style and outlines the theory and application of social learning principles.

The first session was devoted to the methods of observing behavior *per se*, introduction of reinforcement principles, and the importance of record keeping. The teachers were asked to choose a specific target behavior in a given child which required modification. The group was then instructed in techniques which could be used for the observation and recording of behavior, with the goal of determining the frequency of the behavior in question before intervention was instituted (establishing a baseline).

The second session was devoted to a discussion of extinction, the reinforcement of incompatible behaviors, and intermittent reinforcement. The baseline data were examined and suggestions were made by the writer and the group as to what techniques might be employed to modify the target behaviors.

Session three consisted of an examination of the treatment effects by comparing a week of baseline data with a week of intervention data. If the frequency of a target behavior was not changing in the desired direction, different procedures were discussed and decided upon.

The final session was devoted to a re-examination of the treatment effects, again, by referring to the data which had been gathered. The teachers then were asked to complete a course evaluation questionnaire.

RESULTS

Figure 1 is the behavior graph of a second grade girl. The behavior to be modified consisted of the girl's shouting out answers, making disturbing noises and inappropriate sounds.

Prior to the institution of the treatment program the teacher seemed to be reinforcing this inappropriate behavior by attending to it: the teacher would ask the girl to be quiet, reprimand her, etc., contingent upon the girl's shouting out. The child was observed for the same one hour time period for each of the 20 days, and the treatment plan consisted of: (a) ignoring the girl's inappropriate vocalizations, (b) recognizing the girl and dispensing verbal approval contingent upon hand-raising, and (c) dispensing verbal approval, on a periodic basis throughout the day, for quiet behavior. As Figure 1 indicates, the frequency of inappropriate vocalization was reduced to zero.

Figure 2 represents the behavior graph of a ten-year old trainable mentally retarded girl who manifested soiling behavior on a relatively consistent basis, with no evidence of an organic etiology. Prior to treatment, each time the child soiled herself she had to be washed and have a change of undergarments. In addition, the soiled undergarment had to be rinsed.

The treatment plan consisted of placing the child on a 15 minute fixed interval schedule of reinforcement. The teacher played with, praised, and

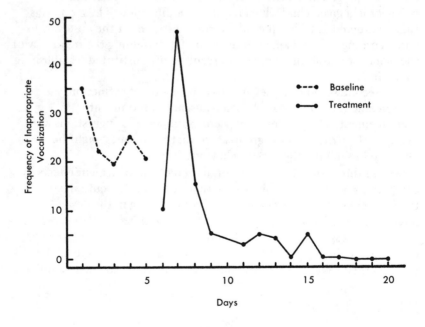

Figure 1

The Frequency of Inappropriate Vocalization for a Second Grade Girl

hugged the child for each 15 minute interval during which she remained unsoiled. During the second week of treatment the teacher moved to a variable interval schedule of reinforcement with an average of 30 minutes. By the end of the inservice training program the teacher had succeeded in reducing the frequency of soiling from an average of seven times per day to one or zero times per day.

Figure 3 represents the frequency with which a seven-year old educable mentally retarded child left her seat during speech therapy sessions. The group consisted of five children and met for two half-hour sessions per week. Prior to treatment the therapist wasted much of her time telling the child to remain in her seat.

Treatment consisted of placing the child on a five minute variable interval schedule of reinforcement, using jelly beans as reinforcers. The speech therapist used a kitchen timer and dispensed jelly beans contingent upon each interval during which the child remained seated. A portion of the five minute variable interval schedule of reinforcement reads as follows: 30 seconds, 5 minutes, 30 seconds, 1 minute, 2 minutes, 30 seconds, 40 seconds, 10 minutes, etc. Figure 3 indicates that in spite of the short period of time the program was in effect (two half-hour sessions per week) the frequency of seat leaving behavior was reduced from an average of five times per 30 minute session to zero times per session.

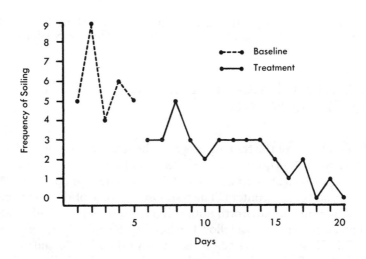

Figure 2

The Frequency of Soiling per day in a Trainable Mentally Retarded Girl

Toward the end of the training project the therapist decided to institute the treatment program with all five children and reported that "the general behavior of the other children in the class had been noticeably improved."

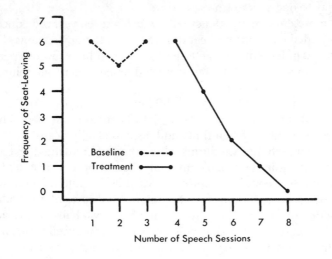

Figure 3

The Frequency of Seat-Leaving in an Educable Mentally Retarded Girl during thirty-minute Speech Therapy Sessions

RESULTS OF COURSE EVALUATION QUESTIONNAIRE

At the conclusion of the training program the teachers were asked to complete an 18 item questionnaire, with a multiple-choice format, concerning such areas as utilization of time, procedures employed by the instructor, and course content. The responses to some of the questions, in terms of percentages, are worth noting. To the question, "Would you recommend this course to a fellow teacher?" 63.6% said, "yes, very highly," 27.3% said, "yes, as better than many others," 9.1% said, "perhaps," and 0% said they probably would not, or decidedly would not recommend the course. If another course were offered in the area of behavior modification, 45.5% of the teachers indicated they would "definitely" enroll and 54.5% indicated that they would "very likely" enroll. In terms of the number of training sessions, 72.7% of the teachers felt that more sessions would have been appropriate while 27.3% felt that four sessions were sufficient. The teachers also were asked to give a subjective estimate of the amount of behavior change observed as a result of their treatment efforts: 36.5% saw a "great deal of change," 37.3% observed a "noticeable" change, 18.3% saw "some change," 0% saw "no change," and 9% ($N = 1$) observed a change in the "opposite" direction.

DISCUSSION

The data obtained from the behavior graphs and from the questionnaires suggest that a short-term teacher training program in the classroom application of operant techniques can be effective in bringing about student as well as teacher behavior change. Two points should be noted: first, the teachers involved in the training program were volunteers and as a result, probably had some motivation to implement treatment programs based on behavior principles. Thus, it is difficult to generalize from this sample to nonvolunteer teachers. Secondly, the teachers were advised to concentrate on relatively simple behaviors. It was recommended that they not become involved in changing very complex behaviors for two reasons: the relatively short time devoted to the training program, and more importantly, the instructor frankly wanted the teachers to be successful in their initial attempts at behavior modification, as this success might motivate them to apply their knowledge of behavior techniques to more complex situations. The behaviors on which the group concentrated were not totally irrelevant or unimportant. If such behaviors as hand-raising, calling out, and seat-leaving could be controlled, perhaps larger and more difficult problems could be prevented.

The final noteworthy aspect of the training program concerns the effective utilization of professional time. Most psychologists employed by school districts face a continuous backlog of referrals. Most would agree that this situation will persist if the individual or clinically-oriented model of service is not modified. Inservice training programs similar to the present one could provide teachers with effective techniques for changing classroom behavior.

References

Allen, K. E., Henke, L. B., Harris, F. R., Baer, D. M., and Reynolds, N. J. Control of hyperactivity by social reinforcement of attending behavior. *Journal of Educational Psychology*, 1967, 58, 231–237.

Allen, K. E., Reynolds, N. J., Harris, F. R., and Baer, D. M. Elimination of disruptive classroom behavior of a pair of preschool boys through systematic control of adult social reinforcement. Unpublished manuscript, University of Washington, 1966.

Buell, J., Stoddard, P., Harris, F. R., and Baer, D. M. Collateral social development accompanying reinforcement of outdoor play in a preschool child. *Journal of Applied Behavior Analysis*, 1968, 1, 167–173.

Hall, V. R., Lund, D., and Jackson, D. Effects of teacher attention on study behavior. *Journal of Applied Behavior Analysis*, 1968, 1, 1–12.

Hall, V. R., Panyan, M., Rabon, D., and Broden, M. Instructing beginning teachers in reinforcement procedures which improve classroom control. *Journal of Applied Behavior Analysis*, 1968, 19, 315–322.

Hart, B., Allen, E., Buell, J., Harris, F. R., and Wolf, M. Effects of social reinforcement on operant crying. *Journal of Experimental Child Psychology*, 1964, 1, 145–153.

Hart, B. M., Reynolds, N. J., Brawley, E. R., Harris, F. R., and Baer, D. M. Effects of contingent and noncontingent social reinforcement on the isolate behavior of a nursery school girl. Unpublished manuscript, University of Washington, 1966.

Hart, B. M., and Risley, T. R. Establishing use of descriptive adjectives in the spontaneous speech of disadvantaged preschool children. *Journal of Applied Behavior Analysis*, 1968, 1, 109–120.

Madsen, C. H., Becker, W. C., and Thomas, D. R. Rules, praise, and ignoring: Elements of elementary classroom control. *Journal of Applied Behavior Analysis*, 1968, 1, 139–150.

Patterson, G. R., and Gullion, M. E. *Living with children.* Champaign, Illinois: Research Press, 1968.

Reynolds, N. J., and Risley, T. R. The role of social and material reinforcers in increasing talking of a disadvantaged preschool child. *Journal of Applied Behavior Analysis*, 1968, 1, 253–262.

Thomas, D. R., Becker, W. C., and Armstrong, M. Production and elimination of disruptive classroom behavior by systematically varying teacher's attention. *Journal of Applied Behavior Analysis*, 1968, 1, 35–45.

Walder, L. O., Breiter, D. E., Cohen, S. I., Daston, P. G., Forbes, J. A., and McIntire, R. W. Teaching behavioral principles to parents to modify the behavior of their autistic children. Paper presented at the meeting of the American Psychological Association, New York, September 1966.

Walder, L. O., Cohen, S. I., Breiter, D. E., Daston, P. G., Hirsch, I. S., and Leibowitz, J. M. Teaching behavioral principles to parents of disturbed children. Paper presented at the meeting of the Eastern Psychological Association, Boston, April 1967.

Walder, L. O., Cohen, S. I., Daston, P. G., Breiter, D. E., and Hirsch, I. S. Behavior therapy of children through their parents. Paper presented at the meeting of the American Psychological Association, Washington, D.C., September 1967.

Walker, H. M., and Buckley, N. K. The use of positive reinforcement in conditioning attending behavior. *Journal of Applied Behavior Analysis,* 1968, *1,* 245-250.

Ward, M., and Baker, B. Reinforcement therapy in the classroom. *Journal of Applied Behavior Analysis,* 1968, *1,* 323-328.

Zimmerman, E., and Zimmerman, J. The alteration of behavior in a special classroom situation. *Journal of the Experimental Analysis of Behavior,* 1962, *5,* 59-60.

Unlike most of the other studies in this volume, with the exception of that by Andrews, the paper by Wetzel is concerned only indirectly with modifying the behavior of students. It focuses instead on the training of paraprofessionals, a field which has been more-or-less neglected until recently. Unlike many research projects, which use grades in classes or teachers'ratings as their dependent measures, the present study attempted to assess changes in the actual behavior of the aides as they interacted with the children and even changes in the children's behavior when instructed by the aide to perform a task.

Behavior modification techniques were used at two levels in this program: They comprised both the methods used to train the aides and the content of the material the aides were to learn. The design of the project implicitly and explicitly involved having the training staff model all the behaviors they wished the aides to display. The aides were provided with the kinds of learning experiences they were supposed to present to the students with whom they would be working: having someone carefully observe their own behavior, seeing appropriate behavior modeled, having chances to practice new responses, receiving immediate corrective feedback, and proceeding from simple and concrete behaviors to more complex and abstract ones.

Unfortunately, the results of this study are not presented in detailed form, so that the reader cannot really assess the effectiveness of the techniques. However, the detailed presentation and rationale behind them would suggest that they are certainly worthy of consideration in the training of paraprofessionals and quite possibly in the training of teachers themselves.

Behavior Modification Techniques and the Training of Teacher's Aides

Ralph J. Wetzel*†

Auxiliary classroom personnel—aides, volunteers, and parent participants—are appearing in public school classrooms with increasing regularity and in various roles. Welcomed by some teachers as additional instructional agents, many aides have been given real teaching responsibility. Others have not been regarded as having the requisite teaching skills and have been assigned tasks of material preparation, clean-up, and custodial supervision. State departments of education have wrestled with the tasks of role definition, training, and career development, while individual teachers alternately lament and praise the addition of new classroom personnel.

By most original definitions, the aide is regarded as one who can relieve the teacher of any number of preparatory, organizational, and supervisory duties so the teacher will be more free to "teach." In most systems the aide is not regarded as an instructional agent. Such a definition is based on a concept of teaching restricted to formal instruction in certain traditional academic skills. Everything we know about learning processes suggests that it is hardly possible for an aide to be a "non-teaching" individual. As an adult member of the classroom's social environment, the aide's behavior can be a rich source of model behaviors that children will imitate. The aide can provide a range of cues that will affect children's social, academic, and deportment repertoires.

Whatever the role and training of classroom personnel ultimately entails, it seems crucial that they have some grasp of behavior principles

* Ralph J. Wetzel, "Behavior Modification Techniques and the Training of Teacher's Aides," *Psychology in the Schools* 7(1970): 325–330. Reprinted with permission.
† University of Arizona

that will enable them to predict and observe the many ways in which their behavior affects that of the student. Over the past 2 years we have been developing training programs to meet this need. This paper describes one such program and some of the measures used to evaluate its effectiveness.

THE TRAINING PROGRAM

The program was designed for the personnel of two federally-supported child day care centers. There is nothing, however, that would make the program inappropriate for schools as well as preschool situations.

SUBJECTS

Five trainee groups, each composed of a teacher and two or more aides and volunteers, participated in the 4-week training program. Earlier experience taught us that to train aides in new skills without teachers is to court disaster. With the exception of one teacher, all of the Ss were women with a mean age of 38 years. All were married with from zero to seven children. Seven Ss were Negro, five Mexican-American, and two Anglo. Aides were drawn from poverty area populations; six had completed high school or had obtained an equivalency certificate.

TRAINING GOALS

The goals of the program were derived from a series of naturalistic observations made in the day-care centers prior to training. These observations suggested that behavior modification was needed in the following areas:

1. High-frequency custodial and menial behaviors on the part of the aides, much standing around, little or no involvement in instruction.
2. Little use of positive reinforcement by the aides with high-frequency threat and punishment; poor contingency management with much positive attention going to the child who was hurt, angry, crying, isolate, or demanding attention; no attention to a wide array of good behavior; little systematic use of positive reinforcement for skills.
3. Low-frequency planning and organizing behaviors on the part of the staff.

The training program therefore stressed:

1. Setting behavioral goals.
2. Contingency management, especially the shaping and positive reinforcement of goal behaviors.
3. The evaluation of methods and procedures.

Focus throughout the 4 weeks remained on the behavior of children and adults with no attention given to concepts such as needs, emotional disturbance, self-concept, or personality growth.

TRAINING METHODS

During the first 2 weeks of the 4-week program, the trainees and 10 children from their own center population spent 2 morning hours in our Pre-school Laboratory. The laboratory provides one-way mirrors and closed-circuit TV observation of the classroom. It is staffed by graduate and undergraduate psychology students at the University of Arizona. We found from earlier work that the use of center children reduced the trainees' belief that their own children were unique and impervious to all management attempts. Also, it may promote transfer of management skills from the training situation back to the center. We asked the staffs to bring their 10 worst-behaving children. The children's activities in the laboratory included breakfast, stories, lessons, music, art, exploration, and free choice. The second 2 weeks of training took place in the centers, where a full day program was maintained.

The training methods might be described as a kind of behavioral engineering. Each day began with demonstration and guided observation of modeled behaviors. No trainee was asked to engage in a behavior that the staff had not demonstrated. When the time came for practice in the classroom, every trainee was accompanied by a trainer for on-the-spot shaping and reinforcement of appropriate behaviors. The trainer provided verbal feedback, demonstrated, and had the aide practice. Inappropriate behavior was ignored or labeled as "wrong" if the appropriate behavior could be demonstrated and the trainee could practice it. Verbal labels were supplied for all behaviors demonstrated or practiced.

As an example, a day might begin with all trainees in the observation room. A trainer might say, "Today, let's look for some good behavior and reinforce the children doing good things by giving them a big smile and saying something nice to them." Then would come a period of identifying and labeling good behavior with the trainer praising, observing, and labeling behavior. Then would come observation of the staff's behavior—smiling, speaking to the children, the contingencies, their mistakes. Usually it was easy by this time to get one or two trainee volunteers to enter the classroom to try it. A trainer accompanied them, helped them select behaviors and helped with the timing. For example, the trainer might say, "Wait until he's finished putting the box on the shelf" and help decide what to say ("My, you put that away nicely") in praise of a good job. The rest of the trainee group observed and discussed until all trainees had entered the classroom to practice smiling and saying pleasant things to children contingent upon good behavior.

Brief lectures, discussions, written materials, and short prepared assignments followed each day's observation and practice session. Again an attempt was made to supply and repeat verbal labels for the behaviors observed and practiced by the trainees and the contingencies between these behaviors and those of the children.

SPECIFIC TRAINING PROCEDURES AND TECHNIQUES

It is, of course, impossible to convey all the procedures and techniques of a 4-week training program in this brief paper. The following are illustrative of principles used in the instructions to the trainers:

1. *Teaching Observing Behavior.* Trainees do not necessarily and automatically engage in observing behaviors in an observation room. They may use the time for visiting, relaxing, and socializing. Thus, trainees were never left alone in the observation room. Observation is modeled by the trainer, who sits or stands looking through the glass and commenting on what he sees. He instructs the trainees to look and watch and asks questions and points out aspects of the program that are obvious (*e.g.*, ignoring a crying child or use of reward). We repeat this "sitting and looking" many times in the 2 weeks at the laboratory. Hopefully, the trainee comes to accept this behavior as a valuable source of information and develops considerable skill in observing behavior.

2. *Modeling by the Training Staff.* It is important that the training staff perform instructional and shaping functions in the classroom. They may take the roles of both teacher and aide. This modeling removes the stigma of "They talk a lot, but let's see them try to work with the children." Also, the trainers themselves can model behaviors of special interest. For example, "Today I am going to use tokens. First I'll teach the children what tokens are, and I'll try using them as rewards during the lessons. You watch and then we'll talk about how well this worked." Or, "Today I'm going to be the hard-working aide during story time. Watch me and later we'll talk about what I did and why."

3. *Providing Corrective Feedback.* The trainers attempted to develop a
frankness and willingness to see errors. First, the newness of some of our
college classroom staff was clarified. For example, "Miss Smith is going to do
the lesson today for the first time. Let's see how it goes." Or, "This is Mr.
Jones' first day in the lab, but notice how well he's rewarding good behavior."
Second, our staff modeled discussion of their own errors and the acceptance
of instructions. Third, the training staff always admitted ignorance and would
say something like, "I don't know the answer, but I'll find out today and let
you know." Or, "I don't know what we're going to do with Bobby; let's
discuss it in staff today." Trainers usually dealt directly with inappropriate
verbal behavior. If a trainee said, "The child has a complex" the trainer
might say, "We don't call that a complex any more. Nowadays we just look
on that as behavior." The same was true for "flaw in personality," "born
mean," "bad home," *etc.* If a trainee engaged in incorrect classroom
behavior, the trainer told her it was incorrect, either told her what to do or
demonstrated correct behavior, had the trainee correct immediately, and
praised her. If this corrective procedure could not be established, the
incorrect behavior was ignored. There was never *ex post facto* criticism.
Corrective feedback always ended with praise. Incidently, we have never
observed a child attend to or in other ways respond to this trainer-trainee
interaction in the classroom.

4. *Discussing Behavior.* Discussion in the daily staff meeting was used sparingly
at first to prevent the trainees from emitting a lot of behavior that would
have to be corrected or ignored. At first, the trainers reviewed the morning
and labeled or explained the observed behaviors. Later, simple assignments
became the focus of example, For example, The Good Behavior Assignment:

> "For every child in your group, list his name, and three good
> behaviors he already has. Try to find at least one behavior at which
> the child is especially good. Practice rewarding the child for good
> behavior. Write down one thing you did, tell who it was, what he
> did, and what happened. Bring this to the lab."

REPRESENTATIVE TRAINING TOPICS

The identification and reinforcement of appropriate behavior was a
central training topic. There were several others during the 4-week period
(*e.g.*, handling time out, record keeping, staff meetings). One of these
topics will be discussed to illustrate the programming.

Instructional Skills. The trainers begin shaping instructional skills in
aides, one at a time. Each trainee experienced these sessions repeatedly
with different trainers. The sessions began with the trainee asked to select
a child with whom she likes to work. Those who wanted to choose the
worst-behaving child were discouraged and told they'd work up to that.
As the trainee became more skilled, a second and third child were added
so that the aide could handle a small group.

The trainer begins by modeling the teaching task and then hands the task to the trainee, interspersing comment, direction, and more demonstration as needed. Our main point was to make the task clear and simple so that the trainee could imitate successfully and receive praise. We used concrete stimulus objects and kept the task structured so the aide could follow the steps. Techniques suggested by Resnick and her colleagues at the Pittsburg R & D Center (Resnick & Wang, 1969) were employed. We did not attempt to teach the aides the subtle and elaborate skills that one finds in the repertoires of many teachers.

Usually a stimulus object is presented with the goal of teaching the child a label, a function, one or more attributes, comparisons, or the like. Correct responses are reinforced. Of particular importance was the teaching of rapid prompting in the absence of correct and appropriate responses by the child. Many classroom personnel do not know what to do if a child does not respond to instructions or questioning, will not prompt, and may make the situation aversive. This program taught a rapid prompt, followed by the correct response by the child, followed by immediate reinforcement. This by-passed long waits, nagging, begging and involved aide verbalizations. The aides were taught to provide the same sense of excitement and reward for a prompted response as an unprompted one. This was difficult for many aides to carry out and required practice. Aides also were taught the management of art lessons, story telling, and question asking.

By the last 3 days of the laboratory training, the classroom was being managed by the trainees. The trainers had faded out and acted only in an advisory capacity and as participants in the training staff meetings. The final 2 weeks consisted of helping the trainees adapt their skills to conditions in their own centers.

EVALUATION

This paper is largely descriptive, but it is impossible to discuss fully a training program and the issues and techniques of assessment in a single paper. In an earlier paper presented at the American Educational Research Association (Martin *et al*, 1969), the data from four training assessment procedures used with this program were presented. They are mentioned briefly here.

1. *Video Tapes* of the aides in the centers before and after training appear to show training effects. This is a very subjective judgment at this time, since no

one has yet undertaken the tasks of editing and analysis. We will look particularly at participation behaviors of the aides and the frequency of aides in instructional roles. (We do not see any arm-folding behaviors in the post-training tapes.) There are many technical difficulties to work out before video tapes provide good training assessment data.

2. *Behavioral Measures of Training Effects.* Using a modification of the TIA Scale developed at our center by Rosenthal, Underwood, and Martin (Rosenthal *et al*, 1969), observers recorded the approval and disapproval dispensed by trainees and the targets of these incentives. Targets were either individual children or groups of children, and reinforcers were categorized as verbal, gestural, or physical. The data show an over-all significant pre-post increase in recorded approval and a decrease in disapproval. Trainees also responded more to individual children than to groups after training and showed a significant increase in the use of both verbal and physical positive reinforcement.

3. *A Behavioral Task.* Trainees were asked to have children perform a standard bean drop task before and after training. During the first presentation, coordination among teachers and aides was rather poor, performance by the children variable with many inappropriate behaviors (*e.g.*, throwing beans) evident. Post-training presentation produced better adult coordination, a higher child performance level (with good adult reinforcement) and no inappropriate behaviors. The achievement measures for the control group dropped in the second administration. They rose significantly for three of the five training groups.

4. *Attitude Measure.* The instrument used covered three areas: The use of reward and punishment, why children behave as they do, and the use of written records in day-care centers. Trainees agreed unanimously prior to training on such items as: "When a child is doing something good you should let him know it"; "A friendly smile or saying 'good' can be a big reward for some children"; "Children should be rewarded for the good things they do"; "It helps a child to learn when you tell him what he is doing right"; "You can teach a child to be friendly." The aides talked a very good game, but none of our behavioral measures indicated any corresponding classroom behaviors. In fact, we had to introduce smiling, hugging, and praise lessons during training. The trainees could verbalize the value of reinforcement but could not put it into use. They felt initially that reinforcement should be used optimally and almost exclusively in response to need, crisis, and sorrow behaviors, rather than to appropriate, happy, and capable ones.

This training was centered on the modification of trainee behaviors in this area. It was in this area that maximum change occurred in survey item ratings. One of the principal effects of this training program was to bring verbal behavior regarding reinforcement and use of reinforcement in the preschool into congruence.

References

Martin, Marian, Patterson, J., and Wetzel, R. Techniques of training assessment. Paper presented to the American Educational Research Association, Los Angeles, February 1969.

Resnick, L. B. Design of an early learning curriculum. Working Paper #16, Learning Research and Development Center. Pittsburgh: University of Pittsburgh, 1968.

Rosenthal, T., Underwood, B., and Martin, M. Assessing classroom inventive practices. *Journal of Educational Psychology*, 1969, 60, 370–376.

This article focuses on the practical problems which arise when one is trying to establish a token reinforcement program in a school and attempts to answer the types of questions which are most commonly asked. One such issue frequently raised by school administrators is that of the expense. Although the cost of the back-up reinforcers may seem rather high, as O'Leary points out, the use of rewards provided by the parent or of privileges within the classroom may substantially reduce the cost. Even the cost of consultants' fees is minor compared to that of traditional therapy or counseling for the problem students. The cost in time at the beginning of a token program may be substantial, too; however, O'Leary mentions that the time required to operate such a program is often compensated for by the reduction in time spent on discipline.

Based on an exhaustive review of the material published on token reinforcement programs in the schools, O'Leary presents a detailed list of suggestions for teachers and administrators to follow in designing and implementing such a program. Before putting any new token program into operation, it may be a good idea to see to what extent it needs to be changed to encompass the suggestions so clearly presented here.

Establishing Token Programs in Schools: Issues and Problems

K. Daniel O'Leary *†

Any attempt to establish a token reinforcement program in a public school will prompt a barrage of questions from principals and teachers. Some of these questions are little more than reflections of resistance to change, but others are well-intentioned and often probe at the critical issues inherent in a token program. It is to the latter type of question that my presentation will be directed. Since a large proportion of you may be deciding whether or not to establish a token program in your schools, I will try to answer questions frequently posed by administrators and teachers themselves when proposals for token programs are presented to them.

The questions posed by principals frequently concern cost, necessary consulting time, teacher training, and probability of success. Let us discuss the cost of reinforcers first. Consider a class of 15 disruptive children in an elementary school. If they all received back-up reinforcers worth 25¢ every day for one month (20 school days), then received 40¢ prizes every other day for one month, received 60¢ prizes every third day for one month, and finally received $1.00 prizes every fifth day for one month, the cost of back-up reinforcers would be less than $300.00 for a 4 mo. program.[1] If the aim of the project director is to transfer control from back-up reinforcers such as candy and toys to praise and other social

* Paper presented in a symposium, Tribulations of Token Programs in Hospital and School Settings, at the American Psychological Association, Washington, D.C., August 31, 1969. Printed with permission.

† State University of New York at Stony Brook

[1] One might use less expensive back-up reinforcers *and* quickly increase the behavioral criterion required for various reinforcers in order to maximize the possibility of maintaining prosocial behavior after the tangible back-up reinforcers are withdrawn.

reinforcers, one should make a transition to social reinforcers as soon as possible. From my own experience with children from first to fourth grade, such a transition could certainly be made within 3 to 4 months without loss of appropriate behavior.

In a junior or senior high school the transition to social reinforcers would probably take longer and the cost of back-up reinforcers would undoubtedly be greater. However, McKenzie et al. (1968) have significantly changed the academic behaviors of ten to thirteen year old children in a learning disabilities class by using grades as tokens and allowances as back-up reinforcers. The parents managed the exchange of tokens for back-up reinforcers under supervision of the experimenters, and since the parents were accustomed to giving their children allowances, neither parents nor the school assumed added costs.

Although some school systems or organizations like the PTA, the Rotary, and Kiwanis have provided for the cost of back-up reinforcers for children, most published studies of token reinforcement programs have had government or university research funds cover such costs. The use of token programs has grown dramatically, but because of the dearth of outcome and follow-up research with token programs in classrooms, it seems best to continue to have the cost of back-up reinforcers covered by research funds where possible. In fact, it is my contention that any token program would be best conducted on a research or "pilot study" basis— even if it is not the intention of the psychologist to publish his results. Having an observer or teacher keep some records of the child's progress provides all people concerned with constant feedback and evaluation about the effectiveness of the program—one of the most beneficial effects of the whole behavior modification thrust.

Administrators and teachers will also wish to know about the necessary consultation time. It is of prime importance that a token program get off to a good start and I suggest that any program receive at least one hour of consultation time per day during the first week of the program from someone knowledgeable in the application of learning principles to classroom management. The consultation time could then gradually taper off to two hours per week. Compared to the number of therapist hours spent in more traditional therapeutic centers where children are seen individually outside the classroom setting, such consulting time is probably an extremely effective use of professional services.

It has been demonstrated that teachers can use a token program and effect some change in children's behavior without participating in a course in learning principles or without having extensive consultation (Kuypers, Becker, & O'Leary, 1968). However, care must be taken not to rely solely on the "heavy duty" back-up reinforcers since only partial change will result. Token and back-up reinforcement is but *one* method of producing change in the children's behavior, and it is critical that attention be paid to the types of cues, threats, and frequency and consistency [of] social reinforcement the teacher uses on a minute to minute basis. Particulary important is the effective shaping of the children's behavior in the time between the distribution of ratings or token reinforcers. In addition, adherence to the rules concerning exchange of back-up reinforcers is critical. Several years ago I dealt with a teacher who became so frustrated with the children that she occasionally allowed them to take any back-up reinforcers—regardless of the amount of token reinforcement. As you might guess, the program had little effect on the children's behavior.

The amount of time a teacher has to spend in giving out the token and back-up reinforcers may be a teacher's greatest concern. Even where we used ratings which were placed in children's booklets every 20 or 30 minutes, the amount of time it took the teacher to place a rating in each of 20 children's booklets and give just a few words of feedback to each child was only 3 to 4 minutes. Furthermore, we have found that after a token program has been in effect, the teacher can use less aversive control and spend less time in simple classroom management. Thus, the initial time spent in giving ratings and exchanging back-up reinforcers may be well worth the effort. It also should be emphasized that simply having the teacher send home a statement about the child's good behavior or giving the child a plastic token which the parent knows is indicative of good behavior can be used to effectively change a child's classroom behavior with a minimum amount of effort and time.

Questions about the probability of success of such a program are much more difficult to answer. From a review of token programs now being completed by Ron Drabman and myself, I would estimate roughly that 70 to 80% of the children in a token program in a pre-school or elementary school class for emotionally disturbed, retarded, or educationally disadvantaged children would show significant gains in appropriate social behavior and that these gains would be appreciably greater than those shown by control children in a regular special education class (O'Leary & Becker, 1967; O'Leary, Becker, Evans, & Saudargas, 1969). With regard to academic improvement—and particularly to changes on standardized tests—conclusions are more difficult to make, but studies by Birnbrauer, Bijou, Wolf, & Kidder, 1965; Hewett, Taylor, & Artuso (1969); Miller & Schneider, 1969; Walker, Mattson & Buckley (1968), and Wolf, Giles, & Hall (1968) suggest that academic behaviors per se can indeed be significantly enhanced by a token program. However, it should be emphasized that a token program is no panacea for increasing the academic repertoire of children. A token reinforcement program is a means of effectively reinforcing behavior, but any token program is intrinsically bound to the adequacy of the presentation of academic materials. In a sense, a token program is an emergency device for prompting and maintaining academic and social behavior but it tends to remain a prosthetic device if the presentation of academic material is boring and poorly programmed.

It has been quipped that behaviorally oriented psychologists are wart removers while analytically oriented psychologists are the heart surgeons of psychological problems. This remark may be particularly relevant to men who apply token programs but worry little about academic programs and the factors that will control the child's behavior after he has graduated from the token program. With regard to this issue of generalization, the question posed by an administrator or teacher is simply: What will happen when the token program is withdrawn? The answer to that question is straightforward. If special procedures are not devised specifically to maintain the children's appropriate behavior when the program is withdrawn, the children's appropriate behavior will decline. On the other hand it appears that if some procedures are followed, the appropriate behavior of the children can be maintained after the formal token program is withdrawn. Because the problem of maintaining gains in a token program is presently such a key issue, a number of suggestions for enhancing long term effects of token programs will follow:

1. Provide a good academic program since in many cases you may simply be dealing with deficient academic repertoires—not "behavior disorders."
2. Give the child the expectation that he is capable and that his good behavior is the result of his own efforts. This suggestion has been amply followed in the Engelmann-Becker Follow-Through Program where immediately following a child's correct answer, the teacher very enthusiastically says "Yes, that's a smart answer; you're a smart boy!" In this regard, it should also be emphasized that the teacher should convey an attitude that she feels or expects the token system to work and succeed.
3. Have the children aid in the selection of the behaviors to be reinforced, and, as the token program progresses, have the children involved in the specification of contingencies—a procedure effectively used by Lovitt & Curtiss, (1969). For example, the child rather than the teacher could specify the amount of recess he should earn for a certain number of correct responses.
4. Teach the children to evaluate their own behavior.
5. Try in every way possible to teach the children that academic achievement will pay off. For example, pick something you know a child likes, e.g. clothes, and tell him how he will be able to buy many nice clothes if he studies hard and gets a good job.

6. Involve the parents. Most published studies on token programs in classrooms have not involved parents—probably for reasons of experimental control. However, I have not yet been involved in a token program where it was not thought that its long term effectiveness could have been enhanced by parent involvement. The effective use of parents in school-related token programs has been well illustrated by McKenzie, Clark, Wolf, Kothera, & Bensen (1968) and by Walker, Mattson & Buckley (1968).

7. Withdraw the token and the back-up reinforcers gradually, and utilize other reinforcers existing within the classroom setting such as privileges, recess, and peer competition, e.g. boys vs. girls and group contingencies.

8. Reinforce the children in a variety of situations and reduce the discrimination between reinforced and non-reinforced situations. Most of the evidence at this point strongly suggests that behavior is very situation specific and when it is clear to the children that their behavior pays off in one situation but not in another, they behave accordingly.

9. Prepare teachers in the regular class to praise and shape children's behavior as they are phased back into the regular classes, and bolster the children's academic behavior—if needed—with tutoring by undergraduates or parent volunteers.

10. Last, in order to maintain positive gains from a token program it may help to look at the school system as a token system writ large with a whole chain or sequence of responses and reinforcers from the children to the teacher, to the principal, to the school superintendent, and finally to the school board. When viewed in such a manner, the consultant or research investigator should attempt to facilitate the process of reinforcement not only for the children but for the teachers, the principal, and the school board. Praise to a teacher from a principal, frequent feedback and follow-up results given to the principal from the investigator, and some publicity about the program in local papers sent especially to school board members are but a few examples of the types of interactions which may serve to maintain interest in both the long and short term effects of token programs.[2]

In conclusion, a word of encouragement and a word of caution is in order. First, there definitely are a number of studies which demonstrate that a token program can be successful in changing the behavior of children in a classroom. However, a token program is but one of a variety of techniques which can be used to help a teacher. Because of the problems of withdrawal of token and back-up reinforcers, other procedures should be tried first, such as making rules clear, using praise and shaping, ignoring some disruptive behavior, diminishing the use of threats and verbal reprimands, and focusing on a good academic program.

---

[2] Consulting fees paid to the teachers for their extra time commitment, university course credit, daily feedback concerning the behavior of the teacher and the children, frequent discussion with the teacher by the principal investigator, and modeling and rehearsal of appropriate teacher behavior have been especially effective for us in gaining control of teacher's behavior.

Where such procedures fail and where there is a great deal of peer reinforcement for disruptive behavior (not just one or two disruptive children in a class), a token program may well be a very useful procedure for you.

References

Birnbrauer, J. S., Bijou, S. W., Wolf, M. M., & Kidder, J. D. Programmed instruction in the classroom. In L. Ullmann & L. Krasner (Eds.) *Case Studies in Behavior Modification.* New York: Holt, Rinehart, and Winston, 1965, p. 358-363.

Hewett, F. M., Taylor, F. D., & Artuso, A. A. Santa Monica Project. Evaluation of an engineered classroom design with emotionally disturbed children. Journal-Council for Exceptional Children, 1969, 35, No. 7, 523-529.

Kuypers, D. S., Becker, W. C., & O'Leary, K. D. How to make a token system fail. *Exceptional Children,* 1968, 35, 101-109.

Lovitt, T. C., & Curtiss, Karen A. Academic response rate as a function of teacher and self-imposed contingencies. *Journal of Applied Behavior Analysis,* 1969, 3, 49-54.

McKenzie, H. S., Clark, Marilyn, Wolf, M. M., Kothera, R., & Benson, C. Behavior modification of children with learning disabilities using grades as tokens and allowances as back-up reinforcers. *Exceptional Children,* 1968, 34, 745-752.

Miller, L. K. & Schneider, R. The use of a token system in Project Head Start. Unpublished Manuscript, Dept. of Sociology, University of Kansas, Lawrence, Kansas, 1969.

O'Leary, K. D. & Becker, W. C. Behavior modification of an adjustment class: a token reinforcement program. *Exceptional Children,* 1967, 33, 637-642.

O'Leary, K. D., Becker, W. C., Evans, M. B., & Saudargas, R. A. A token reinforcement program in a public school: a replication and systematic analysis. *Journal of Applied Behavior Analysis,* 1969, 2, 3-13.

Walker, H. M., Mattson, R. H., & Buckley, N. K. Special class as a treatment alternative for deviant behavior in children. Monograph Dept. of Special Education, University of Oregon, 1969.

Wolf, M. M., Giles, D. K., & Hall, V. R. Experiments with token reinforcement in a remedial classroom. *Behaviour Research and Therapy,* 1968, 6, 51-69.

Homme's article is not the only one in this book which has utilized high probability behaviors or reinforcing events as rewards, but it is the only one which has focused on the theoretical aspects of doing so and which has attempted to specify the conditions necessary for a high probability behavior to serve as a reinforcer. He states that for a reinforcing event to be effective it must remove the organism from the situation and never be present when an undesirable response occurs, although it is fine for the desired response to occur in the presence of two or more stimuli.

Some of the problems which can occur when attempting to utilize the Premack principle, even by experts trained in the use of these techniques, are illustrated in this article. Although he favors the use of self-control and self-management of contingencies, Homme points out that a group of experts in behavior technology were unable to successfully utilize these techniques to develop a program for themselves which would be successful in the long run for increasing the frequency of exercises. Attempts to train people to use these principles in controlling their eating and smoking behaviors have generally also been less than totally effective. It may be the case that some kind of external monitoring of a self-control program is necessary for it to be successful.

Many of the specific suggestions made by Homme are directly applicable to the classroom situation, such as his suggestion that a classroom have two separate areas, one for task-relevant behaviors and one for reinforcing events, or his suggestion that exceptions should never be permitted to occur. He also points out that the great fluctuation from hour to hour in a person's behavior probabilities need not be a problem but rather an advantage to a teacher, as it indicates that there will almost always be some behavior which can feasibly be used as a reinforcer. Alertness on the part of the teacher and a conscious effort to manage the contingencies rather than simply observe them are the only extra resources or skills that a teacher need possess to carry out a behavior modification program utilizing his suggestions.

Contiguity Theory and Contingency Management

Lloyd E. Homme*†

ABSTRACT

It is proposed that contiguity theory provides a base for specifying when Premack's differential probability hypothesis (Premack, 1965) will and will not identify effective reinforcers. Four implications of contiguity theory for contingency management are discussed and illustrated by showing how the contiguity implication has been applied to the contingency management of children and to the engineering of self-management of contingencies. Relationships between contiguity theory, the Premack principle, and reinforcement principles are discussed. It is concluded that propositions derived from these three sources are in agreement and can be tested in non-laboratory situations, particularly in the teaching of self-management.

* Lloyd E. Homme, "Contiguity Theory and Contingency Management," *The Psychological Record* 16(1966): 233–241. Reprinted with permission.
† Westinghouse Electric Behavioral Research Laboratory, Albuquerque, New Mexico.

"Theories exist in science because they are useful. There is no pretense that they are in any other sense 'correct' " (Logan & Wagner, 1965, p. 104).[1]

THE PREMACK PRINCIPLE

The differential probability hypothesis, a generalization which has also been called the Premack principle (Homme, C.deBaca, Devine, Steinhorst, & Rickert, 1963), has been stated in elegant simplicity: "For any pair of responses, the more probable one will reinforce the less probable one" (Premack, 1965, p. 132). In order to strengthen a lower probability response, then, one simply arranges that a higher probability response be made contingent on the execution of the lower probability one. That the Premack principle has proved to be a most useful generalization in the control of behavior can scarcely be doubted. It has proved effective in the control of nursery school children. (Homme, et al, 1963), preschool, non-English speaking Indian children (Homme, 1965a), psychotics (Homme & C.deBaca, 1964), the mentally retarded (Homme, 1964), high-school dropouts (Homme, 1965a), and normal, middleclass children (Berger, 1965; Homme & Tosti 1965).

Yet these instances of effectiveness should not obscure the fact that psychologists' control of behavior still, to say the least, leaves something to be desired. This shows up most clearly in the area of self-management or, more precisely, the teaching of self-management. We cannot yet teach another human being how to condition himself with anything like the precision with which a teenager can be taught, using a standard laboratory manual (Homme & Klaus, 1962), to condition a white rat. Slack (1965) refers to an advanced stage in the development of a science which produces a workable technology as "coffee, milk science" (CMS), the stage at which teenagers who know nothing about the laws of electricity can, knowing only about the technology of operating switches, make excellent coffee and cool milk perfectly. Once this stage *has* been reached in psychology, the signals ought to be clear enough. Mental illness, for example, ought to become as oldfashioned as whooping cough.

Scientific statements are made to be taken literally. The Premack principle implies that nature does not care who arranges the

---

[1] This point is made early so that psychologists of a different persuasion—those looking for experiments which will provide crucial tests of theoretical propositions to serve as thesis topics for next fall—may be spared the time to read this article; they are thus free to go back to worrying about other matters.

contingencies between lower and higher probability behaviors. Presumably this includes the organism whose behavior is to be controlled. Note, too, that, according to the principle, *any* behavior can reinforce *any* lower probability behavior. Experimentation in the teaching of self-management (Homme, 1965b) emphasizes that the Premack principle, useful as it may be, is incomplete as it stands. The conditions which must be met in order for contingency management to be effective have not been completely specified. Breathing, for example, is without question a high probability behavior. Yet, in self-management, to use breathing as a high probability behavior in order to strengthen some lower probability behavior is not, in the long run, going to work. But there is nothing in the Premack principle which specifies that this is so. In view of considerations such as these, it is important that the eminently practical Premack principle be re-examined in the light of contiguity principles to see if it can thereby become still more practical and useful.

GUTHRIE'S CONTIGUITY THEORY

Guthrie himself summarizes his own position in the following statement: "The best information we can gain concerning how a man will behave in a given set of circumstances comes from the record of what he last did in these circumstances" (1952, p. 16). In other words, the stimuli which are present and, presumably, attended to (Wyckoff. 1952) when a response gets made are going to exercise control over that response. Contiguity theory has some important implications for contingency management, both of self and others.

Of particular interest to the present discussion are the stimuli which are present just prior to the emission of a high probability behavior (HPB). These stimuli are important enough to deserve a special name. For the purposes of this discussion, they are called *preparatory stimuli*. They are undefined except for the specification that they are present just prior to a HPB. For example, when a child's HPB is running-to-the-playground, the stimuli just prior to this event are preparatory stimuli. Presumably these would include the feel, sight, and, just possibly, the smell, of his uniform for this event. Prominent among the preparatory stimuli is the subset generated by the S's own behavior—his verbal and imaginative behavior—his coverants. Similarly, when getting-a-cup-of-coffee is a HPB for an adult, the preparatory stimuli would include the sight of an empty coffee cup and coverants concerning how the coffee will taste, and so on.

IMPLICATIONS OF CONTIGUITY THEORY FOR CONTINGENCY MANAGEMENT

It is the plan of this paper to examine four implications of a contiguity analysis of contingency management. For each, the general principle will be discussed and illustrated by specifying how the contiguity implication has been applied to the contingency management of children and how it applies to the self-management of contingencies.

The HPB Should Remove the Organism from the Situation

According to Guthrian theory, the basic function of a reinforcer is to remove the S from the stimulus situation in which he has just made a response (R), so that a competing response (R) cannot be made and thereby attached to the stimulus situation. It is clear that the execution of HPB ordinarily serves this function beautifully. Since the HPB and the low probability behavior (LPB) are different behaviors, they generate different stimuli. Therefore, the HPB can be said to take the organism out of the stimulus situation in which the LPB is made. It follows, then, that the more immediate and complete the stimulus change brought about by the HPB, the more likely R is to be controlled by the stimulus situation. Stated another way, a HPB which only partly removes the S from the stimulus situation will not be as effective as a HPB which more completely removes the S from the situation. Perhaps a word of clarification is in order here.

The phrase, "removes the S from the situation," is not intended to have a solely geographical referent. A "change in the stimulus situation" may, indeed, refer to a geographical change, but it need not. A morsel of food in a hungry dog's mouth causes a change in the stimulus situation, whether or not the dog must leave the room to accomplish this. Nevertheless, in managing contingencies of humans, one may as well play it safe in this regard and let the reinforcing events occur in an area separated from the task area. For example, in managing the contingencies of preschool, non-English speaking Indian children (Homme, 1965a), the completion of a short task ratio resulted in a light signal to run to the reinforcing event (RE) area. Once in the RE area, the S was presented with a RE menu (Addison & Homme, 1966) from which he selected the event most reinforcing at the moment. He then set an automatic timer and engaged in the RE. A bell on the timer was the stimulus which controlled his running back to the task area. (The reason he ran back, rather than dawdled, was that he was intermittently reinforced, "given a free one," simply for getting back quickly.)

Self-management, particularly in the case of adults, clearly illustrates that "getting out of the situation" need not be interpreted in its geographical sense. For example, an S may be instructed to make contacts with himself, such as this: "As soon as I successfully work one more physics problem, I will permit myself to read my novel for ten minutes." [2] In situations like this, the S may even remain at the same desk, but the stimulus situation generated by the high probability activity of novel reading causes a considerable change in the stimulus situation. However, it is often a simple matter to arrange for two desks or work spaces to correspond to the task and RE areas as described below.

A Unique Stimulus Situation Should be Selected to Control the Response

The word *unique*, in this context, needs some explanation. It is intended only to emphasize that a given stimulus situation cannot control both a response (R) and a competing response (R). This means that a stimulus situation must be selected which is not likely to be present when R is likely to occur.

In the contingency management of children, this consideration underlies the use of two separate areas for the task and reinforcement areas. Only task-related behaviors get conditioned to the task area, and only play to the RE area. Similar considerations govern practical matters such as rules concerning the behavior of visitors or observers of projects, such as the child-shaping project described. For example, visitors are not allowed in the task area at all because they tend to evoke Rs. At the very least, visitors should not be allowed to talk in the LPB (task) area. The RE area is another matter. Here the visitor may be encouraged to do anything which may contribute to a jolly (reinforcing) atmosphere including, if he wishes, walking on his hands while singing "The Stars and Stripes Forever." In the RE area, behaviors incompatible with reinforcing behaviors must also be prohibited. For example, weeping and moaning in the RE area are out.

In one of the examples given above, it was asserted that breathing, although a HPB, was impractical to use as a reinforcing response for lower probability behaviors. This is so because, since it goes on continually,

---

[2] D. T. Tosti (personal communication, 1966) points out that this example also illustrates the importance which coveranting events-to-come can have, not only in establishing incentive conditions, but in comprising a large, quite possibly major, portion of the set of preparatory stimuli for a behavior.

every conceivable behavior gets made in the presence of its preparatory stimuli. Therefore, any momentary strengthening effect it may have on the behavior it follows is quickly dissipated.

From a practical standpoint, it is important in teaching self-management to caution the S not to demand LPB in a situation in which stimulus objects, such as other humans, will have a strong tendency to evoke Řs. The most frequent remark self-management Ss make is, "I meant to do it, but I forgot." If S is questioned, it will turn out that some stimulus object, usually another human's talking, distracted him. This suggests the care which must be taken, in writing behavioral prescriptions, to specify the stimulus conditions under which LPBs are to get executed as well as the HPBs which are to follow.

More Than One Stimulus Can Control the Same Response

Because, in contiguity theory, only one of two incompatible responses can be attached to the same stimulus, it is sometimes overlooked that there is no restriction on the number of different stimuli which can come to control the same response. In other words, the preparatory stimuli for several momentarily HPBs can control or set off the same response. For example the preparatory stimuli for teethbrushing can set off some response, R_1, a class of coverants (Homme, 1965b), let us say; the preparatory stimuli for getting-shoes-out-of-the-closet may set off the same response, R_1; preparatory stimuli for sitting-down-to-breakfast may control the same response, R_1; the preparatory stimuli for getting-into-the-car may control the same response, R_1; and so on.

In the contingency management of children, one may wish to strengthen some class of behaviors currently at low strength, such as spelling. In this case, the contingency manager will call for this class of behaviors in the presence of preparatory stimuli for a large variety of HPBs. For example, "Spell *winner;* then we'll play a game of chess." And "Spell *bottle;* then you may run and get some pop." "Spell *tackle;* then you may go out and play football," and so on.

Not completely understood, but an interesting possibility, is that of conditioning responses ordinarily called emotional by the same technique. That is, one would call for the quasi-emotional response, or a response with emotional components, in the presence of preparatory stimuli for HPBs.[3]

---

[3] P. C.deBaca (personal communication, 1965) reports that, in a school for emotionally disturbed children, one child was particularly despondent and lethargic one day. C.deBaca, the contingency manager, demanded the shout, "I feel great!" to the preparatory stimuli for running-to-the-playground. Then he demanded the same response, "I feel great!," in

The Weakening Of S—R Connection.

Contiguity theory says that all that is required in order to displace R from the control of some stimulus population is that Ř occur in its presence. The fact that a habit, that is, an S—R connection, is not always broken in a single trial should not obscure the fact that as soon as Ř *does* get made in the presence of S, weakening occurs. (A theoretical account of how the appearance of gradual weakening of a response may be reconciled with all-or-none postulates is given in Estes [1959], Homme [1956], and elsewhere.)

Contiguity statements about how S—R connections get broken, of course, are highly reminiscent of James' famous dictum: "Never suffer an exception to occur . . ." (1912, p. 68). In present terms, this is translatable to, "Never let Ř occur in the presence of a stimulus meant to control R."

In managing children's contingencies, this dictum is more difficult to abide by than it may appear. This is because children typically have learned to remove themselves from the learning situation by comments like, "I'm tired," "My stomach hurts," "Let's go emit some HPB now," and so on. Remarks such as these are strong signals for the knowing contingency manager. He does not permit the S to "get out of the box" in this way; he does not say, "All right, we'll stop now and get back to it later"; he does not say, "Come on, now, do a few more for me"; he does not say, "Do not con me, you little monster." He does not say anything. This is no time for debate; it is time for extinction of behaviors which compete with the LPBs.

In self-management, the allowing-an-exception-to-occur is particularly likely unless special precautions are taken. One group of Ss[4] decided to use leaving their desk area as a HPB which was made contingent upon physical exercises. They required themselves to do at least one exercise before they left their desk area. Similarly, they required themselves to do at least one exercise (such as an isometric or deep knee bend) before they resumed their seats at their desks. At a given instance in time both of these behaviors, leaving the desk area and sitting down again, are HPBs; therefore, both ought to strengthen the behaviors upon which they are contingent. The first day the contingency seemed to be having an effect. Everyone reported exercise frequencies of well over a hundred. On the

---

the presence of the preparatory stimuli for going-down-a-playground slide (letting go the sides). Other children witnessed this performance; before long every child who got to the top of the slide was screaming at the top of his lungs, "I feel great!" The extent of the emotional component of this response is unknown, but it is reported that this response successfully competed with the "I don't feel so good" response-class for the rest of the day.

[4] Thanks are due to the members of the Westinghouse Research Behavioral Technology Department who participated in these experiments.

second day, the frequencies dropped sharply. By the third day, the frequencies declined still further and, by the fourth day, frequencies were virtually zero. It will be noted that the stimulus situations were well geared for competing responses to intrude. When a person left his desk, it could well be because some other human had called him, or because he was talking to the other human. Similarly, on returning to his desk, he might see work to be done and "forget" the exercise. To mitigate these tendencies for R to occur, the stimulus situation for the exercises was moved. This time it was designated as the washroom. It was agreed that before anyone left the washroom, that is, opened the door (to change the stimulus situation), he was to do at least one exercise. This kind of stimulus control was much more successful, but even here the exercise response tended to fall off. Reasons given were: "I was so busy, I forgot." "I was thinking about something else, and forgot." And so on.

There are problems remaining to be solved in the behavioral engineering of self-management.

RELATIONSHIPS BETWEEN CONTIGUITY THEORY, THE PREMACK PRINCIPLE, AND REINFORCEMENT PRINCIPLES

Sometimes people speak as though there are two opposing schools of thought in psychology, contiguity theory as opposed to "reinforcement theory," e.g., Hilgard (1956). As the quotation marks indicate, it is the standpoint of this paper that this view is in error. Principles of reinforcement are generalizations from data and thus are difficult to argue with. For example, there is very little which is theoretical about the behavioral effects of various reinforcement schedules (Ferster & Skinner, 1957).

The differential probability hypothesis, on the other hand, is somewhat more theoretical in that the differential probability condition is asserted to be not only sufficient but necessary for reinforcement to occur. Yet for purposes of developing a contingency management system, one need only demand to know the circumstances under which the differential probability condition is sufficient.

It is to be hoped that the examples cited illustrate that a contingency manager's orientation vis-á-vis the triple intersection of reinforcement principles, the Premack principle, and contiguity theory is quite simple. He proceeds just as any other operant conditioner applying, as best he can, the principles of behavior control carefully worked out over the last twenty-five to thirty years in operant conditioners' laboratories (Skinner, 1938; 1953).

But, before he can do this—apply the principles of reinforcement—he has to have a reinforcer he can control. This is where Premack comes in. The operant conditioner of animals typically has one reinforcer, e.g. food, the reaction to which remains stable not only within experimental periods but from one day to the next. For the contingency manager of nondeprived humans whose behavior probabilities fluctuate wildly from one moment to the next, things are not so simple. One moment getting-a-drink-of-water may be a HPB; the next moment playing-with-the-little-blue-car may be the momentary HPB; the next, talking-about-the-little-blue-car may be the HPB. And so it goes, with one behavior replacing another as the HPB throughout the experimental session. This tremendous fluctuation of behavior probabilities turns out to be an advantage if one takes the Premack principle seriously. Any responses to be strengthened can be demanded as a prerequisite for any or all of the various HPBs. Thus, the number of reinforcers available to the contingency manager is as large as the number of HPBs he can detect from moment to moment.

As indicated above, contiguity theory appears to be consistent, as good theory should be, with both the body of data based on conventional reinforcement principles as well as that based on the differential probability hypothesis. However, as the discussion also has attempted to show, contiguity theory makes possible further refinement in the application of these principles.

It will also be noted that this paper has tried to take scholars like Kantor seriously when he says, "Applied sciences are legitimate members of the scientific family . . . they . . . help to test and verify scientific propositions . . ." (Kantor, 1959, p. 171). To help test the propositions of reinforcement principles, the Premack principle and contiguity theory, they have been tried out in real life situations, including the most difficult test—the teaching of self-management.

SUMMARY AND CONCLUSIONS

Although Premack's differential probability hypothesis has proved to be an extremely useful formulation, experience with the teaching of self-management and the contingency management of children has shown that certain conditions must be met in order for a response to be strengthened when followed by a HPB. These conditions are specified by

Guthrie's contiguity theory (1952). Implications of the contiguity assumption are:

1. The reinforcing response should be of the sort that removes S from the situation which is to control the response.
2. The stimulus situation which is to control the response should be uniquely present when R occurs (not present when Ř occurs).
3. The same response can be attached to more than one stimulus.
4. As soon as Ř gets made in the presence of S, weakening of the S—R connection occurs.

In exploring the relationships between contiguity theory, the Premack principle, and reinforcement principles, we can conclude that the three classes of propositions are not in conflict, and that propositions derived from these three sources can be tested in nonlaboratory situations, particularly in the teaching of self-management.

References

Addison, R. M., and Homme, L. E. 1966. The reinforcing event (RE) menu. *NSPI J.*, V. 1, 8–9.

Berger, R. J. 1965. A test of the Premack hypothesis with responses to audio and visual stimuli. Unpublished doctoral dissertation, Arizona State University.

Estes, W. K. 1959. The statistical approach to learning theory. In S. Koch (Ed.) *Psychology, a study of a science.* Vol. 2, New York: McGraw-Hill. Pp. 380–491.

Ferster, C. B., and Skinner, B. F. 1957. *Schedules of reinforcement.* New York: Appleton-Century-Crofts.

Guthrie, E. R. 1952. *The psychology of learning.* New York: Harper.

Hilgard, E. R. 1956. *Theories of learning.* (2nd ed.) New York: Appleton-Century-Crofts.

Homme, L. E. 1956. Spontaneous recovery and statistical learning theory. *J. exp. Psychol.*, 51, 205–212.

Homme, L. E. 1964. Technical progress report no. 1, a demonstration of the use of self-instructional and other teaching techniques for remedial instruction of low-achieving adolescents in reading and mathematics. Submitted to U.S. Office of Educ., October.

Homme, L. E. 1965a. Final report, a system for teaching English literacy to preschool Indian children. Submitted to U.S. Department of Interior, Contract No. 14–20–065001506, October.

Homme, L. E. 1965b. Control of coverants, the operants of the mind. *The Psychol. Rec.*, 15, 501–511.

Homme, L. E., and C.deBaca, P. 1965. Contingency management on the psychiatric ward. Unpublished paper. January.

Homme, L. E., C.deBaca, P., Devine, J. V.,Steinhorst, R., and Rickert, E. J.1963. Use of the Premack principle in controlling the behavior of nursery school children. *J. exp. Anal. Behav.*, 6, 544.

Homme, L. E., and Klaus, D. J. 1962. *Laboratory studies in the analysis of behavior.* Albuquerque: TMI.

Homme, L. E., and Tosti, D. T. 1965. Some considerations of contingency management and motivation. *NSPI J.*, IV, 7, 14–16.

James, W. 1912. *Talks to teachers on psychology: and to students on some of life's ideals.* New York: Henry Holt.

Kantor, J. R. 1959. *Interbehavioral psychology.* Bloomington: Principia Press.

Logan, F. A., and Wagner, A. R. 1965. *Reward and punishment.* Boston: Allyn & Bacon.

Premack, D. 1965. Reinforcement theory. In D. Levine (Ed.), *Nebraska symposium on motivation* 1965. Lincoln: U. of Nebraska Press.

Skinner, B. F. 1938. *The behavior of organisms.* New York: Appleton-Century-Crofts.

Skinner, B. F. 1953. *Science and human behavior.* New York: Macmillan.

Slack, C. W. 1965. The therapy machine and other stories. Unpublished manuscript, January.

Wyckoff, L. B. 1952. The role of observing responses in discrimination learning. Part 1. *Psychol. Rev.*, 59, 431–442.

Although the major focus of this book is on the use of behavior modification by a classroom teacher, the article by Woody discusses some of the implications of behavior therapy for the school psychologist and counselor. In his paper Woody summarizes and illustrates some of the major techniques used by behavior therapists which might be relevant to a school psychologist. Among those procedures which have not been emphasized in the rest of this book are classical conditioning of sphincter control, reciprocal inhibition and emotive imagery, play therapy sessions involving the parents, isolation, aversive conditioning with electric shock, and verbal conditioning of responses in a counseling situation. Although a classroom teacher would probably not utilize these techniques without consultation, he might do so with assistance from the school psychologist or other consultants. He might also want to recommend to parents that they seek expert advice if their child has a problem which might be successfully treated by behavior therapy.

As Woody points out, the efficacy of psychotherapy, particularly insight therapy, has not yet been established. Part of the reason for the lack of adequate data is the nature of the "cure" expected. If no clearcut criteria for improvement are established then it is almost impossible to have an unequivocal assessment of whether or not improvement has occurred. Because behavior therapists specify precisely those changes they expect to occur, collecting valid data is possible. The evidence is overwhelmingly supportive of the hypothesis that these techniques can change behavior, and school psychologists and teachers can expect to see observable improvement in their students if these procedures are appropriately utilized. Woody discusses some ways of applying behavior modification techniques and the implications of such involvement for the training of school psychologists.

Behavior Therapy and School Psychology

Robert H. Woody*†

ABSTRACT

The question of whether counseling
and psychotherapy should be
emphasized in school psychology
remains unresolved. There seems to
be agreement that the school
psychologist does have the
responsibility for helping students
with behavior problems, but
controversy develops over the role
the school psychologist should play
in working with these students. That
is, should it be as a consultant or a
therapist? Perhaps some of these
concerns will find resolution in a

* Robert H. Woody, "Behavior Therapy and School Psychology," *Journal of School Psychology* 4(1966): 1-14. Reprinted with permission.
† The author, Robert H. Woody, is an Assistant Professor in the School of Psychology at the State University of New York at Buffalo. He holds an EdS degree in school psychology from Western Michigan University, and MA and PhD degrees in counseling from Michigan State University. Prior to entering university teaching, he served as a school psychologist.

relatively new approach to behavior modification: behavior therapy. As will be exemplified, behavior therapy places the psychologist in a much different role than is typical for more established forms of psychotherapy. This paper will present a review of selected studies that specifically relate behavior therapy to problems and situations that might be encountered by school psychologists and then a discussion of the efficacy of this approach, the techniques that seem most appropriate for school psychology, and factors that may influence the introduction of behavior therapy into school psychology.

BEHAVIOR THERAPY

London (1964) dichotomizes the major systems of psychotherapy into *Action* and *Insight* categories; the behavior therapies, because of their therapeutic rationale and objectives, are placed in the *Action* group. Wolpe (1964), in defining the conditioning or behavior therapies (the terms are used synonomously herein), states:

> These methods stem from the conception that neuroses are persistent unadaptive habits that have been conditioned (that is, learned). If this conception is correct, the fundamental overcoming of neurosis *can* consist of nothing but deconditioning—or undoing the relevant habit patterns. (p. 9) Learning theory predicts that *unless* there are intervening events that directly recondition neurotic reactions, recovery from neurosis that is radical . . . will be lasting . . . (p. 13)

Taking a similar position, Eysenck (1965a), when contrasting psychoanalysis with behavior therapy, indicates that in learning theory, the basis of behavior therapy, the therapists are:

> . . . Dealing with unadaptive behavior conditioned to certain classes of stimuli; no reference is made to any underlying disorders or complexes

in the psyche . . . behavior therapy concentrates on actual *behavior* as most likely to lead to the extinction of the unadaptive conditioned responses. (p. 402)

Regarding the causes of the behavior disorders, Eysenck (1965a) states:

> Learning theory does not postulate any such "unconscious causes," but regards neurotic symptoms as simple learned habits; there is no neurosis underlying the symptom, but merely the symptom itself. *Get rid of the symptom and you have eliminated the neurosis.* (p. 401)

At this point, it is obvious that many psychologists who endorse systems of psychotherapy that involve insight will feel horrified; it is hoped, however, that these persons will not form a final judgment only on the basis of the rationale, a partial one at that, but will also consider the research behind this approach and its efficacy (both points will subsequently receive consideration). For those who are interested, London (1964) and Eysenck (1965a) present well-written analyses and comparisons of the insight and action approaches.

Within this definition of behavior therapy, three major types of treatment are usually found. First, treatment by positive reinforcement contingencies involves such techniques as relaxation training, reciprocal inhibition, and essay commitment. Second, treatment by negative reinforcement contingencies, usually termed aversive conditioning, uses emetic drugs, electric shock, fatigue, noise, and other punishments. Third, treatment by both negative and positive reinforcement contingencies involves encouragement of desirable habits and punishment of undesirable ones. (Schmidt, Castell, and Brown, 1965)

While the selected studies reviewed in this paper might be placed in these three categories, the flexibility or the scope of potential techniques results in many of the studies incorporating aspects that make categorization difficult. This review of studies especially relevant to school psychology will essentially follow a format that exemplifies the conditioning procedure, e.g., development of a stimulus-response relationship, positive reinforcement with emphasis on reciprocal inhibition and rewards, e.g., objects and acceptance from various types of persons, positive reinforcement combined with punishment through withdrawal of the positive reinforcement, aversive conditioning, and verbal conditioning. This latter, although it is a form of positive reinforcement, is important enough to school psychology to merit separate treatment, and emphasis will be placed on its use in reinforcement counseling and psychotherapy.

THE STIMULUS-RESPONSE BOND

Before considering more complex forms of behavior therapy, a very basic type of stimulus-response conditioning might be used to clarify the process. For example, nocturnal enuresis, a relatively common childhood problem, has been successfully treated by conditioning techniques. A special detector is placed under the child and the discharge of urine triggers off a buzzer alarm; the child develops an association between the buzzer and the wetting. The child, thus, becomes conditioned to awake when the sensation of bladder fullness and sphincter contractions occur (Lovibond, 1964). Young and Turner (1965) also found that this approach was effective and that certain stimulant drugs could facilitate the process. In other words, many behavior problems, such as nocturnal enuresis, may be modified by use of the classical and instrumental principles of conditioning.

POSITIVE REINFORCEMENT

RECIPROCAL INHIBITION

Wolpe's (1964) therapeutic use of anxiety-inhibiting responses—assertive, relaxation, and sexual responses—are based on the principle of reciprocal inhibition, described as follows:

> . . . If a response inhibitory of anxiety can be made to occur in the presence of anxiety-evoking stimuli it will weaken the bond between these stimuli and the anxiety. (p. 10)

The term reciprocal inhibition is derived from the physiological phenomenon in which a set of nervous or muscular activities are functioning in an antagonistic manner to another set and this results in change since both cannot occur simultaneously (London, 1964). A use of reciprocal inhibition might be to induce relaxation to counteract tenseness and anxiety, solicit visual images of pleasant situations to contradict unpleasant similar situations, or use a hierarchy of fears to work up to resolution of anxiety-provoking situations by means of progressively learning to control these situations. This approach is frequently and successfully used with phobics.

Results with this approach seem to be excellent; but most research and clinical applications have focused on adults, and only a few studies are directly related to school psychology. White (1957) was able to cure a 5½-year old girl of refusal to eat and what were seemingly rheumatic pains by use of the principle of stimulus substitution and the generalization continuum. Hallsten (1965), using desensitization, restored normal eating habits via behavioral treatment for a 12-year old girl who possessed a pathological food avoidance.

Lazarus and Abramovitz (1962) present a reciprocal inhibition technique, titled "emotive imagery," that seems applicable to school psychology. Essentially, the procedure is to establish the characteristics (range, intensity, and circumstances) of the child's fears, draw up a graduated hierarchy, have the child imagine selected related events, and therapeutically involve the anxiety-provoking and anxiety-inhibiting emotions into the imagery. The assumption is that these induced emotions have autonomic effects that are incompatible with anxiety. Using the subjectively evaluated results of nine case studies with phobic children (ages 7 to 14 years), the authors assert that seven of the children "recovered" in only 3.3 sessions, and follow-ups for up to one year did not reveal a relapse or a symptom substitution. This brevity of treatment supports claims made by Wolpe (1964).

REINFORCEMENT: REWARDS

Behavior modification has been accomplished by giving rewards to reinforce more appropriate or acceptable behavior. Two specific types of rewards seem to be most commonly used: objects and recognition.

Regarding the use of objects as rewards, Miller (1964) used food reinforcement in conjunction with flash cards in an effort to influence and control the study behavior of a normal 17-year old high school girl. Although she was given enough food at breakfast to guarantee strength enough to attend school, she had to earn all other food by means of her study behavior. The girl had a D average for the semester prior to the experiment, a B- average during the semester of the experiment, and a regression to the D average during the two semesters following the semester of experimentation. In a study by Patterson, Jones, Whittier, and Wright (1965), a 10-year old hyperactive brain-injured boy was conditioned to more acceptable classroom behavior. An auditory stimulus was paired with rewards of candy and pennies, and the boy was fitted with an earphone that could be activated by a radio device during his classroom activities. When his poor behavior, e.g., movements in his chair, were controlled by the boy, e.g., sitting still in his chair, the radio device would transmit the auditory stimulus indicating that the boy had earned a reward for his behavior. Although this might best be considered an exploratory study, the experimenters feel that the data offers "strong support for the efficacy of behavior modification techniques for the control of the hyperactive child" (p. 223). Since there have been a number of studies on the learning and conditionability of persons who are mentally retarded (Ellis, 1963), it will suffice to say that conditioning techniques are effective with the mentally retarded, but the intellectual deficit introduces numerous unique factors to the conditioning process. Regardless, as pertinent to this paper, Birnbrauer, Wolf, Kidder, and Tague (1965), in an experimental classroom for retarded children studied the effects of knowledge of results, verbal approval, and tokens as rewards, with special emphasis on the necessity of keeping the token rewards as part of the reinforcement program. During the period when no tokens were given, increased errors in classroom work were noted for 67% of the students, and a few revealed an increase in disruptive behavior. It seems, although more specialized research is necessary, that behavior therapy is of potential value for the mentally retarded and may assume a new importance in the area of retardation since previous efforts of counseling and psychotherapy have been of questionable success (Stacey and DeMartino, 1957).

Reinforcement by rewarding certain behaviors by recognition has been assessed by several studies. Zimmerman and Zimmerman (1962) report the change of unproductive classroom behavior for two emotionally disturbed boys by structuring the situations in a manner that the poor behavior had no social consequence. For example, the teacher totally ignored the subject's attempt to get a reaction from the teacher for a misspelled word; no response was made by the teacher until a correct spelling or, to be more general, an acceptable behavioral response was performed, and then the teacher gave recognition in the form of a commendation, that is reinforcement of the acceptable response, and allowed for progress to the next step in the lesson. It was found that the number of inappropriate or unreinforced responses decreased with each successive spelling word. Brown and Elliot (1965) studied the control of aggressive responses of 27 nursery school boys (age 3 and 4 years). To condition the children, the teacher systematically ignored aggressive responses and attended only to responses that were incompatible with aggression. After a relatively brief conditioning period, analysis revealed that physical, verbal, and overall aggressive responses were significantly modified. Davison (1964) has presented evidence that even non-professionals can be trained in the conditioning approach to modifying the behavior of emotionally disturbed children.

Patterson (1965) provides what might be considered a combination of recognition, reward, and play therapy. Patterson posits that school phobia develops because the separation of the child from the parents serves as an eliciting stimulus, which leads to an anxiety reaction, which evolves to escape or avoidance behaviors, which are manifested in a phobia for school. Doll play, with the eliciting stimulus presented in a graduated series to initially accommodate a low intensity escape and anxiety reaction, similar to the aforementioned hierarchy used by Wolpe, was used to condition the child out of his phobia for school; a total of twenty-three 20-minute conditioning sessions, 20 bags of chocolates, and structured 10-minute interviews with the parents resulted in significant behavioral changes.

If a teacher can be a reinforcing agent, it would seem logical that parents, with affective factors strengthening their significance, could be used to benefit the behavior of their children, and this has been supported by several studies. Successful use of parents as positive reinforcers for behavior problem children has been reported by Bijou (1965), Russo (1964), Straughan (1964), and Wahler, Winkel, Peterson, and Morrison (1965). Basically, the idea is to have the parent carry out most of the conditioning used in the treatment, usually involving verbal and recognition reinforcement, thereby placing the parents and child in a relationship that can be supervised by the therapist and that can be directly and consistently continued by both the parent and child when they leave the treatment setting and return home. This should alleviate the problem stated by many parents of behavioral problem children who have received counseling that the parents are capable of increased understanding while with the therapist but are unable to carry this over to daily activities with their children, and, furthermore, it might be considered highly important to the overall success of child therapy to involve parents in psychologically changing with their children. To be more specific about this method, the child might be participating in play therapy with his psychologist; and during the first few sessions the child would be allowed to become familiar with the play therapy setting and, concurrently, his mother would be receiving an orientation to the therapeutic procedures from another psychologist. She might be trained to react to certain of the child's acts in an entirely different manner than she typically would at home: if he breaks the rules, she must not react, but when he behaves properly she must consistently react to reinforce the behavior. In this manner, socially approved behavior would be reinforced by the mother by the giving of recognition, attention, and approval; and the therapist would be on hand to help the mother overcome the emotional responses she has relied upon for years. Since it is highly essential to the success of the therapy that the parental reinforcing role be maintained in the home, it is logical that the most desirable format would be to have both parents, and possibly siblings, involved in the behavior therapy. In assessing parental involvement, Russo (1964) reports that feelings, emotions, and behavioral controls change with the primary subject, the child, and that the experience helps the parents to become more emotionally relaxed. It is quite feasible that this exposure to behavioral modification may serve as an impetus for some parents, who may reflect as many behavioral difficulties as their children, to seek professional help in changing their own social roles.

It is apparent that children's behavior may be readily influenced by persons with whom they come in contact. In addition to teachers and parents, peers are capable of reinforcing specific behaviors by recognition and verbal rewards. In a study of 36 nursery school children (age 4 and 5 years), Hartup (1964) found that, with the peers·saying "good" and "fine" to show verbal approval, the children's rate of marble-dropping was better maintained when the reinforcing agent was a disliked rather than a liked peer. Similarly, Tiktin and Hartup (1965) studied the effects of verbal reinforcement on the marble-dropping performances of 84 elementary children, and they found a significant increase in response rate when reinforcement was made by an unpopular peer; the performance did not change when the reinforcing person was an isolate and it tended to decrease when the peer was popular. The influence of a different type of peer behavior may be seen in a study by Walters and Parke (1964), where 84 boys (mean age 5 years and 11 months) were randomly assigned to one of the four subgroups: film model rewarded for deviation, film model punished for deviation, no consequence to film model for deviation, and no film. The children who had viewed the film where the child had been rewarded and also where nothing had happened to the child (no consequence) deviated readily during their own play sessions, as had the child in the film, but the children who saw the film of the child being punished for his play or did not see any film deviated very little from previous play patterns.

POSITIVE REINFORCEMENT COMBINED WITH PUNISHMENT

The term punishment in this section takes on a slightly different connotation than it will carry in the section dealing with aversive stimuli. That is, when a child has been conditioned with positive reinforcement, such as the forms of rewards mentioned in the previous section, the process of taking away the reinforcement actually assumes the properties of punishment. In a study of ten 6-year olds, Baer (1961) found that the withdrawal of a positive reinforcement, e.g., viewing a cartoon film, served as a punishment and depressed a recently strengthened behavioral response, e.g., bar pressing to receive a peanut. And in a similar subsequent study, Baer (1962) found additional support for the belief that the withdrawal of positive reinforcement serves as punishment; nursery school children with an unusually high rate of thumbsucking were conditioned out of their behavior by giving them positive reinforcement, e.g., viewing a cartoon film, and by withdrawing the positive reinforcement as punishment, e.g., programming interruptions of the films. In a case study by Burchard and Tyler (1965), a 13-year old delinquent boy received the following conditioning procedures: he was perfunctorily placed in an isolation room when he displayed any unacceptable behavior; to avoid positive reinforcement with this punishment, a radio played during the waking-hours to eliminate the possibility of his communicating with other boys in neighboring isolation rooms; the room was kept free of non-essential objects and the staff members were instructed not to pay unnecessary attention to the boy; and for each period that he maintained good behavior while in isolation he received tokens as rewards, and he was subsequently allowed to purchase material, e.g. cigarettes, and non-material, e.g., recreation, rewards. A steady, gradual decline in the frequency of unacceptable behavior was achieved; for example, a 33% decline in the number of times that the boy was placed in isolation was measured between the first and fifth months of the operant conditioning processes.

AVERSIVE CONDITIONING

The use of aversive conditioning or treatment by negative reinforcement contingencies involves such stimuli as drugs, electric shock, noises, fatigue, or other conditions that are unpleasant to the subject. With these manipulative and sometimes severe techniques, it is not surprising that the use of aversive stimuli has been limited, especially with children. With adults, however, aversive stimuli have been applied to various behavior disorders with success (Grossberg, 1964). It is interesting to note that these techniques seem to have received more acceptance in Great Britain than in the United States.

Aversive conditioning, particularly involving electric shock, has been used with autistic children. Ferster (1961) provides clarification on why this childhood schizophrenia is potentially amenable through conditioning. Lovaas, Schaeffer, and Simmons (1965) found that painful electric shock could successfully modify the behavior of two 5-year old identical twins who had been diagnosed as childhood schizophrenics. Certain pathological behaviors, such as self-stimulation and temper tantrums, were eliminated. After developing an association between adults and shock reduction, the children approached adults, and their affectionate and other social behaviors in relation to adults increased. In response to this study, Breger (1965) admits that the results demonstrate the possibility of simple shock avoidance learning in schizophrenic children, but questions that there is evidence that transfer of this behavior is indicated.

VERBAL CONDITIONING

A form of reinforcement that has received a great deal of attention, particularly in counseling and psychotherapy, is verbal conditioning. Krasner (1965) states:

> Verbal conditioning is the systematic application of social reinforcements to influence the probability of another person emitting a specifiable verbal behavior . . . Verbal conditioning is an excellent technique for learning how human verbal behavior is systematically influenced by situational events; what are the conditions for effectively modifying such behavior; what other behaviors are associated with changes in verbal behavior; and what is the effect on verbal behavior of the interaction of subject-examiner variables. (p. 213)

Experiments by Greenspoon (1951; 1955) attracted the attention of psychologists and a number of subsequent studies have essentially confirmed Greenspoon's findings that stimuli can be used to reinforce classes of verbal responses (Hildum and Brown, 1956; Binder, McConnell, and Sjoholm, 1957; Sapolsky, 1960; Vogel-Sprott, 1964). In a recent review, Williams (1964) concludes that the majority of studies on verbal conditioning are most relevant to psychotherapy. Applications of verbal conditioning in school settings, however, have been somewhat limited. The most appropriate studies seem to be those done only recently, where verbal conditioning is applied to school counseling.

Ryan and Krumboltz (1964), in a study of 60 male college students, found that: when counselors reinforced deliberation responses during counseling sessions, the counselees increased the frequency of deliberation-type responses, and this type of response decreased when the reinforcement was withdrawn; similarly, decision responses increased when the counselor reinforced them, and decreased when the reinforcement was withdrawn. The reinforcing stimuli were verbal responses such as "good," "fine," "that's a good idea," and other approval-oriented verbal expressions. It is interesting to note that counselors varied in reinforcing effectiveness. Krumboltz and Thoresen (1964) randomly assigned 192 high school students to individual and group counseling and gave them one of four types of treatment: reinforcement of verbal information-seeking behavior, presentation of a tape recorded model counseling interview followed by reinforcement counseling, presentation of a film or filmstrip with a discussion period for a control group, and an inactive control group. As in the previous study, the reinforcing stimuli were verbal expressions that indicated counselor approval of the client's verbal expressions. It was found that both the model-reinforcement and the reinforcement counseling produced more information-seeking behavior outside of the counseling sessions than did the control procedures. When using a male model on the tape recording, model-reinforcement counseling achieved greater success than did reinforcement counseling for the males but not for the females. Group and individual settings seemed essentially equal in effectiveness. In relation to this last study, Varenhorst (1964) found that a video tape recording of a model female counseling client was effective with female clients. Perhaps these two studies might be interpreted as suggesting that the use of tape recordings, either video or audio, of a model counseling client facilitates the reinforcement counseling process, but the model and the client should be of the same sex. Krumboltz and Schroeder (1965), with a design similar to the aforementioned study by Krumboltz and Thoresen (1964), studied 54 high school students seeking educational and vocational counseling. It was found that, after two counseling sessions one week apart, the students who received reinforcement counseling, including those who also had the benefit of a tape recording, engaged in more information-seeking behavior outside the interview than did the controls; furthermore, it was found that the ratio of information-seeking responses to other types of responses in the counseling session was positively correlated with information-seeking behavior outside of counseling. Rogers (1960) has also found support for operant conditioning of verbal behavior by use of quasi-therapy situations. And Johnson (1964) found that elementary school children after receiving reinforcement from their counselor for verbal participation showed increased verbal participation in their therapy session and in the classroom. Krumboltz (1965) presents the rationale for reinforcement counseling and emphasizes that the central purpose of behavioral counseling is to help the client resolve the problems that brought him to

the counselor; this is, obviously, compatible with the rationale for
behavior therapy that was set forth early in this paper.

DISCUSSION

One of the major problems confronting psychotherapists has been and
will continue to be the assessment of change due to the therapy. Since
behavior therapy has a very clear criterion for change, the removal of the
problem or symptom, empirical documentation of its efficacy has been
possible and, to say the least, is impressive. Forms of psychotherapy that
rely on achieving insight have had much less success in achieving truly
empirical data to support efficacy; in fact, two reviews by Eysenck (1952;
1965b) conclude that there are reasons to doubt that insight therapy
achieves much more "recovery" than spontaneous remission of the
problems. Obviously, the basic problem hinges on the differences in the
criteria for cure or even improvement between behavior therapy and the
insight therapies. Suffice it to say, if the therapist accepts that there need
not be a neurosis underlying every behavior problem, that behavior
problems represent unadaptive habits, and that the primary therapeutic
goal should be to help the client find relief from the problems that
brought him to the therapist, then there are ample research data to
support the efficacy of behavior therapy. Eysenck (1952; 1965a: 1965b),
Wolpe (1964), Grossberg (1964), Schmidt, Castell, and Brown (1965),
and London (1964) present convincing evidence for this point. It appears
that behavior therapy can efficiently and permanently remove behavior
problems, and that substitute behavior problems will not develop. There
is the fact, however, that while there are experimental studies on
behavior therapy, many of the theoretical principles and applied
techniques are still based solely on clinical case studies; this is evident in
several of the studies cited in this review. Therefore, more research on
behavior therapy is definitely needed, and the use of these techniques
with children, as might be encountered by a school psychologist, is an
especially fertile area for research.

From the studies reviewed, it seems that many of the principles and
techniques of behavior therapy are applicable in school psychology. For
example, the reciprocal inhibition technique of emotive imagery
described by Lazarus and Abramovitz (1962) seems promising for use in
schools. Likewise, the studies by Krumboltz and his colleagues provide
strong evidence that reinforcement counseling can be effective in school
counseling activities. If the school psychologist is serving as a consultant,
as opposed to being a psychotherapist, he is in a good position to

promote certain conditioning techniques for the control of behavior problems in the classroom. The evidence supports that rewards and recognition can successfully modify behavior in an educational setting. In view of established classroom procedures, this usage will undoubtedly be difficult and perhaps temporarily impossible to execute in a regular classroom; but it seems quite feasible that rewards and recognition as reinforcement may be used with small special education classes, either with mentally handicapped or emotionally disturbed children, or with individuals or small special groups removed for brief periods from their larger regular classroom for specific behavioral difficulties. In relation to this, the use of peers by the therapist for purposes of reinforcement, as noted in the studies by Hartup (1964) and Tiktin and Hartup (1965), seems to have potential value for school settings.

The possibility of involving parents in the behavior therapy (Russo, 1964; Straughan, 1964) seems to be an excellent means of introducing behavior therapy to school psychology. Since some of these new and unique therapeutic techniques may meet with reserved acceptance from other educational personnel and the general community, the involvement of the parents will serve to eliminate their concerns, facilitate the child's (and possibly the parents') changes in behavior, and, moreover, alleviate the school psychologist's uncertainty about pioneering in behavior modification. On this latter point, Woody and Herr (1965) found that doctoral-level psychologists believe that certain conditioning techniques are of value for numerous problems encountered in schools, but they were definitely uncertain as to whether contemporary philosophies and practices in education were ready for the use of these techniques by school psychologists (Woody and Herr, 1966).

There seems to be ample research to support that verbal conditioning can be used to accelerate counseling and psychotherapy, and that the school psychologist can use these reinforcement techniques to modify certain behaviors that occur in the school that disrupt the classroom learning activities. For example, it would seem that a child using extremely vulgar or profane words in his classroom conversation could be conditioned, through verbal reinforcement, not to use this type of vocabulary while in the school; this could be accomplished with relatively short behavior therapy sessions.

Aversive conditioning has been quite effective with certain types of adult behavioral patterns and, in a limited number of studies, with emotionally disturbed children. The acknowledged effectiveness of this type of conditioning necessitates further consideration of this type of stimuli for modifying problems encountered in school psychology. But, since the use of punishment contradicts certain philosophical constructs inherent to contemporary public education, it seems highly unlikely that aversive conditioning is ready for introduction into school psychology. With further research in this area and the successful use of other forms of behavior therapy in schools, however, this opinion may be changed.

The use of behavior therapy in schools will necessitate changes in the training of school psychologists. If behavior therapy is to be emphasized in the future, school psychologists will need more academic training in aspects of experimental psychology, with special emphasis on learning theory. It may be that these techniques can be used by school psychologists with essentially the same level of training that is currently required for certification; but in order to fulfill ethical and professional commitments, the school psychologist should have both academic training and supervised clinical experience for the use of behavior therapy, and the supervised clinical experience must be provided by a professional of higher qualifications who has been specially trained in behavior therapy. Obviously, this may create a number of curriculum and personnel problems for some university training programs.

Behavior therapy has a natural alignment with school psychology. Behavior therapy is based on learning theory and learning theory is the basic premise for education. Needless to say, it would certainly be ironical if members of the same theoretical family could not complement the activities of each other.

SUMMARY

A great deal of research and applied interest has been focused recently on behavior therapy, an approach to behavior modification that is based on the assumption that behavior problems are persistent unadaptive habits and that there need not be an underlying neurosis. A review of studies especially relevant to school psychology reveals successful usage of positive reinforcement with emphasis on reciprocal inhibition and rewards, positive reinforcement combined with punishment through withdrawal of the positive reinforcement, aversive conditioning, and verbal conditioning as used in counseling and psychotherapy. The results of the selected studies provide support for the belief that behavior therapy is effective for changing the behavior of children, and that the school psychologist can apply these techniques within the school setting. Recommendations are made for introducing behavior therapy into school psychology.

References

Baer, D. M. Effect of withdrawal of positive reinforcement on an extinguishing response in young children. *Child Develpm.*, 1961, 32, 67-74.

Baer, D. M. Laboratory control of thumbsucking by withdrawal and re-presentation of reinforcement. *J. exper. anal. Behav.*, 1962, 5, 525-528.

Bijou, S. W. Experimental studies of child behavior, normal and deviant. In L. Krasner and L. P. Ullman, *(Eds.) Research in behavior modification.* New York: Holt, Rinehart and Winston, 1965, Pp. 56-81.

Binder, A., McConnell, D., & Sjoholm, Nancy A. Verbal conditioning as a function of experimenter characteristics. *J. abnorm. soc. Psychol.*, 1957, 55, 309-314.

Birnbrauer, J. S., Wolf, M. M., Kidder, J. D., & Tague, Cecilia E. Classroom behavior of retarded pupils with token reinforcement. *J. exper. child Psychol.*, 1965, 2, 219-235.

Breger, L. Comments on "building social behaviors in autistic children by the use of electric shock." *J. exper. res. Pers.* 1965, 1, 110-113.

Brown, P., & Elliott, R. Control of aggression in a nursery school class. *J. exper. child Psychol.*, 1965, 2, 103-107.

Burchard, J., & Tyler, V., Jr. The modification of delinquent behavior through operant conditioning. *Behav. res. Ther.*, 1965, 2, 245-250.

Davison, G. C. A social learning therapy programme with an autistic child. *Behav. res. Ther.*, 1964, 2, 149-159.

Ellis, N. R. (Ed.). *Handbook of mental deficiency.* New York: McGraw-Hill, 1963.

Eysenck, H. J. The effects of psychotherapy: an evaluation. *J. consult. Psychol.*, 1952, 16, 319-324.

Eysenck, H. J. Learning theory and behavior therapy. In G. Lindzey and C. S. Hall (Eds.), *Theories of personality; primary sources and research.* New York: John Wiley and Sons, 1965, Pp. 398-410. (a)

Eysenck, H. J. The effects of psychotherapy. *Int. J. Psychiat.*, 1965, 1, 99-142. (b)

Ferster, C. B. Positive reinforcement and behavioral deficits of autistic children. *Child. Develpm.*, 1961, 32, 437-456.

Greenspoon, J. The effect of verbal and non-verbal stimuli on the frequency of members of two verbal response classes. Unpublished doctoral dissertation, Indiana University, 1951.

Greenspoon, J. The reinforcing effect of two spoken sounds on the frequency of two responses. *Amer. J. Psychol.*, 1955, 68, 409-416.

Grossberg, J. M. Behavior therapy: a review. *Psychol. Bull.*, 1964, 62, 73-88.

Hallsten, E. A., Jr. Adolescent anorexia nervosa treated by desensitization. *Behav. res. Ther.*, 1965, *3*, 87–91.

Hartup, W. W. Friendship status and the effectiveness of peers as reinforcing agents. *J. exper. child Psychol.*, 1964, *1*, 154–162.

Hildum, D. C., & Brown, R. W. Verbal reinforcement and interviewer bias. *J. abnorm. soc. Psychol.*, 1956, *53*, 108–111.

Johnson, C. J., Jr. The transfer effect of treatment group composition on pupil's classroom participation. Unpublished doctoral dissertation, Stanford University, 1964.

Krasner, L. Verbal Conditioning and psychotherapy. In L. Krasner and L. P. Ullmann (Eds.), *Research in behavior modification.* New York: Holt, Rinehart and Winston, 1965, Pp. 211–228.

Krumboltz, J. D. Behavioral counseling: rationale and research. *Personnel guid. J.*, 1965, *44*, 383–387.

Krumboltz, J. D., & Schroeder, W. W. Promoting career planning through reinforcement. *Personnel guid. J.*, 1965, *44*, 19–26.

Krumboltz, J. D. & Thoresen, C. E. The effect of behavioral counseling in group and individual settings on information-seeking behavior. *J. counsel. Psychol.*, 1964, *11*, 324–333.

Lazarus, A. A., & Abramovitz, A. The use of "emotive imagery" in the treatment of children's phobias. *J. ment. Sci.*, 1962, *108*, 191–195.

London, P. *The modes and morals of psychotherapy.* New York: Holt, Rinehart and Winston, 1964.

Lovaas, O. I., Schaeffer, B., & Simmons, J. Q. Building social behavior in autistic children by use of electric shock. *J. exper. res. Pers.*, 1965, *1*, 99–109.

Lovibond, S. H. *Conditioning and enuresis.* Oxford: Pergamon Press, 1964.

Miller, L. K. A note on the control of study behavior. *J. exper. child Psychol.*, 1964, *1*, 108–110.

Patterson, G. R. A learning theory approach to the treatment of the school phobic child. In L. P. Ullmann and L. Krasner (Eds.), *Case studies in behavior modification.* New York: Holt, Rinehart and Winston, 1965, Pp. 279–285.

Patterson G. R., Jones, R., Whittier, J., & Wright, Mary A. A behaviour modification technique for the hyperactive child. *Behav. res. Ther.*, 1965, *2*, 217–226.

Rogers, J. M. Operant conditioning in a quasi-therapy setting. *J. abnorm. soc. Psychol.*, 1960, *60*, 247–252.

Russo, S. Adaptations in behavioural therapy with children. *Behav. res. Ther.*, 1964, *2*, 43–47.

Ryan, T. Antoinette, & Krumboltz, J. D. Effect of planned reinforcement counseling on client decision-making behavior. *J. counsel. Psychol.*, 1964, *11*, 315–323.

Sapolsky, A. Effect of interpersonal relationships upon verbal conditioning. *J. abnorm. soc. Psychol.*, 1960, 60, 241–246.

Schmidt, Elsa, Castell, D., & Brown, P. A retrospective study of 42 cases of behaviour therapy. *Behav. res. Ther.*, 1965, 3, 9–19.

Stacey, C. L., & DeMartino, M. F. (Eds.). *Counseling and psychotherapy with the mentally retarded.* Glencoe, Illinois: Free Press, 1957.

Straughan, J. H. Treatment with child and mother in the playroom. *Behav. res. Ther.*, 1964, 2, 37–41.

Tiktin, Susan, & Hartup, W. W. Sociometric status and the reinforcing effectiveness of children's peers. *J. exper. child Psychol.*, 1965, 2, 306–315.

Varenhorst, Barbara B. An experimental comparison of non-verbal factors determining reinforcement effectiveness of model-reinforced counseling. Unpublished doctoral dissertation, Stanford University, 1964.

Vogel-Sprott, M. D. Response generalization under verbal conditioning in alcoholics, delinquents and students. *Behav. res. Ther.*, 1964, 2, 135–141.

Wahler, R. G., Winkel, G. H., Peterson, R. F., & Morrison, D. C. Mothers as behavior therapists for their own children. *Behav. res. Ther.*, 1965, 3, 113–124.

Walters, R. H., & Parke, R. D. Influence of response consequences to a social model on resistance to deviation. *J. exper. child Psychol.*, 1964, 1, 269–280.

White, J. G. The use of learning theory in the psychological treatment of children *J. clin. Psychol.*, 1957, 15, 227–229.

Williams, Juanita H. Conditioning of verbalization: a review. *Psychol. Bull.*, 1964, 62, 383–393.

Wolpe, J. The comparative clinical status of conditioning therapies and psychoanalysis. In J. Wolpe, A. Salter, and L. J. Reyna (Eds.), *The conditioning therapies.* New York: Holt, Rinehart and Winston, 1964, Pp. 5–20.

Woody, R. H., & Herr, E. L. Psychologists and hypnosis: psychotherapeutic theories and practice, *Amer. J. clin. Hyp.*, 1965, 8, 80–88.

Woody, R. H., & Herr, E. L. Psychologists and hypnosis: II. use in educational settings. *Amer. J. Clin. Hyp.*, 1966, 8, 254–256.

Young, G. C., & Turner, R. K. CNS stimulant drugs and conditioning treatment of nocturnal enuresis. *Behav. res. Ther.*, 1965, 3, 93–101.

Zimmerman, Elaine H., & Zimmerman, J. The alteration of behavior in a special classroom situation. *J. exper. anal. Behav.*, 1962, 5, 59–60.

Bandura's article is the only one in this book which focuses primarily on the therapeutic rather than classroom uses of behavior modification. It is also the only one which does focus on the ethical problems governing the use of behavior modification techniques. Far from merely defending the deliberate manipulation of behavior by behavior therapists, Bandura attacks the traditional clinician, and by implication the traditional teacher, who purports to see control of another as immoral but who in fact attempts such control on a covert level. Bandura states that traditional psychotherapy, and probably traditional teaching, involves a conversion of the client or student to the belief and attitudinal system of the teacher or therapist, often in the name of self-actualization. Specialists in behavior modification, on the other hand, explicitly specify the behaviors to be changed and often permit the person involved to identify his own problems and goals. Bandura would thus conclude that the major criticism of practitioners of behavior modification occurs because they are both more honest in specifying what they are going to do and more effective in carrying out their goals than those who take a more "humanistic" approach.

A second point Bandura makes is that controlling another's behavior may be an important way to increase his freedom of choice. A person's own inhibitions, his lack of education and skill, and restraints placed by society on those who behave in certain ways may severely limit the options available to him. By directly manipulating his behavior to teach him new skills or free him from inhibitions, a behavior therapist can increase his freedom and permit him to achieve his goals. Alternatively, he can be trained in the principles of behavior modification and devise his own techniques for self control.

Relatively few teachers are willing to wholeheartedly endorse as "radical" a philosophy as that which Bandura espouses. An interesting project might be to present this point of view to a group of traditionally trained teachers and note the reactions to it. A teacher or therapist who practices behavior modification should be aware of the ethical arguments in favor of the use of these techniques so that he can answer criticism and provide evidence of the validity of his own position. In this short excerpt from his book, Bandura has managed to do both.

Ethical Issues of Behavioral Control

Albert Bandura*

SELECTION OF OBJECTIVES AND ETHICAL ISSUES OF BEHAVIORAL CONTROL

Behavioral objectives are frequently unspecified in order to avoid acknowledging the value judgments and social influences involved in the modification of behavior. Psychotherapists who subscribe to conversational methods customarily portray their form of treatment as a noncontingent social influence process in which the therapist serves as an unconditionally loving, permissive, understanding, empathizing catalyst in the client's efforts toward self-discovery and self-actualization. In contrast, behaviorally oriented psychotherapists are typically depicted as antihumanistic, Machiavellian manipulators of human behavior (Jourard, 1961; Patterson, 1963; Rogers, 1956; Shoben, 1963). In truth, to the extent that the psychotherapist—regardless of his theoretical allegiances— has been successful in modifying his clients' behavior, he has either deliberately or unwittingly manipulated the factors that control it. It is interesting to note in this connection that conditions that are undesignedly imposed upon others are generally regarded with favor, whereas identical conditions created after thoughtful consideration of their effects on others are often considered culpable. There exists no other enterprise which values incognizance so highly, often at the expense

* From Chapter Two, from *Principles of Behavior Modification* by Albert Bandura. Copyright © 1969 by Holt, Rinehart and Winston, Inc. Reprinted by permission of Holt, Rinehart and Winston, Inc.

of the client's welfare. One suspects that this therapist-centered value system would change rapidly if therapeutic contracts required financial remuneration to be made at least partially contingent upon the amount of demonstrable change achieved by clients in the interpersonal problems for which they seek help.

In view of the substantial research evidence that psychotherapists serve as models for, and selective reinforcers of, their clients' behavior (Bandura, Lipsher, & Miller, 1960; Goldman, 1961; Murray, 1956; Rosenthal, 1955; Truax, 1966; Winder et al., 1962), it is surprising that many therapists continue to view the psychotherapeutic process as one that does not involve behavioral influence and control.

In later writings, Rogers (1956), a leading proponent of the anticontrol position, has acknowledged that psychotherapists do in fact manipulate and control their clients' behavior within the treatment setting. He contends, however, that this benevolent external control yields "self-actualized," "flexible," and "creatively adaptive" persons whose post-therapy behavior is under internal control and no longer subject to the psychotherapist's influences. The actual outcomes, however, are considerably at variance with these idealized pretensions. A brief comparison of interview protocols of cases treated by Rogerian therapists with those of clients seen by therapists representing differing theoretical orientations clearly reveals that, far from being individuated and self-actualized, the clients have been thoroughly conditioned and converted to the belief system, vernacular, and interpretations of reality favored by their respective psychotherapists. Such conformity in verbal behavior is partly achieved through selective reinforcement. Sequential analyses of verbal interchanges in cases treated by Rogers revealed that the therapist consistently approved certain behaviors and disapproved others (Murray, 1956; Truax, 1966). As treatment progressed, approved responses increased in frequency while disapproved verbalizations diminished.

In the often quoted debate between Rogers and Skinner (1956) concerning the moral implications of behavioral control, Rogers distinguishes among three types of control; this provides an excellent illustration of the use of propitious relabeling to minimize the ethical decisions that confront therapists and other agents of change. In the first category, designated as *external control*, person A creates conditions that alter person B's behavior without his concurrence. The second and presumably more humanitarian form, labeled *influence*, involves processes in which A arranges conditions that modify B's behavior, to which he gives some degree of consent. The distinction between external control and influence, however, is more apparent than real. In many instances certain conditions are imposed upon individuals without their agreement, knowledge, or understanding, from which they can later free themselves by willingly changing their behavior in a direction subtly prescribed by controlling agents. Thus, for example, persons who have been legally committed to mental hospitals or penal institutions may voluntarily enter into treatment programs to acquire the types of behavior that will improve their living circumstances in the institution and ensure a speedy discharge. A more fundamental ethical distinction can be made in terms of whether the power to influence others is utilized for the advantage of the controller or for the benefit of the controllee, rather than in terms of the illusory criterion of willing consent.

Internal control, Rogers' third category, involves a process in which a person arranges conditions so as to manage his own responsiveness. Although self-monitoring systems play an influential role in the regulation of human behavior, they are not entirely independent of external influences. Self-monitoring systems are transmitted through modeling and reinforcement processes. After a person has adopted a set of behavioral standards for self-evaluation he tends to select associates who share similar value systems and behavioral norms (Bandura & Walters, 1959; Elkin & Westley, 1955). The members of his reference group, in turn, serve to reinforce and to uphold his self-prescribed standards of conduct. A person who chooses a small select reference group that does not share the values of the general public may appear highly individualistic and "inner-directed," whereas in fact he is very much dependent on the actual and fantasied approval and disapproval of a few individuals whose judgments he values highly.

During the course of psychotherapy, clients likewise adopt, through modeling, their therapists' values, attitudes, and standards of conduct for self-evaluation (Pentony, 1966; Rosenthal, 1955). Responsiveness to modeling influences is apt to be particularly enhanced in a relationship in which a person has developed a strong positive tie to a prestigious model (Bandura & Huston, 1961; Henker, 1964; Mussen & Parker, 1965), a condition which is emphasized considerably in most forms of psychotherapy. Studies of modeling effects further disclose that persons tend to perform the model's behavior in his absence (Bandura & Kupers, 1964; Bandura, Ross, & Ross, 1963), and they respond to new situations in a manner consistent with the model's dispositions even though they have never observed the model's behavior in response to the same stimuli (Bandura & Harris, 1966; Bandura & McDonald, 1963; Bandura & Mischel, 1965). These findings indicate that after the model's attitudes and behavioral attributes have been adopted, he continues to influence and indirectly to control the subject's actions, though he is no longer physically present. In fact, in Rogers' (1951) conceptualization of maladjustment, introjected parental values are construed as continuing pathological influences that maintain disturbing incongruities in the clients' self-structure. However, after internalized parental values are supplanted by adoption of the therapist's attitudes and standards, the client is flatteringly portrayed—by the psychotherapist—as self-actualized, flexibly creative, and self-directed!

Much of the controversy between Rogers and Skinner centers around their own value preferences for others. Skinner advocates that people be made "truly happy, secure, productive, creative, and forward-looking"; Rogers argues in favor of self-direction and self-actualization of potentialities as the prescribed objective of social influence. It might be noted parenthetically that in the context of proclaiming the self-actualization objective, Rogers argues vigorously against self-actualization in Skinnerian directions. The leitmotif in this discourse appears to be one of belief conformity rather than self-realization. As usually happens in disputes over therapeutic outcomes, "happiness" and "conformity to societal norms" are selected as examples of unwholesome outcomes equated with slothfulness; self-actualization, on the other hand, is proffered as an ennobling aim. To balance the evaluative scales, it should be noted that the self-centered ethic of self-actualization might be equally questioned on moral grounds, particularly by innocent victims of self-actualized despots or less notorious but selfish, self-directed persons. Universally accepted goals are difficult to come by because all the various patterns of behavior enthusiastically promoted by therapists of different persuasions can be used to produce inimical human effects.

The most remarkable feature of the foregoing, seemingly humanistic, rhetoric is that neither participant acknowledges that the choice of behavioral objectives is rightfully the *client's*. A person may seek from therapy neither Skinner's security nor a Rogerian conversion in the guise of self-realization. We shall return shortly to this issue of value standardization and the inclination of therapists to impose their own cherished objectives upon their clients.

Contrary to the beliefs of Rogers, Shoben, and other critics, behaviorally oriented approaches usually involve considerably less unnecessary control and manipulation of attitudes and values than do the procedures based upon the psychodynamic model. In the latter treatments, any behavior, no matter how trivial or apparently irrelevant, tends to be viewed as a derivative of concealed psychodynamic forces and is therefore subject to analysis and reinterpretation in terms of the therapist's theoretical predilections. Thus virtually no aspect of the client's life—his social, marital, and sexual behavior, his political and religious beliefs, his vocational choice, his child-training practices—escapes the therapist's repeated scrutiny and influence over a period of several years. Since this approach tends to regard behavioral difficulties as superficial manifestations of more fundamental and often unconscious internal events, influence attempts are primarily directed toward subject matters of questionable relevance. It is not uncommon, therefore, to find clients whose belief systems have been thoroughly modified despite little amelioration of the behavioral difficulties for which they originally sought help.

In contrast, behaviorally oriented therapists generally confine their therapeutic efforts to the behavioral problems presented by the client. These are labeled as learned styles of behavior rather than as expressions of esoteric unconscious processes or as manifestations of mental disease. Moreover, the procedures and objectives are undisguised, the treatment is typically of shorter duration, and clearly goal-directed. To be sure, within this highly structured interaction, the therapist must exercise responsible control over conditions affecting relevant segments of the client's behavior if he is to fulfill his therapeutic obligations. In this type of approach, however, the psychotherapist is less inclined to condition and to shape his client's belief systems in accordance with his own views. Paradoxical as it may seem, the psychotherapists who pride themselves on being nonmanipulative and noncontrolling are, albeit unwillingly, often engaged in a more disguised and manipulative enterprise than is true of most behaviorally oriented practitioners. It should be made clear, however, that behavioral principles do not dictate the manner in which they are applied. Undoubtedly some behavioral therapists encroach on people's rights to decide the direction in which their behavior will be modified, and act as therapeutic agents devoid of consideration and regard for values.

ESTABLISHMENT OF FREEDOM OF CHOICE THROUGH BEHAVIORAL APPROACHES

Discussions of the moral implications of behavioral control almost always emphasize the Machiavellian role of change agents and the self-protective maneuvers of controllees. The fact that most persons enter treatment only as a last resort, hoping to modify patterns of behavior that are seriously distressful to themselves or to others, is frequently overlooked. To the extent that therapists engage in moral agonizing, they should fret more about their own limited effectiveness in helping persons who are willing to undergo financial hardships to achieve desired changes, than in fantasizing about their potential powers. The tendency to exaggerate the powers of behavioral control by psychological methods alone, irrespective of willing cooperation by the client, and the failure to recognize the reciprocal nature of interpersonal control obscure both the ethical issues and the nature of social influence processes.

In discussing moral and practical issues of behavioral control it is essential to recognize that social influence is not a question of imposing controls where none existed before. All behavior is inevitably controlled, and the operation of psychological laws cannot be suspended by romantic conceptions of human behavior, any more than indignant rejection of the law of gravity as antihumanistic can stop people from falling. As Homme and Tosti (1965) point out, "either one manages the contingencies or they get managed by accident. Either way there will be contingencies, and they will have their effect [p. 16]." The process of behavior change, therefore, involves substituting new controlling conditions for those that have regulated a person's behavior. The basic moral question is not whether man's behavior will be controlled, but rather by whom, by what means, and for what ends.

The primary criterion that one might apply in judging the ethical implications of social influence approaches (Kelman, 1965) is the degree to which they promote freedom of choice. It should be added, however, that if individualism is to be guaranteed, it must be tempered by a sense of social obligation. Custodial institutions created by societies are highly populated with socially injurious individualists. A person's freedom of self-expression can be restricted in several ways, each of which presents somewhat different ethical problems in the reestablishment of self-determination.

Self-restraints in the form of conditioned inhibitions and self-censuring responses often severely curtail a person's effective range of behaviors and the types of options that they are likely to consider for themselves. In many instances, for example, persons are unable to participate freely in potentially rewarding social interactions because of severe phobias; they are unable to engage in achievement, aggressive and heterosexual activities; and they deny themselves socially permissible gratification because of austere, self-imposed standards of conduct. Treatment programs designed to reduce rigid self-restraints are rarely viewed as ethically objectionable, since they tend to restore spontaneity and freedom of choice among various options of action. Ethical issues arise only if a change agent uses his influence selfishly or to make his clients socially irresponsible.

Behavioral deficits also greatly restrict freedom of choice and otherwise curtail opportunities for self-direction. Persons' positions in various status and power hierarchies are to a large extent determined by their social, educational, and vocational competencies. The degree of control that one can exercise over one's own activities, the power to form and to modify one's environment, and the accessibility to, and control over, desired resources increase with higher status positions. Persons who have developed superior intellectual and vocational capabilities enjoy a wide latitude of occupational choices; they are granted considerable freedom to regulate both their own activities and the behavior of others; and they have the financial means of obtaining additional privileges that further increase their autonomy. By contrast, high school dropouts who lack sociovocational proficiencies are relegated to a subordinate status, in which not only is their welfare subject to arbitrary external controls, but they are irreversibly channeled into an economic and social life that further restricts their opportunities to use their potentialities and to affect their own life circumstances. Eliminating such behavioral deficits can substantially increase the level of self-determination in diverse areas of social functioning.

Societally imposed restrictions on freedom of self-expression occur as responses to deviant behavior that violates legal codes. Chronic alcoholics, drug addicts, sexual deviates, delinquents, psychotics, and social nonconformists and activists may have their liberties revoked for fixed or indefinite periods when their public actions are judged to be socially detrimental and therefore to be subject to social control. Special ethical problems are most likely to arise wherever restoration of his freedom is made contingent upon the individual's relinquishing socially prohibited patterns of behavior. If an agent of change acts in opposition to the society which supports him institutionally, then he evades his broader social responsibilities with which he has been entrusted. If, on the other hand, he imposes conditions upon his captive clients designed to force conformity to social norms, he is subverting the client's right to choose how he shall live his life. These moral dilemmas are less difficult to resolve in cases where the person's behavior injures or infringes the freedom of others. Such persons have the choice of regaining their autonomy by undergoing changes within a broad range of socially tolerated alternatives, or setting no limits on their own behavior and having society restrict them to institutions. The ethical dilemma is more serious when conventional norms are questioned by many members of society and new standards of behavior are advocated. Today there are open controversies over the morality of homosexuality, premarital sexual intercourse, use of nonaddictive drugs, civil disobedience to unjust rules, and many forms of social behavior that are publicly defined as illegal. In such cases as these, therapeutic agents may support changes in socially prescribed directions or give legitimacy to deviant patterns, depending upon the social and personal consequences of the behavior, the client's preferences, and the therapist's own value orientation.

Most people whose freedom is curtailed by societally imposed restrictions and who voluntarily seek psychotherapeutic help are not that strongly wedded to deviant behavior; but because it is powerfully reinforcing, or because they lack more satisfying alternatives, they have difficulty relinquishing it. The establishment of self-control and the reduction of positive valences associated with deviant activities may sometimes require the use of aversive procedures as part of the treatment program. The use of aversive methods is apt to be criticized as being, if not anti-therapeutic, then certainly antihumanistic. But is it not far more humanitarian to offer the client a choice of undergoing a brief, painful experience to eliminate self-injurious behavior, or of enduring over many years the noxious, and often irreversible, consequences that will inevitably result if his behavior remains unaltered?

Restrictions of behavioral freedom arise also from *socially sanctioned discrimination*. In such cases a person's freedom is curtailed because of his skin color, his religion, his ethnic background, his social class, or other secondary characteristics. When a person's warranted self-determination is externally restricted by prejudicial social practices, the required changes must be made at the social systems level.

It is often mistakenly assumed (London, 1964) that traditional psychotherapies fervently embrace humanism whereas behavioral approaches, for reasons never explicated, are supposedly uninterested in the moral implications of their practices or are antagonistic toward humanistic values. In fact, behavioral therapy is a system of principles and procedures and not a system of ethics. Its methods, and any other effective procedures for that matter, can be employed to threaten human freedom and dignity or to enhance them.

When freedom is discussed in the abstract it is generally equated with nondeterminism; conversely, automatonism is associated with a deterministic position. Whether freedom and determinism are compatible or irreconcilable depends upon the manner in which causal processes are conceptualized. According to prevailing theories of personality, human actions are either impelled from within by concealed forces or externally predetermined. If individuals were merely passive reactors to external influences, then their behavior would be inevitable; it would be absurd to commend them for their achievements or to penalize them for their transgressions. It would be more sensible, from this point of view, to praise and to chastise the external determinants. But since these events are also unavoidably determined by prior conditions, the analysis results in an infinite regression of causes. Some degree of freedom is possible within a deterministic view if it is recognized that a person's behavior is a contributing factor to subsequent causal events. It will be recalled from the previous discussion of reciprocal influence processes that individuals play an active role in creating their own controlling environment.

From a social-learning point of view freedom is not incompatible with determinism. Rather a person is considered free insofar as he can partly influence future events by managing his own behavior. One could readily demonstrate that a person can, within the limits of his behavioral capabilities and environmental options, exercise substantial control over his social life by having him plan and systematically carry out radically different courses of action on alternate days. Granted that the selection of a particular course of behavior from available alternatives is itself the result of determining factors, a person can nevertheless exert some control over the variables that govern his own choices. Indeed, increasing use is being made of self-control systems (Ferster, Nurnberger, & Levitt, 1962; Harris, 1969; Stuart, 1967) in which individuals regulate their activities to fulfill their own wishes by deliberate self-management of reinforcement contingencies. The self-control process begins by informing individuals of the types of behaviors they will have to practice to produce desired outcomes, of ways in which they can institute stimuli to increase the occurrence of requisite performances, and of how they can arrange self-reinforcing consequences to sustain them. Behavioral change procedures that involve role enactment also depend upon the self-determination of outcomes through clients' regulation of their own behavior and the environmental contingencies that reciprocally influence it. Contrary to common belief, behavioral approaches not only can support a humanistic morality, but because of their relative effectiveness in establishing self-determination these methods hold much greater promise than traditional procedures for enhancement of behavioral freedom and fulfillment of human capabilities.

References

Bandura, A., & Harris, M. B. Modification of syntactic style. *Journal of Experimental Child Psychology*, 1966, 4, 341–352.

Bandura, A., & Huston, A. C. Identification as a process of incidental learning. *Journal of Abnormal and Social Psychology*, 1961, 63, 311–318.

Bandura, A., & Kupers, C. J. Transmission of patterns of self-reinforcement through modeling. *Journal of Abnormal and Social Psychology*, 1964, 69, 1–9.

Bandura, A., Lipsher, D. H., & Miller, P. E. Psychotherapists' approach-avoidance reactions to patients' expressions of hostility. *Journal of Consulting Psychology*, 1960, 24, 1–8.

Bandura, A., & McDonald, F. J. The influence of social reinforcement and the behavior of models in shaping children's moral judgments. *Journal of Abnormal and Social Psychology*, 1963, 67, 274–281.

Bandura, A., & Mischel, W. The influence of models in modifying delay of gratification patterns. *Journal of Personality and Social Psychology*, 1965, 2, 698–705.

Bandura, A., Ross, D., & Ross, S. A. Imitation of film-mediated aggressive models. *Journal of Abnormal and Social Psychology*, 1963, 66, 3–11.

Bandura, A., & Walters, R. H. *Adolescent aggression.* New York: Ronald, 1959.

Elkin, F., & Westley, W. A. The myth of adolescent culture. *American Sociological Review*, 1955, 20, 680–684.

Ferster, C. B., Nurnberger, J. I., & Levitt, E. B. The control of eating. *Journal of Mathetics*, 1962, 1, 87–109.

Goldman, J. R. The relation of certain therapist variables to the handling of psychotherapeutic events. Unpublished doctoral dissertation, Stanford University, 1961.

Harris, M. B. A self-directed program for weight control: A pilot study. *Journal of Abnormal Psychology*, 1969 (in press).

Henker, B. A. The effect of adult model relationships on children's play and task imitation. *Dissertation Abstracts*, 1964, 24, 4797.

Homme, L. E., & Tosti, D. T. Contingency management and motivation. *Journal of the National Society for Programmed Instruction*, 1965, 4, 14–16.

Jourard, S. M. On the problem of reinforcement by the psychotherapist of healthy behavior in the patient. In F. J. Shaw (Ed.), *Behavioristic approaches to counseling and psychotherapy: A Southeastern Psychological Association Symposium.* University, Ala: University of Alabama Press, 1961.

Kelman, H. C. Manipulation of human behavior: An ethical dilemma for the social scientist. *Journal of Social Issues*, 1965, 21, 31–46.

London, P. *The modes and morals of psychotherapy.* New York: Holt, Rinehart and Winston, 1964.

Murray, E. J. A content-analysis method for studying psychotherapy. *Psychological Monographs*, 1956, 70, (13, Whole No. 420).

Mussen, P. H., & Parker, A. L. Mother-nurturance and girls' incidental imitative learning. *Journal of Personality and Social Psychology*, 1965, 2, 94–97.

Patterson, C. H. Control, conditioning, and counseling. *Personnel and Guidance*, 1963, *41*, 680–686.

Pentony, P. Value change in psychotherapy. *Human Relations*, 1966, *19*, 39–46.

Rogers, C. R. *Client-centered therapy*. Boston: Houghton Mifflin, 1951.

Rogers, C. R., & Skinner, B. F. Some issues concerning the control of human behavior: A symposium. *Science*, 1956, *124*, 1057–1066.

Rosenthal, D. Changes in some moral values following psychotherapy. *Journal of Consulting Psychology*, 1955, *19*, 431–436.

Shoben, E. J., Jr. The therapeutic object: Men or machines? *Journal of Counseling Psychology*, 1963, *10*, 264–268.

Stuart, R. B. Behavioral control of overeating. *Behaviour Research and Therapy*, 1967, *5*, 357–365.

Truax, C. B. Reinforcement and nonreinforcement in Rogerian psychotherapy. *Journal of Abnormal Psychology*, 1966, *71*, 1–9.

Winder, C. L., Ahmad, F. Z., Bandura, A., & Rau, L. C. Dependency of patients, psychotherapists' responses, and aspects of psychotherapy. *Journal of Consulting Psychology*, 1962, *26*, 129–134.

What kind of study is most likely to be helpful to teachers, parents and therapists who want to change the way someone acts? Baer, Wolf and Risley argue for the value of applied studies, which deal with problems of interest and importance to society and which focus on specific behaviors which can be measured and observed. They also suggest that demonstrated control of a behavior is a measure of the adequacy of the program and they discuss the importance of replicability or reliability in ascertaining the extent to which such control exists. For a study to be of value to others they require what they call a "technological description," analogous to what others might call an operational definition. Unless the procedures can be specified in sufficient detail to permit a typical teacher to reproduce the method, then the description should be made more precise, according to the authors.

Two more characteristics which relate to the practical importance of an article are the size and the generality of the effect produced. If a procedure produces only a small change in the behavior or if very little generalization can be programmed, Baer, Wolf, and Risley would consider the value of an applied behavior analysis to be lessened. Their article, in other words, sets up standards of conceptual and practical adequacy against which to measure articles purporting to provide analyses of behaviors relevant to practical problems, including almost all the articles in this book. Although the rigor of their approach should not dissuade you from testing out ideas and techniques of your own, referring to this article may provide guidelines to ascertain the applicability of your own and other's research.

Some Current Dimensions of Applied Behavior Analysis[1]

Donald M. Baer,
Montrose M. Wolf,
and
Todd R. Risley*†

The analysis of individual behavior is a problem in scientific demonstration, reasonably well understood (Skinner, 1953, Sec. 1), comprehensively described (Sidman, 1960), and quite thoroughly practised (*Journal of the Experimental Analysis of Behavior*, 1957—). That analysis has been pursued in many settings over many years. Despite variable precision, elegance, and power, it has resulted in general descriptive statements of mechanisms that can produce many of the forms that individual behavior may take.

The statement of these mechanisms establishes the possibility of their application to problem behavior. A society willing to consider a technology of its own behavior apparently is likely to support that application when it deals with socially important behaviors, such as retardation, crime, mental illness, or education. Such applications have appeared in recent years. Their current number and the interest which they create apparently suffice to generate a journal for their display. That display may well lead to the widespread examination of these applications, their refinement, and eventually their replacement by better applications. Better applications, it is hoped, will lead to a better state of society, to whatever extent the behavior of its members can contribute to the goodness of a society. Since the evaluation of what is a

* Donald M. Baer, Montrose M. Wolf and Todd R. Risley, "Some Current Dimensions of Applied Behavior Analysis," *Journal of Applied Behavior Analysis* 1(1968): 91-97. Reprinted with permission. Copyright 1968 by the Society for the Experimental Analysis of Behavior.

† University of Kansas

[1] Reprints may be obtained from Donald M. Baer, Dept. of Human Development, University of Kansas, Lawrence, Kansas 66044.

"good" society is in itself a behavior of its members, this hope turns on itself in a philosophically interesting manner. However, it is at least a fair presumption that behavioral applications, when effective, can sometimes lead to social approval and adoption.

Behavioral applications are hardly a new phenomenon. Analytic behavioral applications, it seems, are. Analytic behavioral application is the process of applying sometimes tentative principles of behavior to the improvement [2] of specific behaviors, and simultaneously evaluating whether or not any changes noted are indeed attributable to the process of application—and if so, to what parts of that process. In short, analytic behavioral application is a self-examining, self-evaluating, discovery-oriented research procedure for studying behavior. So is all experimental behavioral research (at least, according to the usual strictures of modern graduate training). The differences are matters of emphasis and of selection.

The differences between applied and basic research are not differences between that which "discovers" and that which merely "applies" what is already known. Both endeavors ask what controls the behavior under study. Non-applied research is likely to look at any behavior, and at any variable which may conceivably relate to it. Applied research is constrained to look at variables which can be effective in improving the behavior under study. Thus it is equally a matter of research to discover that the behaviors typical of retardates can be related to oddities of their chromosome structure and to oddities of their reinforcement history. But (currently) the chromosome structure of the retardate does not lend itself to experimental manipulation in the interests of bettering that behavior, whereas his reinforcement input is always open to current re-design.

Similarly, applied research is constrained to examining behaviors which are socially important, rather than convenient for study. It also implies, very frequently, the study of those behaviors in their usual social settings, rather than in a "laboratory" setting. But a laboratory is simply a place so designed that experimental control of relevant variables is as easy as possible. Unfortunately, the usual social setting for important behaviors

---

[2] If a behavior is socially important, the usual behavior analysis will aim at its improvement. The social value dictating this choice is obvious. However, it can be just as illuminating to demonstrate how a behavior may be worsened, and there will arise occasions when it will be socially important to do so. Disruptive classroom behavior may serve as an example. Certainly it is a frequent plague of the educational system. A demonstration of what teacher procedures produce more of this behavior is not necessarily the reverse of a demonstration of how to promote positive study behaviors. There may be classroom situations in which the teacher cannot readily establish high rates of study, yet still could avoid high rates of disruption, if she knew what in her own procedures leads to this disruption. The demonstration which showed her that would thus have its value.

is rarely such a place. Consequently, the analysis of socially important behaviors becomes experimental only with difficulty. As the terms are used here, a non-experimental analysis is a contradiction in terms. Thus, analytic behavioral applications by definition achieve experimental control of the processes they contain, but since they strive for this control against formidable difficulties, they achieve it less often per study than would a laboratory-based attempt. Consequently, the rate of displaying experimental control required of behavioral applications has become correspondingly less than the standards typical of laboratory research. This is not because the applier is an easy-going, liberal, or generous fellow, but because society rarely will allow its important behaviors, in their correspondingly important settings, to be manipulated repeatedly for the merely logical comfort of a scientifically sceptical audience.

Thus, the evaluation of a study which purports to be an applied behavior analysis is somewhat different than the evaluation of a similar laboratory analysis. Obviously, the study must be *applied, behavioral,* and *analytic;* in addition, it should be *technological, conceptually systematic,* and *effective,* and it should display some generality. These terms are explored below and compared to the criteria often stated for the evaluation of behavioral research which, though analytic, is not applied.

APPLIED

The label applied is not determined by the research procedures used but by the interest which society shows in the problems being studied. In behavioral application, the behavior, stimuli, and/or organism under study are chosen because of their importance to man and society, rather than their importance to theory. The non-applied researcher may study eating behavior, for example, because it relates directly to metabolism, and there are hypotheses about the interaction between behavior and metabolism. The non-applied researcher also may study bar-pressing because it is a convenient response for study; easy for the subject, and simple to record and integrate with theoretically significant environmental events. By contrast, the applied researcher is likely to study eating because there are children who eat too little and adults who eat too much, and he will study eating in exactly those individuals rather than in more convenient ones. The applied researcher may also study bar-pressing if it is integrated with socially important stimuli. A program for a teaching machine may use bar-pressing behavior to indicate mastery of an arithmetic skill. It is the arithmetic stimuli which are important. (However, some future applied study could show that bar-pressing is more practical in the process of education than a pencil-writing response.[3])

In applied research, there is typically a close relationship between the behavior and stimuli under study and the subject in whom they are studied. Just as there seem to be few behaviors that are intrinsically the target of application, there are few subjects who automatically confer on their study the status of application. An investigation of visual signal detection in the retardate may have little immediate importance, but a similar study in radar-scope watchers has considerable. A study of language development in the retardate may be aimed directly at an immediate social problem, while a similar study in the MIT sophomore may not. Enhancement of the reinforcing value of praise for the retardate alleviates an immediate deficit in his current environment, but enhancement of the reinforcing value of 400 Hz (cps) tone for the same subject probably does not. Thus, a primary question in the evaluation of applied research is: how immediately important is this behavior or these stimuli to this subject?

BEHAVIORAL

Behaviorism and pragmatism seem often to go hand in hand. Applied research is eminently pragmatic; it asks how it is possible to get an individual to do something effectively. Thus it usually studies what subjects can be brought to do rather than what they can be brought to say; unless, of course, a verbal response is the behavior of interest. Accordingly a subject's verbal description of his own non-verbal behavior usually would not be accepted as a measure of his actual behavior unless it were independently substantiated. Hence there is little applied value in the demonstration that an impotent man can be made to say that he no longer is impotent. The relevant question is not what he can say, but what he can do. Application has not been achieved until this question has been answered satisfactorily. (This assumes, of course, that the total goal of the applied researcher is not simply to get his patient-subjects to stop complaining to him. Unless society agrees that this researcher should

---

[3] Research may use the most convenient behaviors and stimuli available, and yet exemplify an ambition in the researcher eventually to achieve application to socially important settings. For example, a study may seek ways to give a light flash a durable conditioned reinforcing function, because the experimenter wishes to know how to enhance school children's responsiveness to approval. Nevertheless, durable bar-pressing for that light flash is no guarantee that the obvious classroom analogue will produce durable reading behavior for teacher statements of "Good!" Until the analogue has been proven sound, application has not been achieved.

not be bothered, it will be difficult to defend that goal as socially important.)

Since the behavior of an individual is composed of physical events, its scientific study requires their precise measurement. As a result, the problem of reliable quantification arises immediately. The problem is the same for applied research as it is for non-applied research. However, non-applied research typically will choose a response easily quantified in a reliable manner, whereas applied research rarely will have that option. As a result, the applied researcher must try harder, rather than ignore this criterion of all trustworthy research. Current applied research often shows that thoroughly reliable quantification of behavior can be achieved, even in thoroughly difficult settings. However, it also suggests that instrumented recording with its typical reliability will not always be possible. The reliable use of human beings to quantify the behavior of other human beings is an area of psychological technology long since well developed, thoroughly relevant, and very often necessary to applied behavior analysis.

A useful tactic in evaluating the behavioral attributes of a study is to ask not merely, was *behavior* changed? but also, *whose* behavior? Ordinarily it would be assumed that it was the subject's behavior which was altered; yet careful reflection may suggest that this was not necessarily the case. If humans are observing and recording the behavior under study, then any change may represent a change only in their observing and recording responses, rather than in the subject's behavior. Explicit measurement of the reliability of human observers thus becomes not merely good technique, but a prime criterion of whether the study was appropriately behavioral. (A study merely of the behavior of observers is behavioral, of course, but probably irrelevant to the researcher's goal.) Alternatively, it may be that only the experimenter's behavior has changed. It may be reported, for example, that a certain patient rarely dressed himself upon awakening, and consequently would be dressed by his attendant. The experimental technique to be applied might consist of some penalty imposed unless the patient were dressed within half an hour after awakening. Recording of an increased probability of self-dressing under these conditions might testify to the effectiveness of the penalty in changing the behavior; however, it might also testify to the fact that the patient would in fact probably dress himself within half an hour of arising, but previously was rarely left that long undressed before being clothed by his efficient attendant. (The attendant now is the penalty-imposing experimenter and therefore always gives the patient his full half-hour, in the interests of precise experimental technique, of course.) This error is an elementary one, perhaps. But it

suggests that in general, when an experiment proceeds from its baseline
to its first experimental phase, changes in what is measured need not
always reflect the behavior of the subject.

ANALYTIC

The analysis of a behavior, as the term is used here, requires a believable
demonstration of the events that can be responsible for the occurrence or
non-occurrence of that behavior. An experimenter has achieved an
analysis of a behavior when he can exercise control over it. By common
laboratory standards, that has meant an ability of the experimenter to
turn the behavior on and off, or up and down, at will. Laboratory
standards have usually made this control clear by demonstrating it
repeatedly, even redundantly, over time. Applied research, as noted
before, cannot often approach this arrogantly frequent clarity of being in
control of important behaviors. Consequently, application, to be
analytic, demonstrates control when it can, and thereby presents its
audience with a problem of judgment. The problem, of course, is
whether the experimenter has shown enough control, and often enough,
for believability. Laboratory demonstrations, either by overreplication or
an acceptable probability level derived from statistical tests of grouped
data, make this judgment more implicit than explicit. As Sidman points
out (1960), there is still a problem of judgment in any event, and it is
probably better when explicit.

There are at least two designs commonly used to demonstrate reliable
control of an important behavioral change. The first can be referred to as
the "reversal" technique. Here a behavior is measured, and the measure is
examined over time until its stability is clear. Then, the experimental
variable is applied. The behavior continues to be measured, to see if the
variable will produce a behavioral change. If it does, the experimental
variable is discontinued or altered, to see if the behavioral change just
brought about depends on it. If so, the behavioral change should be lost
or diminished (thus the term "reversal"). The experimental variable then
is applied again, to see if the behavioral change can be recovered. If it
can, it is pursued further, since this is applied research and the behavioral
change sought is an important one. It may be reversed briefly again, and
yet again, if the setting in which the behavior takes place allows further
reversals. But that setting may be a school system or a family, and
continued reversals may not be allowed. They may appear in themselves
to be detrimental to the subject if pursued too often. (Whether they are
in fact detrimental is likely to remain an unexamined question so long as
the social setting in which the behavior is studied dictates against using

them repeatedly. Indeed, it may be that repeated reversals in some applications have a positive effect on the subject, possibly contributing to the discrimination of relevant stimuli involved in the problem.)

In using the reversal technique, the experimenter is attempting to show that an analysis of the behavior is at hand: that whenever he applies a certain variable, the behavior is produced, and whenever he removes this variable, the behavior is lost. Yet applied behavior analysis is exactly the kind of research which can make this technique self-defeating in time. Application typically means producing valuable behavior; valuable behavior usually meets extra-experimental reinforcement in a social setting; thus, valuable behavior, once set up, may no longer be dependent upon the experimental technique which created it. Consequently, the number of reversals possible in applied studies may be limited by the nature of the social setting in which the behavior takes place, in more ways than one.

An alternative to the reversal technique may be called the "multiple baseline" technique. This alternative may be of particular value when a behavior appears to be irreversible or when reversing the behavior is undesirable. In the multiple-baseline technique, a number of responses are identified and measured over time to provide baselines against which changes can be evaluated. With these baselines established, the experimenter then applies an experimental variable to one of the behaviors, produces a change in it, and perhaps notes little or no change in the other baselines. If so, rather than reversing the just-produced change, he instead applies the experimental variable to one of the other, as yet unchanged, responses. If it changes at that point, evidence is accruing that the experimental variable is indeed effective, and that the prior change was not simply a matter of coincidence. The variable then may be applied to still another response, and so on. The experimenter is attempting to show that he has a reliable experimental variable, in that each behavior changes maximally only when the experimental variable is applied to it.

How many reversals, or how many baselines, make for believability is a problem for the audience. If statistical analysis is applied, the audience must then judge the suitability of the inferential statistic chosen and the propriety of these data for that test. Alternatively, the audience may inspect the data directly and relate them to past experience with similar data and similar procedures. In either case, the judgments required are highly qualitative, and rules cannot always be stated profitably. However, either of the foregoing designs gathers data in ways that exemplify the concept of replication, and replication is the essence of believability. At the least, it would seem that an approach to replication is better than no approach at all. This should be especially true for so embryonic a field as behavioral application, the very possibility of which is still occasionally denied.

The preceding discussion has been aimed at the problem of *reliability:* whether or not a certain procedure was responsible for a corresponding behavioral change. The two general procedures described hardly exhaust the possibilities. Each of them has many variations now seen in practice; and current experience suggests that many more variations are badly needed, if the technology of important behavioral change is to be consistently believable. Given some approach to reliability, there are further analyses of obvious value which can be built upon that base. For example, there is analysis in the sense of simplification and separation of component processes. Often enough, current behavioral procedures are complex, even "shotgun" in their application. When they succeed, they clearly need to be analyzed into their effective components. Thus, a teacher giving M & M's to a child may succeed in changing his behavior as planned. However, she has almost certainly confounded her attention and/or approval with each M & M. Further analysis may be approached by her use of attention alone, the effects of which can be compared to the effects of attention coupled with candies. Whether she will discontinue the M & M's, as in the reversal technique, or apply attention with M & M's to certain behaviors and attention alone to certain others, as in the multiple baseline method, is again the problem in basic reliability discussed above. Another form of analysis is parametric: a demonstration of the effectiveness of different values of some variable in changing behavior. The problem again will be to make such an analysis reliable, and, as before, that might be approached by the repeated alternate use of different values on the same behavior (reversal), or by the application of different values to different groups of responses (multiple baseline). At this stage in the development of applied behavior analysis, primary concern is usually with reliability, rather than with parametric analysis or component analysis.

TECHNOLOGICAL

"Technological" here means simply that the techniques making up a particular behavioral application are completely identified and described. In this sense, "play therapy" is not a technological description, nor is "social reinforcement." For purposes of application, all the salient ingredients of play therapy must be described as a set of contingencies between child response, therapist response, and play materials, before a statement of technique has been approached. Similarly, all the ingredients of social reinforcement must be specified (stimuli, contingency, and schedule) to qualify as a technological procedure.

The best rule of thumb for evaluating a procedure description as technological is probably to ask whether a typically trained reader could replicate that procedure well enough to produce the same results, given only a reading of the description. This is very much the same criterion applied to procedure descriptions in non-applied research, of course. It needs emphasis, apparently, in that there occasionally exists a less-than-precise stereotype of applied research. Where application is novel, and derived from principles produced through non-applied research, as in current applied behavior analysis, the reverse holds with great urgency.

Especially where the problem is application, procedural descriptions require considerable detail about all possible contingencies of procedure. It is not enough to say what is to be done when the subject makes response R_1; it is essential also whenever possible to say what is to be done if the subject makes the alternative responses, R_2, R_3, etc. For example, one may read that temper tantrums in children are often extinguished by closing the child in his room for the duration of the tantrums plus ten minutes. Unless that procedure description also states what should be done if the child tries to leave the room early, or kicks out the window, or smears feces on the walls, or begins to make strangling sounds, etc., it is not precise technological description.

CONCEPTUAL SYSTEMS

The field of applied behavior analysis will probably advance best if the published descriptions of its procedures are not only precisely technological, but also strive for relevance to principle. To describe exactly how a preschool teacher will attend to jungle-gym climbing in a child frightened of heights is good technological description; but further to call it a social reinforcement procedure relates it to basic concepts of behavioral development. Similarly, to describe the exact sequence of color changes whereby a child is moved from a color discrimination to a form discrimination is good; to refer also to "fading" and "errorless discrimination" is better. In both cases, the total description is adequate for successful replication by the reader; and it also shows the reader how similar procedures may be derived from basic principles. This can have the effect of making a body of technology into a discipline rather than a collection of tricks. Collections of tricks historically have been difficult to expand systematically, and when they were extensive, difficult to learn and teach.

EFFECTIVE

If the application of behavioral techniques does not produce large enough effects for practical value, then application has failed. Non-applied research often may be extremely valuable when it produces small but reliable effects, in that these effects testify to the operation of some variable which in itself has great theoretical importance. In application, the theoretical importance of a variable is usually not at issue. Its practical importance, specifically its power in altering behavior enough to be socially important, is the essential criterion. Thus, a study which shows that a new classroom technique can raise the grade level achievements of culturally deprived children from D– to D is not an obvious example of applied behavior analysis. That same study might conceivably revolutionize educational theory, but it clearly has not yet revolutionized education. This is of course a matter of degree: an increase in those children from D– to C might well be judged an important success by an audience which thinks that C work is a great deal different than D work, especially if C students are much less likely to become drop-outs than D students.

In evaluating whether a given application has produced enough of a behavioral change to deserve the label, a pertinent question can be, how much did that behavior need to be changed? Obviously, that is not a scientific question, but a practical one. Its answer is likely to be supplied by people who must deal with the behavior. For example, ward personnel may be able to say that a hospitalized mute schizophrenic trained to use 10 verbal labels is not much better off in self-help skills than before, but that one with 50 such labels is a great deal more effective. In this case, the opinions of ward aides may be more relevant than the opinions of psycholinguists.

GENERALITY

A behavioral change may be said to have generality if it proves durable over time, if it appears in a wide variety of possible environments, or if it spreads to a wide variety of related behaviors. Thus, the improvement of articulation in a clinic setting will prove to have generality if it endures into the future after the clinic visits stop; if the improved articulation is heard at home, at school, and on dates; or if the articulation of all words, not just the ones treated, improves. Application means practical improvement in important behaviors; thus, the more general that application, the better, in many cases. Therapists dealing with the development of heterosexual behavior may well point out there are socially appropriate limits to its generality, once developed; such limitations to generality are usually obvious. That generality is a valuable characteristic of applied behavior analysis which should be examined explicitly apparently is not quite that obvious, and is stated here for emphasis.

That generality is not automatically accomplished whenever behavior is changed also needs occasional emphasis, especially in the evaluation of applied behavior analysis. It is sometimes assumed that application has failed when generalization does not take place in any widespread form. Such a conclusion has no generality itself. A procedure which is effective in changing behavior in one setting may perhaps be easily repeated in other settings, and thus accomplish the generalization sought. Furthermore, it may well prove the case that a given behavior change need be programmed in only a certain number of settings, one after another, perhaps, to accomplish eventually widespread generalization. A child may have 15 techniques for disrupting his parents, for example. The elimination of the most prevalent of these may still leave the remaining 14 intact and in force. The technique may still prove both valuable and fundamental, if when applied to the next four successfully, it also results in the "generalized" loss of the remaining 10. In general, generalization should be programmed, rather than expected or lamented.

Thus, in summary, an *applied* behavior analysis will make obvious the importance of the behavior changed, its quantitative characteristics, the experimental manipulations which analyze with clarity what was responsible for the change, the technologically exact description of all procedures contributing to that change, the effectiveness of those procedures in making sufficient change for value, and the generality of that change.

References

Journal of the Experimental Analysis of Behavior. Bloomington: Society for the Experimental Analysis of Behavior, 1957-.

Sidman, Murray. *Tactics of scientific research.* New York: Basic Books, 1960.

Skinner, B. F. *Science and human behavior.* New York: Macmillan, 1953.

Topical Index

Instead of a traditional index, this article index will list for each topic those articles which are relevant to enable you to classify them in various ways.